FORMING A COLONIAL ECONOMY, AUSTRALIA 1810–1850

N.G. BUTLIN

CAMBRIDGE
UNIVERSITY PRESS

Published by the Press Syndicate of the University of Cambridge
The Pitt Building, Trumpington Street, Cambridge CB2 1RP, UK
40 West 20th Street, New York, NY 10011-4211, USA
10 Stamford Road, Oakleigh, Melbourne 3166, Australia

Printed in Australia by Brown Prior Anderson

National Library of Australia cataloguing-in-publication data
Butlin, N.G. (Noel George).
Forming a colonial economy, Australia 1810–1850.
Bibliography.
Includes index.
1. Labor – Australia – History – 19th century. 2. Finance,
Public – Australia – History – 19th century. 3. Australia –
Economic conditions – 1788–1851. 4. Australia – Economic
conditions – 1788–1851 – Statistics. 5. Australia – Population
– History – 19th century. 6. Australia – Colonisation. 7. Great
Britain – Economic conditions – 19th century. I. Title.
330.99402

Library of Congress cataloguing-in-publication data
Butlin, N.G. (Noel George)
Forming a colonial economy, Australia 1810–1850 / N.G. Butlin.
Includes bibliographical references and index.
1. Australia – Economic conditions. 2. Australia – Population.
3. Great Britain – Colonies – Economic policy. I. Title.
HC604.B883 1994   94–16623
330.994'02–dc20   CIP

A catalogue record for this book is available from the British Library.

ISBN 0 521 44006 8 Hardback

CONTENTS

iii

TABLES

FIGURES

ACKNOWLEDGEMENTS

This book is the second volume of Noel Butlin's posthumous economic history that began with *Economics and the Dreamtime,* published by Cambridge University Press in 1993. This book covers the economic history of the colonial economy until about 1840. The perspective it takes is shaped by two important issues — labour and capital — and the account begins with two extended essays on these themes. From this point, the book develops an account of the economic growth of the several settlements, and develops an estimate of the overall level of economic activity including both the Aboriginal and colonial populations.

Noel Butlin died before completing the full account. What is included in this book is the material as he left it, taking into account various corrections, ambiguities, checking and bibliographical amendments. The picture is complete except for an account of the first major depression in Australia, the economic collapse of the 1840s. The notes to the beginning of that chapter sketch out the intended direction of the analysis, and preface the incomplete material that he left. The material and its suggestions for further work are left for other scholars of Australian economic history to take up.

The generosity of Jules Ginswick, initially in providing access to a substantial body of unpublished work and subsequently in clarifying and correcting material used in this volume, is gratefully acknowledged.

Thanks are due to a number of Noel Butlin's former colleagues at the Australian National University. Wayne Naughton took on the task of checking all the tables and provided invaluable technical help, while Barry Howarth put together the bibliography. Graeme Snooks provided helpful comments on structure and content, and assisted with resources. The financial support from the Reserve Bank of Australia and the Australian Research Grants Committee is also gratefully acknowledged.

I would record my appreciation of the efforts of Cambridge University Press, and Robin Derricourt and Marion Fahrer in particular, for their efforts in this project.

Note: While every effort has been made to provide accurate references (in the text) and sources (for the tables and figures), a number of these were incomplete at the time of the author's death and have not been able to be located.

M.W. Butlin

PART I

FORMING AN ECONOMY

INTRODUCTION

It is manifestly obvious that the beginnings of Australian colonial history lie in Britain in the 18th century. The decision, however taken, to form a convict or convict–imperial colony in the late 18th century began that record. The turbulent events between 1788 and 1815 in Europe, and throughout the world, overwhelmed any likelihood that this distant project should receive coherent attention and, indeed, such was the case.

While the shipment of the first three fleets suggested a degree of determination on the part of the British government, the flow of convicts and the degree of policy attention altered radically after 1792. This was reflected in various ways including the long interregnum when officers ruled without a governor to replace the first, Governor Phillip, and the adaptation already outlined in the preceding volume *Economics and the Dreamtime* from a penal organisation to a highly privatised form of penal-capitalist organisation. This was accompanied by the concentration of access to assets firstly in the hands of officials and subsequently in those of a small number of merchants, free arrivals and ex-convicts, the gradual development of agriculture, and the first efforts, particularly by large owners, towards pastoralism.

There followed the emergence of land grants and, through those, the development of private land and goods markets despite, or perhaps because of, the prominence of the government store and distributing agency, the Commissariat. Private property became prominent along with the growth of extensive urban trades and service activities — all illustrating a basic adaptation from any initial concept of a penal settlement. By 1809, powerful private local interests were arrayed against local officialdom and intricate webs of relationships had been established between local individuals and powerful interests in Britain.

A small number of officials, free merchants and immigrants and a few leading ex-convicts had certainly radically altered what might have been an original concept of a prison colony that might evolve into a gradually freed society of ex-convicts engaged in self-support. There was little prospect, in 1809, that the settlement could remain a prison. Changes of governors and different attitudes of governors towards opposing and participating in the private interests of the colony further limited that prospect. The explosion of tensions that ended in the deposition of Bligh forced a much more formal redesign of the colony together with its adjuncts of Norfolk Island and Van Diemen's Land, in constitutional, social and economic terms.

It is scarcely conceivable that Britain could maintain a close supervision of such a distant undertaking even with this redesign and the introduction of a strong military presence and new official faces to the local scene. Not only distance but local pressures and peculiarities negated much of any British objectives, and decisions had perforce to be made — even if sometimes forced also to be reversed on order — because of delays in communication. Nevertheless, the new constitutional authority under Macquarie, and throughout his decade of administration, turned the settlements into a new and more viable direction. Essentially, though it took a decade to be revealed fully, it was a direction towards a more conventional mixed economy in which a more or less conventional public sector coexisted with an expanding private sector and in which convictism flourished beside ex-convict and free society.

There was plenty of scope for 'fits and starts' in the process. But, from a local point of view, 1810 seems the more effective point from which to begin an account of 'Forming an Economy' in Australia.

Major adaptation occurred from 1821 following the reports by Commissioner Bigge into the affairs of the Australian colonies, but though these codified and clarified issues, many of the recommendations were already emergent in action prior to 1820. They included such large matters as the extension of the settlements, the preferred assignment of convicts to private employers, the encouragement to private investors, efforts to relate land grant sizes to persons with resources (not very successful) and, not least, the institution of the redesign of the British-colonial fiscal system.

This does not mean that we can tell the story of 'Forming an Economy' merely from 1810. We have to go back far into British 18th century history in social, military and economic terms. But this is background and preconditioning for the post-1810 story.

How far was the Australian settlement externally driven? How much did it pull? How much independence of action did it have? Perhaps most importantly, to what extent did a synergism develop between British and Australian events and influences? This synergism is different from, though related to, the question of the extent to which the colony became enmeshed in a small/large economy relationship with Britain though this, too, is an important matter to consider.

The beginning is unquestionable. Also impressive are the flow of convicts that developed particularly after 1812 and the resources that Britain poured into the colony(ies). But as these human and physical and fiscal resources were supplied, there was a related and not wholly dependent development within the settlements. Synergism developed most obviously from the early supply of considerable numbers of convict women, along with free women, to the settlements. But so too did a process of primitive capital accumulation (in the Marxist sense) as local development proceeded on the basis of resources supplied. Sustained relatively high living standards, combined with British fiscal support and individual initiative, helped to generate, as suggested in the preceding volume, a great deal of local trades and dealing activities that had no immediately obvious place in a predominantly penal establishment. And, of course, the progressive freeing of prisoners meant persistently changing social relations and status groups. Here was a complex confusion of both dependence and synergism.

This synergism has tended to be underplayed in Australian history and hence attention is called the more prominently to it. At the economic level, it shows up most prominently in labour force and demographic levels and in the whole process of public (British and colonial) funding and private capital development in the colonies. There were powerful British drivers of the local economies. But they are not the exclusive explanators of the fundamental processes of change.

We might, then, begin the account with the convict story and the record of the fitful and then surging flow of convicts with eventually some 160 000 or so arriving in New South Wales (NSW) and Van Diemen's Land (VDL). This was a massive contribution of human resources, substantially all of workforce age, a high proportion with considerable skill and long years of workforce age in front of them.

Such an approach takes us inevitably back into the economic, social, criminal and judicial history of Britain in the 18th century and this is attempted briefly in this book. But it is an interrupted story largely due to the Napoleonic Wars and this is one of the reasons that a more coherent local account should start at about 1810. Relatively few convicts arrived by 1809 — perhaps only 11 000 of the eventual total and almost half were delivered in the first five years of settlement. The subsequent episodic arrivals were turned around after 1810 following the Inquiry into Transportation in that year.

Around the time of the arrival of Macquarie as governor, far more impelling events in Britain were moving towards the resumption of convict transportation. The economic effort in the war against Napoleon was approaching its peak in 1810. Shipbuilding and port construction, in which convict services were demanded at home, also peaked, reducing the inclinations to retain convicts in Britain. A financial crisis developed and, with it, the belief in, and possibly the actuality of, increased criminality in Britain. Moreover, the gathering pace of the industrial and urban changes in Britain extended the opportunities and incentives for crime. Finally, the peaking of the naval pressures against Europe meant the opportunity to release shipping for non-military purposes, including convict transportation. These conditions represented some of the immediate background to the resurgence of convict flows that followed particularly after 1812.

So we can follow, from this point, the story of the rise and fluctuations in convict flows to Australia, the assignment process, the termination and assignment and cessation of transportation to NSW in 1840 and to Van Diemen's Land in the early 1850s. This is the story that emphasises — overemphasises? — convictism in Australia and has been excellently told by Shaw (1966), O'Brien (1950) and others. It remains an appropriate emphasis up to 1830 — temporised by the importance of a moderate number of free immigrants — but quickly ceases to be so thereafter. There are two reasons. It does not take adequately into account the rapidly changing nature of the workforce after 1830. And, most importantly, it fails to reveal the age, sex, skill and workforce structure of the colonies. It misses out on the full demographic picture — the population as a whole, which was in the process of quite dramatic change. These factors all need to be brought to light and display a strong synergism between the two societies by the 1840s.

The unfortunate fact is that we have no thorough demographic history of Australia and least of all for these early years. It is essential to try to do something about this, even if with somewhat heroic remedies. Pedagogically, the trouble is that it requires numerous statistics and these can be boring. Robinson (1985) has gone far towards alleviating some of the tedium but even she is forced into statistical presentation. So we can choose the convict path, search for some of the possible determinants of the flow of transportees and combine that story with the account of the free immigration project (Madgwick, 1937). But readers should be warned that it is almost inevitable that any analytical effort requires statistical representation and no easy narrative. Reconstruction of the population imposes that condition.

There is an alternative way to begin. This was not merely a convict or even convict–imperial project. Initially, it was a major act of British public investment. This is a story that has certainly never been told and one that needs to be brought to light and even perhaps to life. It too requires some statistical representation but it is possible to make it more of a narrative. This may be more palatable even if it is a fiscal and financial account. Here again, we have comparable issues of driver, dependency, independent action and synergism wrapped in a complex parcel. Given that Britain provided not only human capital but resources to support the people concerned, the volume, nature and access to those resources become acutely interesting. In this case, the beginning is not 1810 but takes us back to the 18th century British practices and the curious incipient modes of funding that developed in the colony from the beginning.

Nevertheless, these early obscure but interesting manoeuvres also become clarified in 1810 with Macquarie's arrival, at least in the public fiscal area. These changes are more definitively declared after the Bigge investigations. The British government, from 1822, took a firmer hand in the control of resource supplies and sought greater fiscal restraint as private assignment of convicts proceeded. It also sought an increased local fiscal support from the colonies.

Perhaps what was done was with some recollection of the events of the American Revolution. Perhaps it was a consequence of the penality that was still redolent in the colonies. But the British avoided pushing the colonists into a position in which strong fiscal resistance developed locally. Tensions certainly developed, particularly over controls of Crown lands and their revenues. Britain certainly succeeded in withdrawing a great deal of its early fiscal support and bringing the Commissariat effectively under military control. This both enhanced that restraint and allowed the colonists to leave military protection a British function. At the same time, during the 1820s, Britain moved towards a stronger encouragement of private investment in the colonies just as conditions in the colonies were developing to provide attractions to that investment — again a complex process of driver, independence, and synergism.

Fundamentally, this volume deals with the formation of the economy from 1810. But it is, and must be, preceded by chapters back in 18th century Britain. It focuses firstly on the two central issues from Britain and the way these evolved in relating to Australia — funding and human capital. This means running these accounts throughout the whole period. Thereafter, the chapters take up the local story of 'Forming an Economy' from 1810 but even here a great deal of British background is inevitable.

The later chapters on the forming of the economy confront what is to me the crucial, if implicit, policy issue — do we explain the process as a story of staple development or is there something else at least equally important to deal with? It is proposed here that the colony(ies) sought to move in two directions and did so with considerable effect. One was, indeed, in the direction of natural resource exploitation. The other was in the dramatic use, in urban activities, of skilled labour supplied from Britain. One might say, given the supply of those skills, this was an exploitation of the problem of isolation. The two together would have been impossible without skills and heavy British public and private support. Equally, the way in which human capital was used also depended on available natural resources and the way in which they were exploited. The staple approach and the development of urban activities are intimately interconnected, but it cannot be said that either dominated or led the other. Each was the product in large measure of special conditions.

This, I suggest, is the policy division that has been dominant in Australia throughout its entire modern history. So long as standards of living in Australia remained relatively high, the ambivalence did not strike home. So long as we continued to receive a high level of skills from abroad, isolation could be a positive advantage. So long as primary resource use was relatively non-labour intensive, persons accustomed to exercising skills in urban environments could continue to practise those crafts. This pattern was set in these years and laid the foundation for a long-sustained tradition from which we have not escaped but which has perhaps become intensified.

PART II

THE COLONIAL PEOPLING OF AUSTRALIA: 1788–1850

1

INTRODUCTION

The demographic history of Australia between 1788 and 1850 is a story of two conflicting experiences — a rapidly declining Aboriginal and an escalating colonial population. It is possible, though there is no prospect of affirming this confidently, that the total population of Australia was less, and perhaps much less, in 1850 than it had been in 1788. My own guesstimates of Aboriginal population suggest that their numbers may have fallen from 1 million to less than half that figure in the course of some 62 years. In the meantime, introduced colonial population rose from a round figure of 1000 to 400 000. On this basis, the total Australian population fell during these years following colonial settlement. In the light of this, how do we assess colonial 'achievement' to 1850? How far did it depend on and acquire special advantages from the displacement of Aborigines?

Australian colonial population grew at extremely high rates, close to 9 per cent per annum compounded over the 1788–50 period. There were fluctuations in this process, but the average rate of expansion was extraordinarily high. Does a high rate of population increase, particularly one in which external inflows are major influences, encourage or discourage efficiency or productivity? How does such a rapidly expanding population depend on the combination of this labour with the available natural resources? To what extent are in-built human capital characteristics vital for achieved performance? These are major questions at the end of the 20th century and some that are prominent in the rest of this book.

Here we are concerned with the demography of the colonists. They came originally from 'outside', essentially from Britain. This invites the impression that colonial population growth and the related increase in workforce was the product of an inflow of population from Britain. In other words, external inputs dominate the explanation. A vital issue arises immediately: How far, in fact, was the increase of population and labour due to external factors?

We need to distinguish carefully between the determinants of the increase and components of the colonial population on the one hand and of the workforce on the other. Stress on external determinants in the literature has led to the focus, given data constraints, on convicts and supposedly free immigration (with a subset of the latter in terms of unassisted and assisted immigrants from Britain). In practice, population growth was the product of external inflow and outflow and of net reproduction within the colony(ies). There was an interactive process between external flows and local net reproduction, which yielded the population growth. The locally born have been, to a considerable degree, until the publication of Robinson's *The Hatch and Brood of Time*, literally the forgotten children of Australian history.

This external-local interaction is not peculiar to demographic change. It applied also, as we will see in the next part of the volume, to the development of capital assets where joint external and domestic inputs need to be considered. External factors played a vital role in early Australian colonial development. But in both demography and in factor inputs, it was the synergism of external and domestic components that explains the historical outcome.

The ingredients of colonial population increase were convict arrivals, civil and military officials, non-convict immigration, emigration, births and deaths. It is unfortunate that we have no major research publications on early Australian demography in general, so that even total population estimates are subject to considerable doubt. This strongly influences the structure of this part of the volume. It is essential to disentangle, as much as possible, the growth in the workforce from the increase in population.

It is important, also, to reconsider the prevailing understanding on convict versus 'free' immigrant inflows. We need also to consider colonial population increase as the accession of human capital. This requires some attempt to identify the qualities of the external inflows, the way this external influx was turned to account or was forced to adapt to new conditions and the way in which the locally born developed characteristics different from those from outside.

Accordingly, this chapter attempts to do three things. Firstly, it explores the scale and determinants of the gross additions to the Australian colonial population — convicts, free immigrants and the colonial born. Secondly, it attempts, through population projections, to outline the components of the population stock and the workforce of New South Wales and Van Diemen's Land in terms of civil status, age and sex. Thirdly, it introduces some of the issues in relation to these gross additions as human capital.

Convictism looms so large in early Australian history that emphasis on it is inescapable. The attempt to identify the determinants of that influx inevitably takes us back to Britain. One may reasonably raise some doubts about the division between convicts and immigrants. One possible area for future research is the concealment of convicts under the cloak of assisted immigration.

2

GROSS ADDITIONS TO THE AUSTRALIAN POPULATION

The Determinants of Convict Inflow to Australia

Even though, as suggested previously, there may have been other imperial motives behind the British settlement of Australia, there is no doubt that the transportation of convicts to the Antipodes was a convenient solution to social, judicial and budgetary problems in Britain in the 1780s. Britain had, at the time of the American Revolution, been accustomed to shipping out to the plantations an annual average of the order of 1000 transported convicts. The Revolution cut off that outlet (the West Indies and Africa remained available). Australian settlement did not offer the cheap American solution of disposing of convicts to private masters. The more expensive arrangement of passing transportees into the hands of the colonial governor for disposal had, of necessity in the first instance, to be adopted. But for a distant imperial venture, with no prospect of indigenous labour to engage, the use of unfree convict labour under public discipline and direction may have appeared to have considerable merit. A possible counterfactual, the free occupation of Australia by individuals from the beginning, seems beyond the bounds of plausible consideration. There is, then, no necessary conflict between imperial and penal motives in the colonial settlement of Australia.

Nevertheless, the expense of such a convict–imperial undertaking was and remained an important consideration and, indeed, after a mere three decades of settlement it was possible to adopt a general policy akin, though not identical, to the old American-style solution of convict assignment to private employers. Expense is a matter for the next part of the volume, dealing with the public funding of the Australian colonies.

It is doubtful if any society has solved the problem of dealing with its deviants and most of all with its criminal deviants. Many of the arguments that pervaded Britain in the second half of the 18th century and first half of the 19th century persist, with equal lack of resolution, at the end of the 20th century. Britain, in the last quarter of the 18th century and increasingly so during the first half of the 19th century, lacked or had lost the means either to punish or to reform. Since the Restoration in 1688, they had also lost much of the enthusiasm for Tyburn and its annual eight days of execution. British towns outside London may never have fully shared the liking for the older and final solution. Thus Shaw (1966) estimates that in Britain in the early 17th century perhaps 2000 persons per year were executed. By the second half of the 18th century, he proposes that the numbers had dropped towards one-tenth of this, despite a substantial increase in population and a widespread belief in the prevalence and increase of crime. Transportation to the plantations had, to 1776, significantly reduced the incidence of the ultimate punishment.

The choice of Australia as an alternative transportation outlet did little for almost a quarter of a century to provide Britain with a means of disposing of its unwanted citizens. The Napoleonic Wars were a major interruption to any penal plans in the Pacific though the early experience certainly pointed the way and, in the meantime, the demands of war opened up opportunities, within Britain, both of increased housing and increased productive use of convicted criminals. The mass flow of convicts might be dated from the closing years of the wars. Between 1812 and 1850 there were, however, large fluctuations in numbers transported and remarkably little evidence of a rising trend after 1820. These fluctuations and this trend characteristic conflict with much of the criminal and penal experience of Britain. The lack of any simple correlation makes for a complex array of the determinants of transportation to Australia.

It is too easy, as much of the literature invites, to discuss transportation generally in the context of the 'disturbed state' and judicial severity of Britain during 1788–1850. Without intending to build up a highly formal model, we need to examine the question of the determinants of transportation in three steps. What determined the supply of criminals? What determined the number of convictions? Of those convicted, what determined the number of transportees? It will also be proposed that there is a hidden question: What determined the relationship, if any, between transportation and migration?

The supply of criminals

Until the 1820s, it might be said, with a certain measure of justification, that Britain lacked many of the essentials of an administrable penal code — a consistent judicial system, a workable philosophy of punishment and reform, or an organised means of housing its criminals. As the reluctance to execute increased throughout the 18th century, the number of crimes classed as capital offences escalated. To this increasing array of capital crimes (rising from about 50 in 1688 to over 200 in 1815) were added transportable offences that did not attract the death penalty (Shaw, 1966). By the end of the 1830s, transportation to NSW officially ended. Then Britain had radically reduced its capital offences (to a mere four), had introduced the modern concept of an impartial jury and embarked upon gaol construction, organised police forces and was instituting philosophies of domestic reform of criminals.

What then might have determined the supply of criminals? Many contemporaries in the late 18th and early 19th centuries were convinced that there was 'a criminal class' and that this class was increasing. Moreover, there was a similar belief that crimes were predominantly against property. Without accepting such a concept, one might think that the numbers of potential criminals might be in part correlated with population size. A second variable would, perhaps, be the degree of population concentration supplemented by a third, the extent of disturbance arising in the process of concentrating. A fourth variable, still relevant today, although in a different form, was drug abuse. Finally, crime is what is classified legally as crime and the remaining variable in determining the supply of criminals is the change in the legal code. An additional special variable might be summarised, as a special category, in one word: Ireland — the problem of Ireland and Anglo–Irish relations called forth a special category of 'criminal' through political activisim or repression. Because Irish transportation is to some extent *sui generis*, and we can make some statistical comparisons of non-Irish indictments, convictions and transportation, let us leave this aside for the moment.

The historical counterparts can be dealt with summarily. Few of the suggested variables operated consistently or persistently throughout 1788–1850. British population, according to such estimates that we have, appears to have increased by about 50 per cent in the 18th century and to have doubled again between 1800 and 1850. Particularly from about 1770, there appears to have been a sustained compound rate of expansion at about 1 per cent per annum, enlarging the potential pool of criminals. Most of this population increase occurred in the context of massive economic and geographical restructuring in the course of the Industrial Revolution during the 100 years up to 1850. The Industrial Revolution will receive more attention later.

It is sufficient for the present purposes to note the increasing concentration in towns and the relative decline of rural populations, the greater exposure of urban populations to opportunities for crime and for persons, through problems of survival in urban conditions, to be led by example or necessity to criminal behaviour. That potential could have been accentuated in periods of special hardship during business recessions and reduced in booms. Thus the Napoleonic Wars created high employment conditions but, particularly after 1812, led to high inflation. The post-war slump was followed by a series of business fluctuations, with recessions producing substantial episodes of increased unemployment and the inducement to supplement resources by criminal action (business fluctuations are delineated in Gayer, Rostow and Schwartz (1953). Gatrell and Hadden (ed. Wrigley, 1972) have demonstrated a close though not exact association between criminal behaviour and business fluctuations during the first half of the 19th century.

Since it received such prominence in contemporary commentary, one of the special conditions of urban life was the exposure to alcohol and access to taverns. This attracted attention from several magistrates such as Colquhoun (1800) who saw this as a primary cause of criminal behaviour in the young even though the worst excesses of the 'gin parlours' were over.

If this were a sufficient environment for increasing crime, there is no doubt that contemporaries believed crime to be prevalent during 1788–1840 and, above all, in urban conditions. One of their initial responses, as already indicated, was to extend the list of capital offences greatly and to enlarge the list of acts that, if not subject to the death penalty nevertheless, could yield substantial prison sentences and transportation. It is this great extension of acts classed as criminal that has been central to the view of an extremely harsh judicial system and of many Australian transportees as being, in a modern perspective, petty criminals.

Whether this extensive codification was intended to be harsh, or merely to appear this way, might well be debated. There can be no doubt that the proliferation of legal offences greatly enlarged the supply of executable criminals up to the years immediately after the Napoleonic Wars. Then the process was partially reversed and the number of capital crimes was drastically reduced by mid-century (and particularly during the 1830s) though long lists of non-capital criminal offences remained. This apparent amelioration was concentrated at a time when transportation to NSW was drawing to a close. But, for various reasons, it seems doubtful that one should assume that a high proportion of Australian convicts were, in fact, petty criminals. To appreciate this, one needs to look at some of the conditions of conviction.

The supply of convicts

To be convicted, a person had to be caught, indicted, found guilty, judged and sentences finally reviewed. These were all distinct stages before, if ever, the punishment fitted the crime. Changing procedures and principles at each stage formed the basis whereby these distinct steps acted as variables to separate the flow of convicts from the supply of 'criminals'.

Tobias' evaluation (1967) suggests a contrast between two 'states of society' before and after 1775. In much of the 18th century, few criminals were apprehended and those that were caught and judged guilty were dealt with severely. From 1775 and particularly after 1815, the proportion of criminals apprehended seems to have risen progressively but they were generally judged with increasing leniency. The meaning of leniency, however, deserves some consideration.

Firstly, as to apprehension — with little in the way of an organised police force until the 19th century, capture depended on a variety of processes — thief takers, in London the Bow Street Runners, hue and cry, being taken redhanded by employers or owners of goods, and the formation of 'vigilantes' (such as local associations of residents or businessmen). In 1815, London presented a miscellany of 'police forces' but there was little elsewhere.

From 1815, capture procedures improved steadily as changes were made leading to the Metropolitan Police in London in 1829 and the extension of police organisations occurred in the major towns outside London particularly from the mid-1820s up to 1840 (Tobias, 1967). Technical and social change progressively enhanced the efficiency of these changing procedures. The lighting of towns improved rapidly from the late 18th century and throughout the first quarter of the 19th century, with an acceleration after the end of the Napoleonic Wars. The assumption seems reasonable that an increasing proportion of criminals or suspected criminals were being captured over the period 1788–1850.

Once apprehended, a suspect remained to be indicted. This meant a considerable disparity between arrests and indictment, let alone conviction. For much of the 18th century, the private costs of embarking on a criminal charge were substantial and probably deterred many appellants. The introduction of the Parliamentary Reward system whereby costs of prosecutors and witnesses were met (up to a limit) by Parliament reversed this disinclination and from the time of the foundation of Australian settlement, there were positive encouragements to be litigious and also to be a thief taker. The Criminal Law Act 1826 (UK) established standard public systems of payment of expenses for felonies and misdemeanours and provided a

much more definite incentive to embark on indictments. This remained the position
to the mid-1840s.

Between apprehension and indictment, prisoners were commonly held in what
were essentially privately operated lockups until the 1820s. There they faced
squalor, disease and malnutrition, another set of hurdles with death separating the
supply of criminals from the supply of convictions (we will return to gaols later).
Once assembled for indictment, their cases were generally considered, in absentia,
by Grand Juries (in England magistrates sometimes exercised summary justice,
in Ireland more often) who either threw out the evidence or advised trial by open
jury.

Ordinary juries, until well into the period of Australian transportation, were typically not anonymous faces but persons drawn in with knowledge of location and
persons related to cases. The frequent judgment in the literature appears to be that
the tendency to personalise juries, given the severity of the nominal penalties, often
led to acquittal or judgment on less significant charges than those in the lists. Indeed,
it appears that Court records typically took only one or a few items in an indictment
as the evidence on which a case was found proven. This has an important bearing on
the supposed pettiness of much of Australian criminality. In this respect, at least,
Tobias (1967) appears to have a strong case in proposing that British Court records
before 1850 are suspect.

Justices themselves appear to have become, from the mid-18th century, less and
less willing to impose the full majesty of the law and increasingly to find with
severity but not capital determination on less substantial charges in indictments. This
had an ambivalent outcome. If death sentences were less readily handed down, some
other sentence could more easily be. This may be part of the background to the
apparent arbitrariness of the administration of British justice. In general, there
appears to have been a lift in the proportion of convictions to indictments in the
closing years of the Napoleonic Wars and for the proportion to rise persistently until
1850 (see figure 2.1, right).

The supply of transportees

What did this judicial background mean for Australian transportation? It is unfortunate, that, as yet, we cannot closely link the total numbers of persons transported
from the different major areas of the United Kingdom with the location of trial and
conviction. In particular, many Irish persons appear to have been convicted in
Ireland, shipped to and transshipped from Britain. This need not be confusing except
to the extent that the persons transported from England, Wales and Scotland will
overstate the true number of non-Irish transportees to Australia.

Let us, with this understanding, compare the numbers transported from and
convicted in England, Wales and Scotland. We have conviction data for England and
Wales during 1805–50 and for Scotland from 1830. A rough approximation,
extrapolating the Scottish figures back to 1805, has been made on the assumption of
the average Scottish/England and Wales ratios from 1830. This probably overstates
the earlier figures somewhat and will further exaggerate the proportions of
convictions ending in transportation to Australia.

As will be seen from figure 2.1 the number of indictments rose sixfold and the
number of convictions to almost eight times their 1805 level between 1805 and

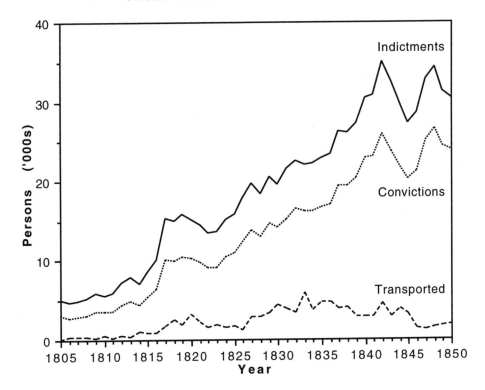

Figure 2.1: Indictments and Transportees: England, Scotland and Wales, 1805–50

1850. Bear in mind that this still excludes Ireland. Both indictments and convictions were boosted rapidly from the closing years of the Napoleonic Wars until 1817. After a decline to 1823–4, both series climbed steadily (though at a slowly declining trend rate) to a peak in the early 1840s. So far as numbers transported to Australia go, there is a broadly comparable increase in numbers between 1812 and 1820 and a decline to around the mid-1820s. Although transportation increased again, its peak was reached in 1833 after which time the numbers trended downwards despite the continued rise in convictions.

One might then propose a relationship between convictions and transportations as follows:

- a comparatively rapid response of transportation to convictions from the closing years of the wars but with the rise of transportation to a peak in 1820, as much as three years later than the peak in convictions;
- a similar time lag in the response of transportation in the course of declining convictions in the early 1820s, with transportation continuing to fall to 1825 although convictions were rising by 1823;
- transportation rising after 1825 much more rapidly than convictions up to 1833; and
- a following trend decline in transportations despite the persistent increase to the early 1840s in the numbers convicted.

England, Wales and Scotland were, then, not 'shovelling out' their convicted criminals in a manner closely related to the available supply of convicts. In other

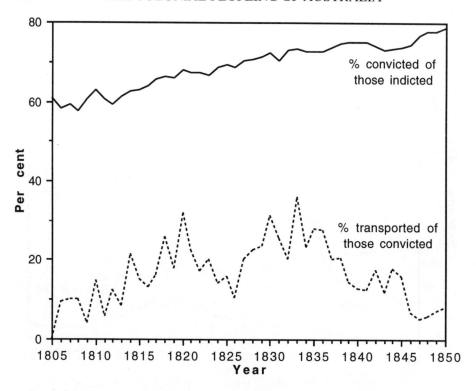

Figure 2.2: Convicted and Transported: England, Scotland and Wales, 1805–50

words, the factors that determined the supply of indictments and convictions are far from adequate as an explanation of transportations, even though they may have supplied general background conditions.

This is confirmed, and two other important features of the relationship between convictions and transportations are raised in figure 2.2. Whereas from the close of the wars to early 1840s the numbers convicted rose and and proportion of those indicted increased in a relatively stable manner, the fraction of those convicted who were transported fluctuated quite wildly. Secondly, although there were marked peaks in about 1820 and in the mid-1830s, those transported were always a minority and typically less than one-fifth of the numbers convicted were under indictment for criminal offences.

The instability of the proportion transported is as interesting as the relatively limited proportion put on transports. England, Wales and Scotland not only disposed generally of a very small minority of its convictions through transportation but seem to have done so in a somewhat erratic manner. Most obviously, from the mid-1830s the proportion transported fell heavily so that throughout the 1840s, despite transportation to Van Diemen's Land, the numbers of convicts shipped out made little contribution to solving Britain's penal problem.

It is important to appreciate that while arrests and indictments were the product of decisions dispersed throughout Britain and subject to arbitrary and inconsistent decisions by different judges, the decision actually to transport (as distinct from judgments of transportation) were more centralised. The flow of transportees, in other words, was exposed to pressures bearing more directly on the central government of Britain. Certainly, there were dispersed issues that determined how many persons might be dealt with by the central government. These included such matters as the judicial decision to impose physical punishment (typically whipping or the stocks), to sentence prisoners (often for only a few months), to send persons to corrective institutions (particularly the Brideswells) or to concede 'rights of clergy' particularly to the more literate.

In practice, the ability to house persons in British penal establishments became very slowly a centralised matter from the end of the 18th century and began to concentrate during the wars. The Brideswells were enhanced by the decision to place persons in marine hulks and the number of hulks proliferated during the Napoleonic Wars. Until the early 19th century, hulks were places of considerable ill-fame. Prisoners in both institutions were increasingly expected to work while under sentence and for efficiency reasons as well as increasing humanitarian concerns the quality of treatment improved. This was marked, in the case of the hulks, by the introduction from 1805 of hospital ships moored with hulks and the provision of substantial dietary allowances. It is relevant that this dietary allowance flowed over to Australian transportees whose nominal rations allocation of meat and bread, at least, was substantial.

The increase in the supply of hulks during the wars was partly due to the use of captured French ships for this purpose. In addition, the demand for convict employment on, or in association with, wharves and shipbuilding yards increased as the British war effort rose to its peak in about 1810. The ability to house convicts and to use them productively therefore increased significantly during the 23 or so years after 1788. Another side benefit of the wars was that convicted persons could be offered the option of enlisting in the army or navy.

On the other hand, the capacity to transport was not only constrained but subject to considerable fluctuations. In part, these were due to budgetary factors but, possibly most importantly, they were influenced by the ability to deploy shipping committed to 'normal' commercial operations and to the blockade of France. The supply of shipping seems a prime factor. British shipbuilding escalated during the early 19th century to peak in about 1810. Then shipping supply was more ample and this condition turned to a surplus of shipping at the end of the wars. This is one major reason for the increased shipment of convicts from 1813 to 1820. This change had its obverse in the declining demand for productive employment at the same time. But it was also associated with post-war inflation and recession, unemployment and rising crime.

From 1820, central budgetary constraints appear to have limited shipments of transportees. At the same time, more strict central planning for gaol accommodation was beginning to get under way, typified by the opening of the Millbank Prison in 1822. Notions of incarceration and reform were increasingly prevalent. Unfortunately for British decision makers, these hopes were largely dashed. The Millbank Prison turned out something of a planning disaster through poor hygiene conditions and the crime rate rose persistently. Increased transportation took up the slack in penal accommodation until the early 1830s when a large-scale policy review of penal provision and transportation occurred under the Molesworth Committee during 1832–37.

During this period, a programme of gaol construction was slowly set underway to house criminals in Britain. At the same time, more stern and coherent views of punishment carried weight in the declaration of objectives to reform through isolation and instruction. By no means irrelevant, it had, by the 1830s, become apparent that conditions of transportees in Australia were generally relatively favourable in the light of these more stern reform objectives. Transportation had become more a benefit to the mass of transportees than a means to punishment. The fact that many had 'reformed' having been given new opportunities to social and economic advantage in Australia does not seem to have carried much weight. The inability to achieve 'punishment and reform' in Australia was a major factor determining the policy change, effectively made by 1836, to cease transportation to NSW and to terminate private assignment. Thereafter Van Diemen's Land remained as a limited and short-term disposal outlet that ceased in 1853.

There was, however, another outlet for convicted criminals in Britain apart from the growing gaols. This has not entered Australian literature and its implications, when fully explored, could turn out to be substantial and long term. This was that persons indicted could be sentenced not only to execution, transportation, gaol or whipping but to another institution. This was the workhouses under Poor Law codes.

An association between gaols and workhouses had long been noted in Britain, basically in terms of the workhouses being staging and training grounds for criminals or alleged criminals. This was particularly so in urban conditions where the unemployed and dislocated individuals, particularly, but not exclusively, juveniles, found temporary refuge.

The old Poor Law of Britain had been established essentially in conditions of a rural society. It did not function effectively in increasingly urban conditions and the Poor Law Act 1834 (UK) set about a major restructuring. Administration was centralised, work and training was required and it was designed that both living conditions and food should be less attractive than in the developing national gaols. On the other hand, as the criminal code and the extending police net caught an increasing proportion of the British population, there appears to have been a growing tendency for magistrates and judges to treat more and more individuals as 'vagabonds and rogues' and to divert them to the workhouses, even to the extent of providing small sums of money to provide immediate necessities there.

If there was, in fact, a direct route from court to workhouse, there was certainly an increasing lack of attraction, after 1834, of the workhouses as refuges. The 19th century view of the workhouse as a breeding ground for criminals, especially young criminals, seems to have at least some justification.

But after 1834, in particular, conditions developed to encourage inmates, whether court-directed or not, to consider or be open to another alternative to crime in Britain or enforced transportation. This was assisted migration. This matter deserves careful research. It raises the question of whether some, perhaps a significant fraction, of assisted immigration was a form of proto-transportation. If correct, it would not mean that persons were removed from Britain or arrived in Australia with convict sentences, though it would mean that the distinction between convict and assisted migration became shadowy. We may need to reconsider the accepted view of 'transportation' ending in NSW in 1840 and of the proportion of 'criminals' transported declining from the mid-1830s. Did Britain, in fact, find (the word does not imply a calculated decision) an even cheaper solution to some of its criminal problem by exploiting Crown land sales in the colonies and the workhouses at home as an alternative to transportation? It is appropriate then to turn to the question of 'free' immigration to Australia.

Immigration into Australia

Nine categories of individuals can be identified as 'immigrants' to Australia during the 1788–1850 period. These are:
- military and civil officials and their families;
- former Australian officials;
- convicts' families;
- ex-convicts having departed and returning freely;
- indentured labourers;
- assisted (pauper) immigrants;
- privately supported persons arranged by colonials;
- ex-officials of the British Empire or armed services outside Australia; and
- free immigrants and their families.

The theory of immigration, in simple terms, can be stated in the following form. Persons may move between countries when the capitalised value of the differential in expected lifetime earnings abroad as compared with those at home exceeds the transfer and relocation costs. Any such calculation is subject to information costs and the risk of error in the available information as well as the possibility of subsidies towards transfer and relocation costs. More crudely and more simply, migration tends to rise in deteriorating and fall in improving conditions at home relative to prospective destinations. How far is this simple general model relevant to Australia?

It may seem contradictory to say that this model applied in both an overwhelming and a minimal way. While a massive flow of people occurred from Britain to North America between 1788 and 1850, the flow to Australia was relatively minute. The cash fares to Australia for much of the period were about eight times that to North America and possibly represented for wage-earners in excess of a full annual wage; to these fares had to be added support for a journey that took four to six times as long. Prospective outlays for a family were almost prohibitive. In addition, the flow of information about prospects in North America and the presence there of relatives or acquaintances greatly reduced information costs. In Australia, the reputation of convictism served for a long time as a special disincentive.

In conformity with the simple model, then, it is not surprising that migration flows to Australia were tiny relative to trans-Atlantic movements. The theory might also be taken to explain why migration to Australia was dominated by 'assisted' migration, though the word assisted has several connotations. But once 'assistance' is introduced, the motivation for transfers becomes much more complex than the theory can easily accommodate. We need to add additional considerations because many methods of assistance became available.

In broad terms, 'free' immigration into Australia was very restricted until the early 1830s. Then, with the introduction of assistance schemes, the numbers rose relatively rapidly largely due to the introduction of bounties and public subsidies. But this numerical change should not be allowed to conceal the character, scale and conditions of pre-1830 immigration. It is inconceivable that we could recover, with any accuracy, the flow of 'migrants' before 1830 and more particularly the net inflow. Convicts escaped, ex-convicts left and returned (having realised the benefits of Australian residence), officials were sent to, and withdrawn from, Australia on British command, some officials with their families chose to remain, convicts' families were sometimes able to follow them. At best, we have to rely on gross inflow in most cases and, frequently, guess at these.

Nevertheless, it is essential, in order to understand Australian economic development, to try to acquire some idea of the numbers of and the attractions to these pre-1830 immigrants. Madgwick (1937) ignores officials. Yet, clearly, they were vital influences not merely in the government of the colonies but in the early development of local enterprise and those who chose to give up official roles and remain in Australia had major long-term influences (cf. Macarthur or Marsden in NSW and Kemp in Van Diemen's Land). The small number of merchants and tradespeople were similarly acutely important in the development of Australian trade. As the colony developed in its first few decades, other officials, not of Australia but of the British Empire or the army and navy, once retired, were attracted to Australian prospects.

In all these cases, there were specific reasons why the costs of transfer and location and the costs of information were reduced in a relatively special manner. Delivered at no private cost to Australia, the early arrivals could learn at first-hand of the opportunities at their disposal. Those earliest on the scene faced least competition in locating. They were allowed, for long periods, under the rules of the prevalent game, to secure public subsidies of land grants and convicts together with ration allocations to facilitate their decision to stay. As we will see in the part of the volume dealing with the establishment of a bridgehead economy, the early comers had other equally lucrative support. 'Assisted' immigration was a very early phenomenon.

Table 2.1 shows some available estimates for official movement. The first column is the only approximation to a partially net immigration series that we have, derived from annual changes in the recorded official populations. Some will have, in due course, left the colony so that the long-term inflow was less (particularly the first marine contingent). Some will have died. But it indicates for NSW something of the relatively large and erratic fluctuations that occurred. Inflow into NSW continued beyond the early 1820s as administrations changed but the significance of new additions of ex-officials had largely ended by then. The second column, relating to Van Diemen's Land, is intended to indicate the dimension of gross flows. Relative to the colonial population they were large. One of the problems in dealing with official movements is illustrated — Australian colonies increasingly became staging points for shifting officials around the empire in the Pacific and Indian Oceans. There is no possibility that these numbers remained for long in Van Diemen's Land.

One of the important elements in this very early inflow both of officials and the very small number of non-official immigrants which influenced migration decisions was an official and non-official imperial network.This network became increasingly important from the close of the Napoleonic Wars and particularly so during the 1820s. Personal contacts throughout the Empire and with Britain were important in delivering information to a particular set of individuals that played a major role in development throughout that period. After the wars, there was an increasing number of imperial and service officials retired or released — army and navy officers, colonial administrators in India etc. — with whom Australian colonial residents were acquainted.

Table 2.1 Indicators of Official Movements, New South Wales and Van Diemen's Land

Year	New South Wales (a) Gross official increase including families	Year	Van Diemen's Land (b) Gross military arrivals including families
1788	273	1829	339
1789	0	1830	595
1790	42	1831	356
1791	282	1832	167
1792	0	1833	970
1793	0	1834	241
1794	90	1835	471
1795	18	1836	268
1796	47	1837	391
1797	0	1838	358
1798	34	1839	341
1799	161	1840	293
1800	0	1841	589
1801	0	1842	854
1802	0	1843	1030
1803	0	1844	1581
1804	120	1845	1665
1805	0	1846	1635
1806	800	1847	485
1807	0	1848	985
1808	200	1849	451
1809	0	1850	238
1810	0		
1811	0		
1812	0		
1813	0		
1814	0		
1815	0		
1816	0		
1817	13		
1818	600		
1819	0		
1820	0		
1821	0		
1822	0		

Sources: (a) New South Wales: Butlin, Ginswick and Stathan in Vamplew (1987).
(b) Van Diemen's Land: Shipping arrivals at Hobart (Tas. Arch. Microfilm).

They were persons of some, if not great, substance — enough at least to qualify for transfer and settlement subsidies that the British government offered as reward for imperial or war service. Although their inflow was not readily supported within the colony before 1820, it was this group that was given active support both in Britain and Australia after 1820. Most importantly, after 1826, half-pay officers were singled out for support in settling in NSW and Van Diemen's Land (*HRA*, series I, vol. 12: 593).

Land grants and convict labour allocations, sometimes of considerable dimension, represented substantial assistance for such ex-officials from Britain and the Empire to relocate in Australia. The 1828 Census indicates that much of the free flow into

THE COLONIAL PEOPLING OF AUSTRALIA

both NSW and Van Diemen's Land between 1820 and 1829 appears to have been made up of this type of free, but very definitely assisted, immigrant to be the land-owners and capitalist employers of a large fraction of the convict workforce. These landowners and their convict and ex-convict employees were in the forefront of the transfer of lands from Aborigines to colonists.

Table 2.2: Free Immigration, Gross Arrivals, Australia, 1788–1850

Year	NSW(a) Non-Official	Year	NSW(a)	VDL(b)	WA(c)	SA(d)	Total
1788	26	1821	190	110			300
1789	0	1822	230	545			775
1790	38	1823	260	283			543
1791	40	1824	250	530			780
1792	19	1825	300	603			903
1793	11	1826	310	405			715
1794	7	1827	360	690			1 050
1795	7	1828	440	765	0		1 205
1796	15	1829	370	274	669		1 313
1797	17	1830	486	847	1 337		2 670
1798	42	1831	457	901	256		1 614
1799	18	1832	2 006	2 025	15		4 046
1800	50	1833	2 685	2 585	118		5 388
1801	80	1834	1 564	1 236	167		2 967
1802	60	1835	1 428	1 215	72	0	2 715
1803	40	1836	1 721	512	27	546	2 806
1804	70	1837	3 477	1 024	53	0	4 554
1805	10	1838	7 430	1 037	106	0	8 573
1806	50	1839	10 549	800	128	477	11 954
1807	40	1840	8 486	910	182	2 992	12 570
1808	40	1841	22 483	1 144	374	776	24 777
1809	30	1842	8 987	1 835	593	0	11 415
1810	70	1843	1 142	1 666	246	1 213	4 267
1811	20	1844	4 687	854	133	1 114	6 788
1812	40	1845	1 096	353	32	2 336	3 817
1813	50	1846	402	695	111	4 458	5 666
1814	120	1847	816	924	67	5 645	7 452
1815	70	1848	9 104	1 097	211	7 664	18 076
1816	100	1849	19 340	1 583	221	16 166	37 310
1817	80	1850	8 593	1 774	625	10 358	21 350
1818	80						
1819	80						
1820	130						

Sources:
(a) NSW: (1) to 1800 based on Vamplew (1987).
　　　　 (2) 1800–28 based on interrogation of 1828 Census subject to assumed standard death rates.
　　　　 (3) from 1829 from Madgwick (1937).
(b) VDL (1) 1821–28 estimated as residual of Madgwick's departures for NSW and Van Diemen's Land (VDL) and Census estimates for NSW.
　　　　 (2) 1829–50 Shipping arrivals at Hobart (Tasmania Archive microfilm)
(c) & (d) Western Australia (WA) & South Australia (SA) from Vamplew (1987).

Many of the early Australian 'capitalists' were, then, in a real if special sense, 'assisted immigrants' whose relocation but not transfer costs were publicly assisted. The conventional dating of assisted immigration (as the term is generally understood, it implies in Australia the subsidising of transfer but not relocation costs) began in 1831. By then, several disparate changes had occurred.

The settlement of Western Australia in 1829 as a free Crown colony was designed, amongst other things, to establish capitalist interests responsible for importing free rather than convict labour. Though that settlement struggled for survival, its establishment signalled the beginning of a change of policy in Britain to encourage free migration progressively leading to the outflow of paupers or of wage-earners unable to meet transfer costs but employable in Australia. That policy, applied to the eastern colonies, was designed to be funded by colonial land sales and to that extent depended on simultaneous expansion of truly unassisted persons of means as potential employers of labour. Land grants were abandoned, sales of Crown land were adopted as the rule and the revenues proposed by Britain to be reserved for immigration (on the fiscal dispute arising, see part III). Shortly after, in 1836, came the Wakefieldian experiment in the foundation of the South Australian colony designed, amongst other things, according to Wakefield, to limit access of wage-earners to landownership and hence to preserve the supply of wage-earners in the colony.

Though one might see this extension of settlement to the south and west as part of the process of British acquisition of the whole of Australia, this, and the accompanying policy changes, derived also from a basic shift towards colonisation and the outflow of persons from Britain. That change derived in part from the persuasive zeal of colonial reformers such as Horton and Wakefield. But it also stemmed from the increasing acceptance of Malthusian views on the growing population problem that Britain was believed to be facing and on increasing fiscal pressures that British authorities confronted.

There can be no doubt that the views of the colonial reformers, represented in publications and in many appearances before a wide range of committees investigating the colonies, population questions, the Poor Law etc., significantly influenced action. British policy had begun to respond to those views, initially of Horton, from the end of the Napoleonic Wars in the encouragement of migration to Canada.

There was still a good deal of incoherence in that policy until the proposals for the elimination of land grants and for assisted immigration funded by land sales in eastern Australia were put into execution in 1831. Those changes had the crucial implication of tying migration to Australia with land revenues raised in Australia. So far as the British government was concerned, it eliminated the question of differential transfer costs between Australia and Canada. Even then, administration of schemes of assisted immigration were not highly organised, with competing and decentralised systems for selection and despatch of assisted migrants.

In 1837, the establishment of the position of Agent General for Emigration in Britain, in combination with funding of migration support through colonial land sales and the abandonment of colonial land grants in eastern Australia, provided Britain with the essential administrative and fiscal machinery to carry through a purposive system of assisted migration to Australia. This administrative arrangement counterbalanced a colonial organisation ultimately in the form of Committees of Immigration in association with subsidiary bodies (such as Ladies Committees) to evaluate arrivals. Though this administrative arrangement changed in detail over time, the essentials of the organisational structure were established (see Madgwick (1937) for qualifications and variations).

Within this structure, two systems of assisted immigration, supplementing a modest flow of unsubsidised migration, were established. One was the so-called bounty system, the other the government system. Administratively, these were divided partly in terms of the share of land sales revenue allocated to each (basically one-third to the bounty system) and partly by the mechanism for nominations and selection.

The British government claimed the right to determine supply under the government scheme leaving individual colonists to nominate and the colonial governments to requite bounty claims. Under the government scheme, free passages were supplied. Under the bounty scheme, repayable advances were offered to migrants with returns to shippers for delivery. In practice, many advances were unpaid and, in that respect, the differences between the two systems narrowed.

But there was a fundamental difference in selection procedures. Bounty agents became prominent and these spread information, misinformation and disinformation about conditions in Australia in order to fill ships. Though this introduced a form of publicity about Australia throughout large areas of Britain, the impact of this information on potential migrants was qualified by the growing control of the (British) Agent for Immigration and the persistence of shippers in filling passenger space. The colonial governments attempted to establish some degree of supervision by the appointment of ships' surgeons to review selections but this was not a close oversight.

There was, then, the potential for considerable conflict of interest on the British supply side and the Australian demand side for assisted migrants. Wakefield's theory of colonisation that strongly influenced land and migration policy from 1831 envisaged little difference of interest between colonists and Britain. Wakefield perceived the British population problem as being essentially one of surplus rural population containing skills that land rich colonies found in short supply. With that perception, he proposed three basic principles:

- the abandonment of land grants and the sale of land exclusively at a 'sufficient' price that would prevent wage-earners acquiring access to land and would force them to compete within the labour market, thereby keeping wages suppressed;
- the allocation of land revenues to meet migration costs; and
- the establishment of a central British administrative control.

The bounty system that allowed colonists to express demands directly and for agents to operate separate from British government control was a British concession that partly disrupted the neatness of the Wakefield principles. Had Wakefield been correct in postulating a simple relationship between colonial rural landowner–employers and a surplus British rural population, the colonial demand for labour might seem a relatively simple function.

On the assumption of a *de facto* gift of transfer expenses to migrants, colonial demand for (wholly rural) labour would continue to the point where land purchase sums (expenses of migration) equalled the capitalised value of the increased marginal product of the (skilled rural) migrants plus the savings accruing from lowered wage rates in the colony. To the extent that some bounty payments were actually recouped, the demand for migrants would be higher. The British rural slums and the Poor Law outlays would be reduced, surplus rural population would be gainfully occupied in the colonies while colonial productivity would rise, activity expand and colonial wages would fall. There would be neither gainers nor losers in Wakefield's Empire.

Even within this narrow construct, problems arose. The colonists wanted active young adults. The surplus British rural population did not necessarily conform to that simple specification, representing a spectrum of ages and, among unemployed, persons whose incentives to work had been affected by long periods of unemployment and dependence. The displaced rural population of Britain frequently also had families of varying ages and bounty rates were offered for man, wife and children. Colonial demands therefore had to accommodate to the possibility of dependents, altering the colonial calculus. Persistent colonial criticism of received migrants arose in terms of the undue youth and number of dependents in migrating families.

Married women and girls sufficiently old to have been trained for domestic tasks were, however, in high demand. This partly reflected the sex imbalance in the colonies and a demand for sexual partners. But it also represented the pressures in economic terms to supplement the market economy with household production by females. Men were perceived as possessing a comparative advantage in farm production, females as the deliverers of household services. To the extent to which this was true (and it clearly was not without substantial qualification), the subsidised immigration of females allowed improved factor allocation, males being released to concentrate on tasks for which they had this comparative advantage (colonial marginal product would rise even without an accession of male migrants). But the condition required of females was that they should be young, appropriately trained in domestic skills, of good morals and, to put it bluntly, be 'biddable'. The rural workhouses of Britain were not ideal sources of supply of such women and the colonial record is full of complaints about inappropriate age of women and girls, their lack of training and their 'low moral character'.

Insofar as Britain was concerned to reduce the population of its workhouses, both rural and urban, a collision of British colonial interest was almost inevitable. But the Wakefield assumptions about the colonies were patently incorrect in two other respects. Rural landowners were not the only employers of rural labour. The squatters who continued to occupy land without payment beyond the declared limits of settlement were direct competitors. Wakefield's proposal was to shoot them!

There were also urban employers of labour seeking skilled craftsmen and female domestics. These two groups were largely free riders in the immigration market (though some revenue was derived from urban land sales). The calculus of the rural contributors of land revenues was then much more restrictive in that a substantial part of their contributions was poached by other employing groups. What this served to do was to make their criticisms of the immigrants the more vociferous, particularly in terms of the reluctance to leave the towns.

Nevertheless, despite the protestations about the quality and mobility of immigrants, rural land buyers were not simply losers to the extent to which urban employers diverted part of the flow to urban employment. The colonial towns supplied a wide range of services, not merely port services, to rural landholders. Some externalities accrued to the latter from urban development. The original calculus could be adjusted to add the capitalised value of the stream of externalities. But it was an obscure advantage.

There were, then, a considerable number of reasons for the colonists to be prepared to criticise the influx of assisted immigrants even under the bounty system.

The crucial weakness of the bounty system from the point of view of rural land buyers was the prohibitive cost facing most individual employers to select, transport and hold migrants. Some very large ones, such as the Australian Agricultural Company, were able to import indentured rural labourers from Britain and the South Australia Company also acquired indentured Indian servants. But indentured employment was of little importance in Australia. Most land buyers had to accept a common mechanism of selection. That mechanism became, for much of the 1830s, a confused mix of bounty hunters and shippers with some relatively indirect oversight by colonially chosen ships' surgeons and the British Agent (later Agent General) for Emigration.

All these individuals engaged in selection and almost inevitably found their prime source of supply in the British workhouses in both town and country. But the same source of supply and the same supply determinants applied to the larger migrant flow organised as the government scheme, directly controlled by the British government through its Emigration Agent (General). Whatever demand conditions might be expressed in the colonies, they could be, to a very large extent, frustrated by supply-side considerations. Colonial criticisms may have carried some weight; the selected ships' surgeons may have exercised some selection; the Emigration Agent may have tried, as Madgwick puts it, to 'select the best possible' recognising that the best was impossible. But the workhouses could scarcely be thought of as reasonably representative of the socioeconomic structure of Britain. The workhouse authorities, the Poor Law authorities, local parsons and others connected with the British paupers highly praised the operators of both migrant schemes as they served the objective purpose of assisted migration, to remove British paupers.

At best, the workhouses provided two types of potential migrants that might have served colonial interests. Firstly, there were the juveniles who to age 14 had, in fact, spent their time in training and some form of education throughout their childhood. Persons of this age were significant amongst the assisted immigrants but they scarcely dominated the flow. Rather, the colonial criticism on this score was that very few such young trainees arrived. The second possibility was that, in periods of business fluctuations, the recently unemployed might have been given brief refuge in the workhouses and be attracted into migrating without having experienced the degradation of long-term unemployment.

The statistics of immigration into NSW do, in fact, show two years of extremely high immigration, in 1841 and 1849, when numbers arriving in those two years amounted to approximately one-third of the total influx during 1831–50. Both 1841 and 1849 were years of British recession. It is possible that a short-term migration market worked to colonial benefit. There is, however, another explanation and one that influences the whole of the assisted migration process.

As to Britain facing great pressure on its Poor Law facilities between 1815 and 1850 there can be little doubt. This, as has already been suggested, was not merely a matter of rural displacement and poverty but also of urban dislocation. Facing massive readjustment in both rural and urban areas, Britain was also confronting two crucial fiscal changes. One was the long-term pressure to control government expenditure and revenue raising. The other was to readapt from the funding procedure, particularly in the imposition of income taxes, during the Napoleonic Wars. The abandonment of income taxation at the end of the wars threw the weight of revenue raising back on customs and excise and property taxation. The expansion of urban populations and industrial activity was part of the pressure behind the reform of the Corn Laws and the movement towards free trade, threatening the supply of customs revenue.

In the circumstances, property taxation became increasingly prominent as the basis of British revenue sources and placed property owners under growing pressure from the tax gatherer. Given the dependence of Poor Law Relief on local rates (i.e. local property taxes), it is not surprising that the workhouses were under pressure to reduce their expenditures. Britain's response, in 1834, to make workhouses unattractive as refuges was in line with its enthusiasm for assisted migration and closely timed with it. From the British government's point of view the more dependent paupers were, the better did they appear as candidates for emigration. Madgwick indicates that they virtually targeted emigration authorities and agents in order to reduce the pressure on their resources (i.e. on property owners). To avoid an outlay at no cost required little in the way of calculus. The more they could shift the long-term unemployed, the more certain they could be of a reduction in outlays. Contact with those engaged in selection was easiest in towns (and with shippers in port towns) so that, as with convicts, the supply bias was strongly towards the urban poor. This conforms to colonial complaints that they failed to acquire adequate supplies of farm skills through either the bounty or the government schemes.

But one question, at least, remains. Was it merely the poor who were assisted after 1831? The colonists certainly were active in their comments on the apparent criminal proclivities of many of the delivered immigrants. Was this merely the pot having a chance to call the kettle black or were there real foundations in these comments? Did the assisted migration schemes offer an alternative route whereby criminals were diverted to Australia without being formally transported? (And one might ask whether similar questions might be raised in connection with assistance schemes to other colonies including Canada.) This is something on which one can only speculate. Tobias (1967) appears to suggest a direct connection between court-room and workhouse but the evidence so far presented is slim. The Poor Law authorities certainly appear to have considered girls over 14 years of age taking refuge in workhouses as often passing from one criminal act to the next. The colonists appear to have agreed with this judgment, at least in principle. This is a matter for further research and a project beyond the scope of this book. It would entail a detailed study, relating trials, workhouses and gaols.

It would have a peculiar interest in relating Australia's first large assisted immigration scheme to that after the Second World War when massive flows of displaced persons occurred. Many were merely refugees, many from concentration camps, some were war criminals. Was there a historical echo between the two experiences?

The prime recipient of assisted immigrants to 1850, Wakefield's theories and his experiment in South Australia nothwithstanding, was New South Wales. Van Diemen's Land took little part, perhaps because of the massive land grants that had been made on the island. As it lost population to Port Phillip after 1836, it took a somewhat more prominent role in the closing years of the 1840s. Neither South Australia nor Western Australia was administratively organised as very young settlements to take much part. Accordingly, table 2.3 indicates only the flows into NSW. Assisted immigration is shown along with unassisted to indicate the much larger level of the former and also the much higher proportion of juveniles amongst the assisted group.

Table 2.3: Assisted and Unassisted Immigration, NSW 1832–50

Year	Assisted Immigration			Unassisted Immigration			Total Assisted & Unassisted
	Males	Females	Children	Males	Females	Children	
1832	140	455	197	679	251	284	2 006
1833	177	728	348	661	418	353	2 685
1834	52	299	133	519	297	264	1 564
1835	33	426	86	518	218	147	1 428
1836	73	595	140	551	212	150	1 721
1837	688	840	1 136	437	200	176	3 477
1838	1 928	1 673	2 501	764	438	126	7 430
1839	3 137	3 017	3 262	1 151	576	406	11 549
1840	2 631	2 733	1 273	1 129	427	293	8 486
1841	7 467	7 985	4 651	1 334	569	477	22 483
1842	2 590	2 532	1 701	1 193	462	509	8 987
1843	3	4	4	642	295	194	1 142
1844	1 362	1 337	1 440	336	131	81	4 687
1845	174	178	146	267	144	187	1 096
1846	0	0	0	210	117	75	402
1847	0	0	0	405	237	174	816
1848	2 741	2 919	2 225	712	329	178	9 104
1849	5 155	6 298	4 320	1 728	968	871	19 340
1850	1 712	3 323	1 020	1 189	833	516	8 593

Source: Madgwick (1937: 223).

The dominance of NSW and Van Diemen's Land until the last few years of the 1840s can be seen by reference back to table 2.2 (p.22). In the late 1840s, South Australia (SA) shot to prominence. One should be cautious about interpreting these separate colonial series. There was a good deal of intercolonial migration making it difficult to disentangle the experience of individual colonies particularly after 1840. This includes substantial gross outflows from South Australia so that the net intake by that colony was considerably reduced.

The Colonial Born

The third gross addition to population and workforce was those born in the colony(ies). As with convicts and immigrants, they were affected by outflows and by deaths. Concentrating on the gross numbers firstly, there were several sources of the colonial born populations. They have, as Robinson (1985) indicates, been treated, if at all, as discarded and unwanted children of convicts for much of early history. In reality, however, locally born were due to several sources as children of:
- officials and their arriving wives;
- officials and convict or ex-convict alliances;
- migrant parents particularly after 1832;
- migrant and ex-convict or convict alliances;
- convicts and ex-convicts;
- wholly colonial born alliances themselves from about 1818–20; and
- colonial born and any of the above groups from about 1818–20.

There is an eighth category of colonial born that should be mentioned though it

Table 2.4: Colonial Born According to the NSW Census, 1828

Age	Male	Female	Total	Approximate Birth Date
0			608	1828
1			510	1827
2			556	1826
3			504	1825
4			458	1824
5			437	1823
6			363	1822
7			415	1821
8			290	1820
9			292	1819
10			306	1818
11			258	1817
12			253	1816
13			246	1815
14			229	1814
15	108	92	200	1813
16	88	99	187	1812
17	89	88	177	1811
18	98	106	204	1810
19	80	87	167	1809
20	89	86	175	1808
21	81	76	157	1807
22	80	78	158	1806
23	67	64	131	1805
24	48	58	106	1804
25	58	59	117	1803
26	32	44	76	1802
27	32	38	70	1801
28	39	32	71	1800
29	22	22	44	1799
30	36	47	83	1798
31	18	17	35	1797
32	16	36	52	1796
33	21	26	47	1795
34	17	18	35	1794
35	7	14	21	1793
36	6	11	17	1792
37	0	11	11	1791
38	2	7	9	1790
39	3	2	5	1789
40	1	1	2	1788

Source: 1828 Census of NSW. Note that the data from the Census are accepted for this purpose subject to excluding those with gaol sentences. Robinson (1985) suggests that up to 1813 the Census may have overcounted the true colonial born by about 10 per cent.

has rarely, if ever, been acknowledged and is very difficult to handle. This is the progeny of colonists at any level having temporary or long-term alliances with Aborigines. That this happened not infrequently is clear enough. But just as the early colonial born tended to be categorised as children of convicts and when counted in Musters listed with their convict parent, so it seems most probable that the product of unions between European colonists and Aborigines were treated — and almost certainly behaved — as Aborigines. They might be expected to have helped, in part, to restore a little of the early population losses to which the Aborigines were subject. However, it is not possible to take this component into account and the discussion below relates only to European children born in Australia.

The strong sex imbalance in the colony(ies) inevitably limited the local production of European children. This did not apply so much to the group of officials though even in this case only a relatively small fraction of military personnel was allowed to bring wives to the settlement. Some supplement to convict progeny came when non-convict spouses joined their convict mates as migrants. On the other hand, there was an important feature of Australia during the first few decades that affected the increase in the colonial born. This was the absence of many of the communicable diseases of childhood to which their parents in Britain had been subject. So far as gross additions to the colonial born are concerned, this may not have mattered for the first two decades. But because a significantly higher proportion of colonially born infants survived to maturity, their own rate of reproduction was faster than would otherwise have been expected.

In other words, the progeny of the first generation of the colonial born contributed abnormally to population growth particularly from about 1818. Disregarding the civil status of the eventual partner of the first generation, as Robinson shows, they married young and reproduced relatively prolifically. Moreover, with the exception of a few specific years, it appears that, predominantly, they stayed in Australia. Forming together with their parents as contributors to farming, trades and personal service, they remained to swell the local population.

Clearly some did leave. Departures followed the withdrawal of official parents and, on average, one would expect this to have meant an approximate equality of the

Table 2.5: Officially Recorded Total Births, Australia, 1788–1850

Year	Births	Year	Births	Year	Births
1788	28	1809	269	1830	1430
1789	43	1810	322	1831	1652
1790	64	1811	315	1832	1782
1791	64	1812	339	1833	2195
1792	80	1813	374	1834	2639
1793	83	1814	356	1835	2640
1794	107	1815	311	1836	2952
1795	106	1816	285	1837	3113
1796	95	1817	393	1838	3823
1797	133	1818	376	1839	4490
1798	101	1819	449	1840	5622
1799	120	1820	535	1841	6650
1800	101	1821	707	1842	7836
1801	105	1822	622	1843	9531
1802	138	1823	689	1844	10447
1803	140	1824	674	1845	10880
1804	163	1825	800	1846	11028
1805	176	1826	1027	1847	11556
1806	158	1827	1074	1848	11847
1807	142	1828	1191	1849	12922
1808	197	1829	1306	1850	14341

Source: McDonald, Ruzicka and Pyne in Vamplew (1987).

sexes of departing children. We can perhaps derive some statistical hint of the loss by out-migration of the other colonial born by interrogating the 1828 Census (see table 2.4) and noting the sex imbalance of the 1828 survivors in the form of clearly low proportions of males. (Females had little opportunity to depart.) This is a relatively crude test and becomes less meaningful as one moves back towards 1788. Nevertheless, it suggests that there may have been an exceptional departure of colonially born males (other than those of official families) particularly during the years 1790–3, 1795–6, and 1802–4. If correct, this would have delayed the subsequent accelerating influence of the colonial born on total population expansion.

For gross flows from local reproduction, we need data on births. Unfortunately, these records were very incomplete, influenced partly by the inadequate administrative organisation, the lack of compulsory registration until 1841 (VDL) and 1855 (NSW) and sectarian conflict leading to difficulties in having births recorded. Anglican births may have been reasonably well recorded, subject to considerable delays that increasingly distort the annual series as settlement extended. Some other sects kept some records but all are incomplete. Table 2.5 gives the recorded official data to which, on an average for each year, a significant upward adjustment needs to be made. We do have information on religions for large groups of the population and it is suggested that to allow for sectarian constraints and administrative shortcomings the figures below should be increased by about 20 per cent.

What is striking is that, subject to a little uncertainty about Van Diemen's Land before 1820, colonial births exceeded — and typically did so by a considerable margin — the gross inflows of immigrants in every year other than the depression years of 1839–42. This was the case despite the low proportion of females throughout and notwithstanding the migration efforts of the 1830s. Moreover, ignoring years when no convicts arrived, colonial births had outstripped convict arrivals from Great Britain and Ireland by 1838, before transportation to NSW was halted. Clearly, this group eventually had a major contribution to the growth of total Australian colonial population even though death claimed an increasing proportion of infants as communicable diseases were established in Australia.

3

THE COLONIAL POPULATION STOCK

Projecting Population and Workforce Components

Because of its relative novelty, this section requires a good deal of statistical documentation to substantiate a possible picture of the stock of population and workforce derived by population projection techniques. A verbal summary of the main implications is given at the end of the section.

The three major sources of increase, convicts, free immigrants and colonial born, are subject to losses from death and out-migration. One might expect that different factors could determine the growth of each element. So far as inflows were concerned, the first group was located in Australia coercively, the second responded primarily to socioeconomic push conditions and the third had, at best, a tenuous connection with economic incentives. Death rates were influenced strongly by environmental conditions in Australia affecting age-specific life expectations (in a highly favourable manner). And out-migration was subject, above all, to opportunities for absconding by convicts and the financial and legal restraints on the return to Britain of time-expired convicts.

There are several obstacles to defining the contributions of the three major sources of population or workforce. Firstly, the accuracy of the official aggregates at Musters and Censuses is not high. Secondly, even when some of the components are reported in official estimates, there are many obvious errors in the available figures. Thirdly, only very incomplete records are available of the major components. The most satisfactory are the estimates of bond population but even these are confused by the inclusion of many children born to convicts in Australia and the difficulty, in any event, of keeping track of all convicts. Detailed work on the surviving Musters may improve this picture but there appear to be major obstacles to recovering the information accurately. Data on age are not frequently assembled though it would be possible, very arduously, to reconstruct ages within reason. The official record appears better on the gross flows of convicts throughout and 'free' immigrants after 1830. It is less satisfactory on births.

It is possible, as is it necessary, to fall back on indirect methods to estimate trends in the major components of population — age, sex and civil status — by using the record of gross additions — convicts and free immigrant arrivals and colonial births rather than such stock records as exist. It is not suggested that these indirect methods will yield very accurate results. However, they seem promising as indications of the trend changes in total population and workforce and in the structure of these aggregates.

This indirect approach rests on progressive five-yearly population projections. These yield broad pictures of the proportion of the population at these intervals composed of convicts and ex-convicts, of free immigrants and of colonial born as survivors of the three major flows at these intervals. They also provide estimates, for the same dates, of both the age and sex composition of the population.

The fact that they yield an approximate outline and not exact estimates needs to be stressed. There is a second limitation: the projections must be confined to New South Wales and Van Diemen's Land. That these two colonies, even in 1850, accounted for over 80 per cent of the total population means that this is not a major problem, although South Australia at that date warrants some attention. The third limitation is that the projections must depend on a number of key assumptions which may not be universally appropriate.

The three sources of increase are projected for successive five-yearly intervals using the following assumptions based on fairly realistic considerations:

(a) Actual annual records of convict and immigrant arrivals may be taken as underlying inflows. Records of births are adjusted on the assumption of a 20 per cent undercount.

(b) Age structures for batches of convicts on arrival have been taken, up to 1816 based on my own estimates for the period 1788–1816 and thereafter from a 9 per cent sample of all convicts taken by Robson (1965). Attractive as, in many respects, the Nicholas estimates (1988) are, they are not presented in a way easily adapted to normal five-yearly intervals. The age structures, it should be noted, were subject to considerable variance over time so that short-term errors in projections must be expected.

(c) Arriving migrants are assumed to have had the same age structure as that of England and Wales in 1841, subject to a maximum age cut-off at 50 years. This assumption fails to capture the Irish element in immigration. The year 1841 is chosen as the approximate midpoint of the dominant period of immigration, 1830–50.

(d) For all groups, a life expectancy at birth of 35 years is assumed, a level conforming reasonably with the estimated British life expectancy of about 1830. This assumption fails to capture the improvement in life expectancy in Australian conditions, partly because of the exceptional health conditions of children and partly because of the prolongation of life in Australia even for arriving adults. Within this general assumption, age-specific life expectancies have been adopted from Coale and Demeny (1983) for circumstances appropriate to a rapidly expanding population. A more subtle and effective procedure would be to allow for progressive improvements in life expectancy over the period.

(e) No provision is made for out-migration or absconding. Though the latter factor is important in early years, the reputed rate of absconding is highly misleading and often irrelevant insofar as absconding convicts frequently did not actually leave the population. However, in the early years, the population projections overstate both the totals and the various components but, particularly ex-convicts, by omitting out-migration.

In practical terms, survivors for NSW and Van Diemen's Land are projected at five-yearly intervals by combining each two years surrounding nominated dates. A very crude procedure has been adopted to deal with the special death tolls on the Second and Third Fleets.

Tests

The resulting projections have been tested in two ways — by comparing the totals with the official estimates and by comparing the projected and Census age structures in 1841 and 1851. These tests yield some encouragement and some warnings.

A comparison of the projected totals and modern official estimates and contemporary returns is given in table 3.1 (below).

The projections are likely to be doubtful for the first few dates. Shaw (1966) believes that a significant proportion of convicts, time-expired, returned to Britain during the first 15 to 20 years. Thereafter out-migration of convicts became very small. Correction for this factor to 1805 would bring the adjusted projections and the official estimates closer together. It would be necessary for the loss from absconding and return home to average about 20 per cent during 1795–1805 for the corrected projections to match the official estimates. This is, indeed, approximately what Shaw proposes.

Between 1810 and 1817, the Muster of 1817 provides a partial check on later outflows suggesting that less than 1 per cent of ex-convicts left the colony over that period. Thereafter, apart from 1820 and 1825, the projections conform closely to the

Table 3.1: Population Projections and Census, 1790–1850

| | Aggregate Comparison | | | Contemporary Returns | |
Year	Projected	Official	NSW	VDL	Total
1790	2 295	2 056	2 542	–	2 542
1795	4 670	3 466	4 693	–	4 693
1800	6 150	5 217	5 658	–	5 658
1805	8 458	7 707	7 666	757	8 423
1810	11 278	11 566	10 629	1 470	12 099
1815	15 585	15 063	12 911	1 947	14 858
1820	32 190	33 543	25 526	5 519	31 045
1825	48 400	52 505	38 168	14 192	52 360
1830	67 938	70 039	46 302	24 279	70 581
1835	112 034	113 540	71 592	40 172	111 764
1840	181 260	175 462	129 463	45 999	175 462
1845	262 735	279 148	181 556	64 291	245 847
1850	327 624	330 197	265 503	68 870	334 373

recent official figures. The occasions of conflict suggest some caution though there is considerable doubt about the accuracy of the official figures in 1820 and 1825 and in the contemporary and recent official adjustments to the 1828 Census, possibly leading official estimates into significant exaggerations. From 1810, the projections are normally a little below the official figures and this is the opposite of what one might expect. However, until we can discover exactly how the various official estimates were made we cannot be sure that this expectation is justified in this case. In any case, during 1830–50, the comparisons are close enough to be encouraging.

Without seeking to evade the test of comparison with official totals, it is important to make clear that the object of the present exercise is to try to obtain a broad picture of the trends in particular components influencing the population and workforce. Nevertheless, the overall test is important.

The problem in comparing official estimates with these projections may be illustrated with reference to the 1828 Census of NSW. It is generally accepted that this Census was an undercount and internal evidence indicates a considerable number of persons not listed who were nevertheless in the colony. It does not follow, however, that the Census was an undercount to the extent officially believed or indeed that it was necessarily an undercount at all. The official view has led to successive upward adjustment. Early official estimates raised the Census figure of 36 600 ostensibly to provide for an alleged 2500 'unaccounted for' (said to be predominantly absconded convicts). The result was an apparently conservative adjustment to some 38 000. Recent estimates by the Commonwealth Bureau of Census and Statistics (cf. *Demography 1945*) raised this further to a little over 40 000 possibly to incorporate an alleged omission of military personnel (though it could have been a double counting of the supposedly missing convicts).

There are several problems with these later adjustments. Firstly, in their favour, internal evidence indicates that there probably should have been just on 300 more persons in the count than are actually reported. Reports of persons working for employers gave names not recorded in the primary count. Some of these may have come from persons who were included in the count and not at their proper location so that the number could be an exaggeration.

As against this group, there is a larger number (approaching 1000) whose entries have been duplicated and even triplicated in the Census. This arose because the so-called Census was a confusion of Census and Muster. Many persons were included in the Census of 1828 by a master providing lists of employees. Where such employees had more than one work location, sublists were returned, duplicating names. Sometimes an overseer at a sublocation even included the employee's name a second time.

The confusion reached its peak in attempts to enumerate at urban workplace and residence. The Census form confused employment status and residence status so that the same person could be listed as employed at one point and residing at another — separate reports coming from employers and householders. The problems were compounded by slight variations in the spelling of names, sometimes sufficient to defeat the Census clerks. The clerks clearly made some attempt to cope with duplications but the evidence is also clear that they were very far from successful.

If this may offset, in part, the number of allegedly absconded convicts, it is not necessarily the case that all such persons were omitted from the Census. A simple and even a slight change in name could achieve disappearance and re-emergence as another person and particularly someone now dead included in the preceding Muster. The evidence of duplication shows how easy this could be and indeed be done inadvertently. Moreover, it is possible that some, and in the circumstances, perhaps a significant number of allegedly absconded, convicts were dead and not due to be counted in any event.

What is, perhaps, of interest, is the question: Why were so many convicts believed to be missing? The *Sydney Gazette* has many notices of absconded convicts but this does not mean necessarily that the various notices should be summed to a grand total of such persons. The real point is, again, the confusion of Census and Muster. From at least 1810, governors worked from a base list of convicts and ex-convicts adjusted for deaths, departures and new arrivals. That these became progressively muddled is reasonably clear, almost certainly leading to overcount. This may be the reason why relatively large numbers are given in 1825 (the last so-called total Muster). These large numbers plague the attempt to estimate NSW populations during the 1820s, *the official estimates being adapted to conform to them.* Names not found at these Musters were left as persons unaccounted for, though they might be dead, have changed their names or left the colony. It is possible and seems very probable that the number surviving and not counted was a small fraction of the gross figure.

One might believe that an early Census is not likely to be highly accurate and this seems to be borne out by inspecting the 1828 Census. One's intuition might be that persons are likely to be missed. Certainly the 'missing' employees seem to be often on the outskirts of settlement where undercount could be most likely. But the assumption that overall such a primitive Census would yield a gross undercount is much less acceptable after inspecting the entries in detail. There are several factors that could lead even to the opposite result and these factors apply also to the Musters before 1828.

We can make a much harsher test than an aggregate one though it is limited to the years 1840 and 1850, by use of the Censuses of 1841 and 1851. Here we compare age structures, a matter particularly important for workforce populations. The NSW and Van Diemen's Land Censuses, plus the separate Port Phillip count in 1851 give very limited age counts — 0–1, 2–6, 7–13, 14–19, 20–43, 44–59 and 60 plus. These are adjusted to five-year age groups and rearranged as follows in table 3.2.

The major discrepancies are in the 45–59 age bracket in both years and in the 0–14 age bracket in 1851. There are quite remarkable anomalies in the 1851 Port Phillip Census which alone could eliminate the problems in 1851 (an incredibly high fecundity of Port Phillip women). The problems with the 45–59 age brackets are most probably due to the truncating of the age-structures of convicts and immigrants at both dates. Despite these problems, the broad age structures stand up quite well given the simplicity of the projection assumptions.

Table 3.2: Comparison of Age Structure (per cent of total population)

	Age				
	0–14	15–19	20–44	45–59	60+
1841 Census	27.3	7.2	56.8	6.8	1.9
1840 Projection	26.0	6.5	56.2	10.4	0.8
1851 Census	37.6	7.7	44.4	8.9	1.4
1850 Projection	33.5	7.7	45.7	12.2	0.9

Sources: Censuses of NSW and Van Diemen's Land, and Mansfield (1841).

Neither fact is conclusive though each suggests that the projections are not all that widely off the mark as to raise severe doubts about their ability to provide the basis of *trend* characteristics even though the reservations must be larger for some years. However, in breaking the population up into subsets, there is a greater risk of error.

Projection of Population Structure: Civil Status

The 'civil' composition of the European population of NSW and Van Diemen's Land, as projected, is shown in table 3.3.

Table 3.3: Civil Composition

Year	Convicts & Ex-Convicts		Free Immigrants		Colonial Born	
	Number	%	Number	%	Number	%
1790 (a)	2 000	87.1	260	11.3	35	1.5
1795	4 109	88.0	414	8.9	146	3.1
1800	5 330	86.7	365	5.9	454	7.4
1805	7 120	84.2	400	4.7	938	11.1
1810	8 671	76.9	634	5.6	1 971	17.5
1815	11 385	73.1	995	6.4	3 205	20.6
1820	24 244	75.6	2 100	6.5	5 746	17.9
1825	34 954	72.2	5 374	11.1	8 072	16.7
1830	48 214	71.0	7 998	11.8	11 724	17.3
1835	68 811	61.4	21 624	19.3	21 599	19.3
1840	83 963	46.3	55 060	30.4	42 236	23.3
1845	93 768	35.7	88 679	33.8	80 287	30.6
1850	95 391	28.9	119 760	36.3	114 472	34.7

Note: (a) These figures in this row are simple rounded totals that may understate the deaths on the Second Fleet.

As would be expected, convicts and ex-convicts made up the overwhelming majority until the late 1830s, even though their share fell from about 90 to about 60 per cent by 1835.

Only by 1850 did they make up the smallest component. Colonial born were the first to come to some prominence at about one-eighth of the population by 1805 and one-fifth by 1820. The large-scale immigration after 1830 made free immigrants an increasingly significant section, growing rapidly from about 12 per cent in 1830 to become the largest component at 36 per cent in 1850. By the latter date, the three groups were relatively similar to each other in size.

These three groups are identified for present purposes on the assumptions that their experience and status may have had different implications for the operation of the labour market. Much more work needs to be done to develop good statistics of surviving convicts at the various quinquennial points. Convict status, as such, could have more substantial bearing on the nature of the labour market. Some comparisons of convicts and ex-convicts are indicated in table 3.4 (p.38).

These figures cannot be treated as very accurate. There were no ex-convicts derived from convicts in 1788 and certainly not over 300 in 1790. It appears, that in early Musters, the number of convicts is exaggerated because the children born to convicts were included with the bond population. This is more than a little irritating

Table 3.4: Civil Status of Convicts, New South Wales and Van Diemens Land

Year	Convicts	Projected Convicts & Ex-Convicts	Implied Ex-Convicts
1788	717	735	18
1790	1 665	2 000	335
1795	3 358	4 100	742
1800	2 017	5 334	3 317
1805	2 386	7 120	4 735
1820	13 651	24 244	10 953
1825	22 938	34 954	12 016
1835	46 136	68 811	22 675
1840	56 178	83 963	27 785
1845	46 792	93 768	46 976
1850	23 801	95 391	72 590

not only because of the exaggeration but also because of the consequential under-statement of colonial born. The latter problem prevents one simple obvious test of one of the components of the projections.

Nevertheless, table 3.4 suggests substantial swings in the proportion of the free and freed population in the colonies. The proportion of convicts to total convict and ex-convict fall from an original 100 per cent in 1788 to approximately 36 per cent in 1800 and a little below one-third in 1805. By 1820, the proportion of convicts rose to about 70 per cent (possibly this occurred quickly after the end of the Napoleonic Wars) and remained at about this level until the second half of the 1830s from which point it declined steadily to the mid-1840s and then quickly dwindled. It becomes an interesting question whether this 'freeing' of the convict-derived population was reflected in a corresponding freeing of the labour market.

The other special characteristic of the early Australian population is its abnormal sex composition. The projections show this structure in the following form. For simplicity, it is assumed that there was an even split between male and female births.

Table 3.5: Female Population Projection

Year	Convicts & Ex-Convicts	Free Immigrants	Colonial Born	Projected Total	% of Total Persons
1790	363	45	17	425	19.6
1795	715	70	73	859	18.4
1800	1 048	87	254	1 391	22.6
1805	2 030	104	580	2 168	25.6
1810	2 599	217	985	3 233	28.7
1815	3 315	411	1 602	4 613	29.0
1820	4 045	783	2 373	6 473	20.2
1825	6 234	1 885	3 536	9 475	19.6
1830	8 730	3 395	5 862	15 491	22.9
1835	11 444	10 388	10 800	29 918	26.7
1840	13 293	26 242	21 118	58 806	32.4
1845	14 995	42 256	40 143	95 693	36.4
1850	10 715	58 617	57 236	130 848	39.9

On this basis, it would be suggested that female convicts and ex-convicts remained the major component of the female total until 1830 and then shrank rapidly to be comparatively insignificant by 1850. This reflects the low female convict inflow, the emphasis on assisted female immigration after 1830 and the rising importance of the colonial born. Due to the two last flows the relative importance of females in the total population rose very rapidly after 1830. Before then, an extreme sex imbalance existed (and was much more marked at the adult level). By 1850, the sex imbalance was greatly reduced although, because of the large inflow of child immigrants and the recent colonial born, the adult sex ratio was much more grossly distorted than these projections show.

The Potential Workforce

In this section, only the *potential* workforce is dealt with. For convenience, this potential is limited to those aged 12.5 to 59 years although it is recognised that some outside these limits sought or were required to work while some, particularly up to about age 18, were not in the workforce or were, in Census terms, 'helpers'.

Masculinity of the Workforce

The changing population structure necessarily implied a radical alteration in the size of the male workforce in the total population. The increasing numbers of young males and of all females compelled this change as shown in table 3.6 (below).

Inefficient as they may have been, the early convict societies and their predominantly convict and ex-convict structure until 1830 had an exceptional ratio of male workforce (potential) to total population. It is interesting to note that, as we will see in the next two chapters, this special characteristic coincided with very large British

Table 3.6: Potential Male Workforce

Year	Workforce Males	% of Total Population
1790	1 784(a)	77.7
1795	3 692	79.1
1800	4 555	74.1
1805	5 981	70.7
1810	7 100	63.0
1815	9 575	61.4
1820	22 822	71.1
1825	34 565	71.4
1830	47 180	69.4
1835	71 630	63.9
1840	99 982	55.2
1845	128 656	49.0
1850	147 405	45.0

Note: (a) Clearly the juvenile convicts below age 12 were required to work. This figure in particular is too low. On the other hand, a significant fraction of colonial born and immigrants aged 12–20 were not in the *actual* workforce. It would have been possible for Australian labour productivity to fall far below one half that in Britain and still allow a relatively high per capita real income in the colonies.

subventions to the standard of living of the society, generating remarkable 'penal' settlements. No radical change occurred until 1830, but thereafter the Australian workforce/population ratio moved rapidly down towards that in Britain, although with a significant advantage still remaining in 1850.

Although the inference depends partly on information outside this part of the volume, it is worth noting the remarkable opportunities in early Australia. For much of the first quarter-century, it was possible for output per head of labour to be as low as half to two-thirds of that in Britain and yet to deliver what appears to be approximately similar income per head in the two countries. Given that British subventions approximated two-thirds the aggregate product of the colonies on an average over this period (see later chapters) they made possible the importation of goods appropriate to high standards. With marked sex imbalance and high subventions, it would have been possible for Australian labour productivity to fall far below one-half of that in Britain and still allow a relatively high per capita real income in the colonies.

The Civil Status of the Male Workforce

The changing civil structure of the male workforce displays an even greater contrast with the characteristics of the population as a whole. In male workforce terms, convicts and ex-convicts loom much larger in the aggregate workforce than they appear to do in total population. Conversely, in particular, colonial born made a comparatively slight contribution to the male workforce, despite their prominence in the total population.

Until almost the end of the period, male convicts and ex-convicts dominate the total male (potential) workforce — still not so very far short of two-thirds as late as 1845. It is of some interest that skills, whether industrial, service or agricultural, were supplied from Britain. These were embodied, as late as the close of the 1830s, in substantially 90 per cent of the male workforce of NSW and Van Diemen's Land. Little is known of the ability of the colonial born to acquire education or skills though church schools and apprenticeship systems developed early. What is crucially indicated is that it was almost entirely a problem of using and adapting to

Table 3.7: Civil Status of Male Workforce

Year	Convicts & Ex-Convicts Number	%	Free Immigrants Number	%	Colonial Born Number	%
1790	1537	86.2	247	13.8		
1795	3394	91.9	298	8.1		
1800	4282	94.0	261	5.7	12	0.3
1805	5638	94.3	289	4.8	54	0.9
1810	6530	92.0	380	5.4	190	2.7
1815	8606	89.9	517	5.4	452	4.7
1820	20681	90.6	851	3.7	1290	5.7
1825	30501	88.2	2373	6.9	1691	4.9
1830	41397	87.7	3845	8.1	1938	4.1
1835	59299	82.8	9459	13.2	2872	4.0
1840	71310	71.3	23985	24.0	4687	4.7
1845	78795	61.2	41343	32.1	8518	6.6
1850	75955	51.5	54900	37.2	16550	11.2

Australian conditions the supply of British skills embodied in convicts and free immigrants. We need, however, to be cautious in exploring the extent of the skills, the ability to use them in Australia, the capacity of the persons involved to adapt to Australian conditions and the extent to which the skills were deployed. In particular, the matching of skills in Britain and Australia is neither easy nor unambiguous.

The Civil Status of the Female Workforce

The potential female workforce raises many more problems just as it presents an entirely different transformation as compared with the potential male workforce. It should be stressed that the approximate estimates below do not attempt to capture the value of women's work in the household except to the extent to which that work contributed to products and services normally disposed of in the market. In a modern perspective, this is a serious deficiency. On the other hand, many women clearly did contribute extensively to 'market' production, particularly on farms and in a variety of service roles, even though classified as 'married' or 'concubines'. Female convicts shrank much more rapidly in relative importance in the total potential female workforce (on this full-time market equivalent basis) than did their male counterparts; and both free female immigrants and colonial born became correspondingly more prominent.

On this basis, by the early 1830s convict females had become less than half the total potential workforce. Colonial born females remained more significant than immigrant females until as late as 1820. But immigrant women moved rapidly towards their eventual dominance after 1820, to account for close to two-thirds of the total by the late 1840s. In the 1830s and 1840s, Australian society represented a curious social contrast in conflict with the high masculinity of the total population. The potential workforce of females became predominantly free by origin and the potential male workforce was still predominantly convict and ex-convict.

This contrast may remain socially, and perhaps economically, important in a society and economy expanding into rural pursuits in which women could, perhaps, continue to play an important work role. However, the reproductive function of

Table 3.8: Female Potential Market Workforce

Year	Convicts & Ex-Convicts %	Free Immigrants %	Colonial Born %	Total Female
1790	95.0	5.0	—	382
1795	92.4	7.6	—	774
1800	91.9	7.0	1.1	1 141
1805	90.7	5.9	3.3	1 635
1810	84.2	7.8	8.0	2 387
1815	76.0	10.5	13.5	3 363
1820	69.0	14.2	16.8	4 723
1825	57.9	23.2	18.9	6 833
1830	55.5	26.8	17.7	10 955
1835	42.5	43.1	14.3	20 047
1840	29.7	57.9	12.4	37 745
1845	22.0	63.7	14.4	59 238
1850	17.5	62.7	19.8	83 419

women meant an 'imperfection' in their ability to contribute to the workforce in these narrow market terms.

We cannot pay much attention to either birth or marriage rates as a means of measuring the increasing claims of reproduction on the potential female workforce. As far as the overall average goes, the significance of child-rearing depended on the number of births (adjusted as suggested) for those ever 'married' and on the average age at marriage.

It seems that there was probably a profound increase in the number of children per reproductive female aged 15–45 throughout 1788 to 1850 incorporated in the statistical record. This may have been due to changing marriage age and fecundity but certainly the arrival of women and particularly married women with children during the 1830s and 1840s affected greatly the significance of reproduction. It is possible that, on a strict statistical representation, the ratio of children per reproductive female rose as much as seven times between 1800 and 1850. The problem is to determine how far, if true, this influenced market workforce participation rates. Perhaps not much for women on farms. But the increasing 'femininity' of Australian towns may suggest that care of families impeded women's participation in extensive settlement.

It is difficult, in the circumstances of this early and changing society, to determine how far reproduction hampered female contribution to the market workforce. In this early society, women with children clearly performed many roles in the economy. Some addition to the reproductive influence limiting female participation in the market workforce is implied. Nevertheless, the series may give some general indication of the trends towards a *long-term* limitation on women's work in the market. What may be inferred is that the demands of reproduction increased greatly. In particular, the increase in the number of women of workforce age after 1830 cannot be taken to imply a comparable increase in the market workforce insofar as the number of young children dependent on them increased.

Nevertheless, there were significant opportunities for the constraint of reproduction to be relaxed. For example, once the Female Factory was established it provided for some (no doubt crude) economies of scale in which convict women with children could work with some degree of child supervision or constraint.

Much more generally, domestic service employment made it possible for convict, ex-convict and some free women with children to care for their own and other women's children, allowing both female employees and employers, with children, to engage in some market workforce activity. With domestic service available, marriage or concubinage was not necessarily a barrier even to paid work. Perhaps generally, as farming developed, women were able (or found it a necessity) to be 'helpers' (in Census terminology) on farms. Nevertheless, even in the latter case, some substantial deductions from this workforce capability followed the presence of young children.

One other factor encouraged at least part-time work by women with families. It seems to have been relatively rare for low income families in Britain to have been able to survive without, at least, part-time work of wives. In NSW and Van Diemen's Land this may have meant, in the last resort, part-time prostitution. At high income levels there is no doubt that a significant fraction of (the small number of) such women performed important work tasks, including at times high managerial functions.

It is clear that no firm conclusions can be drawn about the size and quantity of the actual female market workforce beyond the fact that it was probably smaller and grew more slowly than that implied by the nominal potential female workforce derived from workforce ages. This problem has always plagued efforts to measure workforce and it is unlikely that we can solve it here. The Musters and Census reports of female occupational characteristics most certainly do not provide a solution. It is essential to recognise that women did more than care for families (and, in modern terms this would be valued) but that, particularly as farming developed, they contributed a good deal of unrecorded output, typically as off-market production. However, as we shall see, so too did males. In both cases, this 'off-market' production of goods and services normally marketed have been included in our domestic product estimates and appropriate workforce allocations made. Many convict women had young children. If *all* women were converted, as is often conventionally done, to 0.6 times that of a full-time equivalent member of the workforce, the structure of the projected market workforce would look like the picture presented in table 3.9. At best, this is a lower bound estimate of the contribution of women to the economy.

Table 3.9: Approximate Projected Full-Time Market Workforce

Year	Convicts & Ex-Convicts Males/Females		Free Immigrants Males/Females		Colonial Born Males/Females		Total Workforce Males/Females		Total Persons
1790	1537	218	247	11	0	0	1784	229	2013
1795	3394	429	298	35	0	0	3692	464	4156
1800	4282	629	261	48	12	7	4555	684	5239
1805	5638	890	289	58	54	42	5981	990	6971
1810	6530	1206	380	112	190	114	7100	1432	8532
1815	8606	1535	517	212	452	271	9575	2018	11593
1820	19458	1954	351	402	793	476	20602	2832	23434
1825	28010	2375	1673	950	1291	775	30974	4100	35074
1830	41397	3649	3845	1761	1938	1163	47180	6573	53753
1835	59299	5117	9459	5185	2872	1723	71630	12025	83655
1840	71310	6729	23985	13105	4687	2812	99982	22646	122628
1845	78795	7802	41343	22314	8518	5111	128656	35227	163883
1850	75955	8747	54900	30820	16550	9930	147405	49497	196902

On this basis, the overall potential full-time workforce rose to almost exactly 100 times its 1790 level in 80 years compared with a population expansion of just on 150 times. The male potential workforce, however, rose to only a level of some 84 times while the imputed female full-time equivalent rose to almost 220 times its 1790 base. By 1850, the female full-time equivalent was about exactly one-third the male level, having shot up from barely one-eighth in 1830.

The Broad Structural Implications

The broad structural shifts may be outlined as follows (see table 3.10, p.44).

In the first period, women accounted for only 12 per cent of the total potential full-time workforce increase of some 51 740. In the second, they contributed 30 per cent of the 143 147 aggregate increase. The contributions here and in table 3.8 (p.41)

Table 3.10: Contributions to Workforce/Growth

	Total Increase	Convicts & Ex-Convicts %	Free Immigrants %	Colonial Born %
Males				
1790–30	45 396	87.8	8.0	4.3
1830–50	100 225	34.5	50.9	14.6
Females				
1790–30	6 344	54.1	27.6	18.3
1830–50	42 924	11.9	67.7	20.4

represent strong contrasts with the factors accounting for total population increase in which colonial born and free immigrants were much more prominent and females as a whole made a much larger contribution to the total increase.

General Inferences from Projections

Drawing all this together, there are 11 inferences that we can draw from the projections:

(a) On all counts, the Australian population grew extremely rapidly and in a relatively stable manner.

(b) Convicts and ex-convicts dominated the population to the mid-1830s, thereafter declining rapidly in importance.

(c) The share of convicts in the convict and ex-convict population went through strong swings with no persistent tendency until 1835 for a formal 'freeing' of the workforce. This should not be taken to imply a corresponding slowness in developing a relatively flexibly operating labour market (see later).

(d) Both immigrants and colonial born began as tiny fractions. Colonial born had become significant by the end of the Napoleonic Wars and rose to about one-third by 1850; free immigrants remained numerically slight until 1830 and then rose rapidly to be the major component by 1850.

(e) The population, throughout, showed a strong but reducing sex imbalance, which was particularly prominent, given the increase of children, amongst the adult population. Amongst females, convict and ex-convict groups accounted, throughout, for a smaller proportion of the female group than did their male counterparts amongst the male population. The major turnaround occurred after 1830 following large-scale free (assisted and unassisted) immigration.

(f) The male full-time workforce accounted for an extraordinarily high component of population, following a declining path from 80 per cent to 45 per cent between 1788–1850.

(g) The changing contribution to the full-time male workforce of the three groups, convicts and ex-convicts, free immigrants and colonial born behaved in a way significantly different from the contribution of these groups in the total population. Male convicts and ex-convicts still accounted for half the full-time male workforce in 1850 and were of overwhelming numerical importance until the early 1830s. Free immigrant males in the full-time workforce rose rapidly from the early 1830s to over one-third by 1850. By contrast, colonial born males remained a very small component throughout.

(h) In turn, the behaviour of the three categories amongst full-time workforce females differed significantly from that in the total population and also from their male counterparts in their gender aggregates. Female convicts and ex-convicts had become a small component by 1850. The dominant group was from free immigrants though colonial born females were more important amongst females than their male counterparts.

(i) The claims of reproduction by females increased considerably over the period though the extent to which this inhibited their contribution to the full-time market workforce is not simply determined.

(j) While population grew to some 40 times the 1790 figure, the lower bound estimates of full-time workforce rose to only ten times. A basic trend adjustment occurred reducing the advantage (in simple numerical terms) of the workforce age groups in the total population.

(k) A basic social transformation occurred with the population as a whole receiving a strong injection of free females after 1830 while the workforce remained highly masculine with a marked convict and ex-convict element.

4

HUMAN CAPITAL IN CONVICTS

Original Occupation and Age Characteristics of the Male Convict Workforce

Given their dominance over most of the period in the male workforce, the greatest interest attaches to convicts and ex-convicts. We need to consider the range and degree of occupational skills contained in and transmitted by these convicts. As a distinct question, we may try to identify the extent to which these skills were actually used in Australia. In doing so, we should appreciate that adaptations were required to contribute more effectively to the relatively primitive Australian conditions. The larger these adaptations, the less important the original skill composition may have been in a direct sense. The smaller these adaptations, the more important the original skill composition may have been.

There is, however, another question. In Australian conditions, there was almost certainly less scope to exploit specific skills to the full. On the one hand, demands of farming compelled the rural use of many with urban skills. The establishment and expansion of farms meant more than shepherding and ploughing. There was considerable demand for building skills, for construction and maintenance of drays and carts, harness making and repair, tool-making etc. This is not the place to extend into the familiar linkages contained in staple theory though it is important to note that as settlement extended it became more important to have such skills accessible on or close to farms. What was needed was multi-skilling. On the other hand, multi-functional exploitation may have allowed only partial use of reputed skills. Moreover, where urban skills were used in trades activities, they were not generally deployed in institutions similar to those to which convicts had been accustomed in Britain.

This section deals with the supply of human capital to Australia through the convict inflows in terms of ages and occupational skills. What is required is a detailed analysis of convict arrivals. A simple sampling procedure over long periods is not very satisfactory unless the sample is very large. The elementary problem is that the occupational composition almost certainly changed over time and it is important to be able to make a considerable number of occupational subdivisions. Small samples mean small numbers and high probable errors in these subdivisions.

Occupational data have limited meaning unless related to age. Here there are conflicting issues. On the one hand, a very young person professing some skill qualification may lack on-the-job experience. In a British society, where work and training started at very young ages, the relatively youthful adults might have had considerable experience. Even so, a good deal of modern studies suggest continued accession of productive potential up to ages 40–45 from experience in skilled trades; allowing for morbidity problems of the early 19th century, one would hesitate to put this peak quality below 35–39. On the other hand, the younger the workforce recruit, the longer the potential workforce life. Australia may have been compromised in accessing so many persons aged below 30 and particularly those below 25 — less developed skill and longer working life.

The question of potential working life has a special significance in Australian conditions in both productivity and welfare terms. We have the earliest Australian life table at 1861 that would significantly reflect, but almost certainly understate, the relatively high colonial survival rates particularly over the period 1800–50. Matching this, there are several life tables for British urban conditions drawn up mainly by insurance companies throughout the first half of the 19th century.

Clearly, no very precise comparisons are possible. But it seems plausible that urban children of Britain transferred to Australia at age five in 1810–20 might have had many, and perhaps as much as 20, years added to their life expectancy. In productivity terms, males aged 20–25 similarly transferred may have achieved an additional life expectancy of as much as ten years. From a welfare perspective, it is likely that convicts, drawn from very low income urban levels could have achieved even larger gains. Better diet, less pollution, a more active and open lifestyle and less stress, even for the mass of convicts, were some of the literally vital rewards of transportation.

There are two main secondary sources on this matter, one by Robson (1965) and the other by Nicholas (1988). Robson provides a small sample over the whole period 1788–1850. It is plain that we cannot place great weight on this information though it is a useful preliminary indication. Convict arrivals after 1820 dominate Robson's group and it must be taken, at best, as referring essentially to the period 1820–50. There were major biases arising from the changing areas from which convicts came, raising serious doubts about the relevance of the overall occupational information to pre-1820 conditions.

The relevance of Robson's age structures is probably higher although this is open to debate. Nicholas' study is a much more extensive one with a much larger sample. It concentrates specifically on the period after 1816. However, data are missing before 1817. For present purposes, this gap has been filled, so far as data are available from convict indents, by taking indent records 1788–1816, using all the occupational and age records that are given. This is not particularly satisfactory in that age data for males are confined to the years 1788, 1791–3, 1795, 1797–1801 and 1813–16. Occupational data are given only for 1788, 1800 and 1813–16. Obviously, there are large gaps and, in the years indicated, many convicts' ages and occupations

Table 4.1: Population Age Distribution

Age group	Male Convicts (Average 1788–1816) %	Robson (a) %	England Scotland & Wales (1841) %	Ireland (1861) %	Nicholas Age group	%
age 10–14	1.2	1.1	11.4	10.8	age 16	5.4
age 15–19	9.2	19.8	10.1	11.6	age 16–20	26.2
age 20–24	28.8	35.2	9.3	10.5	age 21–25	30.3
age 25–29	22.6	19.8	7.8		age 26–30	16.9
age 30–34	14.6	9.9	7.2	12.9 }	age 31–35	7.9
age 35–39	9.4	5.5	7.2		age 36 +	13.3
age 40–44	6.8	3.3	5.5	9.8		
age 45–49	4.0	(Over 45)5.5	17.1	21.0		
age 50–54	2.5					
age 55–59	1.3					
age 60–64	0.6					
over 64	0.3					

Note: (a) Excluding 'not stated'.

are not shown. Future research may be able to recover the material for missing years and persons from British court records.

The reported age structures of male convicts, at time of sentencing, can usefully be compared with the age structure of England, Scotland and Wales. In doing so, we are limited to the average 1788–1850 convict age structure and that of England, Scotland and Wales in 1841. Irish age structures in 1861 are also shown. They are distorted by the Famine but nevertheless do not alter the comparison radically. The comparison is given in table 4.1 (above).

The characteristics of the Second Fleet, if nothing else, are loud warnings that one cannot treat any sample distribution as always relevant to the shipments of particular years. Even so, the various estimates of convicts give strong evidence that, on average, the convicts supplied the Australian settlements with a relatively youthful supply of males particularly after the Napoleonic Wars. Both Robson and Nicholas indicate that about 70 per cent of the male convict inflow from that time were under age 30 with a substantial supplement in the next quinquennial age bracket. There is some contrast with the age characteristics available for the period 1788–1816 when the available data suggest only 60 per cent in the under 30 group. Nevertheless, even this lower proportion contrasts sharply with the approximate 40 per cent for England, Scotland and Wales.

Potentially, on Robson's evidence, they were, on an average, men capable of vigorous effort with a long period of workforce contribution before them, in terms of the ages on arrival. With 50 per cent between the ages of 15 and 24, 68 per cent between 15 and 29, and 77 per cent between 15 and 34, their ability to contribute was constrained by health, physique, skill and incentives; not their age. The British male workforce was, in 1841, very much older. A comparison is made of the occupational/industrial composition of Great Britain and Robson's convict sample in table 4.2 (p.49).

The convict 'skills' or industry are those applying and stated or alleged at the time of sentence. More than 50 per cent of convicts reported industrial skills (excluding the 'not stated'). This would suggest that in the light of its primitive state, the

Table 4.2: Occupational/Industrial Comparisons, Convict Population and Great Britain

Classification	Great Britain 1841 %	Convicts (Robson's Sample) %
Labourers & Agriculture	28.3	39
Transport	3.9	10
Metal Manufacture	7.8	5
Personal Service	5.9	5
Wood, Cane, Decoration etc	2.1	4
Defence	0.9	3
Leather Products	0.9	3
Building Construction	7.4	3
Textile, Clothing	17.4	7
Food, Drink, Tobacco	5.5	3
Commercial, Finance	1.9	2.3
Mining, Quarrying	4.3	1
Clerical	0.8	1
Professional, Technical	2.2	0.5
Fishing	0.5	0.02
Other	9.4	3.2
Not Stated	—	10

Australian society was endowed with a relatively high proportion of industrial skills. It is common to find historical criticism of Britain's failure to deliver farming skills. In fact, it appears to have been industrial skills that were, at least after the first decade or so, very highly prized by settlers; and ex-convicts appear to have set themselves up, very often, selling their skills in these areas.

It was fortunate, perhaps, that textile skills seem to have been relatively under-represented amongst the convicts relative to the British male workforce, but a substantial representation existed of metalworking, woodworking, leather products and food, drink and tobacco, all of which were important as the settlements moved beyond their initial stages. Transport, too, was very strongly represented and a valuable skill in the colonies. All these skills were important. One can too readily treat the early Australian settlements as rural-oriented. As we will see in later chapters, the standard of living and tastes of the settlers provided strong inducement to specialised non-rural occupations. Isolation enhanced these inducements further.

Unfortunately, in making comparisons from Robson's sample it is necessary to combine labourers and agricultural workers. It is reasonably clear that the system of convict shipments provided a relatively low supply of farm workers. It would follow that a good deal of restructuring of labour skills was required in Australia. This may have enhanced the value of industrial skills that were absorbed in farming in Australia, even though 'skilled' arrivals divided their time between 'rural' and 'craft' activities.

Nicholas' sample covering 1817–40 gives an essentially similar picture, more firmly based given the size of the sample, and with a significantly higher representation of skills. His data are shown in table 4.3 (p.50). In this case, the urban and agricultural labourers have fortunately been separated and the agricultural workers have been separated into skilled and unskilled. Nicholas' representation of rural convicts clarifies the confusion in Robson's sample, indicating the very low fraction of rural convicts, whether skilled or unskilled. Dominantly, the male convicts from England were urban workers with a relatively high degree of reputed skill.

Table 4.3: Summary Occupational Classifications, 1817–40

Classification	English Convicts %	UK Census 1841 %
Unskilled Urban	21.6	8.2
Unskilled Rural	4.9	20.3
Skilled Building	8.1	7.9
Skilled Urban	39.2	32.4
Skilled Rural	7.0	6.9
Dealers	2.6	5.2
Public Service	4.0	5.7
Professional	1.5	2.9
Domestic Service	11.2	4.6
Miscellaneous	0.0	5.9

Sources: Nicholas (1988) and from sample ships 1817–40.

The supplementary data that I have assembled covering the few available years during 1788–1816 generally fall between Robson's and Nicholas' picture. None of the attempts to reconstruct skill composition suggests other than that there was a high presence of British skilled trades among the incoming convicts.

The Use of Convicts and Ex-Convicts in NSW

It is one thing to identify reputed skills of convicts at time of conviction and another to establish the extent to which these skills were actually exploited in Australian conditions. The Musters of Van Diemen's Land are not sufficiently clear for any overall occupational analysis. In New South Wales, the various Musters appear to be a confusion of colonial occupational description and a strictly clerical repetition of British skill data with some individuals described in colonial terms and others in British terms. The only plausible evidence appears to lie in the NSW Census of 1828 though even this needs to be treated circumspectly.

Table 4.4: Occupations of Male Convicts Transported to NSW

	1788 %	1800 %	1813 %	1814 %	1815 %	1816 %	Average %
Unskilled, Unspecified	56.4	30.6	22.3	34.3	34.9	35.1	34.3
Rural Specified	2.4	7.5	6.4	4.8	3.3	6.9	5.3
Dealers	2.4	2.3	4.0	5.5	5.4	4.9	4.8
Timber Building	7.9	11.6	17.0	14.0	15.0	11.3	13.3
Metals	2.4	12.1	8.0	7.3	6.2	5.5	6.5
Textiles	6.7	19.1	13.8	9.6	10.9	10.0	10.8
Professional	1.2	3.5	2.4	2.8	1.5	2.6	2.3
Services	9.1	1.7	16.2	12.2	12.3	14.6	12.8
Food, Drink, Tobacco	0.6	4.0	1.3	1.5	1.5	1.5	1.6
Leather	6.1	5.8	6.6	5.8	6.0	4.5	5.5
Miscellaneous	4.8	1.7	2.1	2.3	3.2	3.1	2.8

Source: J. Cobley (1970). Other years from Indents.

A first step method is to relate Census and convict Indent data on occupations on a strictly nominal basis. This is a very arduous collation, selecting names of convicts and ex-convicts in distinct groups together with their occupation, date and ship of arrival. These data, when fully matched in the Indents, provide a preliminary indication of the extent to which British skills were used in Australia. The matching of name, ship and date of arrival frequently breaks down (over one-half of a first (tiny) random sample from the Census failed to match). One would need to invest a large amount of time to determine the matter. A larger random 4 per cent sample, each of convicts and ex-convicts, left about one-third unidentified in the Indents. Of the balance, the Census suggested that of the skills attained in Britain a little over 40 per cent bore little relation to the Australian occupation in 1828. The remaining 60 per cent appears large and would be impressive were it not for two problems. Firstly, the perfect match throughout was achieved for persons of least skill — British labourers remained Australian labourers except where a few claimed the Australian title of farmer. Nevertheless, discounting this, it remains that a little under half the (identified) persons claiming British skills are reported as exercising those skills in Australia.

There is, however, a second major qualification. This is that few convicts employed by government had their occupation attached in the Census. Since a very high proportion were in punishment gangs, it is not impossible that this convict 'occupation' had much relation to their British skills. Adjusting for this factor brings the British–Australian skill match shown below 40 per cent.

This did not necessarily imply either large wastage or a full-scale deployment of skills in Australia. Indeed, in about 10 per cent of the cases, the failure to match arose from upward occupational mobility through personal or skill background allowing adaptation. Thus a soldier appears as a supervisor, a groom as an indoor servant. Or there were lateral transfers, with a ploughman appearing as an Australian fencer. These adaptations raise, however, a basic question in relation to both British and Australian skills as claimed. Did the Indents and the Censuses report (assuming them to be truthful) the predominant or the immediately dated occupational categories? In Britain, there was a far greater probability of specialisation and one might take the Indent description as relatively hard evidence. But in Australia, the probability of exercising a specific skill on a *full-time* basis was very much less.

It is vital to appreciate that many and varied demands were imposed on the entire workforce in the relatively primitive conditions. This was one reason apart from resource limitations why the investigation of the 1828 Census was not taken beyond these purely indicative limits. There were, perhaps, brief periods when freedom of choice of the mass of the workforce could be exercised and this condition may have applied in the 1805–6 Muster. This is a particularly interesting but passing occasion that will be given attention later in this volume. But for most of the first 70-odd years and even when Governor Macquarie, during 1810–21, appears to have made first claim on skilled convicts for building and infrastructure purposes, the common condition appears to have been a multi-functional workforce. This was obviously the case with many free persons who chose multi-functional roles from preference. But it was also imposed on convicts in both urban trades and farming so that skills were diluted.

This does not mean that skills were wasted. There are four important points. Firstly, the ability to acquire skills in Britain may have pointed to a level of intelligence that could have a general value in Australian conditions — a general human capital quality. Secondly, pioneering conditions imposed the need for many skills and the possession of one by each member of the workforce could mean the ability to deploy that skill for important purposes. Thus in establishing farms, a carpenter or bricklayer who may have been an indifferent ploughman or shepherd could nevertheless deliver needed construction labour. A blacksmith turned publican still had considerable scope for the exercise of skills in taverns and transport activity.

Thirdly, convicts were not impressed labour working from dawn to dusk. From the end of the 18th century, they were allowed 'free' time in which to work for private reward. This allowed a person who might be described as a labourer in the Census to engage in skilled activity outside required convict hours. This appears as a vital feature as settlement extended and landowners allowed their convict servants to move in 'overtime' to neighbouring farms to contribute much needed skills. Fourthly, in Australian urban conditions, while specialised skills had a more prominent place than in rural areas, the urban institutional structure differed greatly from that in Britain and imposed or opened the opportunity to multi-functional activity. It was almost inescapable, at the very least, that producers of specific products had also to sell, transport and, in the case of durable items, maintain their wares.

Basically what is urged here is that skill-matching has a limited value and that, in a variety of ways, the British skilled convict played a crucial role in Australian economic development. It was a role that can easily be misrepresented. Australia did not depend on an army of shepherds and ploughmen. Had they been provided, it is highly likely that the early settlements would have failed. This likelihood becomes prominent in subsequent chapters. Skill was an essential pre-condition of early Australian colonial success, though in ways and for reasons that might not be immediately anticipated.

PART III

PUBLIC FUNDING OF COLONIAL DEVELOPMENT: 1788–1850

5

INTRODUCTION

The British convict settlement of Australia represented a major act of public investment. This is not to imply that it was consciously perceived as such, carefully designed or well directed. On the contrary. Nevertheless, the rate of return on British public expenditures — effectively capital transfers to the colonies — became a prominent matter during the 30 years after the first settlement. A widely debated question developed and continues to today: Was there a net benefit to Britain in convict transportation as compared with retaining convicts at home?

Large and often undesigned public outlays were made by Britain during more than 60 years in the transfer of unfree persons and on goods and equipment to sustain the occupation of Australia during formative years and to give initial support to successive convict shipments. This was not confined to the convict settlements and some public British subsidies were rendered to the free corporate colonies that developed from 1829. But these latter subsidies were tiny compared with the capital transfers to the convict settlements. The early occupation of Australia began and was sustained as an extension of the British 'budget' (even though the modern concept of a centralised budget was not clearly established until well into the 19th century).

The transfer of human beings was, from an Australian point of view, a capital transfer, even if, from a British perspective, the human capital involved in convicts may have had a negative value. It is with the monetary and goods transfers that accompanied these and other human transfers that we are concerned here. Britain supplied salaries and allowances for military and civil officials, transport shipping services, food and clothing, stores and equipment and some major items of capital including ships presented for colonial use. It was also induced by action within the colonies to supplement these by other goods and services demanded by the colonists. But, as part of the evolutionary process, local colonial activity developed. Britain was able and became increasingly determined to constrain the specifically British public financial commitment and to narrow the range of support. It sought ways of reducing, to the British taxpayer, the per capita costs of convicts landed in Australia and to limit the total budgetary costs of sustaining colonies made up increasingly of freed and free persons.

One way to achieve these ends was through the auditing of colonial accounts and criticism of colonial behaviour. Given the British bureaucracy of the time and the nature of accounting systems, this route was more a source of mutual British–colonial irritation than of effective constraint. Two other methods were much more significant. Both followed the early success of local colonial economies through private enterprise and became formalised during 1821–3.

One was in the adoption of a policy to encourage the private development of Australia, no longer dependent essentially on convict transfers. Measures to encourage free migration with free or cheap access to land also included provision for wholesale assignment of convicts to private employment after 1821. Convict assignment dates much earlier than this but 1821 marks well enough the determination to give priority to private employment of convicts over public employment. More of convict support and supervision costs were thereby transferred from public to private budgets. In the 1830s, this was supplemented by schemes for assisted migration of free persons to the convict colonies and the formation in 1829 and 1836, respectively, of the free corporate settlements of Western and South Australia. Central to this policy change was the encouragement of private capital transfers from Britain to take over part of the burden of colonial development from the British budget. Accordingly, from the early 1820s, there was a basic adjustment in British capital flows to Australia, with an upsurge of private capital first reinforcing and then gradually replacing public capital transfers.

The second procedure depended on the emergence first of a freed society and subsequently a jointly free and freed population with associated market activity in the colonies. This change provided the opportunity that did not exist in a wholly convict population to divert part of the funding of public activity in the colonies from Britain to the colonies. In other words, there appeared to be the opportunity for colonists to fund part, at least, of the public services of the colonies. The dating of any transition from British public funding to colonial public funding is, however, obscure.

British decision makers were far from consistent in their attitudes to fiscal obligations to and from the colonists. One might say, as has been said, that all governors to 1821, except for the first, left with at least his fiscal reputation tarnished. Intermittent and at times irascible and condemnatory intervention in colonial expenditures reflected, in part, British ignorance and suspicion. In fact, complex colonial fiscs operated almost from the beginning of settlement. They acquired a degree of formality from 1800. Between 1800 and 1821 strictly illegal though formalised fiscs were established in New South Wales. Once given *ex post* absolution, legal, formal fiscs were operating from 1822 (absolution was granted in 1819 but the change not yet formalised). They gradually expanded and, in the case of NSW, surpassed British expenditures by the mid-1830s, absorbing all except convict and defence functions.

An important question that arises in this fiscal transition is the extent to which the colonists came, in fact, to bear so much of the burden of colonial affairs as may appear from the budgetary record. One issue that became central and has been generally given prominence is the growth of revenue from colonial lands particularly during the 1830s. Much, though not all, of these funds derived from purchases of land arising from private capital inflow from Britain. But Britain claimed title to Crown lands and hence to the revenues from them (until 1855). Constitutionally, these revenues were part of the British Imperial fisc, not the colonial one, and to that extent it is debatable whether it was colonial or British funding. Debated it was, indeed, and a strong bone of contention between the colonists and Britain.

This illustrates a conflict between British and colonial interests and raises the age-old question of who is to gain or lose in any sharing process. But already other fiscal conflicts had developed well before 1830. The colonists, as we will see, operated an indiscriminate array of real budgetary processes for several decades and, in the process, succeeded in transferring costs to Britain. Subsequently, both the illegal fiscs from 1800 and the formal legal fiscs from 1822 had a different distributive significance. All (other than land funds) relied fundamentally on customs revenue. This, in turn, was a function primarily of the level of imports. But the level of imports was strongly influenced by the level of public and private capital inflow. In other words, Australian economic dependence on Britain was a prime determinant of the increase in the local fisc whether illegal or legal. One cannot readily conclude that the rise in local public revenues reflected colonial self-support or even, in a simple way, the substitution of Australian public funds for British.

Several themes might be taken up in dealing with the public funding of Australian colonial development. These would include:

(a) What was the rate of return to Britain from transportation?

(b) What were the interrelationships between public and private funding of the colonies by Britain?

(c) In what ways and to what degree did Britain and the colonists share in the public funding of the colonies and direct their development?

These questions are all interrelated. The focus adopted here derives partly from the fact that early Australian public finance is almost unknown territory as is the influence of British fiscal procedures and policies on Australian development. Hence this chapter deals with Australian public finance, including both the British and Australian contributions. Public finance can be extremely dull. It can, however, find some amusing sidelights in the context of penal settlements and even more so in the peculiarities of British military fiscal arrangements.

In what follows, an attempt is made to relate fiscal history to the other two questions and to integrate, to some extent, the process of Australian economic development. If, in the end, we find the first question probably unanswerable, the interconnections between the second and third pose some important questions for Australian history. But, in any event, to begin to comprehend the first two questions, some account of fiscal history of Britain and the colonies is essential. This is the more important insofar as the first settlement was made shortly after the American Revolution in which fiscal issues had some prominence, as Britain was passing through an intensive and far-reaching reformation of its fiscal organisation and was making radical changes in the structure of imperial command, particularly in the army. All these had considerable significance for Australia.

6

BRITISH FISCAL CHARACTERISTICS

On first encounter, the system of public finance established in New South Wales and Van Diemen's Land may seem a quaint colonial peculiarity. Some of its features, in the use of convicts as a fiscal mechanism, certainly were; so, too, were the special drawing rights of the governors on the British Treasury. But many other characteristics such as the lack of conscious processes of appropriations, the incoherence of public finance until the late 1820s, the dependence on fees in cash or kind to support officials, the privatisation of much of the public funds and the remarkable modes of accounting adopted were far from peculiar. They derived from British fiscal procedures of the second half of the 18th century.

The First Fleet sailed at a date almost centred between the beginning and end of a 17-year process of British fiscal reform between 1780 and 1797. The Fleet and the subsequent transfer of the NSW Corps in 1790 carried to NSW essentially pre-1780 fiscal attitudes of Britain, both at the civil and military level. That public finance in NSW became increasingly strange up to the end of the 1820s was partly due to the fact that British reforms were not communicated to the settlement. But, in addition, the British failed to establish fiscal control over the settlement and this made the local Australian approaches increasingly archaic and divergent. This failure was partly due to British preoccupation with the French Wars, the isolation of the settlement and the special colonial drawing rights on the British Treasury. But it was also due to the power for much of the period of the Secretary of State for the Colonies and the administrative limitations of the British Treasury.

It is essential to understand how recently developed the strictly public fisc of Britain was at the end of the 18th century and how incoherent, privatised and uncontrolled were many of British fiscal operations. It is equally important to appreciate that, however distracting the Napoleonic Wars may have been, they meant that for much of the early formative period of public finance in Australia the office of Secretary of State for War and the Colonies were held by one person.

It is possible, here, to make only a few sketchy points on British fiscal back-ground. (For background information see Binney (1958) and Young (1961). Com-plex, decentralised and privatised processes of revenue raising through farming-out of revenues had developed from Tudor times to conduct the affairs of State. This is not the place to trace these features though the longevity of 18th century provisions must be noted. The strengthening of parliamentary influence after 1688 introduced little in the way of centralisation; rather, it appears that patronage and the depend-ence on the market to finance government became more important as parliament sought, with an inadequate bureaucracy, to fund the Crown as the ultimate authority in the State.

By 1760 however, the Crown surrendered authority for most direct British revenue-raising in exchange for a substantial annual appropriation. Prior to the introduction of income tax in 1799, British domestic revenues were made up from three main sources. About half the revenue came from excise and a little less than one quarter each from Customs and Land taxation. The various revenue sources were collected, received and transferred to the Exchequer by a variety of different procedures and by no means always placed in a single central location. Exceptional in 18th century Britain, most excise revenue was raised and transmitted relatively efficiently through salaried officials. The remaining half was assembled through highly privatised processes, depending on privately received fees subtracted from the gross receipts and with long delays (often years) before net revenues were finally placed in the public coffers. In the meantime, not only had substantial fees been reaped but individuals had used accumulated balances for additional private advan-tage. Collectors and receivers were often appointed through patronage or purchased the right to office; indeed possession of the office became valuable property and might even be transferred by bequest.

Expenditure processes were even more incoherent and equally privatised. Parliament did not make appropriations for all the expenditures of different public organisations. Most depended on acquisition of fees for items ranging from salaries to purely house-keeping activities. Thus not until 1782, six years before the first Australian settlement, was there significant parliamentary provision for salaried officials in the British Treasury. The conduct of the forces was much more confused with clumsy arrangements for payments (other than officers' salaries for which appropriations were made late in the century) to be made by Army and Navy Paymasters through bills on the British government. Typically these bills sold at a substantial discount and provided both highly inefficient modes of payment within Britain and lucrative business opportunities for the paymasters. Larger expenditures were provided from time to time by the issue of debentures. Sometimes to very considerable private advantage (cf. Binney, 1958: 153 ff). (This is a matter that students of the British capital market could profitably pursue.)

Because of the role of the military in early Australian history, the fiscal organi-sation of the armed forces has a special relevance. Until the late 18th century, and in certain respects beyond, the provisions for the army and navy had strong private overtones (Guy, 1985). In conditions of war, mercenaries, particularly foreign mercenaries, often made up large elements of total fighting forces. But in conditions of war and peace, military and naval commissions were property rights to be bought and sold and even promotions required personal outlays to secure entitlements. Though salaries and allowances were provided by parliamentary appropriations, these private outlays were career investments on which returns over and above salary provisions were expected both by the individuals concerned and by the British government.

Until the late 18th century, the regimental unit could not unreasonably be regarded as a private enterprise of the commanding officer, with distributive arrangements provided for more junior officers. The paymaster of such a unit was presented with an opportunity for personal gain through the use of company or regimental funds intended to cover forage, housing, equipment and pay of the troops. In war, all might gain from booty. In peace and particularly in imperial service, the conventional expectation was that regimental officers would enhance their official pay and allowances in a variety of ways. These could extend through wartime booty through exploitation of subject peoples to the operation of a truck system within the regiment. In the latter case, highly relevant to Australia, funds appropriated for privates and non-commissioned officers could be exploited for the personal benefit of officers.

Efforts to integrate and deprivatise the British fisc were set in train in a more or less continuous way from 1780 and substantial changes were made between 1785 and 1797. These changes extended over a very long period (it was only in 1870 that patronage was officially ended). It was, however, not until 1797 that any individual, group or institution could grasp the full array of English public finances even in relation to domestic fiscal operations in civilian areas. The armed services remained, still, a heavily clouded area; and imperial finances were far from being captured. Although the number of salaried officials increased, fees remained prominent and the bureaucracy was very small. Policy was dominated by essentially part-time Secretaries and Under-Secretaries, both typically politicians and powerful individuals protecting their own exclusive portfolios, within which high level policy was determined.

In the circumstances, the ability of the fledgling Treasury to centralise and constrain fiscal activity and to exercise economy within Britain itself was extremely limited. So, too, was the effort by parliament to press for economy measures. Once a coherent domestic budget for England was available after 1797, parliamentary pressures for economy became more effective. But these pressures had much less significance for the imperial finances for a number of reasons. Vital changes followed the defeat of Burgoyne at Saratoga after which the British no longer claimed the right to impose colonial taxation to fund imperial defence.

These changes had important implications for the varied assembly of colonies that Britain subsequently acquired after 1783. British troops were dispersed around the colonies (including New South Wales and Van Diemen's Land) at British expense. With these, but in varied civil and military form, grew up a system of Commissariats as supply organisations that were operated formally on British account. Both troop and supply arrangements drew Britain into a number of different and confused relations with revenue raising and expenditure processes in the colonies.

Substantial differences between the array of colonies added to the variety of British–colonial fiscal relations. Colonies acquired by conquest were dealt with differently from those that were settled without conquest; and those with representative systems of government had yet other fiscal arrangements. NSW was not regarded as conquered nor did it have any mode of political representation before 1823. Accordingly the governors in NSW were dealt with in a very special way

(Sierra Leone alone was handled similarly). They received not only sustaining stores and civil and military salaries from Britain but were also granted the authority to issue bills chargeable on the British government. As an offset to this entitlement, however, revenue raising in NSW remained within the prerogative of the British parliament. This became a matter of prime concern during the first 35 years of the settlement; and it remained a source of tension until 1855.

At the beginning of the 19th century, the British Treasury was far from being a dominant actor in imperial finance even though it had shared directly in the setting up of the NSW settlement and even though, until 1813, the Commissariat in NSW was wholly a Treasury organisation. Nor had the British parliament acquired any strong oversight of colonial finance. The growing pressures of the Napoleonic Wars greatly increased the presence of government in the British economy. The nominal taxation system and loan raisings in Britain conceal the modes of financing the wars; much of it was through 'forced' savings arising from inflation. The British parliament became more prominent after the wars as government spending was cut back severely and demands for economy and fiscal reforms became more urgent.

In the meantime, in 1801, the office of Secretary for the Colonies was transferred from the Home to the War Office. Held by one person, the Office of Secretary of State for War and the Colonies became extremely powerful. However low on the priority scale colonial affairs may have been during the wars, the authority of the person occupying the office was impressive. The Secretary might obstruct reforms in respect of the colonies from laziness, ignorance or determination. If the first two factors were important during the first decade of the 19th century, the latter dominated under Bathurst after 1812. Bathurst's position in the Colonial Office until 1827 meant a prolonged period of calculated non-cooperation in colonial affairs with respect to the Treasury and to the fiscal reforms that grew apace in Britain after 1815. Bathurst's expressed judgment of the Treasury was that the officials were 'more anxious to extend their duties than to discharge them' (see Young, 1961: 188).

For a large variety of reasons, the colonial authorities in NSW were able to sustain outmoded and peculiar fiscal and accounting systems and to avoid being subjected to close oversight; and the settlers were able to exploit their special advantage to personal and general economic advantage. Governors were able to introduce and maintain wholly illegal fiscal systems. It is more than doubtful whether the British Treasury or Parliament could meaningfully pose and answer the question: What was the rate of return on the public investment in establishing the colony of NSW? Reform in NSW might be traced to two main processes apart from the general pressure for economy in Britain itself.

Firstly, there were informal relations between particular settlers and influential persons in Britain. Secondly, there appears to have been increasing concern in Britain at least as much with the social and political issues of the colonies as with problems of economy. Probes were made into particular issues in the affairs of Trinidad in 1802, of West Africa and the remaining American colonies in 1812. The despatch of Bigge to enquire into NSW was a step of a different order: this enquiry was the first of a series of general investigations to acquire up-to-date information on the economy, society and the political and judicial system of the British colonies. As such, it signalled a parliamentary intention to increase its understanding and control. It does not follow, despite the fiscal reforms that emerged from the Bigge Report, that there was a comparable increase in Treasury oversight and fiscal constraint.

7

THE IMPERIAL FISC IN NSW AND VAN DIEMEN'S LAND TO 1821

Total British spending on New South Wales and Van Diemen's Land was distributed between several bodies (VDL was separated from NSW in 1825). The Victualling, Navy and Transport Boards organised and paid for the supplying and transporting of convicts to the settlements. The Paymasters (Army and Navy) and Colonial Agent transmitted salaries for military and civil officials respectively, as appropriated by parliament. The Commissary was the Treasury head of the network of Commissariats developed as supply, storage and distribution agencies particularly for overseas establishments. In NSW, this direct civilian link with the Treasury applied only during 1791–1813 after which the Commissariat became a military institution in NSW but remained, so far as Britain was concerned, in the Army subsection of the Treasury. The Audit Office of Treasury was charged with the task of auditing accounts of various spending agencies.

Table 7.1 shows one set of estimates of the reputed expenditures on British account during 1787–1822 by the various organisations concerned with NSW and VDL. These estimates are based on Bigge's papers derived and extended to 1822 by Jules Ginswick (unpub.) MS estimates. Access is gratefully acknowledged.[1]

For various reasons, these estimates, particularly until 1817, need to be treated with a good deal of suspicion. The bills honoured by the British Treasury exceed by a considerable margin those drawn in NSW, VDL and Norfolk Island (cf. the fourth column of table 7.1 and the second column of table 7.2). There may also be double-counting as between column 4 and columns 5, 6 and 7 in table 7.1; or perhaps there was some other British instrumentality issuing bills on account of expenditures in connection with the settlements. Columns 1, 2 and 3 in table 7.1 purport to display

---

1. See 'A Return of the Annual Expenditure ... from the 1st January (1786–1822)' in Appendix to the Evidence of the Bigge Report P.R.O. C.O. 201/130 Folio 69. (Irish Universities Press Edn) Colonial Australia vol. 3, p. 233 and p. 53).

Table 7.1 British Government Foundation Outlays on NSW and Van Diemen's Land, 1786–1822, (£)

Year	Convict Transport	Victual	Stores etc.	Bills	Civil Estab.	Military	Marine	Total
1786	28 339	NA	NA	NA	NA	NA	7	28 346
1787	23 779	NA	2 099	NA	2 877	NA	2 586	31 341
1788	7 393	261	NA	4 728	2 877	NA	2 749	18 008
1789	39 588	21 125	12 853	891	2 877	6 847	3 877	88 058
1790	8 203	1 840	18 402	1 341	4 559	6 576	3 853	44 774
1791	47 356	25 682	25 603	13 064	4 758	9 946	2 611	129 020
1792	34 234	17 261	31 140	2 842	4 726	10 110	4 275	104 588
1793	21 411	19 762	NA	11 411	4 658	10 724	1 996	69 962
1794	15 363	25 470	12 309	11 217	4 795	10 228	NA	79 382
1795	14 909	36 697	4 392	3 814	5 241	10 228	NA	75 281
1796	16 156	31 080	7 931	10 020	5 241	13 427	NA	83 855
1797	7 703	7 092	4 030	78 898	5 524	16 906	220	120 373
1798	38 990	12 033	5 169	26 407	6 157	19 726	3 032	111 514
1799	7 672	6 568	88	43 448	6 017	16 481	NA	80 274
1800	8 276	13 834	11 797	50 707	6 310	18 953	1 107	110 984
1801	61 262	12 126	7 187	17 267	7 146	20 576	NA	125 564
1802	1 612	93 272	11 189	17 837	5 908	19 592	NA	149 410
1803	15 916	16 609	16 204	21 465	9 125	16 223	1 419	96 961
1804	247	NA	306	19 298	10 050	15 386	1 232	46 519
1805	30 196	9 511	10 289	32 351	7 226	15 384	3 640	108 597
1806	13 588	38 782	6 921	13 973	12 819	19 983	1 232	107 298
1807	17 156	21 772	17 067	21 264	12 705	30 663	1 232	121 859
1808	32 275	35 876	1 848	23 222	11 166	25 101	2 058	131 546
1809	19 956	11 901	115	49 921	15 134	26 377	1 232	124 636
1810	40 767	18 136	2 134	78 805	12 269	25 357	1 232	178 700
1811	5 637	55 114	20 748	92 128	13 309	24 312	3 449	214 697
1812	31 115	17 911	1 296	91 019	11 701	31 257	1 248	185 547
1813	79 348	31 760	829	57 948	13 295	33 792	1 763	218 735
1814	55 536	23 009	34 651	74 174	13 298	20 893	3 525	225 086
1815	39 041	18 833	557	86 021	12 788	24 350	NA	181 590
1816	36 504	24 613	16 513	109 118	12 423	17 121	NA	216 292
1817	54 094	31 821	21 927	101 163	12 815	10 765	NA	232 585
1818	77 856	50 382	5 290	145 520	12 605	33 478	NA	325 131
1819	78 496	42 619	2 343	163 465	16 825	24 097	NA	327 845
1820	81 234	48 296	17 391	174 110	17 081	35 204	NA	373 316
1821	73 569	39 892	52 647	207 050	17 081	35 111	NA	425 350
1822	65 260	35 689	47 760	162 677	13 347	40 996	NA	365 729

Notes: (a) See appendix 1.
(b) NA — Not available.
Source: J. Ginswick (unpub.) MS.

the large outlays undertaken in Britain on the transfers of people and goods. As they stand, columns 5, 6 and 7 in table 7.1 are merely parliamentary appropriations for salaries (see appendix 1). They are British expenditures but not all the amounts found their way to the colonies; some were dispersed to British dependents or creditors. The actual transfers need to be sought from the accounts of the paymasters and colonial agents who, amongst other things, acted as taxing agents for Britain.

Table 7.2: Summary Public Expenditure, NSW and Van Diemen's Land, 1788–1821, (£'000)

Year	British Expend.	Commis-sariat	Gaol Fund	Orphan Fund	Police Fund	Locally Funded(b) Total
1788	18.8					
1789	58.1					
1790	44.8					
1791	129.0					
1792	104.6					
1793	70.0					
1794	79.4	98.9				
1795	75.3					
1796	83.9					
1797	120.4					
1798	111.5	129.2				
1799	80.3					
1800	111.0					
1801	125.5					
1802	149.4	57.4	0.9			
1803	97.0		0.8	4.4		
1804	46.5		0.5			
1805	118.6		1.1	2.0		
1806	107.3		0.3	1.6		
1807	121.9	106.7	0.1	1.1		
1808	131.5		NA	NA		
1809	124.6		NA	NA		
1810	178.7				3.3	
1811	214.7				10.9	
1812	185.5	258.8			13.5	
1813	218.7				14.6	
1814	225.1	116.8			13.3	NA
1815	181.5	95.3			18.0	20.0
1816	216.3	120.2			17.8	16.8
1817	232.6	110.2			24.7	19.2
1818	325.1	186.5			31.0	15.8
1819	327.8				40.8	30.3
1820	373.3	414.2			43.0	33.8
1821	425.4				44.5	27.9

Notes: (a) NA — Not available.
  (b) British Parliamentary Papers.
Source: J. Ginswick (unpub.) MS.

The actual transfers on salary account were determined in Australia. Nevertheless, Britain set the upper limit in terms of individuals' pay. The aggregate of salaries was not so clearly set in Britain. The colonies were not adequately supported by officials in the beginning and very considerable amplification of the civil lists occurred. Quite often this was done unilaterally in the settlement (beginning with Phillip's appointment of some convicts as officials). Other unilateral acts occurred with the addition in the colony of special allowances, the employment of persons for additional official functions and so on. These were colonially induced additions to British commitments. The colonists found a large variety of ways, some of which British officials were never able to bring to the surface, to enlarge the burden on Britain. This was particularly through the deployment of convicts as a means of payment for services or for inclusion amongst the staffs of the various colonial departments.

Britain has been criticised for inadequate delivery of goods and equipment. These criticisms are valid in the very early years. But overall, Britain spent heavily on the delivery of these goods and equipment and the deliveries were predominantly at colonial request, not British initiative. It is extraordinary that no accounting of the distribution of these goods flows appears to survive. If, in fact, no accounting was ever made, Britain had no means of testing the validity of the requests. It appears most probable that no accounting *was* ever made over the period indicated in table 7.1 insofar as an accounting entry, only in aggregate form, was entered for only one year — in the beginning of the 1820s — in the Commissariat records. Thereafter, British officials were so incurious or unconcerned as to fail to send invoices of deliveries to the colony (cf. notes in records for NSW Commissariat in *Returns of the Colony of NSW*).

Army paymaster's bills may have had a quite special significance in the initiation of private enterprise by the military in NSW. But the biggest area of colonial initiative lay in the activities of the Commissariat. The Commissaries and their assistants in Australia became the most important instruments for issuing bills drawn on the British government, taking over from the authority originally accorded to and exercised by the first three governors.

The Commissariat in NSW was a peculiar form of the supply agencies, different in many respects from those to which British officials were familiar in other imperial operations. Provision was made for a NSW Commissariat with the First Fleet but the first appointee left the settlement early. An informal replacement was made when Phillip appointed a Deputy Commissary in 1791. The immediate object appears to have been to eke out the scarce stores and to control the distribution of such goods as Governor Phillip could arrange to import. Phillip, himself, issued the bills — raising a charge against the British government — and thereby made foreign exchange available. The relatively informal modes of appointing civilians to the Commissariat continued well into the 19th century. Informal appointments continued until 1810 when direct British appointments were resumed, with British directives to act. Between 1810 and 1813, the Commissariat passed to military control. Neither arrangement revealed much of what was happening fiscally in the colony. Only after 1820 did the Commissariat become a means of delimiting and constraining British commitment to the development of Australia.

A subsidiary of the Port Jackson Commissariat was established at Norfolk Island in 1791. With the formation of the VDL settlement in 1803, subordinate Commissariats were located at Port Arthur; and at Port Dalrymple from 1808. Subsequently, regional stores were placed around the colonies, some of them mobile (e.g. ships in the Hunter River). Deputy Assistant Commissaries were appointed in Norfolk Island and VDL and their accounts were merged in the NSW Commissariat possibly wholly until 1810, thereafter as net transactions until 1826. In 1827, the VDL Commissariat was separated from that in NSW. Unfortunately, the surviving accounts relating to VDL between 1810 and 1827 are very scrappy and often illegible. It should be clearly understood in relation to the rest of this paper that, although the Commissariat Accounts of Norfolk Island to 1810 and of VDL to 1826–27 purport to be included in those for NSW, it is very dubious as to what this inclusion means. It seems probable that for many years, at least, the accounts included in NSW represent only the net NSW commitments to VDL and not the true operations of the Commissariat in VDL itself. The same problem arises, in a minor way, with respect to Norfolk Island.

The Commissariat organisation in the Empire went well back into the 18th century with the Commissary General firmly established as a prominent official of the Treasury (though working closely with the Army) before the departure of the First Fleet. In the 1840s, the Treasury described it as a system that 'provides, keeps in store and issues the provisions, fuel and light for the use of the service abroad' (*The British Almanac 1847*: 37–8). Such a formal description fails to capture many of the crucial features of the Australian Commissariats and their subsidiaries. It is fundamental to an understanding of the bodies in NSW that appointments to manage the Commissariats were made without formal directives from the British Treasury and effectively as local delegations by the Colonial governors during 1791–1810. Certainly, these were stores and distributing agencies. But they quickly became much more than this. They were sources of foreign exchange and of local instruments of exchange; they were, at once, banks and credit agencies. These particular characteristics became so prominent in both NSW and Van Diemen's Land that the Commissariats became the springboards for private banking enterprises. In addition, they were the instruments for encouraging and reallocating productive activity, for regulating prices and subsidies to such an extent that they have been perceived as 'staple markets'.

The Commissariats became, also, the means for paying supplementary allowances to officials, for compensating persons for performing public services for which no British appropriation existed or for totally funding some other public services. Through rations distribution, they effectively paid workers engaged in convict gangs on public infrastructure. This last role was, at times, so far extended that they acted to subvert regulations and provided devices for arranging, through barter deals, access to land occupation by persons while still under sentence. They provided a continuing venue for barter at scattered locations around the settlement, a process that led the officials concerned to treat much of the Commissariats' operations as net transactions and therefore to conceal much of their activity.

If this were all, it would merely imply that the Australian Commissariats were complex public institutions. But they were much more than this. Particularly until 1820, they were central to the privatisation of the settlements, to the concentration of wealth and income and, through this concentration and the development of large private enterprises, to the success of colonial economic development. These adaptations depended, among other things, on their providing limited information on the basis of which British officials could assess colonial affairs.

To understand this, one needs to appreciate the nature and scope of the Commissariat accounts. Forms of accounts for NSW survive continuously from 1791. They relate, however, only to those transactions that could be described as net cash transactions (including bills) originating in the settlement. They failed to disclose the gross cash or barter transactions. They were highly condensed and unrevealing summaries, covering various periods of account. Frequently, they were often made up a long time after the period to which they referred and were audited after much longer delays. Barter transactions appear, at best, only as a net cash equivalent in two-way trade. There is not, except for one year in the early 1820s, any acknow-ledgment of goods received directly from Britain. Nor, perhaps most importantly, is there any accounting of the distribution of goods traded by the Commissariat or received into store directly from Britain.

Fundamentally, the surviving accounts are archaic 18th-century summaries delivered by an inferior to a superior person, not impersonal public revenue and expenditure statements. There was no double-entry system. The accounts served essentially after and over some period, to settle the outstanding personal liability of the accountant for the conduct of his period of office. In doing so, the accountant (the Deputy Commissary or his Assistant) at times appealed to principles of liability declared many years after the event — so late was the record and so concerned was he to avoid some repayment. There was little, indeed, that the auditors could explore and investigate unless they had some supplementary accounts that have not so far come to light.

Should this be taken to be merely frustration of a modern investigator, the follow-ing contemporary judgment may be noted. Messrs Erskine and King, reporting in 1811 to the Treasury, declared it essential to introduce 'Some order and method into what is at present nothing but confusion, the past store accounts being incapable of any regular examination, and having every appearance of having been framed with the express view of frustrating all inquiry' (*Historical Records of NSW*, vol. 7: 569).

Whatever may, in fact, have been the case, there is little doubt that the potential for conduct benefiting private rather than public interest was substantial. That improper conduct in any terms occurred from time to time is explicit. Governor Phillip reported organised theft (*HRA*, series 1, vol. 1: 144, 344). Governor King identified beneficial pricing and kickbacks and fraudulent recording. (*HRA*, series 1, vol. 3: 474). The third Commissary was widely condemned as a rogue. Sometimes in the nature of peccadillo, attempts were made to issue bills to self — Foveaux was caught out after eight years' possession of public money. Bills issued by Commissaries to self must be suspect — some were very large (see Commissariat accounts). Palmer as Commissary ran, amongst other activities, a substantial biscuit-making enterprise, simply withdrawing wheat, flour and sugar from the Commissariat that he controlled. Bligh was extremely generous to himself in the supply of convicts, rations and equipment for his farming.

In the privatised environment of the time, however, there were many other possi-bilities. Circumstantially, the second and third Commissaries at Port Jackson became men of substance with remarkable speed. Some convict officials in the Commissariat (such as Lord) emulated and subsequently surpassed them. The manner of issuing bills was not infrequently almost a guarantee of preference to some individual recipient. Those responsible for the payment of wages to groups of employees on government service commonly received a single bill for the entire (net) wages due. D'Arcy Wentworth was one such beneficiary; so were the masters of colonial vessels as well as other superintendents. Subsequently, Macquarie was able to requite claims (such as very large travel and forage claims) on his own say-so (see Commissariat Accounts).

In between these two types of behaviour, Bligh is alleged to have used the Commissariat massively for his private benefit (*HRA*, series 1, vol. 6). Some of these allegations appear to have been justified. Indeed, in the charge and counter-charge in the Bligh upheaval, the control of the Commissariat, not rum, seems to be a focal issue. Beyond Bligh and during Macquarie's administration came the efforts in both

NSW and Van Diemen's Land to convert the Commissariats to private banks by the substitution of private for public bills by the incumbent Commissaries (S.J. Butlin, 1953).

Such varieties of practice may well have assisted the growth of private enterprise and the success of the settlement. What they did not do was to reveal effectively to British administrators the state of colonial affairs. Indeed, they were part of a piece whereby subterranean public finance could more easily develop in the settlements, enhancing the burdens of private colonial development to Britain and relaxing the pressures on both public and private individuals in Australia.

8

BROAD RELATIONS BETWEEN BRITISH AND AUSTRALIAN FISCS TO 1821

The facts of fiscal dominance of Britain and of the presence of large numbers of convicts in the New South Wales settlement until 1840 inevitably narrow the focus in explaining the origins and development of public finance in eastern Australia. Certainly, various forms of political process influenced fiscal history, including the conflicts of interests of different groups. Nevertheless, it is not possible to seek these fiscal origins and developments primarily through the exercise of choice by free individuals and groups in Britain or in the Australian colonies.

Almost from the beginning, there was a conflict of interest between British officials and NSW residents. At least for the first 52 years of Australian history, NSW was a major convict receptacle for Britain. There is considerable debate as to whether there was also some imperial design in the initial decision to establish the colony. In NSW, the initial penal concept was rapidly altered, firstly by privatisation after 1792 and subsequently through the growth of non-convict activities broadening the range of private interest groups. For Britain itself, the revealed behaviour strongly suggests that there was an increasingly imperial interest in the Australian settlements. The Napoleonic Wars distracted British attention from the internal affairs of the colony and limited the flow of convicts.

Two other issues might be noted. Firstly, there was the extension of settlement to Van Diemen's Land at a very early stage in 1803 to forestall other claimants. Secondly, there were the very extensive naval activities in the Indian and Pacific Oceans throughout the Napoleonic Wars. Even if Australia lay only on the perimeter of these activities, British occupation of Australia helped to limit other European nations. For a Britain committed, in particular, to the defeat of Napoleon until 1815 and thereafter under pressure to reduce drastically the role of government in Britain, the pressure on the colony became a matter of fiscal constraint. But was it merely to achieve a least-cost outcome for a penal settlement? The settlers, on the other hand, whether high or low income groups, had a strong interest in passing as much as possible of the burden of establishing the settlement onto Britain. Those engaged most actively in privatising the colony depended on British support to enhance their fortunes.

Entrusted by Britain initially to combine British convicts and NSW lands owned by the British Crown, officials were at first agents of the imperial power. By 1855, transportation had ceased and independent colonies established, the title to Crown lands transferred to colonial governments and British fiscal support largely withdrawn. Between the two dates lies a convoluted process of shifting fiscal relationships. The pedagogic task of disentangling the fiscal streams is demanding. But underlying most, if not all, of the issues was the fundamental distributive conflict that had reverberated through the American Revolution but was dealt with in a different way in Australia: Was Britain to receive relief from expenditure by output from the colonies in self-support (rations production) or from public funding locally to fund public objects?

The total British budgetary expenditures averaged, throughout 1788–1822, just on two-thirds of local NSW and VDL gross domestic product. This was a very advantageous subvention to the settlement and of particular value to the society that, in NSW during 1800–15, was predominantly non-convict. Apart from the local agency task of officials, to combine convicts and local natural resources, the colonists had three other avenues through which to exert fiscal pressure on Britain. One was in the local purchase of goods; the second was through the issue of bills particularly for foreign purchases; the third was to press for stores and equipment direct from Britain.

The placement of the Commissariat in NSW, with its formal roles as a store and distributing institution and its powers to issue bills on the British Treasury, went a long way, given the distractions of the Napoleonic Wars, to removing British fiscal control over the settlement. The British were committed to a civil and military establishment; it was their decision whether or not to transport more convicts. The primary fiscal variables within these formed accounts lay, however, in the accession of stores and equipment and the issue of bills, both under colonial influence. These items averaged about 40 per cent of the total British subvention to 1822.

Free activity in the settlement after 1792 greatly confused the nature and even the timing of local initiative in respect of these variable items. It is not surprising that most governors after Phillip were subjected to British criticism and ended with at least their fiscal reputations tarnished. Thanks to local initiative and the British continuing to honour obligations both of local Commissariat purchases and of imports on 'official' account, the settlement was able to achieve relatively high living standards and a complex variety of economic activity at a remarkably early stage. Very much more than merely penal and defence costs were passed to the British Treasury.

This is not to imply that had a tight fiscal control been possible during the first 30 years, a lower subvention would have been paid by Britain. The colony might have been less efficient. British officials were less interested in counterfactuals than they were in the manifest wealth of the colonists by the early years of the 19th century and by the mounting costs to the British taxpayer. So long as the settlement remained in control or under the influence of a junta or of cabals — however much confused by internal conflict — the British problem was that any fiscal record was too little, too late and, to a large extent, deceiving. Thus, even when total public rations to assigned convicts were reduced severely, these rations continued to be transferred and to a considerable degree matched by debts to the Commissariat, the debts rising partly because beneficiaries failed or refused to recognise that formerly free goods were now charged. A major reformation in assignment arrangements after 1800 failed to achieve a comparable reduction in British fiscal support. The decline in Commissariat expenditures under King was due more to the termination of sentences and sealing than to his efforts to restrain ration supplies for assigned convicts.

Table 7.2 (p.63) gives a broad, if incomplete, indication of the extent to which, despite the widespread privatisation of the settlement, the colonists escaped the need for substantial local fiscal contributions up to 1822. Set against the total British subvention (column 1), one can see roughly the scale of the Commissariat operations that were largely locally controlled (but included in column 1). For an annual representation of Commissariat operations, see appendix 2. The three conventional local fiscs on the NSW mainland were the Gaol and Orphan Funds beginning officially in 1800 (though the Gaol Fund, at least, was established in 1799); these were replaced by Macquarie with the Police Fund continuing until 1821 (columns 3, 4, and 5 of table 7.2). The final column is from British Parliamentary Papers and is clearly an inadequate representation of local fiscal operations.

Subject to some variations, the local contributions were typically less than 5 per cent of British expenditures; even at the end of Macquarie's administration they were not much over 10 per cent. The scale of the local contribution may be under-stated because of subterranean fiscal operations not revealed in these local funds. The problem is, however, to try to evaluate where the incidence of the subterranean operations fell and it will be necessary to come back to this matter later. Despite the uncertainties, it is reasonably clear that the colonists contributed little to their own public goods or welfare or infrastructure problems at least to the end of the Napoleonic Wars (see table 7.2).

Nevertheless, the local contribution was increasing rapidly from 1810. It was not until the British government acted to withdraw the NSW Corps and its privatised military officials (some remained in the colony) that effective restructuring of mutual fiscal obligations was possible. From that date, a clear, if still limited, shift occurred, with Macquarie providing some local supplements to the British resources deployed in infrastructure. It remained for Bigge to recommend and have adopted the proposal for a much broader fiscal imposition on the settlement and for the beginning of British financial disentanglement.

9

THE BEGINNING
OF LOCAL BUDGETING:
REAL AND
SUBTERRANEAN
BUDGETS

Real Budgeting within the Penal System

New South Wales was never a gaol in a literal sense. Nevertheless, the first local budgetary act began in NSW when the first fish were caught and shared and the first corn produced, stored and distributed. In the first settlement years, unfree labour, working under direction, was under pressure to provide a range of immediately needed goods and services. These included the catching, collection and ultimately the production of food, the assembly of local materials for buildings and other structures, the clearing of land and the distribution of goods supplied by Britain.

To support these activities, official ration allocations of food and clothing were organised through the Commissariat as recipient of British supplies and local output. As receiver, storer and distributor, the Commissariat became a Treasury in kind. Through it emerged a rudimentary fiscal process in real goods and services. Virtually from the beginning, the convict colony was operating a local fisc that can be obscured if one thinks merely in terms of productive and distributive activities. Moreover, the real fiscal operations were relatively complex, depending on the precise equality of rations, variance in the efficiency of different convict groups and the variety of activities in which convicts were engaged. As convicts were assigned for personal use, particularly after 1792, the central fiscal role of the Commissariat began to disintegrate. But it remained a significant fiscal agency throughout the whole period to 1840 in NSW and to 1855 in Van Diemen's Land, although with changing functions. (The later Commissariat in Western Australia was an exception in attempting to service a failing private settlement.)

Where there were differences in productivity between convict gangs, the rationing process taxed the more productive and subsidised the less productive. This transfer process might not seem to be the optimal provision to maximise efficiency. However, this is not as clear as it might appear at first sight. If only progressively less efficient resources were available, the expansion of such a simple prison farm would depend on using these less productive resources. Such a tax-subsidy provision would need to balance general loss of efficiency against the need to expand the total resource use.

Of course the NSW settlement was never so simple. Clearly there was some division of labour — fishing, building, land clearing, cultivation, animal husbandry. In these conditions, where standard rations were issued, they became a subsistence basket. Real budgeting substituted for the market and rearranged consumption of specialised individuals by a network of goods transfer to make up the nominated basket of commodities.

Even general ration increases or reductions contained a tax element. When rations were reduced, present consumption was taxed in favour of future consumption — essentially corresponding to a forced loan to the store. The problems became more complex when differential rations were allowed, as they soon were in NSW. Wherever the recipients of above-average rations were more productive, the real fiscal operation might actually be reduced. In historical conditions, the sustenance of the Marine Corps and its dependants implied a considerable tax-transfer process, until privatisation occurred.

These types of local real budgeting continued so long as the government in NSW produced goods and services capable of being transferred in individual units and included in rations or subsidy transfers. In some degree, they continued into the early 1820s. Their significance declined immediately after the first privatisation during 1792–5 and shrank till after 1800. There then appear to have been some fluctuations in their scope until the second major occasion of privatisation, after Bligh's departure. From that point, real budgeting arising within the penal system was probably a minor matter so far as these rations/subsidy transfers were concerned.

Real Rewards for Official Services

The formal British Parliamentary Appropriation that was provided for civil official salaries was an ambivalent benefit to the settlement. It was an important subsidy but it specifically limited the number and type of officials covered. The list in the appropriations could be expanded gradually but only after long delays in British approvals. In some significant cases, the British government refused to recognise the entitlement of persons to public rewards for performance of certain public functions both in Britain and in the colony.

Whether for reasons of slowness of approval or of outright British rejection of proposals for additional officials, a local solution was needed, given the absence of a conventional colonial public revenue before 1800 or of some means of charging for public services provided. These conditions applied most obviously in performing services in relation to publicly employed convicts (overseers and supervisors including convict police), in the growing demands for such public goods as education and in many judicial proceedings particularly in relation to criminal offences, physical punishment and the like. In these areas, market-like systems could not easily be introduced. In other cases, where a charge could be imposed on beneficiaries an alternative solution could be found (see fees for service below).

There were many relevant official roles omitted in the British appropriations list. The shortfall increased because of the reluctance firstly of the Marines and subsequently of the NSW Corps to perform civil functions. Many of these gaps in recognised officialdom remained for several decades even though the British Parliament gradually lengthened its approved list. In some cases, the British officials approved the local solution rather than seeking an increase in the appropriations (cf. McMartin, 1983).

The particular solution that applied to the more skilled or responsible functions was to reward individuals for full or part-time official services by assigning convicts with their rations as a reward (see later section 'Convicts as Public Servants' for lower level services). Such assignments could raise the consumption standards of recipients (personal service), increase their private productive activity or increase their incomes by hiring-off the assigned services. Whatever the outcome, these convicts were assigned for official reasons and remained officially in the public 'sector'.

It is difficult to assess the numbers of convicts involved but they appear typically to have been a significant fraction of the total from the late 1790s until, at any rate, the late 1820s. Not only did this remain an important subterranean budgetary operation for several decades but it confuses also the relative roles of Britain and the colonists in the total budgetary process and the extent to which the colonists were able to divert British resources to locally perceived needs. (There were reversals of this process: in 1803, monetary salaries of *recognised* officials on the appropriations list were *increased* to compensate for the withdrawal of some servants assigned (*HRA*, series 1, vol. 4: 21; vol. 3: 485–6).)

The type of official roles rewarded in kind varied over time. Possibly the most important example, partly because the procedure persisted for so long, was the provision for the magistracy. Magistrates were not normally rewarded directly in Britain, their part-time services were drawn largely from the gentry (they were established in NSW, with 'normal' magistrates' functions in 1798 (*HRA*, series 1, vol. 15: 689)). The failure of Britain to appreciate the high opportunity costs of such services by actively engaged privatised officials in NSW forced a local solution (cf. *HRA*, series 1, vol. 2: 569). McMartin (1983) refers to the original magistrates as being 'surgeons and chaplains'.

Two were Balmain and Marsden, deeply involved in private business undertakings, quite misleadingly described in these exclusive professional terms. Magistrates were initially allowed eight convicts, subsequently reduced to four with rations plus rations for officials themselves (*HRA*, series 1, vol. 3: 419). McMartin calls this a 'small allowance'. At a level, as valued, of £39 per convict, eight assigned servants implied £312 per annum. A *supplement* that was about one-third of the governor's salary can hardly be described as small. Having done so, however, initially in the absence of a local fisc, the colonists saw no reason why, once a local fisc was established, their own financial resources should be invaded when the cost could remain on Britain through the use of the penal system and the Commissariat. In any event, magistrates remained, for some time, closely associated with penal affairs, including convict assignment and punishment.

Authorised Fees for Official Services

The alternative of fees for services rendered officially could be and was adopted where individual transactions or benefits were identifiable. A system of fees was scarcely relevant to a gaol. But the adjustments from a penal condition and transfers of resources out of the public domain offered opportunities for charging even before individual 'free' activity existed. Once individual transactions in a 'free' society occurred, the scope for a system of charging was greatly enlarged.

Two forms of transactions in property rights appear to be the first for which authorised official fees were introduced and became important after 1792. Privatisation greatly enlarged the process of land grants even though many grants were relatively informal; and the transfer of real estate to private property required authorisation, survey, deeds preparation, certification and approval. At every step in the chain, an official fee for service was adopted and charged, benefiting officials from the governor down. The termination of convict sentences or the grant of tickets of leave were similarly valuable changes in the status of property rights and authorised fees were charged for each, at least from 1795.

The growing social and legal complexity of the settlement introduced a variety of civil decisions relating to status, business rights, licences, registration of contracts, etc. These expanded, from the second half of the 1790s, the areas in which individuals in official roles could claim a price for services rendered.

As actual business transactions increased, an official service could intervene to official benefit. This was most obviously the case where import or (the limited) export business was concerned. Port control and the handling of ships and their cargoes presented a wide range of services from anchorage, wharfage, unloading and placement of goods in bond. The functions of Naval (port control) Officers and wharfingers became important and presented particularly handsome opportunities for the charging of fees for service (McMartin, 1983).

When Macquarie assumed office, he listed (*HRA*, series 1, vol. 7: 450–4) over 100 types of officially authorised fees for official services rendered. Even though, by then, a conventional fisc existed, based primarily on import duties, these fees were frequently omitted from the public accounts. Some provided very large incomes indeed (the Naval Officer's income vied with that of the Governor). The original Naval Officer, Balmain, received 15 per cent of cargoes, reduced later to 5 per cent. The Provost Marshal was also rewarded handsomely with fees; at the lower level, gaolers received fees: for example, each discharged debtor and each disorderly sailor gaoled per night (*HRA*, series 1, vol. 5: 280; vol. 6: 160). Fees provided a system whereby public services were rendered and paid for without formally acknowledging the raising and expenditure of public revenues. Some were payments for actual services rendered; some yielded incomes from which the recipient paid subordinates to render the actual service (as in the case of the Provost Marshal). Macquarie's list was a lengthy one; nevertheless, he did not capture the multiplicity of charges that related to a good many of the services and the fact that several 'officials' could make a separate claim for the same process.

The system of fee for service can be seen as derived from three main sources. Firstly, in property transfers, fees were an established British practice and readily approved by Britain in land transfers in the settlement (cf. instructions to Phillip). Some of these were fees in kind. Thus the Acting Surveyor General in 1794 initially received ten convicts plus rations for the general service of surveying (see Dowd, 'A.T.H. Alt' in Pike, 1966). Secondly, without formal revenue raising powers, the Governors could not easily institute a strictly public service rendered by salaried officials. Thirdly, the early privatisation of the gaol after 1792 was based, in fact, on individual benefits from official service. As private activities increased, the involvement of individuals in fortune-seeking meant that their opportunity cost increased and there was increasing reluctance to deliver to others the benefits of their authority without a reward.

Accordingly, almost anything might attract a fee. Thus when efforts were made after 1800 to fund an Orphan Institution supported partly by cargoes of specific ships the local 'orphans' (and their administrators) were supported by the profits of sale of the cargoes. The Commissary and his clerks, however, made a prior claim, a percentage on the total value of the cargo for 'the trouble' in keeping the accounts.

Privately received fees for service continued at least into the 1830s and were still very prominent in most of the 1820s (nominally, they were ended in 1830 (*HRA*, series 1, vol. 15: 851–2, 744–5). With Macquarie's arrival, however, steps were progressively taken to translate these fees into salaries, the fees themselves becoming public revenues. This was possible once a conventional fisc existed, as it clearly did in a reasonably substantial way from 1810 (see below).

From this shift, a broader bureaucracy was established. This was probably necessary to the extent that the removal of the NSW Corps created something of a vacuum in fee-charging officials and facilitated their replacement by salaried officials. Nevertheless a concerted shift to salaries should be dated from around the mid-1820s. Moreover, the elimination of individually received fees for service was not easy if only because of the local prominence of some of the recipients. This was most obviously the case with the Naval Officer whose wealth and high living (from his high fees) were well known in Sydney. McMartin (1983: 134) believed that the Naval Officer received only these fees; in fact, in the 1820s he had military pay and allowances in addition. In 1826, the position of Naval Officer in Britain itself, and in the Empire, was abolished, replacing it with the position of Customs Collector. It was only after the Naval Officer committed defalcations of public revenues to the extent of £17 000 and made a suicide attempt that this particular change was formally adopted and a different person appointed to the new (salaried) position in 1827.

Convicts as Public Servants

For special reasons, the use of convicts as public servants warrants separate attention. They are a particular category of the general colonial budgeting of human capital which local authorities were required to direct by Britain. Whatever the original British intention may have been, the privatisation of the settlement during the interregnum after Phillip resulted in extensive private assignment of convicts. There was then a human capital budget to arrange between the public and 'private' sectors. In public employment, a great deal of convict labour was engaged in farming and public infrastructure. These two uses of convicts by government could be treated as part of 'public finance'. It is, however, more convenient to take them up in discussing the labour market. The use of convicts as public servants, in the sense of filling positions in the normal operations of government, has a special fiscal interest.

The use of convicts in these official roles was almost inescapable from the very beginning. Given the handful of officials, the refusal of the original marines to cooperate fully in penal management exposed the weakness of the traditional British approach to government. The tasks of an isolated, new settlement, particularly one based on convicts, were fundamentally different from those in Britain. Devolution was required and this meant devolution on selected convicts. Phillip had no option but to place a good many convicts in positions of trust and authority, responsible for many low-level management functions.

Despite the increase in the number of ex-convicts, this early arrangement was not easily reversed. There were too many attractive alternatives for freed persons ready to assume official duties that were not supported by British appropriations. Accordingly, under Governor Hunter, the great majority of constables were convicts; and convicts continued to be allocated to support conventional officials in carrying out their public roles. So long as these appointments were predominantly in the area of security, British officials may have had little concern — the British confusion over military and police functions was deeply rooted in historical practice and the charging of support for such persons to the Commissariat was scarcely exceptionable.

After 1810, when a local conventional fisc was established and grew rapidly, a different situation arose. There was now a significant amount of discretionary revenue and widening claims on its use in the colony. Colonial authority had an incentive to husband this local revenue and hence to claim support of its expanding 'civil service' against the British Commissariat rather than locally collected revenues. Convicts could be appointed, in most instances, at something approaching subsistence though with the additional incentive to them of greater freedom and some authority; and the cost was on Britain.

Until the establishment of the Colonial Fund in 1822, the matter may not have been a source of much contention. As this revenue grew in the 1820s, conflict between British and Australian interest became increasingly prominent. Public services in the colony became increasingly complex and of local rather than imperial benefit; and the British government was more and more concerned to limit its area of fiscal commitment. McMartin (1983: 176) believes that there was very little prospect of manning the colonial public service without primary dependence on convicts before 1825. Certainly, in 1827, the Colonial Treasurer and Colonial Secretary appear to have been almost completely dependent on convicts as a source of clerks. The Office of the Principal Superintendent of Convicts was reputedly composed almost entirely of convicts — supposedly capable of the oversight of all convict records. The principle of setting a thief to catch a thief did not appeal to Governor Darling who complained vigorously about the fiscal and security risks of the over-dependence on convict clerks.

McMartin's judgment is open to some question. The colonial officials chose convicts because they were cheap and their charge loaded on Britain. Had the offer price for clerks been raised, one might expect more free or freed persons to seek the positions. Virtually none of the convict appointees appears as a charge in the Colonial Fund; they were supported by the Commissariat. However, higher offer prices would have required more local public fund raising.

The British government sought, from time to time, to discover how many such convict appointees were made but never succeeded in discovering the answer. It is possible that this problem was a major factor in determining the British course to narrow the general areas of British support to the colony. In fact, it is doubtful if the British could then, or if we could now, provide an effective answer. Perhaps detailed investigation of convict records will, in due course, do so. But there is a basic problem of definition. We are not concerned merely with clerks. Persons assigned to those in official capacity may have been essential or conventional to the conduct of official functions. The obvious example is the number of convicts assigned to Government House; but the same issue applies to other senior officials; and, at the other end of the scale, the listing of convict gangs conceals the trusties and low-level supervisors that were drawn from convict ranks. On a very narrow definition of clerk-like activities, the 1828 Census would suggest that perhaps about 100 convicts were involved. On a broad definition, the number could be closer to 1000. It is not surprising that the British were apprehensive.

Concern over efficiency and security because of the employment of convicts increased into the early 1830s; the risks to local revenues were greater; and the flow of free migrants as potential public servants grew greatly. Moreover, Britain had, by then, reasonably clearly demarcated the defence and police roles that it would support through the Commissariat. In 1835, the Treasury acted to direct the removal of all convicts from the colonial public service in NSW. The days of British subsidy to civil service staffing were over. But this change depended on the creation of a substantial conventional fisc in the colonies.

The Formal but Illegal Colonial Fisc: 1800–1821

At least as early as 1792, Governor Phillip (*HRA*, series 1, vol. 1) had sought approval for introducing indirect taxation. The British officials approved the 'raising' of 'charges' but not revenue by the local Governor (McMartin (1983) misinterprets the accounting terms). Subsequently, Governor Hunter proposed local imposts in 1796 (*HRA*, series 1, vol. 1: 593; vol. 2: 437) in the form, according to him, of a charge on access to imports, not a duty on the goods themselves. The imposition of duties, tolls and licenses were accepted as a prerogative of the British parliament. It is not clear whether Hunter's proposal was to provide the governor, himself, with some local fiscal flexibility or a mechanism to achieve greater control on the landing of spirits and wine. At all events, British officials were unimpressed and, indeed, Hunter's proposal appears devious.

Three problems came to a head at the turn of the century and then British officials raised no immediate protest. One was a welfare issue, the case of so-called 'orphans' — essentially neglected children of the convicts. This was a social problem not provided for by British instructions and scarcely welcome to prevailing social philosophy in Britain. Efforts to provide welfare services for children had been made during the 1790s in several ways through some apprenticeships and most importantly a voluntary welfare organisation supported by private charity (*HRA*, series 1, vol. 2: 536).

A second was the replacement of a gaol in Sydney to control particularly intransigent convicts. The original gaol having been burnt by its occupants, Hunter made a public goods appeal (*HRA*, series 1, vol. 2: 355) to replace the gaol: settlers to deliver cash, goods and labour to provide for their security (*HRA*, series 1, vol. 2: 588); the public sector to contribute goods. Some funds and labour appear to have been organised, under a committee, in 1799. Rebuilding was begun on this basis and continued despite a considerable number of free-riders. Exhaustion of privately subscribed funds before completion of rebuilding led to a proposal for a loan from government. Thirdly, Hunter had been charged to restrain the consumption of spirits and wine in the colony. In this, he manifestly failed and imports of spirits and wines increased rapidly to become a flood in 1800. Parliamentary prerogative or not (in imposing certain duties), a fee for access on landing provided a useful additional regulatory device.

It would be almost too good to be true that incendiarism by the inmates of a gaol led to the establishment of a wholly illegal system of local public finance in NSW. Certainly this would be wholly appropriate in the colony's circumstances. But the matter is a little more complex. The pressure to control the importation of spirits was increasing and ship arrivals were displaying a disastrous failure to exercise control. The mere possession of liquor was not an easily sustainable criminal charge. A local fund that had received no duties on landing was specific evidence of at least a tax misdemeanour.

Although Hunter proposed only a 'temporary assessment' on landing, he did not suggest that the assessment would cease as soon as the gaol was rebuilt. In any event, he was on the point of being replaced and probably only one cargo was subjected to his duties. His successor Governor King was more determined to disregard the prerogative of parliament in his anxiety to regulate the liquor traffic. Tiny as the revenue collected may seem, it was a flood compared with what might reasonably have been anticipated (the imports of liquor in 1800 are what prompted Shaw to believe that NSW settlers consumed six times the level of British consumption per head). Moreover, the tax identified transactions in liquor. King imposed charges of 1/- per gallon of spirits, 6d per gallon of wine; and wharfage duties. Significantly, he declared that the revenue was 'For the Jail and other Public Works'. Incendiarism, at least, was not enough. The Gaol Fund, virtually from its inception, was directed to fund *as yet unspecified* expenditure objects of infrastructure. There was no concept of 'appropriations'.

The so-called 'orphans' were, at least in the view of the voluntary committee in 1799, so well funded that subscriptions for orphan welfare were proposed to be loaned for completion of the gaol. Perhaps it was fortuitous but the opportunity was presented to government to purchase the privately owned residence of an official, Lt Kent, regarded as one of the very best mansions in Sydney (*HRA*, series 1, vol. 2: 525). That this should be chosen for purchase (and extended) to house orphans is a curious incident. In any case, King acted in September 1800 to announce a number of specific shipping and harbour dues. These charges were essentially on entry, anchorage, wharfage and clearing of ships but also included a supplementary charge for a permit to land spirits. With these resources, a distinct Orphan Fund was established, Lt Kent's house duly purchased, reportedly to house 200 children. (For details of indirect taxation, see La Nauze, 1948: 1–17.) Indicative, however, of colonial behaviour, Kent's house was paid for by the British government through the Commissariat (see Accounts), even though the same government had funded its original construction through the assignment of publicly rationed convicts.

Subsequently these illegal charges supporting the two funds were extended and the illegality compounded. Until 1810, each fund had separate revenue sources and distinct expenditure objectives. The Orphan Fund remained as its name implies. The Gaol Fund became a specifically local source of income to provide additional infrastructure that enlarged the construction activity by the Commissariat and that did not need to be reported to and approved by British officials. The Gaol Fund could, thus, reflect special predilections of the governor or be directly responsive to local interest groups capable of influencing the governor. This potential became prominent during Governor Macquarie's administration.

The calculations of the various accounts have been generously made available by Jules Ginswick. For the Orphan Fund, revenue sources extended to public house licenses (1800) auctioneers licenses (1801), regulation on coal and timber (1801); a 5 per cent *ad valorem* duty on any imports from ports east of the Cape together with a similar duty on all spirits and wine and goods from any source not being British manufactures (1802). In 1805, fees from land grants and loans, quit rents and fines were payable to the Orphan Fund. In addition, profits on the sale of certain cargoes of goods provided by the British government were also allotted to this Fund. In 1807, Governor Bligh extended the indirect taxes to include specified export duties. There the revenues of the Orphan Fund remained until Macquarie's arrival.

The Gaol Fund remained until 1809 based on import duties on liquor and wine. The liquor duty per gallon was raised to 1/6d in 1805 and so remained until Macquarie doubled the duty to 3/- per gallon (1810) and abolished the Gaol Fund in favour of the new style of Police Fund (see table 9.1).

Table 9.1: Summary Police Fund, New South Wales, 1810–21, (£, rounded)

Revenue

Year	Balance C/Fwd	Naval (Customs)	Licences	Duties	Other Revenue	Total
1810	0	1 384	1 088	800	0	3 272
1811	769	7 872	1 580	610	108	10 939
1812	5 016	5 579	2 338	481	80	13 494
1813	4 502	5 228	3 810	976	105	14 621
1814	6 016	4 549	2 158	602	0	13 325
1815	1 681	13 197	2 095	1 006	15	17 994
1816	3 327	11 200	2 246	927	82	17 782
1817	5 453	16 125	2 165	843	120	24 706
1818	9 363	17 739	2 624	975	307	31 008
1819	18 900	18 431	2 110	1 313	90	40 844
1820	14 129	22 578	1 593	1 606	3 062	42 968
1821	10 725	27 891	2 675	2 178	1 038	44 507
Total	79 881	151 773	26 482	12 317	5 007	275 460

Expenditure

Year	Salaries	Public Works	Other Charges	Balance C/Fwd	Total
1810	178	2 194	131	769	3 272
1811	878	2 965	2 080	5 016	10 939
1812	1 433	3 259	4 300	4 502	13 494
1813	1 239	4 426	2 940	6 016	14 621
1814	1 351	4 993	5 300	1 681	13 325
1815	3 719	6 350	4 598	3 327	17 994
1816	3 297	5 583	3 449	5 453	17 782
1817	2 598	7 048	5 697	9 363	24 706
1818	2 613	6 219	3 276	18 900	31 008
1819	4 367	16 079	6 269	14 129	40 844
1820	5 674	17 131	9 438	10 725	42 968
1821	7 836	14 700	8 223	13 748	44 507
Total	35 183	90 947	55 701	93 629	275 460

Source: J. Ginswick (unpub.) MS.

The establishment of the Police Fund was designed as more than merely a change in name. It signalled, firstly, a local proposal to assume responsibility for the supposedly strictly local police in NSW (a proposal that did not reach ultimate fruition until the 1840s). More importantly, it centralised the local fisc. The separate sources of revenue for the Gaol and Orphan Funds were abandoned and a general sharing rule for the Orphan Fund adopted: one-quarter of the receipts from indirect taxation to the Orphan Fund, three-quarters to the Police Fund; subsequently, the Orphan Fund was reduced to one-eighth as revenues expanded and expenditure opportunities presented themselves.

Public works absorbed a little over half of the revenue of the Police Fund. Police salaries were not a prominent charge; rather, there was a widening of salaried support for colonial public services. Salaries and public works jointly accounted on an average during 1810–21 for just under three-quarters of the total current outlays. With revenues rising by 1820 (the last full year) to well over four times their level in 1811 (the first full year), there was a veritable explosion of local and substantially discretionary funds at Macquarie's disposal. Although scarcely yet challenging Britain's fiscal dominance in the colony, the local revenues rapidly became a significant component.

In this lies an important characteristic of early public revenues. The original problem of rebuilding a gaol apart, it is doubtful whether there was a clearly planned budgeting process adopted before 1822 (and possibly not until 1834). To a substantial degree, expenditure was designed in response to revenue. There was little concept of providing appropriation for designated expenditure proposals. Expenditure expanded to fill the available revenue space.

The administrative procedures adopted for raising and spending revenues were such as almost to ensure this feature. Governors set the rates of customs taxes with very little consultation; one official (essentially the Naval Officer) collected the revenue and, after subtracting handsome fees, passed the revenues, under simple rules, to the spending body. This was 18th-century British practice.

None of this mattered much before 1809. The upsurge of revenue during Macquarie's regime gave him a financial leverage that no governor before (or indeed after, except possibly for Brisbane) possessed. He was able to exert a strictly public patronage, to influence through local public expenditures important aspects of the colony's economic and social development. It was this fiscal leverage, not that he invented the concept of public infrastructure, that gave Macquarie the reputation of a builder. Before 1810, despite the Gaol Fund, the provision of infrastructure was concealed and dispersed in public convict gangs. Macquarie had not only a greatly enlarged supply of convicts. He also had command of a growing local 'Treasury' that allowed him to use both direct public delivery of infrastructure and, in addition, to use the private market to deliver flexibly the types of infrastructure that he chose to emphasise. The point is illustrated in the special arrangement for a monopoly of rum imports in exchange for the construction of the Sydney hospital; and his focus on construction, such as churches and schools, to improve the quality of life in NSW.

Given his social policies and his fiscal powers together with the rapid growth of local revenues after 1810, it is perhaps not surprising that a local tax revolt occurred (cf. La Nauze, 1948). If nothing else, to those affronted socially and restricted economically by Macquarie's emancipist policies, tax revolution was at least a means of venting their spleen. In 1815, the fundamental illegality of the fiscal system was questioned, but only in terms of proposed new charges. In 1816, the Supreme Court Judge, J.H. Bent, refused to pay road tolls. More seriously, in 1818 another Judge, Field, made the fundamental challenge of an illegal local fisc — the usurpation of the exclusive right of the British parliament to impose customs duties. It was, indeed, time for Commissioner Bigge to appear. The tax revolt, Bigge's critique and the long period of illegal revenue-raising needs to be seen in full perspective. Illegal the taxes certainly were; and the governor was personally liable. But British officials were well aware of what was happening and the Colonial Office accommodated the local behaviour without seeking parliamentary sanction. It was, after all, a means of providing some protection to the British taxpayer.

The summary of the Police Fund is given in table 9.1, by courtesy of Jules Ginswick.

10

THE CONVENTIONAL LEGAL FISC IN NSW: 1822–50

Administrative and Political Changes

The local New South Wales fisc was restored to provisional grace in 1819 when the British parliament legislated to provide retrospective legality to the imposts declared by prior governors. The legislation did not yet clarify the future legality of gubernatorial fiscal action. Bigge recommended, and had accepted, several important changes amongst which was the establishment of a Colonial Fund, under British Treasury scrutiny; and he supported the continuation of locally determined duties. The British government provided, in 1823, for a Legislative Council in NSW, partly to advise the governor on local revenue raising and expenditure. At the same time, it left the raising of duties a governor's prerogative. At least, the continuing authority to raise local revenues was clarified from 1823.

The 1823 Legislative Council did little more than formalise past practice and was a very small appointed body. Enlarged in 1825, its increased *de facto* representativeness gave it more influence to contest the governor's prerogatives. The basis of this influence was strengthened by clause 28 of the New South Wales Judicature Act (4 Geo. IV, cap. 96) whereby the local revenue raising powers were made 'perpetual' (1823). In 1828, legislation provided for local revenue raising to be determined, for the first time, by the Governor in Council. Considerable tensions between the governor and the council remained. The council appears to have been able, briefly, to exercise its appropriating responsibilities in 1828, but it was not until 1834 that a continuous process of appropriation through the council was established. In a very important sense, a modern conventional fisc, based on appropriations by a representative body, might be dated from 1834. Twenty years passed, however, before a wholly elective body became the appropriating instrument, even though the Constitution Act of 1842 provided a partly elective council.

The Structure of Funding

In the meantime, in 1833, a distinct section of colonial accounts was established as 'Crown Revenues' (land sales, leases, royalties and some asset incomes), that formally received revenues from the private access to colonial Crown lands offset by specific expenditures, dominantly but not exclusively on immigration. The dominant source of the 'Crown Revenues' in the 1830s was from land sales and at this point, the British government formally claimed the right to dispose of revenues from the 'waste' or Crown lands of the colonies. Prior to 1832, land revenues in NSW had been primarily from rents and leases though some sales had occurred in the 1820s. The fiscal implications of the British Crown title to colonial lands had not then been significant. After 1833, they came to the forefront. British incentive to assert imperial claims came from the desire to exploit land revenues in the colonies to assist pauper immigration in response to Malthusian fears of overpopulation and stresses on Poor Law relief. Colonists, on the other hand, while supporting free immigration in the 1830s, were also interested in deploying land revenues for other colonial purposes as they had done in the 1820s. This was why the title to Crown lands became a major bone of contention in NSW although the British claims were weakened in principle by the outcome of the Durham Report on Waste Lands in Canada in 1836. The dispute was not resolved in Australia until 1855 when the British government surrendered to colonial claims. Until then, in interpreting colonial land revenues and their use, one should treat them as British and as predominantly British contributions to colonial development.

Although a further fund, the Corporations Fund, emerged in the early 1830s, it had little fiscal relevance. In a fiscal sense, until 1834, all churches were 'established', receiving grants from the British government. The Corporations Fund began to set the State at some length from the Church, making grants for churches and for education (largely church schools). The transfers to the Corporations Fund do not disclose the full outlays on religion or education which are concealed in church expenditures as a private matter.

So, in NSW, a complex fiscal structure gradually emerged, with three nominally distinct accounting processes operating side by side — a British Commissariat Fund, a local Colonial Fund and a third, in dispute, but constitutionally British, recorded as a subset of the Colonial Fund and designated 'Crown Revenues', called here the Crown and Land Fund. The Commissariat Fund was subdivided into a Military Commissariat and a Convict Commissariat. To confuse interpretation further, the inclusion of revenue from land in the Colonial Fund until 1832 makes difficult any attachment of revenues and expenditures to distinct British and Australian sources. To compound the confusion, there were large transfers to and from each fund as expenditure demands arose and Britain made intermittent special transfers to the Colonial Fund. And to make matters worse, Britain and NSW joined, in the 1830s and 1840s, in a local imperial venture in the foundation of New Zealand, with substantial outlays appearing as NSW but in fact related to New Zealand. Any attempt to produce a confident cost/benefit assessment of the NSW settlement to Britain faces extreme obstacles in terms of identifying the British inputs into the colony.

Some of this confusion applies to the other colonies even though the public accounts were often simpler. In Van Diemen's Land, separated in 1825, Commissariat and Colonial Funds were established separate from NSW in 1827. In this case, given British reliance on Van Diemen's Land as its prime convict outlet after 1840, there was less British pressure to clarify and limit its expenditure intentions. Even so, in 1847, a Land Fund was established, indicative of British claims.

The land title issue was different in both Western and South Australia. Crown title remained, but land transfers to private individuals were requited by private investments and private immigration arrangements. In South Australia, the Colonial Fund satisfied public accounting requirements. In Western Australia, where exposure to failure of the settlement was greater, something of a reversal of British treatment of the convict colonies arose. While Britain contributed to administrative support of its first Australian corporate colony, it was compelled to enlarge that support and to introduce a civilian Commissariat to procure supplies. This was an exceptional and minor divergence from the broad British intent after 1821 to constrain its colonial expenditures.

British–Colonial Tensions and Adaptations

In principle, the colonial fiscal developments were closely associated with British design to encourage private development of Australia after 1821. The changes that emerged were part of a piece with the decisions to limit public employment of convicts, to encourage private assignment of convicts, to support private corporate colonies, to encourage private immigration of capital, to exploit land revenues to fund assisted migration of free paupers. Fiscally, the intent was to make the colonies less expensive to Britain and more self-supporting in terms of public commitment.

Four issues dominate this rearrangement of fiscal burdens. Firstly, there was a narrowing of Britain's explicit commitments to the colony. Secondly, British support became progressively less specific and certain. Thirdly, there was the major issue of control over revenue from public lands. Fourthly, the Parliamentary, and more particularly, British Treasury pressure for accountability increased greatly during the 1820s.

Britain's contribution became narrowed, primarily, to support through the Commissariat (apart from movement costs of convicts and assisted immigrants) that was, by around 1810–15, much more firmly under bureaucratic control (despite some continued efforts at private profit making). This narrowing of British commitment signalled the British limitation of its financial undertaking to be primarily for penal and defence purposes. Briefly, the Parliamentary Appropriation for the civil establishment remained until withdrawn in 1827. At that time, separate Commissariat accounting was established for NSW and Van Diemen's Land so that, from 1827, mainland NSW can be considered separately with some confidence (for available VDL estimates, see appendix 3). Recognising the radically changed status of the settlement, the colonists in NSW were left to bear the costs of civil administration and civil objects, leaving Britain to support the penal and defence services. There was some obscurity in this division, most explicitly in relation to police. In turn, this obscurity derived from the combination, in Britain, of military and police roles, police functions having long been performed by the military in Britain. The funding of police services in NSW was reassumed by the Commissariat in 1828 and continued until 1833 when police were phased into the colonial budget. By 1840, police had effectively become a local budgetary commitment, with Britain left primarily with (dwindling) penal and defence obligations.

The colonials faced rapid readjustment with strong pressures to raise revenues in the Colonial Fund to meet expenditures in areas vacated by Britain. To enhance the colonial fiscal problems, convicts were progressively withdrawn from the public service between 1828–35 requiring salaried substitutes in place of British-supported convict bureaucrats. However, as Britain withdrew from explicit commitments, it left a significant degree of latitude for the settlement finances. Rather than acknowledging explicit obligations, the British redesign was to have the resources of the Commissariat become 'in aid' of local resources (see Colonial Fund and Commissariat accounts). This removed any certainty of British fiscal support and encouraged such pressures as those towards the local funding of so-called local defence forces along with the recognition of a concept of 'NSW' or local police forces. But the decision to leave the matter unspecified became important when the disposition of NSW Crown land sales became an issue in the 1830s.

Shares in Outlays

As the colonials contended, if one treated land revenues as local, the growth of expenditures arising through the Crown and Land Funds in the 1830s explains a large part of the colony's claim that its own expenditures surpassed British expenditures on NSW by 1834 and rose far above them thereafter (see table 10.1, p.86). There is, however, no doubt that, legally, the colonial claim was untenable and that British expenditures on the colony remained well above colonial public outlays until the late 1840s. The contemporary picture of the relative level of the two fiscal sources, one British, the other colonial, turned on political arguments. As the British were preparing to face the loss of NSW as a receptacle for convicts, the prospect was opened for the transfer of other unwanted Britishers through migration funded from the disposal of Crown lands. Legally, the revenue from these sales was British, and Britain sought to channel the benefits to assisted immigration, passing the costs of the process to land buyers. Traditionally, land sales have been seen as a corresponding opportunity in the settlement to acquire free immigrants and to accept the selling of land in order to obtain these benefits (cf. Madgwick, 1937).

Table 10.1 gives the gross outlays including balances (these are difficult at times to separate) of the three sources. Greater detail of the NSW accounts are shown in the appendixes. It might, at first sight, appear that we can derive a trend picture of the different British and colonial funding in this way. Overall, it would appear to be implied that total public expenditures rose by 1850 to almost four times that in 1822 (while gross domestic product in current prices rose by about 12 times; also, that the colonial contribution increased greatly from about 25 to 40 per cent; but that in 1850, the British contribution, though greatly reduced, still accounted for the major input of public resources. This would be a constitutional perspective. The colonists, in pressing their claim to the Crown and Land Funds would have contended that the colonial public contribution had risen to almost 80 per cent in 1850 and that the British support had become relatively minor.

There are, however, many problems with this simple representation quite apart from contention over rights to 'Crown revenues' and title to land. In addition to the confusion that arises from the incorporation of balances in the accounts, there are two dominant difficulties. Firstly, from 1828, there were very considerable transfers between the funds, most generally though not always, by way of transfers from the

Table 10.1: British and NSW Gross Public Expenditures (including balances), 1822–50, (£'000ª), (excluding actual transportation costs and direct supplies from Britain)

Year	Commis- sariat	Colonial Fund	Crown & Land Fund	Gross Total
1822	212.2	58.0		270.2
1823	149.7	46.8		196.5
1824	NA	NA		NA
1825	155.0	142.2		297.2
1826	103.3	113.2		216.5
1827	133.7	118.5		252.2
1828	238.0	107.6		345.6
1829	243.2	98.3		341.5
1830	196.8	103.0		299.8
1831	203.6	135.3		338.9
1832	194.3	135.9		330.2
1833	165.5	147.7	9.0	313.2
1834	187.0	203.5	60.8	390.5
1835	250.2	270.0	132.0	520.2
1836	344.4	387.8	263.3	995.5
1837	254.8	360.9	254.9	870.6
1838	363.7	617.4	489.7	1 470.8
1839	474.7	528.3	184.5	1 187.5
1840	389.5	670.5	156.8	1 216.8
1841	278.6	421.3	342.2	1 042.1
1842	247.1	398.2	131.8	771.1
1843	206.0	331.4	45.7	583.1
1844	176.6	257.9	87.7	522.2
1845	272.5	309.1	106.3	687.9
1846	448.8	322.5	146.5	917.8
1847	318.0	325.9	233.6	877.5
1848	264.4	331.1	212.3	807.8
1849	262.5	347.3	296.0	905.8
1850	256.7	441.7	373.0	1071.4

Note: (a) This includes VDL in Commissariat during 1822–6.
   (b) NA – Not available.
Source: Re-estimated from J. Ginswick (unpub.) MS with some adjustments from Commissariat Accounts and Blue Book version of Colonial and Land Funds.

Colonial Fund to the Commissariat. Secondly, very substantial outlays were made for purposes other than those directly connected with NSW. Table 10.2 (p.87) attempts to make the major adjustments to meet these items.

A radically different picture emerges. Overall, the rise in net expenditure between 1822 and 1850 was much less than the gross data suggest, with public outlays overall lifting to approximately three times their 1822 level. Broadly, the picture of the 1820s is unchanged with the colonial public contributions rising quite sharply in the mid-1820s. With some slight fluctuations they accounted for 40 to 45 per cent of netted outlays on NSW until the late 1830s, significantly higher than implied in table 10.1. But it is from the late 1830s that the most radical difference occurs, so much so that the Commissariat appears as a net recipient of colonial funds in the closing years of the 1840s.

Table 10.2: Approximate Net Expenditure on NSW, 1822–50, (£'000)

Year	Commis-sariat	Colonial Fund	Crown Land	Net on NSW	Commis-sariat %	Colonial Fund %	Crown Land %
1822	188.8	66.7		255.5	73.9	26.1	0.0
1823	139.3	53.4		192.7	72.3	27.7	0.0
1824	NA	NA		NA	NA	NA	0.0
1825	152.1	97.3		249.4	61.0	39.0	0.0
1826	98.6	156.9		255.5	38.6	61.4	0.0
1827	128.7	95.6		224.3	57.4	42.6	0.0
1828	230.4	114.5		344.9	66.8	33.2	0.0
1829	235.2	182.7		417.9	56.3	43.7	0.0
1830	189.5	159.6		349.1	54.3	45.7	0.0
1831	189.8	135.3		325.1	58.4	41.6	0.0
1832	185.5	135.9		321.4	57.7	42.3	0.0
1833	153.8	147.7	9.0	310.5	49.5	47.6	2.9
1834	163.2	203.5	50.8	417.5	39.1	48.7	12.2
1835	236.6	270.0	132.0	638.6	37.0	42.3	20.7
1836	317.9	266.9	263.3	848.1	37.5	31.5	31.0
1837	186.3	308.1	229.9	724.3	25.7	42.5	31.7
1838	294.1	492.9	489.7	1 276.7	23.0	38.6	38.4
1839	359.9	540.5	184.5	1 084.9	33.2	49.8	17.0
1840	324.8	486.6	156.8	968.2	33.5	50.3	16.2
1841	257.7	643.2	342.2	1 243.1	20.7	51.7	27.5
1842	209.8	419.7	131.8	761.3	27.6	55.1	17.3
1843	144.2	320.5	45.7	510.4	28.3	62.8	9.0
1844	154.2	274.3	87.7	516.2	29.9	53.1	17.0
1845	192.5	309.1	106.3	607.9	31.7	50.8	17.5
1846	132.7	322.5	146.5	601.7	22.1	53.6	24.3
1847	99.7	328.9	233.6	662.2	15.1	49.7	35.3
1848	7.0	331.0	212.3	550.3	1.3	60.1	38.6
1849	−13.4	347.3	296.0	629.9	NA	NA	NA
1850	−105.3	441.7	373.1	709.5	NA	NA	NA

Note: (a) VDL included prior to 1827.
  (b) NA — Not available.
Source: Returns of the Colony.

The prime reason for the difference in the fiscal picture in net terms is that rising expenditures from these sources were being made on activities outside NSW (note that expenditure on immigration is treated as expenditure on NSW in these fiscal terms). Basically, the Commissariat was the vehicle for making the outlays but the main source of the funds for extra-NSW expenditures was from the Colonial Fund. Large transfers were made from the latter to engage in such activities as the experimental outposts in Western and Northern Australia and, ultimately and most expensively, on the foundation of settlement in New Zealand.

This should not be taken to imply that the Commissariat was performing minimal functions in NSW by the 1840s. In reality, it is difficult to portray, in accounting terms, the role of this body as NSW took, from the end of the 1820s, an increasing role in the further settlement of Australia and New Zealand. Some suggestion of the

Table 10.3: Main NSW Expenditure Components, 1822–50, (£'000)

	Immig. Land Fund	Convict Commisst Fund	Military Commisst Fund	Civil Estab. Col. Fund	Police Col. Fund	Construct Col. Fund	Police Commisst Fund
1822	NA	180.0	27.8	13.1	3.5	1.0	
1823	NA	116.9	27.7	12.1	3.5	1.2	
1824	NA	NA	NA	NA	NA	NA	
1825	NA	86.8	35.9	45.2	14.3	13.5	
1826	NA	68.8	29.8	34.7	18.3	4.6	
1827	NA	91.6	37.0	42.9	19.3	8.9	
1828	NA	118.4	60.3	41.7	NA	6.7	11.2
1829	NA	115.4	68.2	48.0	NA	8.3	19.5
1830	NA	89.7	59.5	47.6	NA	7.2	20.3
1831	NA	89.5	61.3	41.4	NA	1.0	19.3
1832	NA	77.7	67.4	53.3	NA	1.5	16.9
1833	9.0	78.1	53.2	50.8	NA	4.1	19.9
1834	7.9	98.2	65.0	55.5	8.0	8.4	15.8
1835	10.6	105.3	82.7	59.0	23.0	9.2	5.5
1836	11.8	133.5	98.1	69.8	30.2	13.3	5.7
1837	36.5	125.8	83.2	75.5	33.9	34.1	7.5
1838	101.7	127.4	81.0	90.0	52.8	87.9	4.8
1839	156.9	159.2	86.1	101.7	75.5	69.6	0.4
1840	146.0	149.5	88.4	110.5	85.2	61.2	0.4
1841	329.3	118.8	86.4	121.3	91.6	61.7	0.2
1842	110.1	88.0	81.4	110.0	83.8	64.9	0.1
1843	11.5	66.5	61.7	95.8	70.3	34.3	0.1
1844	70.3	54.4	80.5	61.7	60.2	25.9	0.1
1845	15.6	31.6	56.5	62.5	59.3	26.0	0.1
1846	1.1	27.7	51.3	67.3	61.0	30.0	0.1
1847	0.6	25.5	53.3	72.2	59.3	56.0	0.1
1848	113.1	14.7	45.3	82.2	67.3	54.5	
1849	137.4	11.4	41.4	74.9	57.6	39.0	
1850	165.7	10.7	35.0	74.0	56.5	51.2	

Note: NA = zero except for 1824.
Source: Re-estimated from J. Ginswick (unpub.) MS.

distribution of public functions (for more detail see appendix tables) can be made in terms of the major categories in relation to NSW when we firstly exclude all expenditures not directly linked to NSW and then group several major public functions together in table 10.3. It should be reiterated that this picture excludes British outlays on the movement of convicts.

Table 10.3 shows (columns 2, 3 and 7) the changing role of the Commissariat in relation to convicts, the military and police in NSW. Of these, only provision for the military shows a persistent upward trend to 1836 and even that subsided throughout the 1840s. The closely linked Commissariat outlays on police peaked in 1830 and fell heavily after 1834, leaving the colony to provide for its internal law and order. Provision for convicts accounted for the main Commissariat activity until the early 1840s within NSW but subject to very strong fluctuations. Once the decision had been taken (effectively by 1836) to cease transportation to NSW, these outlays dwindled rapidly from 1839 and, by 1850, the Convict Commissariat in NSW was virtually a thing of the past.

The narrowing of the British role to these three areas in the Commissariat and their trend decline relative to gross domestic product placed an increasing burden on the Colonial Fund for internal administration and development in NSW. The sharp increase in the mid-1820s and the progressive rise to 1840 in provision for the civil establishment within the Colonial Fund, for the police and for public works, are the strongest indication of the success of the British government in inducing the colonists to fund their own activities. The depression of the 1840s, however, forced severe cutbacks in colonial expenditures in all these main areas, though not with the severity of the decline in British expenditures.

Expenditure on immigration was much more unstable than any other area, funded from Crown land revenues and from debentures raised through these revenues. This was clearly the most affected by major business fluctuations with a very rapid upsurge in outlays to 1841 and a decline to almost zero by 1847. After 1847, however, a sharp recovery occurred indicative of the restoration of economic conditions in the years immediately before the gold discoveries in 1851.

To a substantial degree there was an identity of British and NSW interest. But there was by no means an acceptance in NSW that land revenues were British or were to be used only for immigration. Initially, the proceeds were merged in the NSW Colonial Fund, then reclassified as 'in aid' of that fund and only separated in 1833. By being obscure about its willingness to support the settlement after 1821, the British government was hoist with its own petard. In fact, very large transfers were made to non-immigration expenditures in the Colonial Fund due to access to the resources of the Crown and Land Fund; and this fund engaged in other substantial outlays apart from immigration.

The British government had a short-lived success in the 1840s when insistence on its legal rights committed the Crown and Land Fund exclusively to immigration. But, by then, the British fiscal presence in NSW was being rapidly phased out and colonists were displaying a strong reluctance to buy land. Expenditures on account of the penal establishment and defence forces declined rapidly after 1840 and, already in 1850, the primary burden for these long-acknowledged British obligations was being assumed by the colony. After 1850, the colonists had little to gain fiscally from Britain. The discovery of gold transformed their prospects of a free society. In 1855, Britain surrendered virtually all its fiscal authority (apart from its determination to control NSW tariff policy) by the transfer of title in Crown lands to the colonial government.

Main Revenue Sources

Detailed revenue data are given in the appendixes. In table 10.4 (p.90), five major revenue items of the three funds are shown, supplemented by three others in notes to this table. In addition, the second column indicates the transfers from the Colonial Fund to the Commissariat, transfers treated by the latter as revenue.

Table 10.4 indicates several major transformations. Firstly, Treasury bills drawn on Britain that had been the dominant sources of total charges raised in NSW and were still so in 1822 dwindled rapidly in relative importance, despite considerable fluctuations and a brief lift at the end of the 1830s in their amount. Insofar as Treasury bills had been amongst the prime sources of colonial fiscal flexibility for the first 30-odd years of the settlement, this trend decline in itself restricted the

Table 10.4: Main NSW Revenue Components, British and Colonial, 1822–50, (£'000)

Year	Commissariat Treasury Bills	Commissariat Transfers Ex-Colonial Fund	Colonial Fund Customs Excise	Colonial Fund Other Indirect	Colonial Fund Income Public Assets	Crown Revenue Land Revenues
1822	230.1	NA	37.9	5.9	2.8	
1823	119.0	NA	23.7	6.8	6.8	
1824	NA	NA	28.8	5.3	7.0	
1825	193.9	NA	48.4	6.5	12.1	(5.5)
1826	59.3	NA	47.7	7.2	5.2	(2.6)
1827	164.6	NA	49.5	10.2	14.8	(2.3)
1828	98.5	NA	64.8	10.7	16.5	(5.0)
1829	154.4	NA	73.2	9.2	9.0	(2.7)
1830	138.7	NA	78.7	9.5	6.6	(1.0)
1831	117.8	NA	87.8	11.1	10.8	(2.6)
1832	114.8	NA	93.9	12.7	20.0	(12.5)
1833	81.0	2.8	108.5	14.8	4.7	26.1
1834	114.9	3.8	124.5	17.1	5.0	43.2
1835	176.9	4.8	140.4	17.7	7.5	89.0
1836	223.4	2.6	153.7	18.6	7.7	131.4
1837	173.9	28.9	163.3	20.8	9.5	123.6
1838	292.5	62.8	145.3	23.5	4.5	120.2
1839	248.0	90.6	153.4	42.5	15.4	160.8
1840	205.6	39.1	192.8	56.1	19.8	325.3
1841	92.1	7.4	216.2	54.4	19.8	105.8
1842	171.5	8.4	215.3	49.3	28.8	44.1
1843	146.9	8.7	164.9	54.8	25.0	29.3
1844	142.8	1.5	151.9	45.8	30.7	20.9
1845	91.2	3.0	157.5	56.8	39.7	28.2
1846	213.7	87.1	151.1	86.2	27.5	38.8
1847	120.4	56.9	170.6	87.2	9.4	77.4
1848	85.4	118.8	168.7	52.7	31.7	51.7
1849	101.9	123.5	186.0	53.0	44.5	90.5
1850	37.7	161.8	219.3	56.7	48.5	65.3

Notes:
(a) Commissariat received specie from Britain as follows : (£'000) 1831, 20.5; 1832, 5; 1833, 15; 1834, 20.8; 1835, 40; 1836, 60; 1842, 15; 1844, 10; 1845, 100; 1846, 85; 1849, 10.
(b) Colonial Fund received transfers from Britain as follows: (£'000) 1822, 9.5; 1823, 8; 1825, 16.6; 1826, 91.7; 1827, 15.2; 1829, 20; 1834, 25; 1835, 55; 1836, 50; 1837, 20; 1838, 25; 1842, 46.
(c) Crown lands — Debentures issued on security of revenues: (£'000) 1842, 48.7; 1844, 75.7; 1849, 77.2; 1850, 57.9.
(d) NA — Not available.

freedom of colonial action in funding settlement development. Added to the British decision to establish a formal and legal Colonial Fund accountable to Britain, local options were greatly narrowed. Moreover with the issuing authority, the Commissariat, under military control, even the Commissariat's freedom to impose costs on Britain was greatly restricted. Treasury bill issues broadly conformed to two factors up to 1840. One was the fluctuating supply of convicts arriving; the other was the demand for British resources particularly from the late 1830s to support the acquisition and settlement of New Zealand.

In revenue terms, the Commissariat served another vital purpose particularly to a growing private colonial economy. Later in the volume, monetary and banking development is discussed, including the transition from dollar to sterling currency. The notes to the table indicate the sterling specie supplies from 1831 as the British government moved to establish a sterling currency standard in the colonies. During the 1830s, part of the inflow was used by the Commissariat to acquire circulating dollars which it then used for purchases of imports. The depression of the 1840s eroded the specie supply by leakage abroad and Britain was called on again in the 1840s to provide large specie supplements. The gold discoveries in 1851 finally ended the colonial dependence on British specie supply and, indeed, Australia quickly became not merely a source of gold for minting but in fact became a source of coinage for other parts of the empire, particularly in India.

Transfers from the Colonial Fund to the Commissariat inevitably imply looking at the expenditure purposes of the former and the revenue side of the latter. Initially, these transfers do in fact reflect increasing British insistence in the late 1820s that services supplied by the Commissariat for general colonial purposes should be requited by colonial payments. Thus, the colonial government came increasingly to purchase 'civil service' goods supplies made available by the Commissariat. But progressively in the 1830s and more so in the 1840s, the relationships between the Commissariat and the NSW colony changed. Given British willingness to support defence purposes an administrative–military institution, not much concerned with convicts, existed in the colony. Transfers to it then became a means of colonial use of this resource, as already indicated, in the development of New Zealand. Though transfers were required, the NSW colonists acquired, due to the presence of the Commissariat, a cheap entry into a local imperial adventure, one in which it had British support. In the late 1840s, these transfers had become the major source of revenue for the Commissariat.

Nevertheless, after 1820, Britain imposed a sterner hand on its public inputs into Australian settlement. While it continued to support Van Diemen's Land as a convict location after 1840 and came to the rescue of the private settlement in Western Australia in the 1830s, it imposed stronger brakes on NSW. This was most severe in the mid-1820s, but thereafter the brakes generally remained applied. NSW, more than any other colony, was compelled to look to its own capabilities to fund public purposes. The sharp lift in revenues in 1825 and the strong trend rise in Colonial Fund revenues to 1840 are indicative, at once, of the speed of growth of the colony and the increasing necessity of the colonial authority to find domestic revenue sources.

Revenue from indirect taxes provided the overwhelming source and, in turn, customs and excise predominated throughout. (As a side issue, income tax was actually collected in NSW in 1810 but as a British tax on defence personnel.) Customs and excise was minor relative to Treasury bills issued by the Commissariat in the early 1820s. This revenue lifted sharply in 1825. By the early 1830s, it briefly rivalled Treasury bills from the Commissariat and peaked in 1841 when it was momentarily more than twice the level of Treasury bills. Although the depression of the 1840s forced contraction, customs and excise during the decade to 1850 was typically the major single source of public funds in the colony.

Even so, this growth in local revenue raising did not keep pace with the expansion of imports or of gross domestic product. Nor did it match the growth of other colonial revenues, either of other indirect taxes or of income from public assets. While customs and excise rose in 1840 to approximately four times their 1822 level, other indirect taxes were almost ten times and income from public assets (excluding land sales after 1832) was well over ten times its 1822 level. The colony over these two decades was becoming much more complex, with a rapidly widening variety of private activities becoming taxable, to pressure from Britain.

The tension over revenues from land sales has already been discussed. In the final column of table 10.4, the numbers in brackets indicate land sales revenues up to 1832 at a time when the British–colonial confrontation was obscured (the amounts were included in Colonial Fund revenues — see appendixes). In 1833, this tension compelled the separation of land revenues and their expenditure purposes. Part of the land revenues derived from leases and rents, part from purchases by colonials, but increasingly they derived from purchases from absentees or new arrivals delivering capital.

During the second half of the 1830s, land sales revenues appear to have been pre-dominantly derived from newly arriving British private capital responding to the prospects of an export boom (private capital inflow is discussed elsewhere). During the 1830s, this revenue source amply funded assisted immigration from the colonial point of view and provided a means to support the clergy and education together with Aboriginal welfare. The collapse of land sales during the depression of the 1840s drastically reduced the ability to shift British paupers to Australia and to support locally these other expenditure purposes. Accordingly, during the 1840s, the colonists turned to a related revenue device, the issue of debentures on the security of prospective land revenues (see notes to table 10.4). So began an Australian prac-tice of public borrowing overseas on the basis of revenue expectations, a practice continued into the 20th century. In this case, the public borrowing was linked closely, as it was in the 1840s, with the inflow of private capital that provided the rationale for higher land prices and thus higher colonial land revenues.

Conclusion

The beginning of British settlement in Australia from one point of view could reasonably be regarded as a phase of total Australian dependence on British public capital support. The original project, to plant a colony some 13 000 miles and over six months in time from Britain, was an extraordinarily risky operation. It is scarcely conceivable that such a project could have been achieved as a private venture. Success depended, in part, on public funding and the ability of a small number of free persons to direct the activities of the mass of unfree. In this respect, early Australian development fits some of the prescriptions of Gerschenkron's thesis of the 'advantage of being backward' — above all, the ability to deploy unfree re-sources through relatively centralised direction. As we will see later, success also depended on the initiative of a small number of free persons and the human capital that they directed. But they, in turn, relied on the ability to secure the witting and unwitting support of the British government.

For the first 30-odd years of settlement, the initial colonial endeavours depended fundamentally on British public funding. But the extent of that funding was not planned, not subject to close scrutiny and was greatly amplified by a large variety of actions taken locally to enhance the British public support. Fiscal operations, in kind, began virtually from the beginning though many were intra-colonial transfers. Supplementary demands on Britain were achieved through colonial rights to issue Treasury bills and through the budgeting of unfree human capital that added to British fiscal support. In the process, an institution that was generally perceived as a military support organisation, the Commissariat, became a central developmental agency with a multiplicity of functions. Through this organisation, Britain channelled much of its support resources in terms of Treasury bill funding, supplies and victuals. As the colony(ies) became more complex, with expanded free and freed activity, the Commissariat became an exceedingly complex organisation.

The growth of local market activity opened the opportunity for colonials to apply 18th-century British techniques of public fund-raising through fees for service (in cash and kind). In the absence of formal British approval, this led to the establishment of a strictly illegal local fisc that persisted until 1819. But it was not until the beginning of the 1820s that the British government determined to limit its public fiscal support to Australian development and to encourage private economic development. From that point, relations between Britain and the colony(ies) began to change and to change quite rapidly as British public funding narrowed, became more uncertain and subject to considerable fluctuations. From the mid-1820s, local fiscal activity rose relatively rapidly in significance in funding the public purposes of Australian settlement.

The transfer from British public to colonial public funding was not without its tensions. There is considerable fiscal evidence that Britain continued to supply crucial resources (such as the supply of specie and special allocations). Nevertheless, as private development proceeded apace, the focal conflict was over the access to Crown lands as a means of supporting the migration of British paupers or other colonial purposes. In the main, Britain preserved most, though not all, of its prerogatives.

By the end of the 1840s, the British efforts to exert fiscal control in the Australian colonies (except perhaps in Western Australia) were severely weakened. In certain respects, Australian ability to exploit the British public purse is encapsulated in the fact that from the late 1830s and through the 1840s, local interests were able, with some colonial subvention, to use the human and organisational resources of the Commissariat to further local sub-imperial ambitions in the settlement of New Zealand. But as the 1840s drew to a close, to a large extent, the colonists were able to fund most public objects from local resources. In doing so, however, they had become intimately dependent on private British capital inflow and the development of colonial enterprise based on that private investment. The gold discoveries in 1851 largely resolved remaining tensions and constraints, opening (except for Western Australia) the prospect of rapid development, free enterprise, considerable wealth and a separation from the public purse of Britain.

PART IV

THE COLONIAL AUSTRALIAN ECONOMY 1810–1840 A HISTORICAL, STATISTICAL AND ANALYTICAL ACCOUNT

11

SUMMARY AND QUESTIONS

During the 30 years from 1810 to 1840, two Australian economies — colonial and Aboriginal — were in direct contention. On the south-east mainland, in the modern New South Wales and Victoria (Port Phillip District) and in Van Diemen's Land, the confrontation was a broad one. It ended in total disaster for the Aborigines in Van Diemen's Land and with only few Aborigines remaining in NSW and Port Phillip. The outlines of this frontal encounter have been told, in terms of impact on Aborigines, in the final part of the companion volume to this one, *Economics and the Dreamtime* and earlier in *Our Original Aggression*. More obliquely, a similar if less destructive series of meetings occurred by the end of the 1820s, firstly in what is now Queensland at Moreton Bay, at Raffles Bay and Port Essington in the Northern Territory and at King George's Sound in Western Australia. These were followed by more direct but still limited farm settlement by colonists in Western and Southern Australia in 1829 and 1836, respectively.

The total collision between Aborigines and colonists was a combination of disease transmission and economic interaction. The economic outcome largely reflected a broad breakout from early colonial bridgeheads in NSW and Van Diemen's Land and partly a dispersed process of British government and private settlers laying claim substantially to the whole of Australia. We are concerned in this volume with the settlement process from a colonial point of view. In exploring colonial performance over this period, the emphasis is on the two main 'convict' colonies, NSW and Van Diemen's Land, with only incidental references to other areas and locations. In particular, the private economies of Western and Southern Australia are taken up more fully in the concluding part when they had acquired rather more significance to the total colonial economy in Australia.

How do we delineate processes of economic development? Formally, change can be defined in terms of aggregate economic expansion, altering relationships between factor inputs and outputs (productivity), increase of population relative to real income or consumption (changing standards of living), alterations in the structure of inputs and outputs, the development of trade *vis-à-vis* domestic activity, market structure and organisation and institutional development. An important question that emerges is whether these different matters are all equally relevant or whether some are better indicators than others of performance in early formative stages.

Economic Expansion

Within New South Wales and Van Diemen's Land, the outstanding phenomenon was the extremely high average rate of colonial economic expansion throughout 1810–40. Figure 11.1 shows, in semi-logarithmic form, the increase of gross domestic product of the two colonies measured in constant 1830 prices. The process of expansion is given for each colony including and excluding the imputed value of livestock increase (this last component is discussed at length later). Taking the series omitting livestock increase, the NSW economy expanded at the very high average rate of not much less than 9 per cent per annum over the 30 years. Van Diemen's Land increased even more explosively at a little below 13 per cent each year, though this exceptional performance derived partly from the fact that the island had been settled only seven years before 1810. Both represented pell-mell increase in activity in the two colonies. The inclusion of livestock increase added about one percentage point to the rate of expansion in each colony.

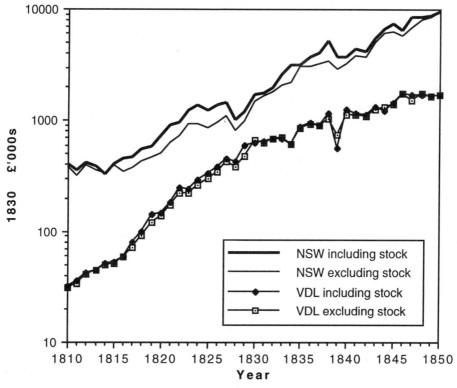

Figure 11.1: NSW and Van Diemen's Land Gross Domestic Product, 1810–50, (1830 prices, £), (including and excluding livestock increase)

Many questions arise in economies increasing at this speed. Are such rates consistent with stability? Do they tend to high levels of inefficiency? Are they subject to strong inflationary influences? Are they feasible only with very simple patterns of activity and with easy access to resources? Are they driven by overseas or domestic market conditions? Was the dispossession of Aborigines an easy matter or did Aborigines directly assist the expansion? These and other questions will be discussed in the following section.

One of the consequences of the significantly faster rate of expansion in Van Diemen's Land was that it quite rapidly caught up in terms of total activity with the original NSW colony. In 1810, Van Diemen's Land gross domestic product (GDP) was less than one-tenth that of NSW. By 1820, it approached 30 per cent and at the end of the 1820s was almost two-thirds of the size of the 'mother' colony. Then its expansion slackened markedly relative to NSW and, by 1840, Van Diemen's Land had regressed to a level of about one-third that of NSW. Despite this relative slackening, Van Diemen's Land had become a major component of the total 'Australian economy'. (To complete the colonial relativities, South Australia after a mere four years' development had risen at the end of the 1830s to equal approximately one-sixth of NSW activity while Western Australia was still struggling, after 12 years development, to achieve only one-eighth the level of NSW.)

External Factor Inputs: Population and Labour

Although the formation of bridgeheads in NSW and Van Diemen's Land by 1809 were crucial first-stage achievements, only tiny bases had then been established. A mere 11 000 convicts had been delivered over 22 years. Over the following period from 1810–40, when transportation to (the present) NSW ceased, some 115 000 convicts were delivered to the two convict colonies — about eight times the rate of inflow of the period 1788–1809.

In 1810, the British Committee of Inquiry into Transportation set the stage for the accelerated flow of convicts, partly in the belief of increased criminality in Britain, partly because of the declining demand for convict labour in Britain as the war effort against Napoleon was peaking. Within two years of this inquiry, the increased rate of convict transport began, rising to the early 1820s, plateauing in the mid-1820s and accelerating again into the mid-1830s. Concomitant with the rising flows of convicts into the 1830s, free immigrants became a visible item in labour and population inputs into the colonies. At the end of the 1830s, free immigration exceeded convict inflow.

No single year marks a very meaningful historical dividing point. But this change in transportation policy in 1810 had a major impact on the affairs of the Australian colonies. It implied, initially, a substantial increase in the proportion of coerced labour in the colonial workforce. But subsequently, as sentences expired, those born in the colony increased and as free immigrants rose in number, particularly after 1831, there was a major reorientation of the labour market, progressively towards a market-determined mode of labour allocation and use. Important issues arise in this transformation. Did the increased flow of convict labour delay the development of market influences in the labour market? Did the emergence of more legally free labour imply a corresponding pressure towards flexibility and price influences? As we will discuss these matters, the answers are by no means clear-cut.

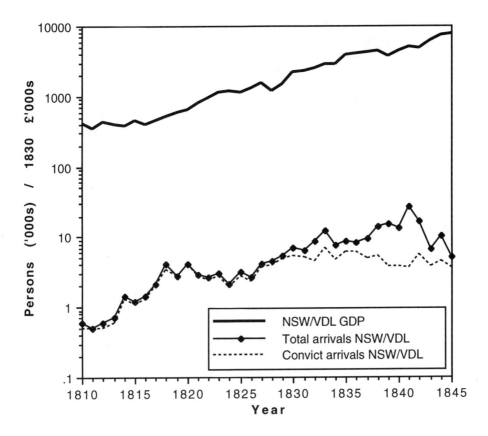

Figure 11.2: NSW and Van Diemen's Land Gross Domestic Product and Gross Arrivals, 1810–45

But there is also a developmental question. Was the influx of external labour and population a prime driver in the rate of economic expansion? Though the point needs to be discussed later at some length, figure 11.2 may give some hint of the general form of the answer. Certainly, its broad implications are worth registering at this introductory level.

In trend terms (least squares regression lines), the rates of increase of total new arrivals and of GDP of the two colonies were not significantly different. What might this mean? Was it the case that there was no significant capital deployed and that there was an essentially constant ratio of land to labour as the scale of enterprises and of the economies expanded? Does it indicate that no labour productivity gain was achieved? Both possible implications need to be considered with some caution, even from an inspection of figure 11.2.

Firstly, the influx of population is not a perfect proxy for labour inputs, particularly in the 1830s so that there may have been less of a trend increase of labour than seems to be implied. Secondly, in subperiod terms, there were very pronounced differences between the rates of growth of total new arrivals and GDP, with arrivals tending at times to increase very much faster than GDP and at other times to fall a considerable distance behind. This implies phases of declining and periods of rising productivity (see section below, Economic Growth: Productivity and Living

Standards). What special conditions of development at these different periods might explain these contrasts? We seem to have a considerable nest of questions arising in relation to labour inputs and, indeed, on any explanatory approach that might turn on production function or factor contribution analysis.

Changing modes of labour allocation, particularly as between the public and private sectors, appear as a prominent element in this formative stage. In 1809, the labour market was predominantly free and freed with the majority of coerced labour absorbed by private undertakings (including self-employment). The proportion of unfree labour in the workforce rose to the early 1820s and then tended to decline so that by 1830 it accounted for about one-third of the workforce (and continued to fall slowly until 1840). But the main policy change followed in 1821 with the determination to concentrate convict assignment on private employers rather than government. This derived from the recommendations of the inquiries conducted by Bigge. It continued in NSW until the closing years of the 1830s and in Van Diemen's Land to the early 1850s.

External Factor Inputs: Capital Inflow

A correlation of this change in labour allocation was the progressive emphasis by Britain on private investment in Australia. In part III, the interaction between British public finance and colonial public funding was discussed, with the shift towards colonial fiscal self-reliance. The obverse of the British withdrawal of British public funding was the switch towards British private investment in Australia. This was, in one sense, not new even in 1810 and, moreover, there was no sudden break during the 1810s.

Partnership and agency associations between British, Anglo-Indian and Australian businesses were established early and trade credit was important even by 1800. These types of short-term capital relations expanded during the 1810s. The years immediately before and after 1820 saw the beginnings of a basic shift towards long-term private investment in Australia. This was not an isolated Australian adaptation but was accompanied by comparable changes throughout other parts of the Empire, particularly in Canada and Africa. It reflected a marked preference for private individuals to develop imperial resources and expand the Empire once Napoleon was defeated. Britain had control of the seas and the British government was withdrawing from direct participation in the demonstrative and imperial mooring. British government willingness to support individual British investors with land and labour allocations was accompanied firstly by the formation of large corporate undertakings in the early and mid-1820s and secondly, from the end of the 1820s, by the establishment of private corporate colonies.

Figure 11.3 (p.101) shows an approximation that can be made, with existing data, to capital inflow and indicates something of the shift during the 1820s and 1830s from a predominantly public to a strongly private presence. It is unfortunate that there is a break in the early 1820s. Subject to this, it is not implausible to combine the slopes of the series for public support to the early 1820s with that of capital inflow afterwards. Unlike the trend relationship between arrivals of persons and GDP (where there was no significant trend difference), the slopes of capital inflow and GDP do appear significantly different, with GDP expanding more rapidly than the level of capital inflow. As in the case of arrivals and GDP, there appears to be a

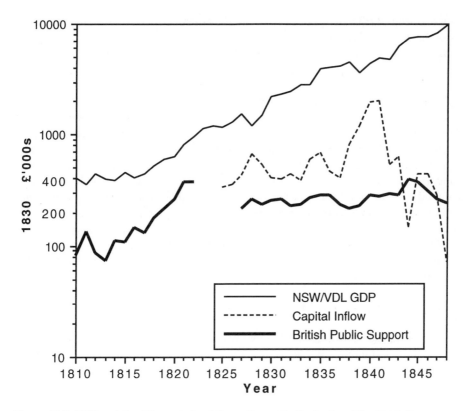

Figure 11.3: NSW and Van Diemen's Land Gross Domestic Product and Capital Inflow

significant set of subperiod contrasts, with capital inputs from outside rising much more rapidly than GDP to the early 1820s and much more slowly between 1826 and 1840.

Again a complex set of questions arises. Was the early public capital subvention inefficient with a low marginal efficiency of capital? Was private capital correspond-ingly very much more efficient? What form did capital inflow take? Were capital goods prominent or was this essentially a 'Crusoe' economy in which development depended on the accumulation of consumption goods (in this case, from outside) so that available labour could be deployed in domestic capital formation and enterprise development? Was private capital increasingly attracted because activity was expanding rather than providing an inducement to that expansion? These and related questions need to be taken up in due course.

The inflow of convicts with an increasing supplement of free arrivals and the cor-responding transition from public capital support to an increasingly private presence might suggest a progressive tying together of the British and Australian economies. In this case, we could be invited to view the development of the 30 years examined as the emergence of a large/small economy relationship. We need, however, to be cautious of any simple large/small links. The willingness of Britain to allow the colonies a high degree of flexibility in accessing the British budget through Treasury bills gave a degree of peculiar independence. By contrast, private trade credit links which tied, in particular, British, Indian and Australian commerce into indirect

networks could generate quite convoluted, though nevertheless dependent, relationships that may not be immediately obvious.

Was private capital inflow determined by opportunities for local gain within
Australia (the transfer of capital by migrants) or how far was it a response to
growing export capability? In turn, did private capital inflow lead to debt obligations
and the commitment to requite investment by interest and/or dividends? Is there a
basic transition in Australian external capital dependence? It would appear that the
British government's subsidy might, in these terms, represent a free gift (even
though one qualified by a determination by Britain to force the colonies to contribute
increasingly to their own and convicts' support). Capital brought in by migrants
similarly represented no external balance of payments commitments unless migrants
returned to Britain with any accumulations. What then was Australian experience
with absentee and corporate investment? Was there a rapidly rising balance of
payments problem during the 1830s or did the Australian colonies escape substantial
commitments even on this account? If the latter, the early experience of Australian
capital inflow would suggest an extremely cheap accession of external capital
support as a first stage in a long experience of external capital dependence.

Economic Growth: Productivity and Living Standards

Growth, in the sense of increased output per unit of factor input or increase in real
income or consumption per head of population, is the widely accepted test of
economic performance. Is this really so relevant to early Australia? There are some
special considerations that need to be looked at. The possible 'growth' measures that
can be derived are shown in figure 11.4 (opposite). These show annual series of
gross domestic product and of gross national expenditure per head (in both cases
including the imputed value of livestock increase) together with estimates of output
per member of the market workforce at five-yearly intervals. The final indicator
mentioned is the best possible but is limited as an indicator of productivity change. It
can be usefully linked to gross domestic product per head of population to suggest
the shorter-term variations. Gross national expenditure per head is an approximation
to living standards and can be thought of, essentially in this case, as gross domestic
product plus capital inflow per head — local output plus external subvention.

In terms of simple end-point comparisons, there is no significant difference in any
of the series between beginning and end productivity and standards of living (as
broadly implied in figure 11.3) at least when we regard the problems arising in the
onset of depression immediately before 1840. But a basic shift is apparent. All series
decline greatly during the first decade and all trend strongly upwards from
approximately 1820.

Several questions immediately arise. Was the high level of 1810 peculiar to the
early bridgehead conditions? Was the decline in the ensuing decade due to problems
of labour absorption as convict inflow accelerated after 1812? Were there major
resource constraints during this first decade arising from the imposed conditions
limiting settlement to close to early bridgeheads? Did the subsequent recovery arise
from a reversal of absorption problems, from relaxation of resource constraints
(partly as settlement spread) or from changing institutional modes as labour assignment altered, private enterprise flourished and private investment expanded? Were
there significant changes in the ratio of workforce to population, affecting the

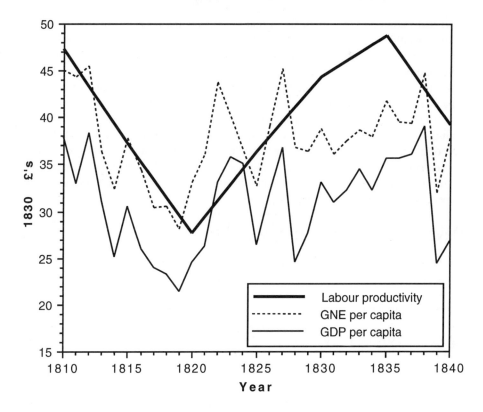

Figure 11.4: NSW and Van Diemen's Land Labour Productivity, Gross Domestic Product per Capita and Gross National Expenditure per Capita, 1810–40 (including livestock increase, 1830 prices, £)

potential for a high rate of labour productivity increase to sustain high output and consumption per person? Were the high levels of all three measures attained in the late 1830s secure or precarious and unstable?

The answers to these questions will affect consideration of others. Thus we have proposed that colonial settlement needs to be seen as a conflict between two types of economy, with Aboriginal losers and colonial gainers. If the gains made by colonists during the two decades after 1820 were securely based, there is an important matter to try to evaluate whether these colonial achievements were made at low or high cost due to conflict with Aborigines. From an overall and not simply from a colonial point of view, there is the question of the *net* loss or gain when both types of societies are taken into account. Whether this is a feasible project remains to be seen. But the answer would be more ironic if the colonial gains to the end of the 1830s were based on insecure foundations.

Leaving Aborigines aside, another peculiarity in strictly growth issues was the changing role of convicts in relation to the colonial workforce. Nominally, convicts were generally accorded a constant real level of consumption through the designated rations provisions. How was any general increase in productivity achieved or improvement in real living standards taken out or distributed in these circumstances? Were convicts losers or gainers by acquiring freedom and losing the provision for fixed real incomes? One might think that the slower the pace of growth, the more likely it would be that many may have been losers. But there were other groups in colonial society, particularly free immigrants and colonial born, who might have suffered from slow growth experience.

A further special growth question was the externally enforced pace of colonial expansion, particularly through the organised rather than market-induced inflow of both convicts and assisted immigrants. In the circumstances, might one then not evaluate 'performance' more in terms of the ability to sustain a high rate of expansion of aggregate activity and to organise the structuring of an expanding economy rather than in terms of growth per factor unit or per head? Certainly, as indicated earlier, the colonies achieved an extremely high rate of expansion. What did they achieve in terms of structural development?

Development of Export Capability

Whatever the answer to the questions indicated above, a marked structural change occurred in that Australian export capability clearly developed greatly during 1810-40. In 1810, a miscellany of export activities, chiefly from maritime resources had been developed, accounting for perhaps 1 to 2 per cent of the GDP of New South Wales and Van Diemen's Land. It is doubtful whether this had lifted much beyond 3 per cent or so by 1820, as sealing declined and wool exports were still little more than promising.

During the 1820s and 1830s, however, wool and whale product exports increased substantially to become the prime export commodities. Supplementing these formal exports, there were conflicting experiences of a trend decline in the sales of agricultural products to the Commissariat (quasi-exports) particularly from the mid-1820s and a trend rise in sales of goods and services to the expanding volume of visiting ships during 1820-40. The intermingling of foreign, intercolonial and Commissariat trade makes it difficult to analyse the rise in foreign exchange earnings. The best that one can do is to make an educated guess but it is unlikely that, by 1840, export earnings from natural resource development were less than 25 per cent of GDP of the two colonies combined. Essentially generated in the course of 25 years, this was a remarkable colonial achievement.

Three important consequences flowed from this trend development. Firstly, with a qualification about visiting ships, the direction of Australian trade shifted strongly away from an early Asian dependence. There was a related reorientation of imports. With flows of people, capital and goods directed towards Britain, a fully integrated large/small economy nexus was established by the end of the 1830s. Secondly, a substantial export capability was achieved, based on natural resource use. Thirdly, the combination of cheap external capital inflow and export earnings provided for an extremely high level of import capacity.

Do we then see a model of early Australian economic change through the staple thesis or export-led development, set in the context of a large/small economy relationship? One can scarcely doubt that such an approach would be helpful in any analytical model.

There are, however, at least two important reservations in exploiting the theory of export-led development. Firstly, can one identify a significant array of linkages from the natural resource industries? Or was the capacity to import exploited through a diffuse expenditure process ending predominantly in the importation of a wide range of consumer goods? If the latter, did this mean an insecure achievement of high living standards that could be eroded particularly by any sudden drying up of capital inflow? The composition of imports and their relevance to the development process needs to be looked at with some care.

Secondly, however, one needs to return to the labour market and the allocation of labour to natural resource activities. How far was convict and free or freed labour absorbed by these areas? If the dominant allocation of labour was not into natural resource production, were the other areas of activity driven by linkages from these natural resource industries? If there is no strong evidence of powerful linkages, we need to look to other models to explain development outside these natural resource areas.

Urban versus Natural Resource Development

Here we are concerned, then, with the domestic structural development of the colonial economies. This is discussed at length later. We have to recognise the high place that urban activities played in the colonial economies throughout the whole period and the possibility that the rate of expansion of urban industries and services may actually have outstripped that of natural resource activities.

Though trend shifts and fluctuations in relative importance occurred throughout the 30 years examined, the colonial economies showed a very strong urban bias with only limited evidence of linkages from staple to urban activities. Undoubtedly some linkages existed and it would be false to suggest a dual economic system. Nevertheless, the willingness and ability of a high proportion of the population and workforce to be occupied in rapidly expanding towns is a peculiar feature of 19th-century Australia that demands attention, to a large extent, separate from the concentration of 'extensive land settlement', staple production and export-led development.

The reasons for this early urban concentration and the relatively rapid growth of urban activities is at least as important as the account of natural resource development. How far was this due to the persistence of the array of influences identified in the development of the bridgehead economy? How far was it due to precariously high living standards? How far did it reflect a problem deeply embedded in much of the literature of Australian immigration history — the problem of labour absorption and the urban battleground of persons coming from Britain? How far is it explicable by low labour/output ratios in natural resource exploitation?

Microeconomic Adjustment: Institutions and Behaviour Patterns

Rapid economic expansion and the allocation of resources to competing ends, the shift from convict labour to a rising influx of free persons, the progressive freeing of convicts, the growth in private investment, the development of export industries and trade, the expansion of local industries, local trade and commerce and services — all these pointed to a progressive development of a market-oriented economy in Australia. In turn, this depended on the extension of principles of private property, freedom of choice, the incentive to gain and to respond flexibly to market signals. But behind this lay the evolution of an array of institutions, value systems and behaviour patterns through or on which market-oriented behaviour operated.

Can we, for the purposes of economic history, take these issues as given and external to an explanation of economic expansion, growth and structuring? The short answer, in respect of any economy, is, of course, no. But in the Australian case, the development of institutions, value systems and behaviour patterns oriented to market conditions have a peculiar significance, given their convict origins. Those origins do not seem to have presented very much of an impediment to the establishment of appropriate institutions and even within the convict system, as we have seen, market procedures emerged in bridgehead conditions. Why was this so?

Basically, it might be suggested that transferees to Australia, whether transported convicts or free immigrants, carried with them a substantial degree of understanding of the economy from which they came, an economy that was then the most advanced in existence. This was more than the 'transmission of technology' — indeed some of the British technology was irrelevant to Australian conditions. What is at issue is what historians have labelled 'intellectual baggage', a useful tag to summarise the understanding of ways of thinking and acting carried in the minds of new arrivals, free or unfree. With important adaptations, the arrivals during 1810–40 transferred a changing understanding of an evolving British market economy and recreated in Australia what they understood of this system. The transfer of this intellectual baggage is a fundamental part of the explanation of early colonial success. It is the central topic of the next section.

The recreation of market forms in the Antipodes did not rely wholly on migration. Some corporate forms were established in Britain for Australian purposes. Moreover, the application of flexible choice did not apply uniformly in different market conditions. Both labour and land markets in Australia were significantly different from those in Britain. In addition, the intervention of gubernatorial authority had a weight that did not apply in Britain. For a variety of reasons, one needs to look at institutional development and behaviour patterns in terms of different markets. All this is the substance of microeconomic adjustment that is and was the foundation of economic expansion, structuring and growth.

What is vital in the approach to microeconomic adjustment in Australia is that the mass of transferees before the Australian gold discoveries of 1851 was concentrated in the period 1810–40. In turn, this was the period of most massive structural adjustment in Britain itself. It was during these 30 years, not in the foundations of the first settlement, that the significance of the so-called 'Industrial Revolution' in Britain unfolded.

We may question the meaning of this concept of industrial revolution, preferring to see a process of massive socioeconomic restructuring affecting both the internal British economy and society, and Britain's relations with the rest of the world. Britain could not be said to have achieved a 'perfect market' in this period. But it did achieve a high level of flexibility and market responsiveness, far more so than other European countries. Moreover, institutional forms improved, from this point of view, particularly after the Napoleonic Wars. Despite their convict origins and possibly partly because of their urban convict origins, the Australian colonies were an early beneficiary of this British development. It is appropriate, then, in considering Australian economic development during 1810–40, to turn now to these micro-economic foundations.

12

TOWARDS A PRIVATE MARKET ECONOMY IN AUSTRALIA: 1810–40

Introduction

By 1810, only a very small number of persons, whether convict or free, had been transferred to Australia. The great inflow of immigrants occurred after 1812, in broad terms accelerating up to 1840 when a sharp reversal occurred. Although the initial bridgehead to 1810 was strongly influenced by British ideas, behavioural practices and institutions, the mass transfer, the mass influence of Britain on Australia during this formative period, occurred after 1810. Though major adaptations in Britain, encapsulated in the concept of the Industrial Revolution, may have influenced the decision to establish a penal colony in Australia, it was after 1810 that the full flow of these British changes affected the colonies.

Historians are accustomed to the idea of the 'intellectual baggage' that came with these immigrants. What has not been explored adequately is the content of this 'baggage' and the way in which it was adapted to Australian conditions. This section addresses these issues. Immigrants to Australia, whether coerced or not, came with various parts of an understanding of how the British economy and British society operated. This implied a degree of understanding of the most advanced market system on earth. It is clear that, during the years of establishing a bridgehead, officials, both military and civil, had a strong appreciation of self-interested behaviour, of the value of private property, of the importance of accumulation and incentive. Subsequently, freely arriving immigrants were similarly attuned to market behaviour.

But it is possible that the mass influx, the convicts, were the most fully accustomed to the ways human beings might adopt, adapt and exploit market behaviour. This is true whether they are considered as potential 'entrepreneurs' or as employees. And Australian conditions, whether from the point of natural resource conditions or physical location, discouraged reversion to self-sufficient behaviour.

On the contrary, it led definitely to specialisation, interaction and interchange. Some convicts, no doubt, were political prisoners. But the vast proportion fell into one of two categories. Many were typically employees in Britain, having experienced over the 30 years after 1810 dramatic structural adjustments, relocations and increasing specialisation in Britain. Nicholas (1988) has proposed that for most, the crimes were work-related. Even if one doubts the strength of his judgment, clearly, it seems to have been the case for many.

The other category were those committing crimes not directly related to the workplace. Here, it is possible that many crimes that were apparently work-related were, in fact, carried out by those aware of the benefits that they could find in job-locations. Their crimes might have arisen from personal dislocation, unemployment or the anomie that accompanied the increasing populations of Britain in large towns. Or they might have been, as many British observers thought, professional criminals or actual or potential recidivists. In any event, many were engaged in a black market, from their own point of view adapting and perhaps perfecting a market system that did not fully meet their needs. The takers and receivers of stolen goods were undoubtedly operating a market whatever may have been the ostensible motivation for their behaviour.

Once principles of private property, private gain and specialisation were established in Australia, as they were by 1810, both coerced and free immigration might then be seen as, in large measure, the relocation of a form of British society and British economy in Australia. *Natura non facit saltum* (nature does not make leaps) and it did not do so in the convict foundations of Australia. The continuity in the transfer from Britain is illustrated in the fact that convicts often brought goods and money with them and that some appear to have been able to buy their early freedom. One of the early functions of banking in Australia was to receive cash deposits from convicts on disembarkation. But most importantly, behavioural practices widely understood and accepted, even though qualified by intermittent lashes for some, were also continuous.

It is an interesting speculation whether Australia could have been founded from a long distance without a high degree of coercion and whether its settlement could have been sustained without the ability to develop rapidly towards a free market-oriented system. In contrast with, for example, the North American pioneer model, there was very restricted scope in Australia for self-sufficient behaviour.

Accessing natural resources and establishing farms required a radically different mode of organisation whether of employees or land-seekers. Resource and climatic conditions limited mixed farming. Isolation of Australia as a whole, and distance within the colonies as settlement expanded, provided strong encouragement to increasing specialisation. But it was specialisation to which the inflowing British were increasingly accustomed during 1810–40. Here we had not the tyranny of distance but the strong incentive to accept the challenge of isolation and distance.

Immigrants, and particularly the convicts throughout this 30 year period and the mass of poor free immigrants in the 1830s, came above all from the British towns. During 1810–40, they experienced the full flood of the restructuring in the so-called Industrial Revolution. Insofar as we see Australian settlement as the transposition of a form of British society and economy, it is in this context that we need to observe most directly the range and nature of British restructuring that had begun earlier but which began, in earnest, in the closing years of the Napoleonic Wars.

The occupational specialisation of the immigrants, derived from this restructuring British economy, is an important aspect of the British/Australian connection. But it is only one. The British towns were the locale not only for specialisation but also its counterpart, interchange. Their growth relative to the rural areas of Britain also implied another important ingredient, the flexible allocation and adaptation of both capital and labour. The towns implied not merely or even primarily industry but also trade, credit, banking, forms of business organisation, professional and personal services, asset ownership, tenancies, contractual arrangements whether for transactions in assets, goods or labour, legal provisions for property rights, systems of order and so on. Moreover, and this bears on Australian isolation and extensive settlement, many of these activities were hierarchically organised into a national structure in Britain and spread networks through much of the known world — increasingly so after 1810.

It is not suggested that each immigrant came with an in-built awareness of all the manifestations of British market behaviour that we can now, *ex post*, reconstruct. But within the intellectual baggage of the mass of Australian immigrants came sufficient awareness of parts of the system to make feasible its rapid application, subject to modifications, in the new territory. What makes the transfer most interesting is that, on the one hand, the British market system was itself developing and altering and, on the other hand, changing ideas and behaviour were being injected into an Australia that was also altering rapidly and in a way significantly differently from Britain.

The so-called 'market' rests on a mosaic of personal assumptions and understandings, of behavioural patterns, rules and institutions that were not consciously created but grew together, sometimes in harmony, sometimes in conflict. This mosaic is not readily amenable to economic modelling. What is important to appreciate is that economic efficiency is likely to increase as different pieces of a massive (and changing) jigsaw fit together. It makes no sense to postulate, for example, the removal of one or a few of the ingredients — the typical procedure of model construction and testing. What we have to try to identify, even though very summarily, is how the intellectual baggage of the immigrants who landed in Australia was exploited and adapted to achieve a viable, dominantly market economy by 1840. As in the case of Britain, it is not suggested that this was complete or 'perfect' by 1840. We are dealing with an inchoate system. Nevertheless, there was a remarkable development in Australia towards a private enterprise and market economy by 1840.

This is the more remarkable because of several obstructive conditions. A large-scale influx of convicts obviously did not supply the conditions for specialised, flexible conditions for labour allocation. British retention of rights to Crown lands in Australia and the adoption of systems of land grants appear in opposition to ready development of land and natural resource markets, together with the enterprises based on them. Imperial restrictions on particular activities such as shipping and trade again seem to present strong constraints on freedom of behaviour. Within Australian conditions, the tasks of learning by doing in a new environment demanded adaptation of understood practices. Nevertheless, these and other constraints were to a high degree overcome by 1840. The year 1810 as distinct from the conventional dividing year at 1821, seems a more appropriate departure point from which to examine this institutional evolution.

Let us turn firstly to the point of embarkation of the baggage and look at some of the major issues of the British economy that seems most relevant to the Australian experience.

The British Industrial Revolution

The so-called 'Industrial Revolution' in Britain has prompted a vast stream of litera-ture about the causes, timing, process of economic change and the outcome in terms of productivity, real wages and per capita real income. This is not intended to be a contribution to that literature but rather a brief conspectus of some of the issues. One cannot possibly do justice to the variety of views. Rather emphasis is placed on recent perspectives, particularly by Deane (1965). In doing so, prominent questions in the literature dealing with increasing real output, productivity and real wages are left aside.

Deane has presented the most coherent picture of what she rather bravely defines as the 'first' Industrial Revolution. One might fairly readily identify comparable economic transformations earlier in other parts of the world, in China, the Middle East and the Mediterranean. There was one vital difference — the printed word that allowed the communication of information and ideas.

If we drop the adjective 'first', there is little doubt but that in the century or so from about the third quarter of the 18th century there was a massive change in the composition of British activity, in the application of technology, in business organi-sation, in the urban–rural composition of the population and in the size of the popu-lation and workforce. Rather than a narrow 'industrial' revolution, one might suggest that radical micro- and macroeconomic changes were occurring to achieve, for Britain, a massive structural adjustment. Deane, along with many other British scholars, dates an acceleration of these changes at about 1780, continuing into the third quarter of the 19th century.

For Deane, the Industrial Revolution is a complex of interrelated 'revolutions' during the second half of the 18th century, even though each component is seen as derived from changes extending much further back in time. This makes more sense as a broad restructuring process rather than merely an 'industrial' revolution. Deane's 'first' Industrial Revolution then becomes an interactive set of 'revolutions' in demography, agriculture, commerce, transport and manufacturing. This should be stressed: it was not merely a series of changes within separate sectors but also rapid and relatively flexible responses of changes within one sector by others. The ability to achieve this interaction was the product of market structure and practices — of modes of responding to market stimuli generally, not simply of achieving a series of distinct innovations in separate pieces of British activity.

At its most general level, the massive restructuring that ensued produced a British economy that was dominantly an urban–industrialised one by the mid-19th century, attuned to market signals. The population greatly increased from the third quarter of the 18th century and was less centred on agriculture, rural pursuits and 'peasant' households, all of which came to be a minority. By the mid-19th century, the greater proportion of the population and the workforce were in towns and, indeed, a high proportion in large urban centres were committed to market activity.

Some hints, at least, of the interaction are essential. Demographic behaviour is, perhaps, the least influenced directly by market indicators. Population growth in Britain appears to have accelerated relatively slowly after about 1730 and to have picked up speed by about 1780, to a rate of about 1 per cent per annum. Modest as this appears, in retrospect in relation to other parts of the world (cf. Australian rates of increase), it was sufficiently rapid to create a large population nucleus by 1850.

Health, cultural and economic factors have all been proposed as part of the explanation for the sustained population growth which subsequently helped to enlarge the domestic market and workforce.

One contributing factor was food supply and, in turn, this is one of the links between the demographic and agricultural 'revolutions'. Possibly fortuitous 'good harvests' before the mid-18th century were part of a continuing process of rural change that transformed the face of rural Britain. It is argued that enclosures aggregated farmlands, the application of capital in farms reduced labour intensity and increased total factor productivity; and the application of science and technology to farm and animal husbandry further enhanced output.

Even where farmlands were not engrossed, many of the new farming practices percolated downwards to small farmers. At the same time, many former 'peasant' farmers became landless. The decline of the relatively self-contained rural household was accentuated, pushing more rural families into the market as wage-earners. As a concomitant of these changes, farming became increasingly a business with decision-making more and more responsive to market processes rather than parochial security of food supplies.

As Deane argues, it does not follow, as has been claimed in the past, that there was a large-scale release of labour from rural areas to meet rising demands from urban centres. A good deal of rural labour does seem to have been released to other rural activities including the physical process of enclosure; and a good deal of rural poverty emerged, with claims on poor relief. Rather the emphasis is on the proposition that British agricultural output could enlarge without corresponding demand for labour so that the increase in aggregate population could be concentrated in urban activities. Even though substantial rural relocation occurred, many rigidities kept families in rural locations. This limited mobility was one of the conditions that led increasingly to fears of overpopulation particularly after 1815. These fears were instrumental, amongst other things, in stimulating schemes for pauper emigration from Britain and, in due course, to the assisted departure of free migrants to Australia in the 1830s.

In the meantime, however, available rural labour appears as a major factor in simplifying the generation of social overhead capital in rural Britain during the second half of the 18th and first half of the 19th centuries. This capital provided the base of Deane's 'transport revolution' that was a prime factor establishing a nationwide market for both rural and manufactured products. Britain's fortunate status as an island nation and the access to sea transport only partially solved the problem of internal transport costs and the costs of personal movement. Particularly for bulky rural products, costs of land transport were extremely high and the radius of accessible markets limited at the beginning of the 18th century.

Concerns of rural landowners, miners, foreign shippers and urban manufacturers combined to create incentives for the improvement of roads and the development of canals and waterways. Parochial as many of these road and canal projects were, the level of outlay and scope of the total 'network' increased progressively particularly during the second half of the 18th century and for a period after the Napoleonic Wars and the beginning of railways in the 1830s. Transport costs and passenger movement costs fell correspondingly as the rising demands of an increasing British population could be met by internal transport. Particularly, the use of water transport served, despite physical limitations, to increase greatly the mobility of goods and persons and to permit the carriage of greater and greater tonnages of goods throughout an increasingly unified national market. At the same time, this increased mobility, notwithstanding substantial rigidities, assisted the restructuring of the population towards urban nuclei.

This internal mobility was linked to the development of port facilities and through them the growth of British international commerce. In that lay the next of Deane's 'revolutions', the 'commercial revolution'. Most prominently London, but in addition Liverpool and Glasgow became the great British ports developed jointly by public and private enterprise. In the development of the London docks and in the construction of shipping, another Australian link occurred with the use of convicts from the hulks prior to transportation, in port and shipbuilding. Declining demand for British convict labour in these areas as the end of the Napoleonic Wars approached, triggered an upsurge of convict transportation to Australia.

In contrast with the prevalent mercantilist attitudes of the 250-odd years prior to 1800, Britain's international trade depended on multilateralism and on the increasing presence of individual merchants rather than regulated companies derived from the middle ages. Wool that had been the premier industry and trade for several (perhaps hundreds of) centuries before 1800 served to tie British trade to Europe and subsequently to North America. Woollen textile trade with Europe and America remained an important component throughout the 18th century. But its share was progressively reduced by increasing multilateralism and the flow of materials inputs from tropical and semi-tropical parts of the world as Britain's Empire and trade grew during the 17th and 18th centuries.

Part of this flow was re-exported to Europe. Part was used as inputs into British manufacturing and exported particularly to Europe and North America. Of these inputs, cotton is generally accepted to be the most important providing the foundations of accelerating growth of cotton textile outputs in the second half of the 18th and first half of the 19th centuries. In exploiting these inputs, the development of internal transport to service expanding industrial centres was crucial. But re-export trade in primary materials also rose rapidly from the mid-18th century and into the 19th. Among these, wool was a significant component and it was a combination of British manufacturing consumption and re-export of wool that helped to stimulate Australian production.

The expansion of British overseas multilateral trade during the second half of the 18th and into the first half of the 19th centuries focused above all on London and the development of a great *entrepôt* centre. In London not only commercial expertise and variety developed but also a concentration of financial wealth arising from commerce. Increasingly London was developed to assume the position of funding worldwide activities and also the industrial development of Britain. It was not alone in this; the major British ports had substantial ancillary roles to play, particularly in providing the capital for industrial expansion. Indeed, the subsidiary centres, linked as they became to the locations of prime manufacturing, may have had, along with large landholders, a primary role in funding the Industrial Revolution.

The strictly Industrial Revolution can be seen as a transformation of manufacturing or a much broader integrated development of urban–industrial society and economy. At the level of manufacturing, the focal changes are represented as an array of technical innovations and organisational adjustments predominantly in cotton textiles and iron production. These are taken to be the leading sectors in industrial restructuring in Britain. Cotton textiles are represented as passing through a process of rapidly increasing output, scale of activity, increased efficiency, expanding inputs and a progressive centralisation in 'factory form' in particular locations where large urban centres developed particularly during the first half of the 19th century. Iron production had a much longer prior history of 'capitalistic' production and was not such a 'new' industry as cotton, but it too was transformed technologically and organisationally during the last quarter of the 18th and first half of the 19th centuries. By comparison with cotton, the large-scale changes in iron production had massive ramifications for many other industries through the development of a variety of iron products. The culmination of this influence was the generation of railways in the 1830s and after.

Cotton depended on rising volumes of imports; iron on the replacement of imported ores with British ore and the greatly expanded use of coal (as coal furnaces progressively took over from coke and charcoal). Cotton required increased cargo capacity and iron served to enlarge the size and speed of ships to deliver these goods as imports or exports. In due course, as British exports of both cotton and iron products increased, the capacity of Britain to deliver exports throughout the world depended on the 'transport revolution' and ships' carrying capacities.

Cotton, in particular, is taken as the industry transforming relations between rural and urban populations and workforce. Relying initially on the old skills and physical assets of woollen textile workers in rural households, it swept firstly the spinning activity into factory systems and then, more slowly, the weaving operations. It depended, perhaps, on a progressive transformation in that rural workers provided a great deal of the early capital assets in the form of their own dwellings and were prepared even at considerable personal cost to preserve their independence. Once weaving was mechanised, this independence was threatened and by 1850 the old system of outwork in rural areas was substantially a thing of the past. In its place, cheap labour particularly of women, children and young persons in urban factories was the norm.

This change operated to create not only massive shifts in the location and structure of the workforce, it represented the ultimate proletarianisation of both urban and rural workers, rural poverty, urban stress and dense populations.

One indicator of the scale of transformation that occurred is a comparison of 1801 and 1851 in respect of the urban populations (see table 12.1, p.114). Given the composition of the towns, this change cannot be based on an 'industrial' revolution as such. The comparison has its own defects, not least the limitation to the first half of the 19th century. For what it is worth, it suggests that in a population that almost doubled, the populations of the recognised cities and towns of Britain had almost exactly trebled in population while the large centres outside London, as designated, almost quadrupled in size.

This was a massive socioeconomic transformation in not much more than a contemporary lifetime. It was from these towns that most of the convicts and pauper migrants came over this period to Australia and particularly so after 1810.

This urbanisation reflected more than merely industrial change. Accompanying that industrialisation was an upsurge in commercial and service activity and in urban building. It is not possible to delineate the change in occupational and industrial distribution of the workforce. The best available indication is in the 1851 Census, displaying something of the end-process. The 1841 Census is classified differently and omits many occupied persons. Nevertheless it is included here to try to push back the available data as far as possible.

Table 12.1: British Isles Towns Population ('000)

	1801	1851
Birmingham	71	265
Bradford	13	104
Bristol	61	137
Dublin	?	272
Edinburgh	83	194
Glasgow	77	363
Leeds	53	172
Liverpool	82	395
Manchester	75	338
Sheffield	46	135
Total Major	561	2 375
Total exc. London	1 379	4 975
Greater London	1 117	2 685
Total	2 496	7 660
Approx. Total Pop.	15 500	27 371

Source: Mitchell (1988).

Strictly manufacturing aspects of the Industrial Revolution have been given great and perhaps undue prominence in the past (though they may have high relevance to Australian history). The broader impact of the development of iron and iron products greatly enlarged the skill composition of the British workforce. So, too, did the specialisation that developed in textile production. The emergence of a highly skilled industrial workforce also had a feedback to Australian history in the transfer of human capital, initially by transportation and subsequently through free migration and colonisation. Combined with capital outlays and developing technology, these skills took Britain rapidly into clear pre-eminence as the industrial and trading nation of the world in the first half of the 19th century.

The statistical evidence of the scale of the transformation is very limited and more than a little shaky. Hoffmann's index of industrial production has served at times as an indicator of change over the 18th and 19th centuries but it has a limited coverage and cannot be relied upon. In any event, it does not convey the overall scale of the economic restructuring that occurred. The first reasonably well-founded Census data on workforce distribution are available only by 1851; however, the 1841 returns are also included despite the inadequacies of that Census (see table 12.2, p.115).

Whatever 'guesstimates' might be made of the proportion of the British workforce engaged in agriculture in the mid-18th century, its share displayed by the mid-19th century had certainly shrunk radically. Correspondingly, the representation of manufacturing occupations had become, by 1851, by far the largest sector, with a wide variety of important industry groups within manufacturing.

It was from these towns and from these occupations that most convicts came to Australia. These immigrants to Australia carried British skills. But perhaps even more importantly, they were accustomed, perhaps unconsciously, to the conditions under which an advanced market economy operated and to the detailed mechanisms facilitating flexible decision-making, innovative behaviour and responsiveness to market indicators. It is important, then, to appreciate some of the microconditions that allowed Britain to restructure as substantially and rapidly as it did. That capability was carried over to Australia even though the conditions differed radically.

Table 12.2: Great Britain Census Estimates, Persons ('000)

	1841	1851	1841	1851	1841	1851	1841 %	1851 %
	M	M	F	F	Pers.	Pers.	Pers.	Pers.
Public Administration	40	64	3	3	43	67	0.62	0.71
Armed Forces	51	63	0	0	51	63	0.74	0.67
Professional etc.	113	162	49	!03	162	265	2.35	2.83
Domestic & Personal	255	193	989	1 135	1 244	1 328	18.01	14.17
Commercial	94	91	1	0	95	91	1.38	0.97
Transport	196	433	4	13	200	446	2.90	4.76
Agriculture, Forest. & Fish.	1 458	1 824	81	230	1 539	2 054	22.28	21.91
Mining, Quarries	218	383	7	11	225	394	3.26	4.20
Building, Construction	376	496	1	1	377	497	5.46	5.30
Metal Manuf. Machines etc.	1396	536	14	36	410	572	5.94	6.10
Wood Furniture etc.	107	152	5	8	112	160	1.62	1.71
Bricks Cement Glass etc.	48	75	10	15	58	90	0.84	0.96
Chemicals Oils Soaps	23	42	1	4	24	46	0.35	0.49
Skins Leather Hair etc.	47	55	3	5	50	60	0.72	0.64
Paper Print Books etc.	44	62	6	16	50	78	0.72	0.83
Textiles	525	661	358	635	883	1 296	12.78	13.83
Clothing	358	418	200	491	558	909	8.08	9.70
Food Drink Tabacco	268	348	42	53	310	401	4.49	4.28
Total Manufacture	**1 816**	**2 349**	**639**	**1 263**	**2 455**	**3 612**	**35.54**	**38.54**
Gas Water Electricity	2	7	0	0	2	7	0.03	0.07
All Other Occupied	474	490	41	61	515	551	7.46	5.88
Total Occupied	**5 093**	**6 554**	**1 815**	**2 819**	**6 908**	**9 373**	**100.00**	**100.0**

Source: Censuses of Great Britain, 1841 and 1851.

'Perfecting the Market' for British Restructuring

Throughout much of Western Europe, many limitations on economic and social development survived from the Middle Ages, overlain by other restrictive conditions derived from the post-medieval mercantilist States. Some of this mixture of medievalism and mercantilism remained in Britain into the 19th century. One illustration relevant to Australia was the prohibition of the export of wool, a condition that persisted into the 19th century so that, once relaxed, a significant British export trade in wool began only in 1820. Symptomatic of the issues to be discussed, the lifting of that restriction by Britain and the scaling down of taxes on wool (even a brief imperial preference to NSW wool) were preconditions of the development of a British re-export trade in wool, a trade from which Australia gained handsomely. In reality, this is a superficial and incidental remnant of a vast array of physical and artificial barriers that had been lowered to permit a flexibly operating market system.

Britain did not achieve a 'perfect market' in its industrial restructuring between 1750 and 1850. But the trend towards a large-scale reduction in constraints was striking, particularly so in comparison with France and the still semi-feudal States of Germany. To appreciate the British achievement and the nature of the heritage for Australia, one needs something of a British-European comparison. This is even more important given the unfree conditions with which Australian settlement by Britain began.

Only a broad illustrative sketch is possible here. Mercantilism that Adam Smith (1776) so roundly condemned may be seen as a system of State regulation of internal affairs, external relations and colonial development. Mercantilism was developed in Britain relatively weakly as compared with the continent. Nevertheless, in all areas, it is perceived as evolving from attempts, initially, to break down the restrictive parochialism of medieval life and to deal with relations between 'unified' States and their growing imperial interests. From Smith's standpoint, mercantilist policies restrained the development in size of markets, limited opportunities for scale and specialisation, impeded the growth of trade, restricted multilateralism and the most advantageous use of national endowments, and muted responsiveness generally to the market.

Medieval life had offered points of security for recovery after the collapse of the Roman Empire. Those points, outlined below, nevertheless served to contain opportunities and expectations within very narrow horizons. The medieval view of the world was strongly parochial and, for most individuals, insecure and short term. Plague and war, the fear of death and the Devil, high mortality and short life-expectancies, containment for most to a local environment, fear of hunger, commitment to legal constraints on individuals, and the sharp definition of status were conditions that changed slowly and intermittently. Local regulations on industry and trade and on rural life were essential characteristics even though they might be relaxed over time. In terms of internal economic activity, a central object of medieval regulation was for separate local groups in individual towns to secure the basic supplies for survival (however distributed by status and force).

The unification policies pursued by mercantilist States were designed to break down this particularism. Local medieval policies had led to widespread differences in regional treatment of conditions to which 19th century people took a universalist approach in order to achieve ease of communication and understanding. Peculiar local weights and measures, local barter and currency rules, special laws and regulations, localised modes of contractual arrangements, enforcement methods and penalties, particular tolls, taxes and fines, separate rules for each town in the regulation of apprenticeship and promotion in different trades illustrate the underlying obstacles to widening markets.

The breaking down of this particularism was a slow process. In Britain, where the process began relatively early and was most complete by the early 19th century, change took a long time. Thus efforts to unify weights and measures began with the *Magna Carta*. A great reduction in variety was achieved by 1700. A wholly uniform system universally adopted in the United Kingdom was not finally achieved until 1835. Even so, Britain was then far ahead of Western Europe.

Weights and measures required a mind that was capable of exact quantitative measurement and of appreciating its advantages. So, too, did the adoption of a uniform currency (a problem that was to plague the first 40 years of Australian settlement). Again, Britain was a leader in this unification process, beginning with Henry II and substantially achieved in legal terms under Henry VIII's laws against debasement of the coinage. France, Britain's nearest mercantilist rival in unification in this area, achieved a nominally standard currency early but retained different regional valuation systems into the early 19th century.

Until about 1700, local town or parish organisations continued to charge local tolls for the use of British roads and waterways without doing much in the way of transport improvement. These charges were essentially a monopoly rent based on location. As already indicated, building operations, particularly on waterways, but also to some extent on roads, grew apace during the 18th century in Britain. But now the charges were less merely a claim for monopoly rent and increasingly a means of rewarding improvement (still to local monopolies).

The contrast with Europe lay in the persistence of regional division and of charging what the traffic would bear along water and road routes without much effort to improve. This was a prime contrast for two different reasons. Firstly, Western Europe possessed major river systems well-suited for long-distance movement internally and indeed depended on these water routes for extensive long-distance movement. High charges and frequent toll points imposed, up to the end of the 18th century, almost prohibitive taxes on the transfer of goods.

In Britain, the island structure made sea carriage a substantially toll-free link to all coastal towns and even some distance from river mouths. As overseas trade developed rapidly during the 18th century, British merchants did not face a comparable obstacle to those in France and Germany. Moreover, access to the sea in Britain reduced the value of the local monopoly locations in inland waterways and made them less opposed to either improvement or to their replacement by new business-like trusts.

For physical and economic reasons, it became much easier to achieve market unification in Britain, to allow relatively unimpeded movement of goods and persons to adopt national contractual systems and practices of commercial law and to achieve the domestic market scale that, in Adam Smith's judgment, was crucial to the specialisation that was necessary for rapid industrialisation.

This physical condition may have been part of the reason for the different treatment in Britain and Western Europe of the medieval urban centres, their internal practices and controls and, above all, the role of the gilds in relation to commerce, manufacture and rural activities. Town centres and urban gilds in France and the German States appear to have actually increased their impeding influences in the course of unification, whereas in Britain, the gilds largely withered away after about 1700. Their decline was fundamental to the development of generalised commercial legal systems. Both French and British outcomes followed attempts at 'unification'. In the British case, there were vital implications for contractual procedures of business and customers and for the introduction of new ways to train the workforce and to reorient it.

After the Black Death, both Britain and France attempted to establish centralised enactments to regulate and codify the working conditions and the mobility of labour. But the crucial centralised effort at national regulation of labour occurred in both countries in 1581, in Britain's case with the Statute of Artificers. Britain established a relatively loose and comparatively inefficient system of national regulation that was in harmony with the highly privatised mode of revenue-raising generally. It allowed labour mobility except for the poor. In doing so, it facilitated the British response particularly to the development of international trade and of a rising domestic market.

France, on the other hand, established a highly centralised bureaucracy for revenue-raising and for administration of labour conditions. In doing so, it accepted the power of urban centres and of the gilds. It tended to prevent labour moving from rural areas to towns and even between towns. Its national administrative system became regionalised (with regional 'intendants' and 'inspecteurs' nominally responsible to Paris but located in regional centres). In accepting and dealing directly with the gilds at specific urban centres, it enhanced their restrictive power and influence throughout the 18th century. Not only was their spatial monopoly preserved but inter-industry mobility was constricted. The French Crown exploited a nationally recognised gild system for fiscal purposes by enhancing their restrictive power.

It is not the purpose here to follow through the variety of artificial obstacles to nation-wide market operations. As a centralised monarchy that accepted a high degree of regionalism under national authority, the French system remained undisturbed until 1789. The various interest groups were adapted to this inhibiting system. Then the French Revolution destroyed many of these pressure groups and in the process freed France from a set of institutions that had left it increasingly behind Britain in terms of economic restructuring and development.

Britain's successive adaptations might be seen as a product of natural advantages (particularly the sea), regal efforts to incorporate towns at the national level and, perhaps above all, the series of breaks in succession in the British monarchy. The pre-Tudor struggles for access to the Crown disposed of many vested interests; the succession of the Stuarts brought the whole of England, Scotland and Wales together; the execution of Charles I and the departure of James II radically weakened a strictly royal centralism. Behind these events there were underlying political and economic changes introducing non-royal but extremely powerful interest groups into positions of dominant influence. The capture of the unified State by non-royal interests might be signalled in a variety of ways. It is not the least significant indicator that George III surrendered royal rights to revenue raising in exchange for a handsome pension in 1751.

Finally, the success of the American Revolution helped to break down, for Britain, much of the external and colonial trappings of centralised mercantilist policies. The consequential destruction of the Navigation Acts and the attenuation of efforts to adapt colonial development to serve the interests of Britain were in tune with other changes developing on a global scale that a centralised British government could not effectively control. The old regulated monopoly companies were increasingly unable to sustain substantial advantage over large distances even though national recognition might give them some preferred entry into the growing London metropolis and *entrepôt* port by the mid-18th century. By the time of the foundation of Australia, one significant company remained, the East India Company. Its presence did inhibit some activity for a time in Australia, though less in reality than in form. Its monopoly was already much in question by 1788 and it was eroded during 1813–19 so far as control of trade and shipping in the Pacific and Indian Oceans were concerned.

Towards Conventional Australian Markets: Deprivatising Officials

Given the role of the governors in the colonial history of New South Wales and Van Diemen's Land one might focus on autocratic processes in the settlements after 1810. Such a focus helps to make a major dividing point in 1821 with, amongst other changes, British recognition of a pastoral and agricultural prospect in Australia and British determination to substantially divert all convict assignment to private and away from public employment. Other changes in the early 1820s, including the establishment of a consolidated colonial fiscal system and of a small advisory system to the governor, operated to move the settlements along the road to free colonial societies.

This focus is not adopted here. The ostensible decisions of the British government may have facilitated change after 1820 but they largely formalised prevalent colonial (including gubernatorial) opinion and extended private and official action already underway in the settlement. A different policy issue, basically a structural and procedural matter, was at stake in the Rum Rebellion, the enforced withdrawal of the military junta and the replacement of Bligh by Macquarie in 1810. To appreciate the significance of the change, we need to recapitulate summarily some of the characteristics of the pre-1810 economy and of British administrative procedures in the late 18th and early 19th centuries.

The conditions of settlement 'success' in economic terms between 1792 and 1810 included the installation of the basic principles of private property, profit-making and personal choice. Market behaviour extended beyond a few wealthy individuals and even beyond all free persons to the treatment and behaviour of convicts themselves. Public assets of land and human beings could be acquired only through official sanction and administrative decisions. But once transferred to the private market, transactions in these resources and the output that they generated were dealt with by market processes. The services of convicts could be, and were often, retained compulsorily by masters but both masters and convict servants had options open to them in market behaviour that appear to have been widely exercised. Admittedly, the market included the Commissariat but, however administratively conducted, it too operated extensively as a market institution within the settlement.

The peculiarity about this early market behaviour, and one that largely, though not wholly, distinguishes it from the post-1810 system, was the intimate interconnection between official positions and market behaviour. There was a widespread confusion of public and private interest so that, in creating market systems, officials used their official positions to gain private benefit and to launch enterprises for personal gain. In the process, they were able to establish conditions in which many ex-convicts followed suit though, in their case, they frequently depended on official decisions and actions (in allowing land grants, convict assignment, provision of business licences etc.) that were made on a fee-for-service basis.

What this meant was that officials, including governors, were actors in the play and not primarily directors of it. In filling official roles and pursuing personal business interest at the same time, they simultaneously established the rules of the game and played actively in it. As already indicated, this was a local interpretation of official behaviour that, in general form, was widespread in 18th century Britain and the Empire. But it was simultaneously a local adaptation of British market principles and procedures to which the officials, convicts and ex-convicts were accustomed. In its significance for economic development but not in its form, it did not differ radically even from the privatised and semi-privatised gaols of Britain. The outcome in the Rum Rebellion *was* a little special. It was not normal for rebellions of officials to occur in British gaols. What was at issue in NSW was the conflict over wealth and property between potential winners and losers in the exploitation of official positions or connections to achieve personal benefit.

The recall of all the officers of the NSW Corps went far towards deprivatising officialdom in the settlement. Some former ex-officers remained along with about one-third of the Corps' privates and some NCOs. Subsequently many Corps officers returned as free settlers once discharged. Those privates and NCOs transferring to the new military command or leaving the army were accustomed to pre-1810 procedures. But the incoming governor and his regiment and subsequent civil official appointees had no such associations. Macquarie was not averse to beneficial use of public funds or making land grants that were to family benefit. Subsequently, Commissaries in both NSW and Van Diemen's Land attempted to construct private enterprises from their official positions but were quickly reprimanded and replaced. This conformed to changing British practice.

Though the break at 1810 was far from complete, there was a profound shift in the relations between colonial government officials and the society and economy that they governed. The British government may have perceived the change to imply the restoration of a penal settlement and appears not to have comprehended the scope of privatisation and free market activity that had developed before 1810. In that context, it waited until 1821 and the Bigge Report to move the British government towards declaration of the potential in Australia for the development of privately conducted agricultural and pastoral enterprise.

But within Australia itself, the privatisation had gone too far to be easily reversed even if British officials ever contemplated such a reversal. This limitation combined with the logic of the completion of convict sentences and the consequential freeing of increasing numbers, if nothing else, imposed a more complex perspective on local colonial officials. But their function was now to govern in a more aloof manner, to determine the rules of the game played by others in the colony(ies), to encourage and restrict the players, perhaps in the process to favour some to the disadvantage of others, but not to participate directly in business activities themselves.

This change was in tune with reform in government in Britain. From the 1790s, a more strictly bureaucratic officialdom evolved. Above all, this change was indicated by the gradual conversion of fees-for-service to salaries for officials, the former fees being paid to public revenues. As the size of the British public service rose during and after the Napoleonic Wars, the presence of salaried officials became increasingly apparent. Reform was a slow process and it was not completed in Britain until late in the 19th century. The change was achieved more rapidly in Australia and the essential reforms appear to have been in place by the mid-1830s.

Indeed, the most prominent alteration began in 1812 and was completed with the replacement in 1827 of the NSW Naval Officer, operating on a fee-for-service basis, with a wholly salaried customs official. Initially, the progression began with doubts being raised about the conflict of interest of a private merchant, Campbell, acting as Naval Officer, with consequential prior public and private access to cargoes. Campbell resigned under pressure in 1813. He was replaced by Piper who continued as a wealthy public servant, with no overt business associations, until 1827 when he was replaced by a fully salaried official. This decision followed earlier similar substitutions in comparable customs positions throughout the Empire. Well before 1820, the privatised official was no longer uniformly approved but strongly under question and scrutiny in Britain and the Empire. Macquarie prepared, in 1814, a list of fees received privately in the settlement that he regarded as at least competing with the opportunities for raising public revenues in NSW. He sacked at least two senior officials for efforts to engage in privatised official behaviour.

The disentanglement of public and private interest after 1810 did not mean merely autocratic rule of subject residents whether free or unfree. Historians' efforts to label one governor or other as more or less autocratic misconstrue the pressures under which governors laboured after 1810. They were subject to often ill-informed British directives to conform either to penal or imperial policies. Other British influences stemmed from fluctuating but typically high rates of convict inflow to 1840 and separate British decisions to reduce capital subventions or to adapt convict transportation to pauper migration. Governors were also subject to pressures from different interest groups within the settlements. In dealing with those pressures, the colonial officials confronted administrative and development tasks that might override some or at times all private interests. But the growth of private interests made it increasingly impossible for governors to disregard those interests. So far as economic administration went, the essential role of government was increasingly to facilitate a private sector market behaviour as the essential *modus operandi* of the economy, notwithstanding the penal character of NSW and Van Diemen's Land.

In the process, a more distinct public sector emerged side by side with the private sector in both NSW and Van Diemen's Land as distinct from the supervision of convicts. A mixed economy in this sense persisted in the latter case until 1840. In NSW, the government largely lost control of much of the settlement after 1830 and its role dwindled sharply. In the 1830s, the NSW economy was perhaps more fully private than it had ever been before and was ever to be thereafter, despite massive convict inflows between 1830 and 1840. The formation of the private colonies of Swan River in 1829 and of South Australia in 1836 meant that private property and private enterprise were the dominant characteristics of the Australian economy as a whole.

In contrast with the British economy, however, this evolving relationship between private interest and public action did not occur in the context of a fully structured economic system. Though private property rights were well established, the Crown laid claim to unoccupied lands in Australia (as it did without question throughout the Empire until the Durham Report of 1836 questioned the appropriateness of this attitude). Principles and procedures were required to transfer land to private hands and the conditions of transfer had major influences on the process of economic development. Similarly, the influx of convicts required decisions about allocation between public and private projects and within the private sector, choices between competing individuals, locations and industries. This issue was strongly influenced by a third major decision-making question. Private individuals might be expected often, at least in the short-run, to prefer private to joint outlays and to underprovide public goods and, in particular, developmental infrastructure. Much of the task of infrastructure development fell to government until the 1830s when the growth of private institutions led to a brief private effort in road construction.

In addition, the government intervened in relation to private action in continuing to operate the public market institution of the Commissariat. In the process, it affected prices and determined quantities of goods bought and sold through this authority. Government attempted to set prices and wages, to limit or orient some types of private enterprise, to control labour mobility and to assert public rights to fix the conditions of convict labour employed privately as well as publicly. One of the more interesting features of some of these types of control is that they sometimes accelerated and sometimes restrained the development of flexible decision making by individuals.

Conditions of Market Operation in Australia

The transfer by way of migration of British understanding of the conditions of market operations was a vital part of the rapid evolution of market behaviour in Australia. Moreover, the replacement of the NSW Corps by the 73rd Regiment and the continued influx of convicts and free arrivals helped to update local awareness of evolving British practice.

But British methods were far from being the only determinant of modes of operation in Australia. Four groups of actors might be seen as influencing the outcome. The British Colonial Office had its own views on the conditions of development in Australia and these were not necessarily merely to copy British domestic achievements. The local colonial officials were a second group, confronting as they did the realities of local conditions and local pressures and forced to act to a substantial degree in terms of local considerations. A third group was the Australian 'private sector' in which free individuals not only transacted between themselves but also dealt, in particular, with local officialdom and the special conditions presented by British penal and imperial interests. The fourth was the presence of Aborigines and the role they played in the conditions of transfer of their natural resources to British control and ownership.

It is convenient to discuss evolving modes of market operation in terms of five sub-sections:

(a) The labour market;

(b) The land market;

(c) Goods markets;

(d) Capital markets and particularly the institutions of money, credit and banking;

(e) Entry into urban business.

In dealing with these, it is important to appreciate that conditions of market behaviour developed on two different planes. One arose in the relations between colonial governments and private individuals. The other emerged in dealings between individuals within Australia or with individuals outside Australia. Government may appear important at the latter level at all times; in fact, one of the interesting issues in Australia is the irrelevance of government in important circumstances even in validating the 'rules of the game', the interpretation or adoption of which was pre-empted by private individuals. In these latter cases, a complete turnaround occurred as compared with the pre-1810 private dependence on official positions or associations with officials. Progressively, particularly in NSW, the importance of the British government dwindled and, within the colony, officials largely lost control of major areas of decision making between 1825 and 1840. The 'rules' became increasingly private. This has already been discussed in terms of relations with Aborigines. The process was, in fact, broader than race relations.

The Labour Market

The supply of convicts as the major input of labour in NSW and Van Diemen's Land implied a specific element of freedom. It does not follow that there was a comparable lack of freedom in terms or response to the market.

Externally, actions in Britain influenced some allocative procedures in dotting small convict outposts around the Australian coast between 1803 and 1827, partly to forestall other entrants. But this affected only a few hundred of the 250 000-odd convicts arriving to the end of transportation to south-eastern Australia. The essential issues lay in the colonies themselves. Britain sought punishment and hopefully reformation. Colonial officials and the colonial private sector were at least as much concerned with the economic use of convict labour. But British fiscal concerns brought the two sides towards a broad coalescence of policy.

One must appreciate the significance of convict labour in the total workforce during 1810 to 1840. Unfortunately, available numbers are scrappy and incomplete and the best one can do is to relate convict numbers and adult population as a whole. The 1806 Muster suggests that convicts then accounted for perhaps 40 per cent of the adult population — significantly less than half. Between 1806 and 1810, this proportion almost certainly fell substantially because of expiry of sentences and low rates of new convict arrivals. From 1813, convict arrivals rose rapidly, subject to some substantial fluctuation. The influx was offset, in part, by expiry of sentences, deaths, the arrival of free immigrants (growing rapidly in the 1830s) and by increasing numbers of persons born in Australia. However, the proportion of convicts in NSW rose quite quickly after 1813 to half and then fluctuated fairly closely around this mark into the 1830s. The proportion was somewhat higher in Van Diemen's Land but even there a large segment of the workforce was free or freed after 1825.

Given the scale of convict influx after 1813, one might speculate as to why a public market in convicts did not develop in Australia as it had done in the United States. In part, this appears due to changed British attitudes to the use of human beings. Within the colony itself, a very limited and partial public market had developed as discussed in 'What a way to run an empire, fiscally!' (Butlin, 1985a). Private assignment was strongly established by 1810, at zero access costs to recipients. The accelerated influx from 1813 soon taxed, for a time, the capacity of both the public and private sectors to absorb the flow. And, far from additional convicts in the few years before 1820 commanding a price, a considerable increase in the granting of tickets of leave was made to dispose of the problem of a temporary surplus. It remained until the settlements extended beyond the immediate bridgehead limits and into the hinterland that complaints of labour shortages developed. By then, however, the system of assignment was too deeply ingrained.

In the absence of a market for convicts, colonial officials were faced with allocative decisions to distribute convicts between public and private sectors and between individuals, locations and industries and, in addition, assumed the task of attempting to determine conditions of convict employment and terms of their release into free labour.

So far as allocation to the public sector was concerned, the demand for publicly produced goods and services such as roads, wharves, buildings, exploration etc. diverted a significant fraction of the total convict workforce to these ends. This fraction appears to have been sustained throughout 1810–40 between 15 and 20 per cent of the total convict supply. It implied allocation without clear market indicators. On the one hand, the allocations depended partly on official view of 'need' for infrastructure and of private compromise with that objective and with acquiring a private workforce for enterprise or own final consumption purposes. And allocative processes were influenced by the acceptance by the private sector of the importance of some publicly provided goods and services on the other.

Relatively close settlement around the Cumberland Plain in NSW and in Hobart

and Launceston in Van Diemen's Land generated early pressures for a communi-
cations network and a variety of administrative structures and social amenities. This
was the focus of attention during the first decade after 1810. Even in that decade,
however, road building began over longer distances around the coast and into the
hinterland. By the beginning of the 1820s, the NSW Commissariat was even
advertising contracts for roads to be constructed 'on the principle of Macadam'.
Pressures for public road construction and local control structures increased substantially as settlement spread into the hinterland during the 1820s and 1830s. This
structural shift occurred more or less simultaneously with two important changes
from the early 1820s. One was the British government direction to give priority to
the private sector in allocating convict services; the other, particularly after 1828
was to withdraw convicts progressively from clerical–administrative positions in the
colonial public service.

Two consequences followed, affecting the significance of market operations in
this context. One was the increasing tendency to substitute public roads with private
toll roads (broadly following British practice) during the 1830s. The other was that
public employment of convicts became increasingly a matter of punishment rather
than economic use (a characteristic that emerged in the late 1820s), deploying this
segment of convicts into building gangs made of persons less manageable or controllable by the more limited supervisory capacity of private employers. In effect, a
private sector selective process became more prominent in intersectoral allocation.
Implicitly, it tended to increase the efficiency of the private sector and reduce the
efficiency of government activity.

No systematic procedures were ever applied effectively in determining allocation
as between individuals, locations or industries within the private sector. The
privatised officials before 1810 had established a pattern of giving preferences to
themselves as against most ex-convicts or even the few free immigrants. In general,
it appears that the implied preferences were for those capable of supervising and
using larger groups of convict employees — in other words, for those with greater
resources; and to favour urban or near urban employment, serving the demands of a
well-to-do society seeking import-competing products or non-tradables rather than
rural output. The subsequent allocations after 1810 similarly favoured the more
well-to-do, heavily subsidised, persons who, in a market environment would have
exercised the larger effective demand for convicts. Consistently, in the Musters and
the 1828 Census and up to around 1837, there was a high degree of concentration in
the size structure of employment of convicts, with a relatively small number of (free
and ex-convict) employers accounting for the majority of assignees.

This size distribution of employment was achieved by varying 'rule of thumb'
procedures in which land grants and convict allocations were given so as to favour
persons with wealth. Though there were frequent official complaints that persons to
whom such allocations were made often overstated their wealth, the outcome nevertheless broadly conformed to an employment structure that a market could be
expected to achieve.

This outcome needs to be interpreted in the light of two conditions. Firstly, the
greater proportion of convict assignees tended to be within fairly closely settled
areas so that, already, the assignment procedures tended to favour the establishment
of population nuclei that progressively emerged as urban centres. The obverse of this
is that, as expansion into the hinterland occurred, labour was less readily available to

sustain the expansion of natural resource exploitation. Secondly, ex-convicts tended to be concentrated within the areas of closest settlement supplying, in accordance with market demands, the products of the skills that they brought from Britain. Official procedures for allocating convicts, that appear arbitrary and inefficient, need to be seen in the context of this large market for freed persons. Officials dealt with the disposition of increments to the workforce and with the introduction of these British convicts to a radically new environment.

In Van Diemen's Land, in the mid-1820s, an extensive provision for very early tickets of leave allowed many convicts to find their own employer (and vice versa). This was a loose adaptation to market procedures. In NSW, efforts were made in the first half of the 1830s to systematise the allocative procedures, to provide reasonably clear rules that would allow escape from criticisms of arbitrariness and personal favours. These had become substantially formulated on paper when, by 1837, it was already known that the assignment system in NSW was to end.

From the late 1790s, hours of work for convicts were declared officially and the opportunity to work for pay beyond those hours was allowed. In effect, beyond an enforced eight hour working day, six days a week, the market operated. In Van Diemen's Land, this procedure provided not only for market activity in labour allocation but also a system of rewards and punishment, underscoring the importance of labour market behaviour: punishment for offences was frequently not the lash but the denial of access of 'free' labour time. Moreover, employers could hire out convicts and convicts could hire themselves out.

We do not know how far the hiring system extended but it appears that working for pay beyond the declared hours was widespread. This practice continued to around 1840. It applied in both settled and frontier conditions. In both cases, the question of convict mobility was at issue. This was provided by the issue of special tickets of leave, in this case, permission to travel so that spatial and occupational mobility was introduced. Such market provisions were particularly important as the settlements extended and convicts, with special British skills, were thereby able to deliver their skills over substantial areas and thus assist individual employers who were otherwise faced with a limited range of workforce capabilities.

This type of market arrangement meant accommodation between individual employers rather than official supervision. Its significance depended on the state of development of each employer's enterprise. At early stages of establishing enterprises, employers faced a considerable range of tasks in clearing land and establishing structures and there was a phased process in which, for a time, convicts' freedom was considerably restricted in any particular location. But once establishment processes were achieved, the ability to retain convicts in cells and chains was drastically reduced. Drovers and shepherds could not be closely supervised or contained. Convict servants travelling with overseers in search of appropriate pasture areas and managing livestock in the process could not easily be physically hampered.

Control, in these cases, was exercised in the last resort by the rights of masters to deliver convicts to magistrates for corporal punishment. The punishment books strongly suggest that a very limited proportion of convicts were exposed to severe punishment, typically a small proportion of recalcitrant convicts who repeatedly refused to accept restraint (a severely damaged convict was not an efficient worker). Increasingly, convicts had a high degree of personal and spatial freedom notwithstanding apparently draconian Master and Servants Acts. Moreover, even apart from 'overtime' work, convicts, almost of necessity, had to be delivered other benefits such as arms and horses if only for personal protection to secure the private property of employers. In other words, their strictly 'convict pay' was increased. Australian conditions beyond urban surrounds offered little option until Aboriginals were no longer a threat.

Without such market provisions, the Australian settlements outside the urban areas faced a major problem of 'concealed unemployment' — conditions in which skilled persons were deployed in tasks not utilising their skills. A great deal of such concealed unemployment existed, but it was greatly offset by the ability to disperse skills in 'overtime' activity. It is possible, though we do not know, that inter-employer hiring may have extended this offset. Clearly, by 1840, the convict labour market failed to incorporate market procedures fully. But it had gone a long distance by a combination of official procedures and private adaptation to achieve a considerable amount of flexibility and freedom for convict workers and for the activities to which they were nominally assigned. Indeed, this was one factor that led Britain to abandon the assignment system in NSW in 1838: conditions appeared too favourable to transportees.

The Land Market

A variety of devices and changes in procedure were adopted to form the conditions for a market in land, including constraints on access. In contrast with convicts, land was abundant relative to employment opportunities. As with convicts, British and colonial officials sought to determine allocation between public and private demands and to control conditions of use as well as access. By 1810, the principle of private property in land was well established though subject to overall British Crown claims to title to so-called 'waste' lands.

Transfers of title to the private sector were accepted by colonial officials as the principle of operation from 1810. What changed progressively were the techniques of transfer and the limitations on transfer. The outcome of the limitations and of the changing conditions of transfer was a progressive loss of government control in NSW (though not in Van Diemen's Land) over the modes and rates of transfer and over operations within the growing private land market. That loss of control in the land market was already emergent by 1810 but became most apparent throughout the 1830s and applied to both the British government *vis-à-vis* the Australian settlements and colonial officials in relation to the private sector. So basic was the land market that these developments radically reduced the ability of government, at any level, to control either the society or the economy as a whole.

The abundance of land implied low prices in transfer from the government. This implication was not fully comprehended by British officials nor by empire reformers such as Wakefield under whose influence experiments were made in the establishment of a wholly free colony in South Australia in 1836. Even with zero access price, private individuals frequently refused even by 1810 to accept limitations on the areas to be used and tended to absorb lands still wholly under Crown title — in colonial parlance, squatted. This began around the Cumberland Plain during the 1810s. It extended with the spread of settlement along the coast and proliferated as occupation of the plains hinterland developed after 1815. *De facto*, the private sector was already determining the control of land use if not the transfer of title to land.

In part, this private response reflected differences in land quality but most importantly a refusal to accept rationing on official terms.

During much of 1810–20, officials were preoccupied with three prime problems in relation to land. One was to try to recapture control and determine the validity of the transfers made by the military cabal after the overthrow of Bligh. Recognising the predominantly private nature of the early economy the cabal rapidly made many hundreds of transfers, mostly to ex-convicts. Under Macquarie's administration, the significance of ex-convicts was also fully recognised and the mass of these prior transfers was confirmed. But the administrative process imposed a lag on new transfers — in other words intensified the rationing process unintentionally and encouraged the emergent illegal occupation of land.

This issue brought into sharper focus the feasible rate at which transfers could be achieved and the appropriate speed of extending the boundaries of settlement. The discovery of access to the NSW plains in 1813 introduced increasing private pressures for extension into the interior and the second preoccupation was then to try to achieve an orderly, officially constrained, occupation of the interior. It was the issue of the speed of this occupation not its appropriateness as an objective that brought Macquarie and Bigge into apparent conflict of purpose. And the issue of the occupation of the interior was one of the considerations that induced the British government in the early 1820s to acknowledge the potential of NSW as a colony appropriate for free enterprise and more extensive and ready access to land. A comparable process applied in Van Diemen's Land where efforts to sell land were made earlier than in NSW and where looser access terms for convicts were adopted from the mid-1820s.

Prior to 1820, Australian officials in both NSW and Van Diemen's Land were confronted with a third issue — order and social and economic arrangement in the established settlement areas. A central derivative of this was the need to establish designated urban locations and to design an array and a hierarchy of towns extending from the government centre. Hence the question of urban land transfers and urban land markets was an important one.

In terms of area, rural lands transferred were undoubtedly vastly larger than urban lands by a factor of many thousands and rural lands actually used by the private sector were larger still in relative terms. However, the value of urban lands, once transferred to the private sector, was not so small relative to rural lands. On the contrary, in confined urban areas, the concentrations of population and activities of the skilled residents, commerce and port activities rapidly led to capital enhancement. To this general stimulus to the value of urban lands was the additional factor of spatial monopoly that was far more substantial than in rural areas (even granted rural quality differentiation). The tendency for a large proportion of the economic activity of the Australian settlements to concentrate in towns makes the manner of organising the urban market a matter of prime importance.

Almost from the beginning, certainly by 1792, different approaches had been adopted to private acquisition of rural as against urban lands. The former was initially acquired by grant, the latter largely though not wholly by lease. Separate as these two appeared, the expansion of settlement areas and population were such that by the decade after 1810, urban land markets had become a confused mix of lease and grant.

This confusion progressed, particularly as the recognised area of Sydney expanded. But it also applied to locations outside Sydney because rural grants were allotted before the town area was declared and rural holdings were contiguous to the original urban area. In essence, lands originally granted as rural had become encircled by expanding urban activity and population, to the considerable benefit of the private owner. To complicate the urban land market even further, some individuals were accorded special treatment in being allowed to convert leases into grants and even to exchange grants outside Sydney for grants within Sydney. Nevertheless, leasing was basic to the urban land provisions until the 1830s.

Urban leases were typically for either 14 or 21 years and usually in allotments less than an acre. During the 1810s, the size of urban leases outside Sydney were occasionally much larger reflecting the confusion of urban and rural land use. The leases were renewable and transferable, could be cancelled or surrendered. In all respects, urban leases followed British market practice where large land ownership, subdivision, leasing and subleasing were common. In Australia, the 'large' landowner was the Crown. Similarly, as early grants were absorbed into urban areas, they too could be subdivided and either sold in segments or leased. Until the 1830s, it appears that leasing or subleasing was the dominant basis of urban land transactions.

So far as direct government leasing was concerned, annual small rents were nominally charged. But they were frequently requited by the absorption by private settlers of additional convicts and, in any event, were often neither demanded nor paid. A similar dereliction of market behaviour occurred between government grantees and the government but not between the lessees/grantees and sublessees. A true market behaviour emerged within the private sector rather than between government and individuals. Leasing was abandoned in the early 1830s and replaced by sale, as were most land transfers from government, officially. The change did not affect grantees. It is unclear whether government shared in the capital gains in urban areas as lessees were required to purchase or surrender leases. Public accounts do not reveal the outcome and the dating of leases spread over time obscure any indication of special increases in public revenues. Obscurity also follows from the simultaneous shift in NSW to the sale of rural lands, producing from that source a sharp increase in the land revenues of government in the 1830s (see table 12.3).

If leasing was the basis of the urban land market, it was not until 1848 that a similar approach became dominant in respect of rural lands. In 1839, a provisional move towards this occurred in NSW when a combination of occupation licenses and poll tax on sheep was made. In the interval, a series of adaptations occurred, partly due to colonial interests, partly from special British pressures. The path to this outcome was a tortuous one. In essence, the outcome was a recognition of government failure of control.

As table 12.3 (p.129) relating to NSW shows, grants of Crown lands to private individuals were long-established procedures. There was little option so long as grants to ex-convicts were adopted — the mass lacked the resources to purchase significant areas. Before 1810, privatised officials were able to protect their interests and purses in the same way. Between 1810 and 1820 in NSW, the granting procedure became a matter of rationing allocations and limiting the geographical spread of settlements. In Van Diemen's Land from the late 1820s constraints in granting land were thrown to the winds with a massive series of Crown land grants made by the governor (see table 12.4, p.130). As such, rationing by grants did more than reflect government acceptance of the ex-convict nature of the settlements. It also acknowledged the limited administrative personnel available to control a spatially

Table 12.3: NSW Land Grants, Urban Leases and Sales

	Cumberland		Hinterland		Total NSW		Sydney	NSW
	Grants Number	Grants Acres	Grants Number	Grants Acres	Grants Number	Grants Acres	Leases Acres	Sales Acres
Pre-1810	1 521	270 028	47	12 955	1 568	282 983	248.79	
1810	6	4 424	0	0	6	4 424	7.96	
1811	6	4 350	0	0	6	4 350	0	
1812	96	17 556	0	10	96	17 566	5.26	
1813	5	8 060	2	400	7	8 460	0	
1814	3	1 645	0	0	3	1 645	3.13	
1815	55	16 852	0	0	55	16 852	1.33	
1816	203	43 522	12	1 340	215	44 862	0.26	
1817	47	17 090	7	7 506	54	24 596	2.97	
1818	130	33 574	0	0	130	33 574	0.44	
1819	234	37 305	0	0	234	37 305	2.99	
1820	3	990	30	2 720	33	3 710	0.31	
1821	90	14 885	9	12 650	99	27 535	0.56	
1822	16	2 601	151	34 621	167	37 222	0	
1823	218	32 805	350	166 489	568	199 294	58.55	
1824	0	0	0	0	0	0	0	
1825	1	185	5	15 900	6	16 085	0	
1826	2	22	0	0	2	22	0.41	
1827	0	0	2	2 800	2	2 800	0.48	
1828	0	0	1	1 000	1	1 000	0.16	
1829	1	1 000	5	6 865	6	7 865	1.41	
1830	31	5 104	7	77 380	38	82 484	0	
1831	226	23 967	20	31 124	246	55 091	0	
1832	3	15	0	0	3	15	0	20 860
1833	48	6 347	108	63 770	156	70 117	0.2	29 001
1834	30	1 995	92	82 413	122	84 408	0	91 389
1835	43	4 632	202	155 525	245	160 157	0	271 947
1836	16	1 524	81	45 509	97	47 033	0	389 546
1837	29	3 881	209	196 417	238	200 298	0	370 376
1838	43	4 547	195	175 382	238	179 929	0	316 160
1839	53	4 597	365	305 653	418	310 250	0	271 610
1840	52	5 472	361	220 270	413	225 742	0	189 787

Note: Grants exclude major grants determined in Britain.
Source: Returns of the Colony.

expanding society and economy. After 1820, grants were increasingly directed to persons ostensibly with the capital resources to develop land. This implied greater allocations to free migrants to whom a zero land price was designed as an attraction.

Formally, grants required land use development and the payment of quit rents. Little effective control in either respect was applied and many grants were transferred in the private market without development, while quit rents went frequently unpaid. This public failure to collect rents was most prominent in Van Diemen's Land. Nor did grantees confine their beneficial use to areas granted, and during the 1810s and later years they moved onto 'common' lands, so-declared, and onto other vacant land. The process of squatting began at a very early stage. Grants were a convenient method of transfer from the public to the private sector so long as the object of settlements was the reformation of time-expired convicts. Small allocations, administrative oversight and relatively concentrated settlement were implied.

Table 12.4: Van Diemen's Land Land Grants and Sales

	Grants Number	Grants Acres	Sales Acres
1824	72	43 420	0
1825	279	111 939	0
1826	109	60 270	0
1827	83	77 186	0
1828	190	164 777	49 425
1829	215	207 620	20 870
1830	156	108 009	0
1831	238	205 807	31 699
1832	35	33 242	75 495
1833	24	23 500	17 351
1834	7	8 820	23
1835	24	8 660	47 048
1836	16	8 054	25 918
1837	43	22 030	21 729
1838	70	44 632	19 971
1839	32	15 036	42 452
1840	22	9 683	88 789

Source: Returns of the Colony.

Unfortunately for officialdom, the theory did not work. In private hands, many small grants were sold and engrossment to what were, in Australian conditions, effective land parcels was achieved within the private sector.

In the late 1810s and increasingly thereafter, the focus of grants shifted to provide attractions to free immigrants with capital. It is relevant that this policy shift did not await the Bigge Report and the British government adoption of a free pastoral prospect for Australia in the 1820s. Certainly after 1821, grants were increasingly allocated to persons with capital or claiming to possess capital. Size of grants was supposed to be proportioned to the capital of immigrants and their ability to absorb convict labour. There was still little recognition that interior mainland Australia required large land parcels for effective British exploitation — official policy moved, to accord with physical reality. But, in NSW at least, the efforts to relate grant size *with precision* to available capital were largely a failure. Free immigrants often provided grossly exaggerated statements of capital (sometimes including expenditure on fares to Australia as part of 'capital') and were often unable to sustain their projects. The British government itself flirted with two chartered companies, the Australian Agricultural Company and the Van Diemen's Land Company, in the first half of the 1820s, with somewhat more but still slow success, making large direct Crown grants (not in the tables above). Some private individuals were often given direct imperial grants in Australia in exchange for major public service to the Crown.

Interest in free immigrants and free pastoral development, partly for the benefit of the British textile industry and partly to achieve a cheap assignment of convicts, even led in the 1820s to attempts at the sale of rural lands. These were very limited in the 1820s in NSW though more successful in Van Diemen's Land. Already, the process of mainland squatting was in the process of superseding grants let alone sales and pastoral success depended more on having learned by doing than having possessed capital. Offered at auction with no reserve price, the small volumes of land sales gave little incentive to local NSW officials to sustain the process.

The experience was different in Van Diemen's Land. Here, for British settlers or investors, the physical conditions were much more akin to those of Britain. Moreover, in Van Diemen's Land, established individuals were active in presenting themselves as investment advisers to prospective investors, migrants or retirees in Britain and throughout the Empire, leading to substantial land sales by government side by side with grants. A zero price and an actual, if low, price for land could coexist given a differentiation in information available to residents as against nonresident private individuals. Distance was not a tyrant but a fairy godmother to selected Van Demonians.

A variety of circumstances helped to extend the attempts to dispose of public lands by sale in the 1830s. The disastrous failure in an immediate sense of the Swan River settlement (based on the concept of free migration with no convicts and on massive grants) provided one line of argument against both the grant system and cheap public land sales. This was part of the case developed by Wakefield for a substantial fixed price for public land disposal. Wakefield probably misinterpreted Western Australia's position where grandiose land allocations to original settlers forced newcomers into uneconomic locations. Another element against grants and cheap land sales was the awareness in Britain, by then, of the substantial pastoral prospects in Australia, the stirrings of which had prompted the company chartering in the early 1820s. In addition, in the beginning of the 1830s, the occupation of the hinterland in south-eastern Australia was well underway. Australia had indeed become attractive to British investors and free immigrants with capital.

While local occupation was essentially illegal, squatting was in full flight in the 1830s. It had extended far beyond lines drawn legally as 'settled counties' in the late 1820s, as a last ditch effort by local officials to retain an administrable area. For outsiders, dealing with government, options to purchase were confined to these delimited areas. Government in Australia could briefly exploit the monopoly advantage of land scarcity in the settled counties which existed by now. Lands were offered for sale now by auction with reserve prices. For Wakefield, grossly misreading the squatting process, the reserve price was too low. His argument was essentially that a low reserve price made land ownership too accessible to prospective wage-earners, raising wages and restraining enterprise. His domestic British objective was to achieve land sales and revenues to fund pauper immigration thereby providing a sustained source of labour for colonial expansion, remove paupers from temptations to criminality and, at the same time, free Britain of part of its poor relief problem.

Wakefield's arguments had impact in both Australia and Britain. They prompted, in Australia, a decade of efforts at public land sales and the use of part of the revenues for pauper immigration. In Britain, they sparked the project for the establishment of South Australia in 1836 as a free corporate Crown colony, exploiting land sales and the attraction of free migrants with capital.

Though land sales were substantial during most of the 1830s, the areas involved were overwhelmed by the scale of squatting. Once again, those with local understanding, aware, if only generally, of the appropriate locations for pastoral development and of the administrative impotence of the government, simply moved in to occupy land at zero cost. There was one obstacle in doing so. Squatting did not achieve a legal transfer to the private sector. No legal land market could be built on this process. For private sector transactions to develop, some degree of recognition of occupancy, capable of transfer, was necessary. This applied not only beyond settlement limits but also beyond grant or purchase areas within the settled counties. Wakefield proposed that squatters should be treated like the squatters with which he was familiar in Wales — shot!

The local officials temporised with the solutions. Official administrative presence was established at Port Phillip. In 1839, certificates to occupy were accorded the squatters, combined with a poll tax on sheep. The tax payments in 1839 and 1840 represented a small fraction of the total herds. It was not until 1848 in NSW that leases, capable of being incorporated in mortgage provisions and transferred in a private market system, were generally adopted. This became the dominant legal instrument for very large parts of the Australian hinterland.

Goods Markets, Currency, Credit and Banking

It is convenient to deal with these various issues together. Up to 1810, the Commissariat was a dominant government store, with functions of buying imports and local output and of selling imports, British official supplies and local output together with the issue of rations. In the process, the Commissariat combined extensive barter transactions with the issue of store notes as a form of local currency and provided credit to buyers. It also delivered, through the ability to write Treasury bills chargeable to the British government, vital foreign exchange. The combination of all these functions in one institution and the experiments in all areas that it conducted after 1810 makes it difficult to separate the issues to be discussed. Moreover, as the settlements extended, subsidiary Commissariats were established so that from Moreton Bay to Hobart, the Commissariat became, in effect, a massive 'nationwide chain store', importer and bank.

However, it needs to be appreciated at the outset that other goods transactions, other currencies, and other credit instruments existed before (and after) 1810. Private transactions and institutions expanded side by side with the Commissariat particularly after 1810. By 1830, the Commissariat's role was dwindling rapidly in NSW and was insignificant by 1840; it continued to have an important place in Van Diemen's Land until after 1840 and a Commissariat was later introduced into the Swan River settlement to cope with the peculiar problems of that free settlement. Most of the changes that occurred in the functioning of the Commissariat and the emergence of sophisticated goods transactions and in banking stemmed from NSW and it is appropriate to focus primarily on that colony.

As at 1810, the settlement operated through barter (predominantly) and a miscellany of Commissariat store notes, personal notes and a mixture of currencies, British, Indian, Spanish etc. Within this miscellany, sterling was frequently employed as a unit of account despite its limited availability as a medium of exchange. The British government saw little reason for supplying a penal settlement with sterling currency for internal or external transactions and the very limited ability to earn foreign exchange meant that any currencies acquired soon shifted abroad. The basic source of foreign exchange was in the form of Treasury bills and bills from the military. Store notes could be aggregated and converted into Treasury bills but under the cabal before Macquarie and in Macquarie's first few years, this convertibility was severely limited. The settlement was driven further back into barter. For a few years after 1810, the Commissariat became, as a purchasing and selling agency, more prominent than it had been previously.

In fact, behind this retrogression, changes were underway in several directions towards a money economy that were perhaps, as S.J. Butlin (1953) has proposed, the most important indication of the growth of a market-oriented capitalistic economy particularly during 1810–20. These changes were contained in a series of public and private endeavours within the settlement. One effort was a local official attempt to equip the settlement with a sterling currency, an attempt that failed because of the monetary constraints on Britain during the later phases of the Napoleonic Wars. In the second effort in terms of currency, the local residents fell back on a currency that they had earlier prized and was common in many colonial areas, the Spanish dollar. Large-scale Commissariat and private imports of Spanish dollars were made during the 1810s and first half of the 1820s. Efforts extended to attempting to establish these dollars, revalued, cut into segments, and with valuations dependent on the transactions involved, as a medium of exchange and a unit of account. This was a highly unsatisfactory outcome that was constrained by the complexity of valuation systems and the tendency for currencies to leak abroad.

In the meantime, two divergent attempts were made to introduce different mediums of exchange. One was in a joint public and private effort in 1817 to establish the Bank of New South Wales with a local charter that, had it been legal, assured the principle of limited liability for the banking entrepreneurs and of long-term finance. In fact, most long-term funding had to await the influx of migrants with capital or the interest of absentee investors. Strongly supported by the governor (and, indeed, a favoured project of his from the time of his arrival), it was formally established in Sydney by a group of some 15 private individuals. Local public intervention was always prominent in the bank, including interest-free deposits of colonial revenue balances with the bank and the *de facto* disregard of the British government's refusal to accept the local charter. The bank was able to continue into the 1820s as if it had limited liability. It served a useful function in providing a mechanism for credit and note and coin distribution. Most importantly perhaps, it signalled the opportunity to others to follow suit in the 1820s and 1830s.

Public action is often a mix of inconsistencies. This is most obviously the case in the organisation of a banking system and a conversion of the goods market to a monetary system. As plans for the bank proceeded, Commissaries successively attempted to compete with the bank by extending the Commissariats in both NSW and Van Diemen's Land into *de facto* 'privatised public' banks. In this case, three Commissaries claiming British authority (which they probably lacked) instituted the practice of issuing their own personal notes in payment for goods purchased locally by the Commissariats in both NSW and Van Diemen's Land. These notes, in fact, became far more important for local currency purposes than the instruments issued by the Bank of New South Wales up to 1820. They were eventually stopped by the beginning of the 1820s by the governors and the notes withdrawn. In their place followed an experiment with the very large-scale importation of Spanish dollars and a concerted effort during 1821–5 to establish the Spanish dollar in the settlements. None of these attempts was sufficient to supplant barter activities. Indeed, the growth of the private sector between 1810 and 1825 was such (given the limitations on currency supplies and the expanding interchange between individuals rather than with the Commissariats) as to encourage widespread barter activity.

These varied attempts occurred against a background of limited export capability, the continued willingness of the British government to subsidise the settlements with supplies and rights to draw Treasury bills and the slowly emerging recognition of the growing private sector in both NSW and Van Diemen's Land. The recognition, by Britain, of the private pastoral and agricultural prospects of the formerly penal settlements was accompanied by a growing British reluctance from the beginning of the 1820s to sustain its level of subsidy and the volume of Treasury bills issued from the colonies. Though that reluctance by Britain meant pressure on the colonies to provide a local system of public financing, it also imposed the need to regularise the currency system and to allow the acquisition of sterling.

Large shipments of sterling currency were initiated in the second half of the 1820s and for several years a dual dollar–sterling system existed. Bad money may drive out good in a wholly private enterprise system. It certainly does not necessarily do so with strong public intervention. The Commissariat was able to assemble much of the miscellaneous dollar currency and substitute it for Treasury bills in purchasing imports during the second half of the 1820s, so that dollars moved rapidly out of the colonies. By the early 1830s, Australia was established as part of the sterling area. By then, too, export earnings were growing rapidly and substantial private capital inflow was occurring. These, with the growth of a more complex banking structure, moved the colonies rapidly into the common use of money, based on sterling.

Banking institutions spread throughout the Australian colonies throughout the 1820s, partly as colonially formed banks, partly as London-based and British chartered banks. A NSW Savings bank in 1819 was followed by the Bank of Australasia in that colony in 1827. Van Diemen's Land saw something of a proliferation between 1824 and 1830 with the Bank of Van Diemen's Land, the Derwent Bank, the Cornwall Bank and the Commercial Bank of Tasmania, followed in the 1830s by two savings banks and the Tamar Bank. This Van Diemen's Land development reflected a highly entrepreneurial spirit encouraging investment in that colony. The Bank of Australasia was perhaps the primary British-based bank operating widely in Australia and playing a special role in the free colonies of Western and South Australia. Banks do not seem to have been envisaged in either of these free colonies in the initial plans and, indeed, a Commissariat was set up in Western Australia in 1831 as a partial substitute until the Bank of Australasia absorbed the Bank of Western Australia established in 1837. In Adelaide, the Bank of South Australia was operating, despite its omission in original plans, in 1837, a year after the first settlement.

By the 1830s, the basic conditions of operating a money economy were established. Barter activity persisted on the fringes of settlement by 1840 but basically the economies functioned as fully established monetised systems. Only in Van Diemen's Land was there still an essentially archaic Commissariat concerned with ration provisions to publicly employed convicts.

Entry into Non-Rural Business

While conditions of access to rural lands indicated the essentially failed attempts by government to determine entry into rural enterprise and the growth of banking was a major instrument facilitating that entry, no comparable controls were exercised over the setting up of urban enterprise. By 1810, Sydney was a thriving urban centre, composed of a large variety of trades and manufactures, import and retail enterprises. This development followed from the combination of British subsidy, the freeing of convicts and the exploitation of their skills to meet local demands.

Nevertheless, there were essentially market-like controls that had been established by 1810 and extended thereafter. Licensing of businesses had been established by the end of the 18th century. Nominal licenses were sometimes provided as substantial restrictions on entry though as restrictive charges were imposed the response appears generally to have been illegal or underground operations — the development of 'black' markets. In some cases such as the auctioning of ships' cargoes, attempts were made to establish monopolies. Occasional repetition of monopoly efforts were made in the 1810s in such cases as the granting of monopoly rights to import spirits as a means of financing Sydney Hospital. Neither this nor other efforts at monopoly were effective. As Sydney's population and skills expanded, business was able to respond to demand conditions to satisfy local tastes with minimal constraints. In a few instances, the government attempted to supply manufacturing projects where substantial capital was needed but these dwindled rapidly during the 1810s.

One constraint of some formal significance persisted until 1819. This was the East India Company's monopoly of trade in the Pacific and Indian Oceans and with that monopoly, limitation of shipbuilding in the settlements. Between 1813 and 1819, that monopoly was officially eroded and with it the limitation of the size of ships built in Australia. In practice, however, the company's monopoly had limited direct influence though it did indirectly channel behaviour in important ways particularly during 1810–20. Shipbuilding and repairing were stimulated too strongly by the sealing trade, and the boom in sealing activity that reached its peak before 1810 had already made the company's attempt at control of limited significance to colonial activity. After 1810, the demands for coastal trade and for participation in whaling generated a strong colonial encouragement of shipbuilding. The elimination of the company's monopoly was followed by the increasing size of ships built in the colonies, with size rising (a rare achievement) to as high as 600 tons in the 1830s in Van Diemen's Land. At the same time, the rising volume of convicts arriving meant increasing ship arrivals and departures. This, more than anything else, loosened the constraints on colonial export and import activity.

If the colonists were not deeply constrained directly by the Company's monopoly, British ships arriving in Australia were. One of the earliest consequences of the erosion of the company's monopoly followed in 1813, when British ships were officially allowed, for the first time, to visit Van Diemen's Land en route to Sydney and to collect cargo from Van Diemen's Land for delivery in Sydney. This was far from being a minor change. Combined with the growth of colonial shipping, the ability to move cargoes around the whole south-eastern Australian coast was greatly simplified. Even where relatively small numbers of British ships were involved, their size allowed a greater two-way flow between NSW and Van Diemen's Land. Interregional mobility was enhanced, providing for the growth of interregional trade, a growth that was significant in allowing Van Diemen's Land to become a large supplier of primary products to Sydney and subsequently to Port Phillip and Adelaide, and to cease to rely on Sydney as an outlet for overseas goods shipments. The relaxation of the East India Company constraint also allowed whalers, as they extended across southern Australia to the west, to provide additional interregional transport facilities. These whalers could visit Australian ports legally for the purposes of provisioning and repairs. A constraint was lifted to allow the enlargement of the local market, with regional interchange, exploiting the sea rather than land for this market extension. Coupled with that widening of the market was the opportunity for specialisation and the development of specific businesses, in trade, industry and primary production.

Some General Implications

By 1840, the Australian economies were still far from providing the conditions for 'perfect markets'. But between 1810 and 1840, institutions, practices, policies and legal arrangements, largely copied or adapted from Britain were being set up to overcome the unfree labour foundations and external administrative controls. A uniform monetary system was in place based on sterling exchange — a gold standard without gold. Specialised commercial and financial institutions were well-established by 1840, allowing for note issues, deposits and advances. British contract law and systems of titles and judicial procedures were established, even though some judicial penalties were apposite only to unfree conditions. No consideration was given to accommodating special Aboriginal legal conditions. Weights and measures were drawn directly from Britain allowing identification of contract terms and exchange arrangements.

Even in areas of convict rights, extensive adaptations of conditions of servitude had allowed convicts a great deal of flexibility in their working conditions and, within at least a substantial margin of their time, able to work for private gain. Moreover, the rapid increase in the proportion of freed and free persons made convict conditions progressively less relevant to the entire labour market. Perhaps it was primarily in relation to land that the preconditions for an effective market behaviour was least fully developed. Here, within the conditions of recognised settled areas, there remained limitations on the ability to mortgage lands and beyond settled limits to acquire transferable title. But even in the latter case, devices had been established by 1838 at least to establish rights to occupy.

Throughout much of this evolution, changes were made by a combination of decisions by authority and by actions by private individuals. The colonies at times ignored British efforts to control where it suited and individuals disregarded colonial authority where ways could be found to defeat constraints.

Many of the changes were not put in place by edicts. Those that were had to be formally recognised, but the initiatives towards them came from the private sector. The different systems of arrangements became progressively consistent with each other and the environment of activity in which they operated. What is vital to understand, however, is that these microdevelopments took several decades to establish and were far from complete by 1840. Structural adjustment, in this sense, takes a very long time. Several pieces had to fall into place before colonists could effectively respond to appropriate market signals. Thus they could exploit natural resources and provide business arrangements for the free and freed, and incentives to convicts, but they could not achieve a substantial export response until constraints on ship movement were removed and until sufficient ship arrivals provided the flexibility to deliver and remove cargoes. However, the structural jigsaw was moving quite rapidly into place in the year or so immediately before 1820 and formal and informal development beyond then allowed the Australian economy(ies) to achieve a relatively efficient exploitation of the human capital delivered from Britain and to combine them with local resources.

13

STRUCTURAL ADJUSTMENT AND DEVELOPMENT: 1810–40

Economists and economic historians tend to focus on the question: How well did an economy perform? In other words, how rapidly and consistently did it perform in terms of rates of growth and stability of real product or consumption per head or per unit of factor input. By contrast, in this chapter, we are concerned with the general question of how and why the Australian colonial economies took the shape that they did in terms of the composition of output and the related allocation of resources.

In doing so, it should be appreciated that right up to 1840, the economies had some special peculiarities. This was not simply convictism. Rather, the most important issues arise from the fact that they were very open economies in terms of factor inflows and, for a long time, relatively closed economies in terms of goods flows. Progressively, they became more open in all respects as export and import capability developed. But even by 1840, they were still very isolated despite improving ocean transport links. There is no very simple application of the theory of international trade to be made even though international trade became increasingly relevant. While export potential is important, so too is the response to four basic domestic conditions — the character of natural resource endowment that encouraged specialised natural resource development rather than self-sufficient activity, the demand for a wide range of goods in conditions of isolation, the presence of British skills and relatively high standards of per capita expenditures thanks to external public and private capital.

These were not static conditions. On the contrary, we are dealing with a formative process in which change is a basic circumstance. By 1840, one might claim that the essential foundations of the 'second' (i.e. the colonial) Australian economy had been laid. There were still many developments to follow, not least of which was the enormous stimulus to expansion that occurred with the discovery of gold in 1851. But the broad patterns based on Australian natural resource conditions and Australian isolation had been laid down by 1840. Moreover, this was achieved over three decades at neck-breaking speed. Expansion ended in a major depression. This is examined in the following chapter.

The story of developing activity of the 'second' economy can be told in a variety of ways. This depends partly on how one chooses to cut the colonial cake either for reasons of history, theory or statistics or simply from pedagogical convenience.

At the most general level, there is, firstly, the division between public and private activity. In this section, we are not concerned with the development of private market procedures and institutions versus control and regulation already discussed but with the dimension and composition of activity. Inevitably, however, some of the issues of market operations enter. For present purposes, attention is concentrated on the circumstances that led, after 1810, to the progressive slowing of public sector expansion, with more general and summary discussion of *relative* stagnation that derived from the speed of expansion of the private sector. It is important to appreciate that, even with the disappearance of convictism in NSW by the early 1840s, the 'size' of the public sector did not decline absolutely. Moreover, convictism was not the sole inducement to strong early government. Even in the supposedly private enterprise colonies, an early centralisation in the public sector occurred.

Once we dispose of the public sector, there is a pedagogic choice to be made. We can move to the next most general question, the conditions of development of external economic activity versus domestic activity. However, there is a case for taking up one aspect of the very general rural–urban division of the economy and considering some of the factors that promoted and sustained urban concentration. In part, this is how Australian history began, with port and town concentrations, and it is, perhaps, more natural to follow the historical course even though this intrudes in part on, but helps us to understand, questions of import replacement and export development.

This intrusion provides a natural progression to the discussion of import replacement activity and of the local production of 'non-tradeable' goods. In combination, the outline of urban development and of non-export production preceding the story of the growth of trade may help to avoid an appearance of restoring export staples and export-led growth as the theoretical basis for explaining early economic development.

The following part of this chapter does, however, move to this more conventional theme, concentrating on maritime and pastoral exports and the local servicing of the increasing numbers of visiting ships. As will emerge, the explanation of maritime and pastoral exports is far from being merely one of achieving supply to distant markets and/or of changing external demands. Interactions between domestic and external conditions are crucial. It turns out that we really have to discuss much of the domestic economy and export development together in order to understand the stimulants to and retardants of exports. In doing so, one should appreciate that development was not merely a stable response. But questions of general instability are left to the next chapter.

Structure and Structural Shange: Statistical Summary

A brief and highly summarised statistical picture of the output structure of the economies of NSW and Van Diemen's Land may help to set some of the contours of activity and economic change to be discussed. This outline derives from estimates of gross domestic product. One should not place too much reliance on the precision of these estimates but they do give an impression that helps to focus attention and to tie together the subsequent discussion. Components of gross domestic product are not the only indicators of economic structure but they do show the final purposes to which factors are allocated.

In principle, one might present these components in either current or constant price terms. Because allocative decisions are made on the basis of current relative prices (whether of goods and services or of assets), the statistics here are given in current prices. In practice, the relative size and changes in the component parts of the two economies do not alter significantly when constant prices are used. The logic of decision making points to a preference for current measures.

The underlying estimates of gross domestic product are subdivided into seven separate groups. For the purposes of this chapter, these have been collapsed into four. The prime object is to attempt to delineate the essentially 'natural resource' and predominantly 'urban' parts of the private sector. These are not finely drawn divisions and this matter is discussed later in the chapter. In the 'natural resource' activities, only two divisions are shown. The pastoral industry is separated from agriculture and maritime activities which are grouped into a 'non-pastoral' segment. Later in the chapter, agriculture and maritime activities are dealt with separately.

The immediate reason for this subdivision is to bring out, from the beginning, the relative significance of the pastoral industry, conventionally regarded as the leading industry on the mainland. So far as 'urban' activities go, manufacturing, commerce, services and rents are lumped together. Clearly some of these accrue in 'rural' locations but these products were dominantly urban. Set beside the private sector and deliberately represented graphically with this 'urban' complex is the product of the public sector. This, too, was dominantly urban though some infrastructure, in particular, as well as a limited amount of farming, was delivered by the public sector in non-urban conditions. It will be clear that there is no intention to suggest precision but rather a broad-brush picture.

There is another question to be raised before moving to the substance of the statistics and graphs. This is the incorporation in or exclusion from pastoral product of the value of the natural increase in livestock. In my book, *Australian Domestic Product, Investment and Foreign Borrowing 1861–1938/39*, I included a component for the imputed value of livestock increase (sheep and cattle only) because ample data were available on both numbers and relevant prices. Twentieth-century official social accounts omit this item. In an economy in which pastoral activity is important, this omission is indefensible. The original estimates of Australian gross domestic product between 1788 and 1860 also left out this item because virtually no livestock numbers are available for NSW between 1823 and 1843 and those before 1823 are suspect. But it does not require much stretch of the imagination to appreciate that, in the two economies with which we are concerned where sheep numbers grew to some 15 millions and cattle to approximately 2.25 millions by 1850, we are dealing with a major source of output.

We have official numbers substantially throughout for Van Diemen's Land (*Statistics of Van Diemen's Land*) and Hartwell (1954) provides enough prices for an approximate estimate. The gap in NSW numbers can be filled in only by somewhat heroic measures, with some slightly more secure methods of deriving appropriate prices. Abbott (1971) attempted a reconstruction of NSW sheep numbers derived

Table 13.1: Sectoral Shares of Gross Domestic Product, New South Wales and Van Diemen's Land, 1810–50 (percentage shares of GDP, including livestock accumulation)

| | New South Wales | | | | | Van Diemen's Land | | | | |
| | Non- | | Total | Other(a) | | Non- | | Total | Other(a) | |
Year	Pastoral	Pastoral	Primary	Private	Public	Pastoral	Pastoral	Primary	Private	Public
1810	46.5	18.6	65.1	24.7	10.2	14.0	30.1	44.1	31.8	24.1
1811	43.0	15.5	58.5	28.7	12.8	15.2	33.0	48.2	31.5	20.3
1812	37.3	23.4	60.7	26.7	12.6	15.6	28.5	44.1	33.3	22.6
1813	34.9	24.0	58.9	27.7	13.4	18.1	26.9	45.0	34.2	20.8
1814	30.7	25.6	56.3	30.0	13.6	21.5	23.3	44.7	36.8	18.5
1815	37.2	20.5	57.7	30.2	12.1	24.4	22.4	46.8	36.3	17.0
1816	27.5	22.9	50.4	35.6	14.0	25.8	21.9	47.7	33.1	19.1
1817	30.8	22.1	53.0	32.7	14.3	18.6	39.8	58.4	30.9	10.7
1818	30.6	23.5	54.0	32.3	13.6	24.3	30.8	55.1	33.6	11.3
1819	32.4	25.5	57.9	28.3	13.9	23.1	38.5	61.5	30.7	7.7
1820	31.7	27.0	58.7	28.0	13.3	25.8	27.2	52.9	38.2	8.9
1821	38.5	22.8	61.3	27.5	11.2	31.8	25.7	57.5	35.4	7.1
1822	36.5	22.8	59.3	30.8	9.9	31.5	31.6	63.2	30.9	5.9
1823	35.0	22.1	57.1	32.7	10.2	26.2	31.2	57.4	35.6	7.0
1824	33.3	23.3	56.6	33.0	10.4	24.8	31.2	56.0	38.0	6.0
1825	30.7	27.7	58.4	32.2	9.4	25.1	29.7	54.8	39.6	5.6
1826	32.0	23.4	55.4	34.7	9.9	25.7	29.7	55.3	39.3	5.3
1827	30.6	22.3	52.9	36.3	10.8	31.8	23.3	55.0	40.3	4.6
1828	29.0	25.2	54.2	37.6	8.1	29.8	26.8	56.6	38.9	4.4
1829	26.9	21.1	48.0	42.7	9.2	22.9	33.7	56.5	39.4	4.1
1830	23.8	19.9	43.8	47.4	8.8	35.3	11.3	46.6	48.3	5.1
1831	22.4	21.6	44.0	47.7	8.3	31.6	19.6	51.2	44.3	4.5
1832	21.3	17.1	38.4	53.0	8.5	28.3	20.0	48.3	47.1	4.6
1833	22.5	20.6	43.1	49.5	7.4	30.1	14.6	44.6	50.4	5.0
1834	27.0	30.6	57.6	37.0	5.4	25.5	19.7	45.2	50.0	4.8
1835	33.2	33.0	66.2	29.4	4.4	28.8	22.2	51.0	45.1	3.9
1836	31.2	25.1	56.3	38.2	5.5	26.7	25.3	52.0	43.1	4.9
1837	20.2	30.3	50.6	43.6	5.8	31.9	23.6	55.6	40.1	4.3
1838	19.5	28.7	48.2	45.8	6.0	26.4	31.2	57.5	38.2	4.3
1839	23.9	27.8	51.6	43.2	5.1	46.0	0.6	46.6	48.0	5.3
1840	26.8	24.9	51.7	43.3	5.0	33.5	27.9	61.4	35.3	3.3
1841	19.5	23.7	43.2	50.8	6.0	33.8	21.7	55.4	40.6	4.0
1842	14.8	25.7	40.5	53.2	6.2	20.6	24.3	44.9	50.5	4.6
1843	14.2	24.3	38.4	55.6	6.0	21.3	25.3	46.7	47.5	5.9
1844	9.3	28.2	37.5	57.0	5.6	27.5	5.6	33.1	57.8	9.1
1845	11.9	27.6	39.5	55.6	4.8	25.4	21.0	46.4	47.6	6.1
1846	13.8	27.6	41.4	54.5	4.1	34.9	18.9	53.8	41.8	4.4
1847	10.0	28.0	38.0	57.8	4.1	27.4	31.2	58.5	37.2	4.2
1848	13.7	30.2	43.9	52.6	3.5	35.3	13.8	49.1	46.1	4.9
1849	13.4	19.1	32.5	63.5	4.0	31.8	16.6	48.4	45.9	5.7
1850	17.7	19.6	37.3	59.2	3.4	29.8	20.6	50.4	44.9	4.7

Note: (a) Comprises manufacturing, commerce, services and rent.

from export volumes. An alternative procedure is adopted here by projecting forward from 1815 (Fletcher, 1976) and backwards from 1843 (*Returns of the Colony, 1841–44*) using assumed lambing/calving rates and death/culling rates for both sheep and cattle. These projections are subject to adjustments in periods of known climatic stress. The two initial projections almost conform when one lowers the lambing/calving rate during 1815–28 and increases it for the period 1828–43. This is consistent with the difficulties confronting the pastoral industry while confined primarily to the coast. Price series are based on Hunter Valley auction prices for small unit flocks (not individual animals) during the 1830s and 1840s (Australian Agricultural Company manuscript records) and extrapolated back to 1810 on the basis of meat and wool prices.

By no stretch of the imagination could the result be regarded as very accurate. Accordingly, the figures which follow show results for the pastoral industry including and excluding livestock increase. What is clear is that, even allowing for very large errors, livestock accumulation was a major factor in the pastoral industry. For individual pastoralists, stock increases could be sold within the industry to new entrants or to those seeking to expand beyond the limits of natural increase. To this extent, they represented cash incentives. For the industry as a whole, these were, of course, merely inter-industry transactions. While the industry was expanding rapidly, natural increase was an important benefit. In times of contraction, high rates of natural increase exacerbated problems. Because of its manifest importance, whatever the true figures, table 13.1, showing shares in industry subdivisions as a whole, includes the estimated stock increases.

Summary Statistics

Shares are somewhat tricky to interpret. Only the most marked features of table 13.1 (p. 140) deserve comment. It will be seen that the public sector in both colonies declined greatly relative to the private sector, in NSW halving in relative importance between 1810 and 1840 and in Van Diemen's Land falling to about one-eighth its 1810 level by 1840. It is important to remember that this is only a product measure and does not necessarily indicate the regulatory significance of government. Even so, the vigour of private expansion in both cases is well displayed and it does not seem plausible to claim, as did Hartwell (1954), that Van Diemen's Land remained essentially a government enterprise in 1840.

By contrast, in trend terms, the conglomerate of activities, treated here as predominantly urban, trended upwards from between 25 to 30 per cent in the two colonies in 1810, occasionally rising to more than 50 per cent in both colonies and generally well in excess of 40 per cent of total economic activity in the late 1830s. While they were not wholly consistent, these activities provided a powerful upward thrust in the expansion of both economies. In other words, they represented important restructuring influences not necessarily dependent on natural resource use. On the other hand, as might be expected, natural resource activity tended generally, though not invariably, to be the major part of both economies. This majority was, however, neither overwhelming nor securely sustained. Indeed, for a few years, they accounted for less than half of total gross domestic product. Generally speaking, they ran between 50 and 60 per cent — very substantial, but clearly not dominant *even though livestock increase is included*. Within the 'natural resource' industries, pastoral activity, including livestock, was generally not the major contributor. It is possible that extensive settlement, in signifying the acquisition of real estate and in encouraging private capital inflow, provided a special incentive to pastoral activity. But this is an asset and a financial, rather than a product, consideration.

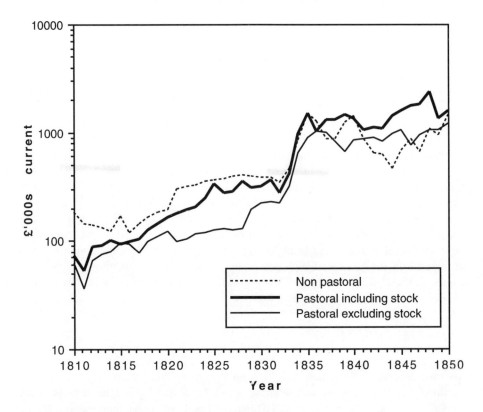

Figure 13.1: NSW Primary Sector Production, 1810–50

Figures 13.1 to 13.4 show essentially the same components in semi-logarithmic terms. In this case, however, pastoral product is shown with and without the imputed value of livestock increase so that the order of magnitude of this factor can be seen.

These figures help to show the rates of expansion as well as the levels of activity by the nominated groups. They display clearly the relative retardation of the public sector and the rapid expansion of the private components. They suggest the extremely high importance of livestock increase in affecting the level rather than the rate of pastoral expansion. In general, they reaffirm the ambivalence of pastoral activity as the prime mover in both economies and the significance of the level and speed of expansion of the 'urban' activities as roughly defined.

The Changing Size of the Public Sector
Functions of the Public Sector

As the statistical outline indicated, the public sector expanded relatively rapidly during the first decade from 1810 and then subsequently its rate of expansion slackened drastically in both NSW and Van Diemen's Land. The post-Bligh colonial governments did not represent a complete break with the pre-1810 experience, least of all in Van Diemen's Land. However, the radical reduction in the personal interest of officials in business after 1810 meant, as already suggested, a much more

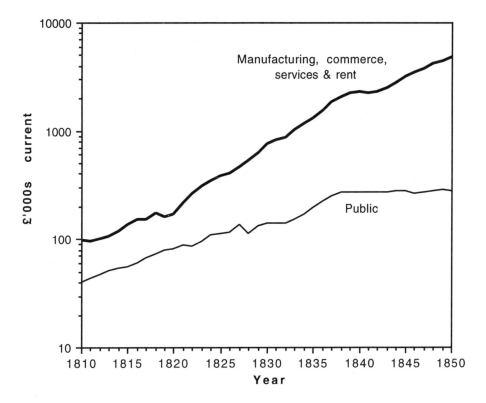

Figure 13.2: NSW Manufacturing, Commerce, Services, Rents and Public Sector Production, 1810–50

distinctive separation of public and private functions. Many of the matters to be resolved by the incoming Macquarie administration derived from action taken by the military junta that deposed Bligh, as in the case of the junta's land grants which required lengthy review. But basically, from 1810, a different tension emerged between British government and colonial governors' policies: in respect of the colonies on the one hand and, on the other, the interests of private individuals who sought, for their own benefit, to influence the actions of both the British and colonial governments.

As a public sector, interacting with private interests and with the British government, colonial governments carried out a large array of functions. They might be listed, without trying to be encyclopedic, in the following summary:

• government reception of convicts, their control and 'housing' and their allocation throughout the economy;
• similar government reception, organisation and disposition of supplies and provisions for convicts and for others entitled to rations, together with financial and marketing arrangements;
• harbour administration and control;
• government manufacturing and farming;
• public construction activity, the local development of building materials supply and the development of infrastructure;

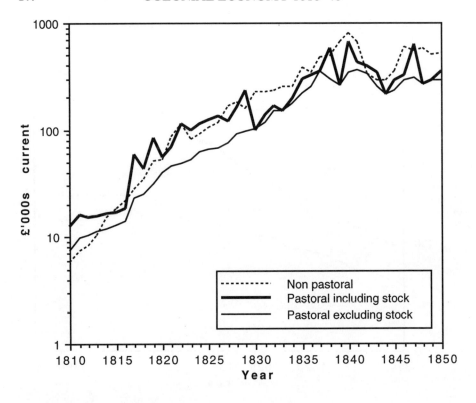

Figure 13.3: Van Diemen's Land Primary Sector Production, 1810–50

- public social provisions for the ordered development of a freed society and relations between convicts, freed (i.e. ex-convicts) and free;
- planning development of urban communities;
- administration of provisions for access to and disposal of land;
- licensing of business and professions;
- regulation of prices, wages and working conditions;
- currency management and banking;
- exploration and surveying;
- welfare and medical services;
- provision for religion and education;
- aboriginal policy;
- law and order; and
- defence.

Some of these major factors that led to the changing 'size' of the public sector are discussed below. The 'size of government' is a complicated concept. Here, it is confined to product and employment neither of which adequately indicates the regulatory significance of colonial governments. In this limited perspective, the size of the Australian public sector was affected by several conditions, three of which are basic.

First was the conventional British practice, to a large extent carried over into the colonies, of severely limiting the number of public servants. Though this limitation might work for a fully developed free society it did not for a highly regulated convict

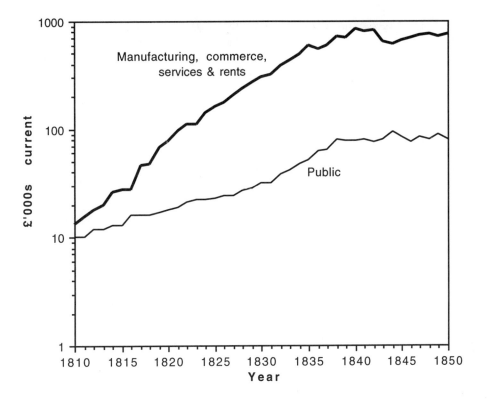

Figure 13.4: Van Diemen's Land Manufacturing, Commerce, Services, Rents and Public Sector Production, 1810–50

settlement and, to some extent, the colonies were forced to expand the numbers of public servants and hence the output of the public service.

Secondly, given the peculiar nature of the convict colonies, the supply and mode of use of convicts provided a special source of public output. Increasing inflows and their allocation to public purposes meant directed public output of convict labour in the public sector in manufacturing, farming and, above all, construction and infrastructure. Convicts were also employed within a more conventional public service in non-construction roles until the 1830s. Hence, the output of the public sector includes services provided by wage and salary earners and these varied products of convicts in addition to infrastructure.

The third condition was the extent to which colonial governments were limited to British fiscal support or could develop colonial revenues for use in colonial public services and other output. The development of a local fisc has been discussed in an earlier chapter but here it is necessary to look at the way in which this fisc supported or limited the production of goods and services by the public sector.

Another condition affected the relative, as distinct from the absolute, size of the public sector. This was the growing viability and strength of the private sector and its increasing ability to discard, ignore or influence public control and public activity. For much of the 1810s, the private sector was strongly constrained by government. Despite public efforts to set boundaries of settlement, private interests progressively moved outside government control during the 1820s and 1830s. At the same time, increasing private intervention by representation in the governing process checked government authority. Both processes tended to limit the increase in the size of colonial government (and, indeed, in its regulatory authority).

Government and the influx of convicts: the development of infrastructure

In the years immediately after 1810, many of the leading actors in the pre-1810 play in NSW had been recalled to Britain or returned to give evidence in the Bligh case. Prospective employment of convicts was more limited to smaller farmers and urban employers. In Van Diemen's Land, the very recently formed settlements were not in a position to absorb large numbers. The surge in convict arrivals from 1812 up to 1820 was not offset by comparable increases in private employment opportunities. For different reasons in the two colonies a high proportion of the new arrivals were retained in public employment.

In the case of Van Diemen's Land, the very recent establishment of the settlements largely imposed the need for public building and construction and other preparatory activity, a pressure intensified by the fact that, for the first several years, the settlements faced near-starvation. In the circumstances, it is not surprising that the public sector looms large in the economy relative to private activity in the first decade after 1810.

In NSW different considerations applied. The maturity that the original colony had attained by 1810 had depended on an emphasis on the establishment of private assets to the detriment of infrastructure. Certainly, a great deal of public building and construction had occurred but these activities were oriented to facilities that serviced private interests of the officers and civil officials and leading merchants. Wharves, barracks, publicly constructed private houses had been preferred to roads, hospitals, gaols, schools etc. Moreover, considerable public resource had been diverted, as it continued to be in Van Diemen's Land, to the establishment of productive enterprises of saw and grain milling, lime and salt making, timber cutting and bricks that serviced both the public and private sectors and for whose establishment there was inadequate private capital. Further constraining the production of public goods in the settlement, the colony in 1810 was predominantly free, with limited public labour resources to be deployed for more general purposes.

As the convict inflow rose rapidly particularly from 1812, it was received during much of the ensuing decade into settlements established in very restricted areas. Theoretically, several responses were possible — to allow a more rapid extension of settlement, to permit greater freedom for convicts, to assign more convicts to small private (ex-convict and ex-soldier) farming or to exploit convict labour in public projects. In fact, all these options appear to have been adopted in part. Exploration was encouraged, a substantial proportion of new arrivals were quickly released, ex-convict farmers were encouraged with convict assignees. But a distinctive feature of the first decade after 1810 was an emphasis on a special range of public infrastructure through public employment of convicts.

Public provision of infrastructure was not a novelty by 1810 nor was the allocation of considerable numbers of convicts to this purpose. One should be cautious about viewing Macquarie as the 'builder', as has sometimes been suggested. Macquarie did divert a relatively high proportion of the skilled convicts to public construction. But the significance of this allocation lay more in the social purposes of the infrastructure. In place of the earlier emphasis on roads, wharves and military barracks, the infrastructure in NSW during 1810–21 was focused on the definition and laying out of towns, the provision of schools, hospitals, churches, gaols (strictly convict barracks) and the construction of roads to link town and hamlet settlements and, as a special project, to push a road from the NSW coast into the newly discovered interior. This emphasis was replicated, in part, in Van Diemen's Land due to Macquarie's direction. In this case, however, the newness of the settlement ensured a greater presence of facilities such as wharves and roads, official buildings, soldiers' barracks etc.; and the special penal conditions of Van Diemen's Land encouraged attention to higher security gaol building. But even in Van Diemen's Land, a strong social orientation was given to expanding infrastructure.

This social infrastructure was put in place within settlements that were spatially limited, essentially, though not wholly, on the Cumberland Plain and around the early Van Diemen's Land bridgeheads. It was consciously designed to recognise the presence of a freed society and to provide for its expansion and for its permanence. Insofar as increasing numbers of convict arrivals occurred, the convict barracks provided a means of securely housing and separating convicts outside working hours and improved social order.

The erosion and breakdown of spatial limitations in the second half of the 1810s challenged this emphasis on public infrastructure. Spatial extension was helped by, for example, road building across the mountains in NSW and hindered, so it was argued, by the diversion of a substantial fraction of the incoming convicts to social infrastructure. The provision of this infrastructure might be seen, *ex post*, however, as an important part of the micro-adjustments that secured the foundations and greater working efficiency of the settlements. To that extent, it laid the basis for a later surge of extensive settlement as more convicts and free immigrants flowed in. The gradual return during the 1810s of those implicated or interested in the overthrow of Bligh brought back into contention potential large private employers of convict labour, a group slowly supplemented by a trickle of free immigrants with capital. As 1820 approached an increasing challenge to spatial constraint on the settlements and to large-scale public infrastructure provision emerged.

This challenge was part of the broader policy issues confronted in the Bigge Reports in the early 1820s. Those reports led to the change in British government policy towards encouragment of private enterprise, the larger extension of the colonial settlements and the increased private assignment of convicts. But already, before the arrival of Bigge in the colonies, internal pressures were increasing towards these ends. Recognising this pressure Macquarie was divided between bending with it and the necessity to preserve order and control. Bigge's Reports essentially settled that policy conflict. With the increased private assignment of convicts after 1821 came the relative decline in public employment of convicts and hence a major component of the output of the public sector. Progressive diversion of convicts away from government, and increased free immigrant arrivals later, implied a sustained relative stagnation of the public sector.

This meant a private expansion after 1821 less and less supported by infrastructure, even the types of infrastructure such as transport facilities that were important to the effective operation of an extensively settled society. Subsequent colonial governments attempted to use part of the convict workforce in these areas but they could not keep pace with the speed of extensive settlement. Increasingly, it was the more recalcitrant convicts, not readily manageable by private supervisors, that delivered a less and less efficient mode of producing public infrastructure.

Settlement extension led to two different and conflicting public activities. One was the successive explorations to learn about the resource endowments of the interior to enhance private exploitation. In principle, exploration was a public goods activity, with much in common with physical infrastructure. In practice, given the nature of extensive settlement into unknown areas, it was private discoveries at the micro level, opening up specific routes and identifying particular areas, that appear to have been far more significant than public exploratory endeavours. The second was to attempt a different mode of containment over much wider areas, through the delineation of areas for legal settlement. So emerged, by the end of the 1820s, the famous Nineteen Counties of NSW, supposedly declaring the limits of settlement. In fact, private settlers were already well beyond those limits. Neither type of public action absorbed much in the way of resources and the latter had a very limited effect on the progress of extensive settlement though it may have encouraged illegal behaviour in the form of mass squatting.

Convict influx: Support, Allocation and Public Commerce

There were many supply tasks and goods allocations to be performed by the public sector. Some of these arose directly from the organisation and distribution of materials and equipment required in infrastructure. Many more derived from the reception, victualling and clothing of newly arriving convicts. Still again, there were similar supply problems for resident convicts retained by government and those assigned to private persons or officials who were given rations support for convicts. Ex-convict and ex-soldier settlers were also an outlet for goods, often including animals, in early stages of farm establishment. The military and civil officials and their dependents were typically granted rations support available in kind from the public sector. Finally, military and defence supplies and equipment also needed to be acquired, stored and maintained. And tied to this commercial operation was the task of transporting much of the goods.

Most of these tasks of acquiring, receiving, storing and dispersing supplies revolved around the Commissariat. (It might be noted in passing that Australian Commissariats were not always geared to convicts. A Commissariat was set up in WA in order to support free settlers as that settlement faced survival problems. Later in the century WA came to accept convicts.) Partly derivative of these goods trans-actions, the Commissariat came to buy and sell commodities within the colonies, and formed a primitive note-issuing and banking service. It is unfortunate that no history of the Commissariat system in Australia has been written. Here we had a large-scale public warehouse and shop engaged in procurement, storage and distribution. Clearly, the Commissariat was a key institution in the early years of the settlements. On the other hand, its initial importance meant a progressive loss of prominence as the settlements became more complex, dispersed and free.

To a very considerable degree, its expansion and decline was a counterpart of the experience with public infrastructure because the numbers of convicts retained by government and the scale of building, construction, exploration and survey activity were all directly linked to goods, materials and equipment flowing into and out of the store. As convict numbers rose rapidly after 1812 and many were retained by government, so the scale of the public output of the Commissariat increased. As convicts came to be increasingly redirected to private assignment after 1821, the expansion of the Commissariat braked strongly. This was the case even in Van Diemen's Land during the 1820s despite the local governor's willingness to be more generous with assignment of convicts with rations to new settlers.

On the side of officialdom, the substantial number of British military and civil officials during the decade after 1810 similarly created a high level of activity for the Commissariats whether as strictly military agencies or to supply rations and other goods to the civil colonial government. British pressure for fiscal constraint led even before 1821 to growing revenue raising in the colonies and the local support for a rising public service (and, indeed, a small amount of infrastructure). These colonial provisions for locally employed officials were more restrictive than those originally provided by Britain, and particularly so in the attachment of public support in kind to many official salaries. Once again, the role of the Commissariat began to narrow. Between 1810 and 1819, the proportion of the population being rationed shrank from 40 to around 33 per cent. The process speeded up during the 1820s and into the 1830s as private assignment of convicts increased and as Britain pushed more local security (police) functions onto the colonies and even induced a greater presence of locally supported military. The point here is that the further these processes went, the fewer strictly commercial functions were left to the Commissariat and hence this component of public output slackened progressively.

Accentuating this trend was the joint public and private development of the settlements. Before 1810 and for several years afterwards, officials tended to acquire locally produced commodities by public assembly and transport, and frequently public redistribution. This was particularly so while bulk transport around the Cumberland Plain depended so much on water carriage, largely organised by government. As local road systems grew, a major organisational change developed with the Commissariat inviting tenders for delivery of specified ranges of goods (or advertising others for sale), with delivery by private individuals into the store as the standard practice. By 1818, the local transport services of the NSW Commissariat had been undermined by its own infrastructure activity even though its significance as a store was not yet reduced. This gradual erosion of public transport by the Commissariat was extended as sub-Commissariats were set up in expanding localities in the Hunter Valley and across the mountains in the interior. Indeed, in some locations as in the Hunter, the sub-Commissariats themselves became mobile, tending to move with settlement and the gangs of convicts that they supported.

The increase in assignment of convicts to private employment was a major element in checking the expansion of public commercial activity, notwithstanding the large numbers of convict arrivals during the 1820s and 1830s. Increasingly, new convict arrivals were relatively quickly moved out of the public support system as effectively unfree private contract workers. This was the basic allocative shift that led to a strong relative retardation of Commissariat activity. There was a slight reversal of this after 1837 as the assignment system was formally ended in NSW. In reality, the peak in the numbers assigned was attained in 1839 and then, for a very few years, convicts were concentrated in government. However, by 1845, only a relatively small number of convicts were recorded, as such, in NSW. One consequence was to divert convict arrivals to Van Diemen's Land where, by that stage, however, the private assignment system dominated.

Trend influences and structural change in other public activities

Most of the remainder of the listed public functions presented less opportunity for major trend changes though there were opportunities for substantial structural adjustments in relative importance. Many such as law and order, licensing, welfare and medical services, religion, education and defence had strong overhead characteristics. In these cases, the public setting up of systems of arrangements to deal with these policy issues tended to be concentrated in the early years of settlement and particularly during 1810–20. Once overhead arrangements were made — e.g. in hospitals or the principle of public support of churches for both religion and education — increasing public outlays were often more in the nature of transfer payments rather than increasing public output. In a slightly different guise, the same process applied in the special case of Aboriginal policy. In the 1810s and 1820s in NSW and particularly in the 1820s in Van Diemen's Land, there was a large public effort in reducing or eliminating Aboriginal threats to incoming colonists. As that threat dwindled, the 'rules of the game' changed to a sort of welfare handling of remnant Aborigines, for which low-cost (low output) protective provisions were made in the 1830s.

As the settlements expanded with increasing freedom, more government attention was given to the rules of a different game, the game of market activity, dependent on some public intervention in the conditions of market operation. In part, this was absorbed in an established overhead administration of law, the servicing of which required only gradual expansion despite the high rate of increase of private activity. In part, the public response was dominantly legalistic and formal, without an increasing administrative input. Regulation of prices, wages and working conditions partly depended on the adoption of regulations or laws but dominantly relied upon published proclamations with very limited administrative backing. To the extent to which backing was provided, as in the case of discipline of privately assigned convicts, the adoption of the part-time magistracy greatly limited the growth of the public service as the colonies expanded.

Possibly the most important change in these areas of public action was in the role of government in access to land as private expansion occurred. Originally beginning with land grants and urban leases, government was deeply involved in land transfers. Initial transfers depended greatly on the governor himself and could be arranged through personal negotiations as occurred with the wealthier settlers or with newly arriving immigrants with capital; or grants could be made in considerable numbers, as was particularly the case from 1825 in Van Diemen's Land, without much concern about administrative oversight. In neither event was much strictly public service input required even though some form of survey and title preparation was required. The lack of this input was apparent in the great shortfall in quit rents and lease payments. No great change in administrative attention followed the efforts at land sales in the 1820s or 1830s. It appears that little attempt to keep pace with the speed of legal land occupation through title resources was made. Indeed, the major survey efforts in the 1820s related to the determination of limits of settlement not the clarification of individual land areas. Even though Governor Darling required a complete review of grants, in the closing years of the 1820s the basic surveys and instruments of title had been completed.

Once the settlement in NSW broke those bounds set in 1829, for the next decade there was little opportunity for the government to begin to regain control of land access. Certainly some general administrative apparatus was set up at Port Phillip, in particular, in *ex post* recognition of private occupation there. But grant, lease and sale processes became less relevant further reducing the role of the government in the economy. Efforts to introduce taxes on livestock and to accord occupancy permits from 1838 represented ineffective and token outputs of the public sector.

Related to these changes in the relations between the public and private sectors were two other issues of substance. One was the determination applied between 1828 and 1835 to removing convicts from the public service. This implied colonial fiscal responsibility to any substitute salaried employees and hence greater local constraint on the growth of the local bureaucracy. But the change occurred over a period during which colonial governors were being drawn into a formal net of influence from the colonial private sector on government policy making. Increasingly, decisions were made not only to spend but also to raise revenues by the Governor-in-Council rather than the Governor and his immediate aides. British subventions were declining, reducing governors' freedom of action and private influence limited the opportunity for local revenues to increase to meet expenditure objectives. In the course of the 30 years from 1810, the public sector had shifted from being a highly subsidised and largely external element to being a set of institutions integrated with, and to a large degree constrained by, colonial private interests.

It should not be assumed from the preceding discussion that it was convictism and its gradual demise that prompted the changing expansion of a public sector. In the free enterprise colonies, Western Australia illustrates a different issue underlying efforts to colonise Australia from a distance. In this case, efforts to establish prior blueprints from a distance were the hallmark of private initiative, in both Western Australia and later in the Wakefieldian experiments in South Australia. In the former, excessive land grants, lack of knowledge of settlers and inadequate logistical support quickly exposed the Western Australian settlement to near disaster. Initially, the British government supplied tiny fiscal and bureaucratic support to the private project. A handful of officials were supposed to manage land allocations and surveys and to provide and distribute essential resources. Within a few years, this was quickly reversed as the threat of starvation prompted several changes. An increase in the bureaucracy was accompanied by access to Treasury bills for essential supplies and the introduction of public import, storage and distribution of rations. By 1835, the supposedly free enterprise settlement was heavily dependent on government.

Thus Western Australia proceeded initially in the opposite direction to that of the convict colonies. In the few years before the depression, the straggling establishment of private farming brought back the relative but not the absolute size of government.

Urban Development: 1810–40

In dealing with the private sector, two separate but interconnected paths need to be pursued. One is a distinctively urban development in Australia. The other is natural resource exploitation. There is a curious symbiosis and conflict between these two paths which need to be exposed. What prompted Australia, in contrast with Canada and the United States, to become quite strongly urbanised at an early stage and to persist with that urban concentration? Why did a complex of manufacturing and commercial and service activities group together in the Australian colonies? Was it due to isolation, the nature of Australian natural resource development, the supply of capital and skills in Australia? The answers to these questions are not clear-cut and a variety of conflicting issues need to be taken into account. In attempting to answer them, let us approach the question of urbanisation in general terms.

Early urbanisation

Some point of initial concentration was largely inevitable in Australian settlements formed by arrivals by sea. In the case of Western Australia, the provision of large land allocations to individuals to some extent accelerated dispersal from the point of disembarkation while, in contrast, the weaknesses inherent in that western settlement led many arriving individuals to cling together. Initial disembarkation points were not necessarily the optimal location for establishing a centre whether large or small. If harbours were a consideration in determining approximate locations for original assembly points, adequate water supply was another physical consideration in concentrating settlement.

These two factors were prime determinants in the location of Sydney, Hobart and Melbourne. In other cases of Adelaide and Perth, other specifically urban planning considerations prompted relocation from points of disembarkation — terrain, immediate access to cultivable land, transport potential, even aesthetics. Even in the earliest towns of Sydney and Hobart, there was a clear presupposition that an urban settlement, a point of long-term concentration was to be established (for the discussion of choice of early cities, see Statham (1989)).

Already, from the beginning of settlement throughout Australia, the dominantly urban backgrounds of the mass of new arrivals created some predisposition in favour of concentration. This was a form of 'urbanisation' and, for a variety of reasons, the chosen locations expanded into formal towns and eventually into cities. As they did, and as extensive settlement proceeded, these urban settlements faced a powerful incentive to disperse. As will be discussed later, rural land use in Australia up to and beyond 1840 was relatively labour-intensive. It remained for increasing pastoral specialisation and the application of new technology and capital equipment after 1840 to create the conditions for low labour/output ratios in the pastoral industry. Hence extensive settlement before 1810 implied movement away from the original centre and a long-term decline in the initial concentration. This was inevitable in terms of successful colonial expansion.

What was not inevitable was that the original concentration points should succeed in retaining a high proportion of the population of every colony. What was also not inevitable was that a hierarchy of smaller centres should be dispersed over areas of expanding settlement, to form urban nodes. One should be cautious of thinking in terms of a clear distinction between urban and rural populations and activities. A century and a half after the first colonial settlement, Sydney possessed a flourishing farming activity on its edges and, throughout the years 1810–40, every town, however large, contained some farming. Moreover, non-farming and farm activities merged at urban limits to blur boundary lines. Equally, on the other hand, tiny hamlets contained a variety of non-farm activities.

These considerations make it impossible to measure accurately the expansion of towns. Coghlan (1918), for example, recorded the population growth of Sydney from 3163 in 1805 to 6158 by 1810, declining by 1815 to 5475 and then increasing rapidly to 12 079 by 1820. No sources are cited. Unfortunately many early records have been deliberately destroyed and Coghlan may have had access to material no longer available. It is possible that these numbers relate to the 'Sydney area' as defined in the Musters or even to persons summoned together and counted in Sydney even though non-resident there.

From 1828, the Censuses of NSW make possible a plausible count within a given defined urban area. Even then, we should remember as already suggested that some farm activity would be captured in such a count. The censuses suggest a progression for Sydney of 10 815 in 1828, 16 232 in 1833, 19 729 in 1836 and 29 973 in 1841. Coghlan's figure for 1820 suggests a little over 40 per cent of the population of NSW in Sydney and the subsequent figures, as a percentage of that population are 29.55, 26.67, 25.59 and 22.91 (see Mansfield, 1841). The latter four figures indicate that Sydney was expanding less rapidly than the total population during the period of extensive expansion and it is certainly not impossible that a fall from about 40 per cent to about 30 per cent occurred between 1820 to 1828 — this covered a phase of very rapid coastal and inland expansion.

The relative decline of Sydney needs to be read within the context of several considerations. It was far from being merely due to expanding rural land use. The years 1810–40 included the growth of subsidiary inland towns such as Parramatta, Liverpool, Windsor and others on the Cumberland Plain during the 1810s; of Newcastle, Morpeth (both subsidiary ports) and Maitland etc. in the Hunter Valley particularly during the 1820s; of Bathurst and others beyond the mountains in the 1820s and 1830s; and last, but not least, of Port Phillip in Melbourne from 1835. Extensive settlement downgraded the relative magnitude of Sydney but, in part, encouraged a subsidiary urban development elsewhere. It is unfortunate that we cannot effectively count this subordinate urban expansion. The 1836 Census (see Mansfield, 1841) listed only the seven 'main' towns apart from Sydney, giving their total population in excess of 9000 or an average of 1300. The total was almost half that of Sydney. There were a good many other smaller centres. When these are taken into account, it seems plausible that the total 'urban' population at the end of the 1830s may have approximated 40 per cent of all NSW colonial population. The society and the economy were far from being preoccupied with rural natural resource development. (The small size of these 'urban' populations indicates the problem of how we classify locations as non-urban. Clearly in Britain such tiny numbers would be "hamlets". But the role of these small centres in Australia is what matters, not their numerical size. Even Sydney up to 1840 would be counted in Britain as, at best, a very small town and perhaps only a large village. But its occupational structure and its role in the total society are radically different from a comparably sized town — or sometimes a very large town — in British terms.)

Basically, a similar picture arises in Van Diemen's Land. According to Rimmer (1969), the population of Hobart (the dominant southern port) was a mere 600 in 1810 (see Abbott, 1971), rising to 3500 in 1820, 6000 in 1830 and 15 000 in 1841, about half the size of Sydney. The rounded figures point to Rimmer's caution about accuracy. Over a third of all arriving immigrants and convicts, according to Rimmer, ended up in Hobart. Again, as in NSW, we have to add other towns and again the urban proportion looks relatively similar to that of NSW even though Van Diemen's Land was much more amenable to arable land use and a higher rural labour/output ratio.

We are not concerned here with the specifics of site selection except perhaps with some of the particular issues that arose in relation to inland and subsidiary towns. What is of interest is why colonials continued to congregate in towns and why, in an extensively expanding economy, urban populations appear to have sustained a high rate of expansion relative to the rest of the society throughout 1810–40. A simple economic explanation might be that urban areas, particularly those serving as ports, attracted commercial, industrial and service activities. This, basically, is the approach adopted by Rimmer in relation to Hobart (see Statham, 1989). If this were the case, we would, indeed, move directly into questions of import replacement and the production of non-tradeables. This is not a satisfactory explanation even though these activities loom large in urban occupations.

Urban congregation needs to be seen as a response to a large range of influences. Immediately available arable land and water supply apart, there were basic logistical considerations in colonies whose population was expanding rapidly by influxes from overseas. Ports became the locale for the delivery of human and goods cargoes, their assembly onshore and the organisation for their (partial) dispersal to other locations. This implied centralisation not merely as a first bridgehead but a continuing aggregation. Assembly control and administered dispersal depended on command systems, systems that were particularly prominent in convict settlements but were also important in free colonies where settlement depended greatly on accession of imports. Such a command base provided overhead institutions from which proliferated other administrative services. Particularly in convict colonies, there was a strong influence towards establishing original port towns as governing centres for expanding colonies. That influence was sustained by the rapid influx of convicts after 1812.

Efforts to exploit natural resources confronted arduous tasks and a very large one of coming to terms with a new environment. This learning by doing could be supported by a fall-back location and this seems to have been a significant factor in both Western and South Australia where, to some extent, difficulties of adjusting to the new environment helped to hold new arrivals in established administrative centres. But this also applied to New South Wales and Van Diemen's Land where the private costs of land exploitation could be reduced by a gradual incremental settlement from an established core. No doubt many individuals, less risk averse or under sentence conditions, were willing or forced to move into isolation. For most, isolation meant not only loss of amenity but increased exposure to Aborigines. Even moving out from an original centre typically led to hamlet formation and the development of minor towns, partly for social reasons, partly for protection from Aborigines. Macquarie's urban planning development and the extension of infrastructure were, in part, a conscious attempt to provide this social structure and protection.

Protection became progressively less important as Aboriginal risks were diminished. But social considerations remained. Here we face the rigidity in Australian society, established in the early years and persisting in the long run, arising from the fact that the mass of newcomers, whether convict or free, were urban in their background. As convicts, they could be directed out of towns and compelled for the duration of sentences to engage in rural activity. To that extent, convicts not only directly supported extensive rural settlement but their status complemented the urban background of many of their employers who were, from access to a convict workforce, able either to be absentee land occupiers or, at the least, to maximise the time spent in urban environments. Some such employers resided in the main centres. Others provided a nucleus for the smaller nodal towns as a place of residence.

Freed or free persons generally, however, appear as showing a strong preference for urban locations. In the large centres, the presence of a publicly provided infrastructure and amenity, the existence of a system of law and order and the opportunities for a wider social interrelation made an offset to any additional labour market competition that they may have faced. They were in an environment to which they were accustomed.

But the environment was more akin to British conditions by, say, 1820, than might seem at first sight. Even Sydney, with a population ranging between around 10 000 in 1820 and 30 000 in 1840 was, in terms of modern Australian towns, apparently no more than a moderately sized country town. Such a perspective would be seriously misleading. Sydney was the centre of government. It was the dominant port, though Hobart came to rival it in the second half of the 1830s. Sydney presented a wider variety of activities, as early as 1810 and more so by 1840, than many of the British towns that were larger than it and, again, Hobart came, in the 1830s, to rival this variety. By the time that Macquarie had carried through his social infrastructure, Sydney (and a similar evaluation could be made for Hobart a decade later) had acquired considerable attractions for any level of society.

In such locations, there was the opportunity for more than merely commercial, industrial or service activities. This brings us to the question of import replacement and the production of non-tradeables. But before embarking upon that discussion, it is important to appreciate the variety and even the quality of much of these activities. By 1840 none of the Australian towns and particularly not Sydney or Hobart can be thought of as having the specialisation of some British towns or lacking the ability to attract high quality service professions. Tertiary service tends to be underplayed in much Australian history and economics and this is true of these foundation years. Sydney and Hobart, in particular, soon attracted a substantial array of medical, dental, educational, legal, architectural and religious service personnel as well as artistic and recreational services. The early colonial 'service sector' included many domestic servants of various sorts. But the more highly skilled and educated services that were present provided a total living environment that added significantly to the attractions and benefits of urban life far beyond those of a substantial country town today or a comparably sized British one in the first half of the 19th century.

These service activities were, in the conventional parlance, sources of a major type of non-tradeables — services delivered face-to-face. In practice, as shipping arrivals from Britain increased and as whaling and other trading activity of both British and American ships expanded during the 1820s and 1830s, another synergism emerged. Such shipping activity enlarged the economic and the social potential of the major port towns. They became valuable havens for ships and for their crew to whom local face-to-face services were delivered, along with repair and victualling services. So-called 'non-tradeables' actually became exports of substance because external customers arrived to enjoy them.

So far, the emphasis has been on placing the conventional urban activities of commerce, manufacturing and services as sources of urban growth into a broader perspective. We now examine these activities in their own right. The following discussion is then to be treated both as a summary of these activities and as part of the explanation of the urban expansion that occurred; two pictures of Sydney give some impressions of the occupational mix at two important dates — 1814 and 1828.

Some Indication of Occupational Composition

Unfortunately, only a few statistical glimpses of the reputed overall occupational or industrial structure can be given during 1810 to 1840, all essentially confined to NSW. The 1828 Census is a key document, providing a personalised account of the mass of the colonial population at the approximate time of the break-out from the restrictions of the officially approved areas for settlement. It conveys a picture of the colony still in relatively compact form though it probably does not capture statistically a considerable number of persons 'squatting' outside limits. It has specific deficiencies, not least of which is the absence of informative data on a large proportion of convicts in government employment. For this reason, the summary tabulation below is confined to the private sector workforce, whether free, colonially born, convict or ex-convict. On the other hand, the detail of the 1828 Census has a special merit in that it permits allocation of individuals to specific locations within the town of Sydney (not always with complete confidence) so that we can develop, for that date, a reasonably good picture of the private activity of Sydney as a town. In this context, the absence of informative statistics on many convicts is much less important in that a large part of the publicly employed workforce was outside Sydney; in 1828, Sydney was dominantly free and private. In particular, the operations of the Commissariat had dwindled so that, relatively, public commercial activity was greatly reduced.

After 1828, the Censuses provide only summary data, too heavily condensed to be of much use for these purposes. Before 1828, the various Musters provide a less certain but still valuable impression of occupational structure with at least strong hints of urbanised activities. None is accurate enough in terms of aggregate count or in occupational designation to define sequential change. For present purposes, a summary outline of the 1814 Muster is presented below. This is chosen primarily because it accords closely with the start of large-scale convict inflows in the closing years of the Napoleonic Wars.

One should be wary of both 'pictures' presented below. In 1814, 'Sydney' meant the 'Sydney area' and the other locations listed are similarly broad. The Muster was far from complete. This can be remedied in part. A good many of the omissions can be filled in as block statistics from other sources though they cannot be linked to particular areas. There remains perhaps 10 per cent of the reputed population of the colony unaccounted for. The essential supplements and omissions are given in notes to the table. Equally important, comparatively little information is given for women included in the 1814 Muster. For this reason, the table is confined to males. Given this gender constraint in 1814, the same treatment has been adopted for the table on the 1828 Census, which also fails to report the activity in which many women engaged.

There is a general proviso applying to both 1814 and 1828. This is that only one occupation/industry is listed. There is no doubt that the convict skills delivered by Britain were widely used in the colony and to considerable advantage. But it would be incorrect to assume that this one occupation alone was relevant. Virtually all members of the workforce were called on to perform a variety of roles whether as employers, self-employed, convicts or ex-convict employees. The two pictures

Table 13.2: Workforce Summary (Number of Males)

Occupation	Sydney Free	Sydney Convict	Liverpool Free	Liverpool Convict	Parramatta Free	Parramatta Convict	Windsor Free	Windsor Convict	Total
Assigned	0	31	0	214	0	216	0	396	857
Farming	159	54	119	1	161	60	390		944
Commerce	33	14			5	2	1		55
Food, Drink, Tobacco	71	7			12	1	3	1	95
Dock	0	22							22
Building	135	204	10	3	39	77	30	63	561
Gaol & Gang	0	52							52
Overseers	13	18	2		7	2	2		44
Administration	74	7	7	2	19	6	15	12	142
Professional	12	20	2	5	8	7	10	6	70
Person. service	34	22			8	30	4	8	106
Watchman	0	7							7
Transport	62	40			3		7	1	113
Labourer	202	114	59	15	143	44	156	2	735
Goldsmith	0	1							1
Metals	27	20		2	9		4	1	63
Leather	29	15			7	3	6		60
Potters	1	2							3
Printer	0	1							1
Textiles	16	11			4	23	3		57
Bookbinder	1								1
Glassmaker	2								2
Jeweller	1								1
Saltboiler	1								1
Silversmith	2								2
Soapmaker	1								1
Watchmakers	4								4
Filecutter					1				1
Sievemaker					1				1
Glazier							1		1
Not Stated	67	15	4	9	16	47	34	71	263
Total	947	677	203	251	443	519	665	561	4266

Notes:
(a) Female Population 1814
Women formed an active part of the total workforce (cf. *The Hatch and Brood of Time*).
Though the Muster gives occupational data for some women they are too sketchy for use here.
The following locates the women recorded in the relevant areas and their reputed conjugal status.

Sydney Free Women	Total	704	(450 Wives, 45 Concubines, 45 Widows)
Sydney Convict Women	Total	372	(162 Wives, 35 Concubines, 7 Widows)
Liverpool Free Women	Total	119	(96 Wives, 5 Concubines, 1 Widow)
Liverpool Convict Women	Total	45	(25 Wives, 3 Concubines, 0 Widows)
Parramatta Free Women	Total	332	(209 Wives, 25 Concubines, 10 Widows)
Parramatta Convict Women	Total	1270	(74 Wives, 7 Concubines, 0 Widows)
Windsor Free Women	Total	408	(274 Wives, 60 Concubines, 15 Widows)
Windsor Convict Women	Total	115	(87 Wives or Concubines 1 Widow)
Total		3365	

(b) Identified omissions from the 1814 Muster
The reputed 1814 population was 13 117. The Muster shows 4266 males and 3365 women or a total of just on 8000. The missing 5000 odd are accounted for as 3116 children, 1151 military, 86 civil establishment, 10 in the commissariat, 272 located at Newcastle and 150 engaged ex-Sydney on colonial vessels.

might indicate the predominant occupation/industry. Or they may, in a good many cases, show how the workforce was engaged at the time of the data assembly. We know that persons functioned as, for example, merchants, landholders and farmers and that convict employees, if only in their free time, pursued crafts that were often not applicable in their prime employment. This is not to deny the advantages taken of opportunities to specialise — far from it. It is likely that, in the Sydney area in 1814 and in Sydney in 1828, far more opportunity was available to sustain specialisation. However, the limitations of the data should be noted. Given this, several points of interest emerge:

(a) The Sydney area still contained a substantial amount of farming. If we assume (almost certainly an overstatement) that those listed generally as 'assigned' were in fact employed by farmers, the 'Sydney' farm total of the recorded NSW male workforce accounted for just on 40 per cent. This conforms broadly to the 1814 land and stock returns, with the Sydney area accounting for almost exactly one-third of land held, almost 40 per cent of horned cattle and about 22 per cent of sheep numbers (see Baxter, 1987: 14).

(b) In terms of the concentration of certain occupations, the Sydney area was far from completely dominant except in the occupations of commerce, food, drink and tobacco (just over 80 per cent of the NSW total). These might all be grouped together in a general distributing category although some processing would then be captured. Even so, the balance of 20 per cent to other locations implied a significant dispersion of distributing activity, chiefly of the localised retailing of food, drink and tobacco. Sydney's importance in commerce derived essentially from its role as a port and boasting the major local goods assembly, importing, wholesaling and distribution.

(c) Next in line, the Sydney area is represented strongly in specialised industrial/ craft activities, including metalworking, leather and textiles plus the more specialised activities of goldsmith, bookbinder, glassmaker, jeweller, saltboiler, silversmith, soapmaker and watchmaker. In these latter specialised crafts, 'Sydney' dominated though it is possible that the single occupation description conceals these activities in the other colonial areas. Sydney's failure to dominate industrially can be partly explained by the strong presence of textiles, and also by significant metal and leather work elsewhere (extra-Sydney textile activities would be more significant if women were included). Here, however, we need to be a bit wary. It is doubtful whether some public 'manufacturing' is adequately represented in the Muster listing — in brick and lime-making, milling etc.

(d) The failure of the Muster to show up a relatively high proportion of administrative and professional occupations in 'Sydney' partly reflects the biased nature of the omissions from the Muster (see notes to table 13.2). Nevertheless, although Sydney was the governing centre of the colony, the Muster returns are consistent in general terms with the fact that subsidiary command and control centres were established throughout the colony forming small urban nuclei.

(e) One other activity in which the Muster shows 'Sydney' as very strongly represented was transport. This is underscored when it is recognised that more persons, engaged on colonial ships, were omitted from the Muster than the total of those actually included. Two factors account for this dominance. One was Sydney's role as the prime colonial port, a role accentuated in 1814 not only because it was the point of arrival of goods and human cargoes but also because Van Diemen's Land was prevented from engaging in sea transport except locally by the East India Company's monopoly. But another factor needs to be stressed, partly because it is less obvious. In 1814, many of the goods exchanged in the colony were transported by water, particularly along the Hawkesbury. As a commercial centre, Sydney was significantly driven by this internal colonial water distribution system in which both the Commissariat and private traders were involved.

Essentially, the 1814 Muster delineated the Sydney area when the colonial settlement was largely confined to the Cumberland Plain. When we turn to the picture of 1828, it bears repetition that the statistics shift to focus on the private sector workforce. No direct comparison can be made in any detail. Deliberately, no attempt has been made to generate consistent classifications and this limits, to some extent, the comparability. However, whereas in 1814 a high proportion of publicly employed convicts were still in the Sydney area, by 1828 this proportion was greatly reduced. Moreover, the government's share of the total convict workforce had also shrunk considerably so that some comparisons between tables 13.2 and 13.3 can be made in general terms, without risk of gross error.

The 1828 summary of the private sector workforce shows Sydney as accounting for less than a quarter (23.8 per cent) of the NSW total. Given the greatly increased scale of population, the shares accounted for by Sydney have a greater solidity than they do in 1814. Substantial deviations in particular occupations/activities above a quarter of the total imply relative concentration in urban Sydney.

Several major points might be noted here:

(a) Sydney, in 1828, had lost much of its rural air. Nevertheless, the area designated as Sydney environs represents essentially the rest of the Cumberland Plain. Here, a little over half the private sector workforce engaged in farming was still to be found. As a budding city, Sydney merged quickly into rural surrounds. On the other hand, some, at least, of the persons designated as engaged in farming in Sydney were clearly absentee farmers.

(b) Distributing activities (commerce, dealers, persons engaged in food, drink and tobacco) remained the most strongly represented in the major urban centre (approximately 80 per cent, substantially the same as in 1814). Sydney had clearly confirmed its role as the dominant commercial centre in NSW. But by now, this dominance was, in fact, essentially private. The role of the Commissariat had dwindled greatly and commercial activity was overwhelmingly conducted by private enterprise. Moreover, that commercial prominence rested firstly on the role of Sydney as a port. But by now, Sydney had two other major roles. One was to serve as a significant export centre, receiving goods from the interior and from the sea for overseas exports. The other was to distribute throughout the colony a considerable range of import substitutes, many of which were produced in Sydney.

(c) By 1828, Sydney was clearly a major centre for (ranked in order) clothing and textiles, manufacture of timber products, production of metal goods, building

Table 13.3: Estimated Distribution of NSW Private Sector Male Workforce, 1828 (Number of Males)

Industry/Occupation	Sydney	Sydney Envir.	Hunter	Total NSW	Sydney (% NSW)	Sydney Envir. (% NSW)	Sydney & Sydney Envir. (% NSW)
Farming	276	4 536	2 111	9 138	3.02	49.64	52.66
Professional	138	73	53	283	48.76	25.80	74.56
Food, Drink, Tobacco	521	380	44	982	53.05	38.70	91.75
Commerce/Dealers	781	131	54	971	80.43	13.49	93.92
Personal Service	114	22	4	146	78.08	15.07	93.15
Metals	173	89	14	305	56.72	29.18	85.90
Woodworking	479	217	31	797	60.10	27.23	87.33
Bricks	30	53	2	95	31.58	55.79	87.37
Other Bdg Ops/Materials	112	72	26	222	50.45	32.43	82.88
Total Building	621	342	59	1 114	55.75	30.70	86.45
Leather	207	205	19	466	44.42	43.99	88.41
Clothing, Textiles	222	66	3	297	74.75	22.22	96.97
Clerical	100	52	38	207	48.31	25.12	73.43
Clergy	28	45	27	176	15.91	25.57	41.48
Overseers	9	39	70	194	4.64	20.10	24.74
Mining	13	8	0	22	59.09	36.36	95.45
Transport	219	45	2	281	77.94	16.01	93.95
Labourers	339	567	53	1 080	31.39	52.50	83.89
Miscellaneous	144	63	4	228	63.16	27.63	90.79
Not Stated	451	293	223	2740	16.46	10.69	27.15
Total inc. Non-skilled	4 540	7 131	2 803	19 066	23.81	37.40	61.21

Note: The difference between the sum of Sydney, Sydney Environs and Hunter Valley and the colonial total covers persons occupied in mountain and transmontane areas.
Source: Estimated from *NSW Census of 1828.*

activity and building products other than timber, and leather working. Many other specialised crafts, individually small sources of employment, have to be concealed under the label 'miscellaneous' and it is these crafts that make the miscellaneous category so large relative to the rest of the colony. As in 1814, there was an array of goldsmiths, silversmiths, watchmakers and the like, mostly practising their crafts in the Sydney centre. Although most of these industrial activities may be classed as import substitutes, it is also relevant that several manufacturing groups were linked particularly to local natural resources — wood products, other building materials and leather working together with some, but far from all, of clothing and textiles. If we question the significance of 'staples' we should not wholly discard the importance of natural resource exploitation in import substitution.

(d) So far as tertiary services other than commerce are concerned, Sydney in 1828 accounted for just over half of the private specialised professionals and clerical personnel. Only the clergy appear to have been distributed relatively closely to that of the population throughout the colony. It is interesting that less skilled personal service is also strongly represented. These include not only domestic servants but, in the present classification, occupations such as boarding housekeeping. Moreover, transport services in 1828 were less associated with goods distribution but more with passenger movement and were also very strongly represented in Sydney.

(e) Outside Sydney, the main subsidiary towns were located in what is designated as Sydney environs. When these surrounding areas (unfortunately not merely towns) are included, the total area was of overwhelming importance in the whole range of commerce, manufacturing, professional and personal services and transport. The shares of all in the Cumberland Plain were far above the corresponding shares in the total area for the aggregate private workforce of NSW (see final column of table 13.3 opposite). The Cumberland Plain may have remained a significant contributor to total farming activity. But it was, by 1828, more non-farming than farming and one may reasonably conclude that in Sydney, and the surrounding towns, was contained a relatively rich array of occupations and skills, servicing not only the immediate population but much of the rest of the rapidly expanding colony.

It is unfortunate that only such a limited statistical delineation is possible. Nevertheless, even these two pictures may help to give some sense of proportion to the following loose institutional description of NSW and Van Diemen's Land at least over the 1810–40 period.

Commercial, Industrial and Service Development

The section on the statistical outline of economic development suggested that the complex of commerce, industry, services and rents, in trend terms, was the most rapidly expanding sector of the Australian economy(ies) up to 1840. The substantial separation of public and private interests in NSW and Van Diemen's Land following 1810 helped, to some extent, to clarify the structure and function of these activities and the role of the institutions involved in them. Before 1810, it is difficult to be confident where private enterprise and public activity began and ended. It bears reiteration that after 1810, with some exceptions, the stimulus to and constraints on private enterprise in commerce and manufacturing in particular were increasingly the product of conscious official acts affecting on private individuals in contrast with the earlier intimate intertwining of public and private purses and resources.

Pre-1820 Conditions

The structure of these activities in the first half of the 1810s was strongly influenced by recession conditions to be discussed later. The other general points are worth nothing. Firstly, there was a very strong public representation among the totality of commercial, manufacturing and professional activities. The Commissariat was, institutionally, by far the largest storage agent, buyer and seller of both imported and basic local products. The colonial government conducted the largest manufacturing enterprises particularly in timber and grain milling, textiles, the production of building materials (particularly bricks and lime as well as timber) and in salt-making. In addition, the government operated boat and shipping services for both goods and passengers on a substantial scale. It also provided key professional services.

Secondly, there was a large variety in private sector commerce, manufacturing and services including:

(a) Substantial and varied enterprises, initially mainly in commerce (see Stevens, 1965) but spreading out of commerce into manufacturing. Those in 1810 had been established as undertakings of now ex-officials both military and civil (such as Palmer), of a few free immigrants (R. Campbell) and of some ex-convicts (Simeon Lord). Such enterprises were rarely specialised, commonly depended on agency or partnership relations and frequently carried through the range of buying and selling local products, imported goods on own account or on behalf of shippers, and spanned the functions of wholesaling, retailing and auctioning. Despite some protestations, their transactions were not confined to private individuals but were also carried on through purchases from and sales to the Commissariat. Though some became bankrupt in the early 1810s, they provided the initial prominent private institutions. It was largely following, or in response to, recession conditions in the early 1810s that some of these individuals began to turn their attention to manufacturing in milling, textiles, metal products, tanning, glass etc. But already, by 1810, some significant manufacturing enterprises had been established (see Abbott and Nairn, 1969), the most notable of which was shipbuilding, linked as it was to local maritime interests and the need for access to the outside world and to move goods around the colony(ies) in the absence of adequate roads. Wentworth suggested that some £250 000 sterling had been invested in private Sydney factories by 1820 (see Abbott and Nairn, 1969).

(b) Subsidiary and often more specialised enterprises such as publicans, lodging-house keepers, private teachers, boat and ship builders, butchers and tanners. Some of these represented the more successful and independent ex-convicts and ex-soldiers; many appear as those who had been earlier the affiliates or subordinates of civil and military officials before 1810. Indeed, for whatever motive, those earlier officials, dependent as they had been on a network of distributors, had established with considerable success a 'small business' that underpinned the auction and wholesale functions of the few large merchants.

(c) Last, but far from least, was the large array of ex-convicts, ticket of leave persons and some still under sentence who carried out craft activities, both processing products and selling their wares in a combination of small-scale manufacturing/commerce (see Musters). These have tended to be lost from sight in discussions of early manufacturing and commerce but they deployed special skills in jewellery, watchmaking, file-making, gunsmithing, sievemaking, furniture and cabinetmaking, tobacco processing, garment making, conducting markets of local produce and in professional services including medicine, the law and education.

Neither government nor private enterprise operated in a specialised way and this continued to be a basic characteristic throughout the 30 year period to 1840. There was, however, one clear trend condition after 1810. As the productive role of government contracted, it became less diverse due to: a progressive decline in the proportion and eventually the numbers of persons supported directly by government; positive public support for private activity, particularly in manufacturing and crafts but also in commerce; and to the successful development of private enterprises as independent institutions, particularly after the late 1810s and into the 1820s.

Post-1820 Changes

The conditions determining this trend after 1810 and the successful development of private commerce and manufacturing can usefully be grouped into supply and demand factors. The supply-side factors included the availability of capital and short-term credit, labour with appropriate skills, supplies of natural resource products both for domestic production and for export, and local transport facilities and shipping access to and from the outside world. On the demand side, private development above all depended on both public and private expenditure levels and the patterns of tastes of the colonists and on the allocative expenditure preferences of the government.

Sydney in 1810 was almost cut off from the outside world. There were few convict and store ships arriving, only a small number of trading ventures with India and the colony's own few ocean ship movements. Hobart, in a sense, was both less and more isolated, with a growing coasting shipping connection with Sydney but few overseas ship arrivals. One important omission or near omission appears in the early 1810s — the virtual absence of American ships that had been important at the beginning of the century. This Australian isolation was only very slowly reduced. In fact, fewer overseas ships arrived in 1815 than in 1810. By 1820, conditions began to change significantly with over 50 overseas ship arrivals, partly due to increasing convict flows, partly to the increasing prominence of whaling visitors and partly to the growing trade of private merchants between Sydney and Calcutta. Some of these ships brought supplies of people and goods, some imports, some foreign customers directly to port and, in 1820, a rare incident still, one ship took away 'a valuable cargo' of colonial produce. Most ships left in ballast or with miniscule and miscellaneous exports.

Until the end of the 1810s, then, Sydney and Hobart were dominantly local ports in terms of harbour activity, receiving a considerable range of products on local water-borne craft from the hinterland and around the coast — salt, lime, wheat, maize, potatoes, barley, oats, timber, kangaroo and sealskins, oil, lime, coal. These local inflows supplied a few items for export, but mostly for local processing and consumption. Some meat was similarly delivered but arrivals mostly travelled to slaughter and preserving locations by land. Throughout the 1810s, the great majority of these products were absorbed by government though a significant local distributive system was set up to service the private market.

The role of that private market grew as the influx of population quickened and the proportion of that expanding population supported by government declined. It expanded rapidly as convicts were increasingly assigned after 1821. But already, before 1820, the Commissariat was progressively changing its mode of operation enhancing the opportunities for private business (cf. *Sydney Gazette*). Whereas its established practice before 1810 had been to declare prices and quantities to be bought in (and indeed often sent out boats to collect produce), it moved rapidly in the late 1810s towards a tender system which allowed both direct producers and local merchants to bid for deliveries. It moved away from slaughtering and meat preserving in its own right to public invitation to deliver subsidised casked as well as fresh meat to store.

This is merely one illustration of public withdrawal from its dominance in access to capital, labour and natural resource products and of the deliberately increased access of private individuals to those basic supply conditions. The change appears as fitting the expectations of and the relative rates of monetary return, in private activity. Before 1810, private farming was a source of security as well as real estate. Private commerce appeared to offer the highest rate of return. The latter expectation was punctured by the recession during the first half of the 1810s. Initially, the colonial government appeared to contribute constraint rather than support in a difficult situation. It retained a high proportion of rising convict supplies, it accentuated its monopoly of access to external capital through the British Treasury and to British stores supplies and even limited the convertibility of Commissariat notes.

Convertibility was quickly restored and currency imported to improve liquidity. Of advantage particularly in processing activity (including processing by small craft producers), the Commissariat allowed access to stores at invoice prices (S.J. Butlin, 1953). But most of all, its tendency to 'monopolise' the flow of convicts led, through its building activity, to two vital changes. Firstly, it rapidly transformed land transport conditions. This not only meant flexible access to the Sydney market but also tended to encourage relocation of the processing of bulky goods closer to points of consumption. This was an important factor in some markets concentrating business in Sydney, in others encouraging dispersal and the development of subsidiary centres. Secondly, its building activity led to rapidly increased demand for a variety of building materials and private individuals responded to this demand (Abbott and Nairn, 1969). The recovery from this early recession appears to have been led, to a considerable degree, by public works activity. But this activity meant more than merely crude materials processing. It also induced the production of the contents of building, spreading the expenditure benefit to private carpenters, cabinet makers, metalworkers etc. as well as private builders. Some merchants who had previously given preference to commerce, transferred available funds to manufacturing and there is a striking tendency for increased private interest in substantial manufacturing ventures from the second half of the 1810s.

Most of this public stimulus depended on Macquarie's willingness to exploit his official access to Treasury bills (external capital) as well as his use of convict labour. By converting public capital to private income, he allowed the private sector to exploit indirectly an expanded access to foreign exchange. As these expenditures rose to 1821, so access to capital within the colonial sector was restored and with it the potential for the recovery of private import business, much of it by persons who had not been prominent before the recession. Many of these 'new' people followed in the same institutional path of their predecessors, establishing links through agencies and partnerships first in India and after 1820 increasingly with Britain. By 1825, the Australia Company could boast that it had 'completed arrangements for establishing a regular intercourse between this colony and the Mother Country' (*Sydney Gazette*, 6/1/1825). Certainly after the early 1820s, the trend of trade connections was set strongly away from India and China and towards Britain.

With that change came a marked shift in the contents of Sydney's and Hobart's stores and the functions of leading merchants. During the 1810s, advertisements certainly included a good many British consumer goods (not necessarily finished goods) for sale. But there were very large volumes of Asian goods at auction, wholesale and retail in Sydney and specialised Asian 'bazaars'. Asian products dwindled rapidly throughout the 1820s and in their place came a full range of British goods. That supply was not geared in any simple way to the development of a viable export trade in wool and oil, though undoubtedly that trade helped to orient trade links and hence the purchase of imported consumer goods, materials and equipment towards Britain. The rising flow depended closely on the achievement of a transition from British public capital support to substantial private capital inflow. It is that transition, occurring in about the mid-1820s, that was at least as important in sustaining imports, the British connection and the commercial and processing activity that depended on those imports.

Composition of Imports

Throughout the entire period, consumer goods dominated colonial imports. Initially, British government deliveries in kind emphasised the supply of ration goods to convicts. This fact is relevant to our perception of imports before the mid-1820s. W.C. Wentworth (1824) attempted to rescue early import statistics from oblivion for the period 1816–23. It is doubtful whether his efforts are useable though they are important in indicating the early high dependence on imports from non-British sources, particularly India and China. Basically, the colonies shifted gradually away from an Asian supply source to imports from Britain after 1820. Wentworth does not disclose the components of imports. But his totals are probably deficient in that he relied on recordings made without a systematic customs procedure (i.e. in which the Naval Officer of the day was concerned primarily with those goods on which import duties were imposed and from when he collected fees as salary). Wentworth's figures probably significantly undercounted total imports in these early years. Nevertheless, sufficient information is available on cargoes to determine the predominance of consumer goods on both public and private account. Moreover, it is clear that a high proportion of consumer goods imported were not finished goods but required local processing. This is even more the case with non-consumer items.

The official import data begin for Van Diemen's Land in 1822 and for NSW in 1826. They have all the defects of the export statistics with some special peculiarities. The chief additional problem in the case of imports was the determination of NSW to treat its fisheries output as both exports and imports. These have to be removed from the NSW import statistics to clarify the relative importance of major groups of imports and their removal is a matter of considerable importance in estimating capital inflows/balance of payments and the shares of commodity groups imported. Once we make this adjustment, it is clear that, whatever the statistical defects, imports were overwhelmingly consumer goods throughout the whole period and the trend significance of consumer goods tended to increase over time.

Essentially, NSW imports of consumer goods ran at around 70 to 80 per cent of all imports (see table 13.4, p.166). Van Diemen's Land shows the same basic characteristic and proportion (see *Returns of the Colony*). This is not surprising. In a primitive, inchoate economy, dependence on consumer goods reflected three conditions. One was the environmental and resource condition limiting local production of a wide range of goods. The second was the absence of large demands for capital equipment. The third was the fact that much of economic development represented a situation in which current consumer support from external sources was sought to allow the long gestation period in establishing a functioning economy.

Even with the changing relations between Britain and the colonies during and after the 1820s, Australia remained an isolated outpost. The number of ship arrivals

Table 13.4: Components of NSW Imports, 1827–50 (percentage shares)

	Food Drink Tobacco	Textiles Apparel	Household Goods	Total Consumer Goods	Metals Materials Products	Building Materials Products	Total Major Components
1827	38.6	26.6	3.2	68.5	7.4	2.1	78.0
1828	44.2	31.0	1.8	77.0	8.8	6.3	92.1
1829	41.5	27.9	2.6	72.0	9.0	7.5	88.5
1830	33.1	34.1	2.3	69.4	9.0	5.0	83.5
1831	30.0	33.7	2.2	65.8	8.9	5.3	80.0
1832	30.9	33.7	3.8	68.5	11.4	4.7	84.6
1833	31.9	35.6	3.4	70.9	13.4	5.7	90.1
1834	35.4	37.8	2.9	76.1	10.5	4.9	91.5
1835	38.8	36.7	3.5	79.0	8.7	5.7	93.4
1836	43.1	28.9	4.2	76.3	8.8	4.6	89.7
1837	32.6	37.9	5.3	75.9	9.6	4.2	89.6
1838	33.2	37.0	5.6	75.8	7.9	3.9	87.5
1839	41.8	33.8	4.2	79.9	7.2	4.0	91.1
1840	39.1	32.5	4.1	75.8	9.9	4.1	89.8
1841	44.5	22.9	4.3	71.7	11.8	4.5	88.0
1842	42.1	27.4	4.7	74.2	8.1	5.0	87.3
1843	38.7	41.2	3.4	83.2	5.1	3.7	92.1
1844	32.0	42.4	1.7	76.1	6.1	3.9	86.1
1845	39.0	41.5	2.2	82.7	6.1	3.8	92.6
1846	38.1	42.5	2.2	82.7	8.8	4.5	96.0
1847	45.4	34.3	2.4	82.1	7.9	3.4	93.4
1848	39.7	35.5	2.5	77.6	11.7	3.5	92.8
1849	34.9	42.4	2.8	80.2	10.0	3.2	93.4
1850	29.4	46.0	2.9	78.4	10.4	3.5	92.3

Source: Returns of the Colony.

certainly rose rapidly in trend terms so that an annual handful of overseas ship arrivals in 1810 had become annual hundreds by the close of the 1830s. Some implied competition of imports to local processing and craft activities. Many carried materials for local processing. Some carried a rising business of ship repair, refitting and victualling. The latter became a major activity for both Sydney and Hobart throughout the 1830s, offering both commercial and manufacturing opportunities. Increasingly regular cargo arrivals allowed colonial merchants to depend less on tenuous agencies and partnerships, with their tendencies to speculative deliveries, and to order goods more according to locally perceived demand.

Occupational/Industrial Composition

But did this mean a rising competitive threat to local Australian business, particularly manufacturing and craft activities? It is not possible to delineate very confidently the development of early Australian manufacturing and still less the small 'craft' enterprises that were clearly conducted extensively. We can pick up statistics of 'factories' for Van Diemen's Land from 1824 and for NSW from 1829. These factories, so-called, relate (in local terms) to significant enterprises, not to small shops. To that extent, given the early evidence of the presence of small crafts and the

Table 13.5: Cumberland Plain Self-Employed by Occupation/Industry, 1828 (Number of Persons)

	Total Private Workforce	Private Self-Employed	Self-Employed % Total Private
Professional	211	48	22.7
Food, Drink, Tobacco	906	230	25.4
Dealers	912	182	20.0
Personal Service	138	41	29.7
Metals	270	105	38.9
Woodworking	706	233	33.0
Bricks	83	41	49.4
Other Building	184	48	26.1
Total Building	973	322	33.1
Leather	425	144	33.9
Clothing, Textiles	288	90	31.3
Clerical	152	28	18.4
Clergy	132	4	3.0
Transport	264	34	12.9

Source: NSW Census.

later 19th-century emphasis in the statistics on very small undertakings, one can reasonably assume the presence of a large number of unrepresented businesses. Some indication can be gleaned from the 1828 Census in NSW. If we take merely the Cumberland Plain where most of the non-farm activity was then concentrated and confine attention simply to self-employed persons in the private workforce, it is possible to show one component not indicated by 'factory' statistics.

Table 13.5 shows the relevant contrasts and includes the main areas of non-farm occupations or industries. The first column gives the total private workforce in designated occupations/industries, the second the self-employed only and the third the percentage of self-employed in the total of the Cumberland Plain. What we cannot do, unfortunately, is identify the widely adopted practice of convicts working in specialised activities during their 'free' time. Episodically, it is clear that these services further enhanced the delivery of skilled craft products.

Here we are faced with a problem of interpreting the returns. Did the occupational designations truly indicate full-time commitment? If all occupations are so interpreted, it would follow that, in single person enterprises alone, we have to add 33 to 40 per cent or more to the strictly 'manufacturing' or processing activities. In principle, it seems likely that single person enterprises were as indicated occupationally and industrially by the Census, while others engaged might be less likely to be so specialised. In this case, the fraction to be added might even be larger. Too much guesswork would be needed to estimate the likely supplements from tiny enterprises with, say, two to four employees, but it is clear enough from the Census that any plausible combination of self-employed and such tiny undertakings would have accounted for at least half and possibly more than two-thirds of the total manufacturing-processing-craft workforce. It seems likely that commercial activities, so labelled, were predominantly small and that these small shops accounted for the mass of the total private workforce.

Even so, the 'factory' statistics reported indicate a wide range of activity in both

Table 13.6(a): Van Diemen's Land Manufacturing, 1824–50, (Number of Enterprises)

	1824	1830	1835	1840
Agricultural Implements		4	10	15
Breweries	3	11	13	22
Candles		2	2	5
Cooperage		2	3	12
Coaches			2	2
Distilling	1	2	3	
Dyers			3	4
Engineering			6	7
Fellmongering		4	3	5
Foundries		1	3	4
Furriers			2	10
Mast Blocks			1	1
Mills, Steam			1	NA
Mills, Other Power	5	36	46	53
Potteries		2	1	1
Printing	1	3	5	7
Rope	1	1	1	1
Sails	1	1	3	5
Sawmills	1	2	2	NA
Shipwrights			4	6
Snuff			1	
Soap	1	1	1	
Sugar			1	
Tanneries	6	19	12	14
Woolstaplers		1	3	5

Source: Statistics of Van Diemen's Land.

colonies. In reading them, one should bear in mind that a high proportion of these so-called factories would also be multifunctional, operating as producers, direct sellers and in many cases deliverers (transporting) to customers. The Van Diemen's Land statistics suggest a number of industries in which local natural resource inputs would have been large — most obviously in candle making, fellmongering, milling and sawmilling, in tanneries and woolstaplers (see table 13.6(a)). In the NSW statistics, there would have been a comparable high input of local materials in brewing, soap, candles, wool cloth and tanning and possibly also in hat-making. It is not credible that grain milling was not also conducted extensively in NSW. However, in other factories, even where some local inputs would have been present (distilling, coach-making, pottery, for example) the value added component of total output was much higher than in simple processing operations. For the rest, and partly for these industries using some local materials, activity depended heavily on imported materials.

Clearly a considerable proportion of these 'large' enterprises depended on the increasing supply of local materials, in agriculture, the pastoral industry, in whaling and in the direct industrial exploitation of local timber, clays, stone, lime etc. This may invite the assumption that there was a strong staple dependence and that Australian manufacturing developed predominantly around (a) food and drink, (b) clothing and textiles and (c) building and construction, with one other prominent group in metal goods production a special non-staple category using imported materials (Abbott & Nairn, 1969). This is at best partially true. There are two basic problems with this. Firstly, many foods and drinks were imported subject to local

Table 13.6(b): NSW Manufacturing, 1829–40, (Number of Enterprises)

	1829	1830	1835	1840
Distilleries	3	3	2	2
Rectifying				3
Breweries	6	13	10	8
Soap, Candles	6	15	4	5
Tobacco		2	2	4
Wool Cloth	6	11	7	4
Hats	2	2	2	1
Ropes	1	3	2	3
Tanning	11	34	17	14
Miscellaneous	2	1	29	48

Source: Vamplew (1987).

processing while a great deal of clothing and textile activity used non-woollen materials. Secondly, to reiterate, this 'factory' grouping conceals the scale and variety of manufacturing and processing carried on in non-factory enterprises and there is reason to believe that these not only accounted for the greater part of total output, but also displayed a much wider variety of products and materials, many of them imported. Once we incorporate very specialised activities (watchmaking, jewellery, silver- and goldsmithing, pipe-making etc.) and add their activities where they match with those conducted in factories — we have a radically different picture of import competition and replacement.

Enough has been said about the supply of imported skills to indicate the variety of human capital to exploit small business oportunities and to suggest that the local ability to compete in terms of skills existed. It has also been indicated that con-victism was not an insuperable barrier to considerable flexibility in the use of these skills. Enough has been said, also, about the external resources supplied publicly and privately to sustain expenditure standards and satisfy a wide range of preferences in the colonies. In the next section, the staple supplement to consumption standards, the growth of exports will be taken up. This supplement provides part of the structural development of early Australia. The specific question that now remains is whether declining isolation with increasing ship arrivals throughout 1815–40 attenuated the opportunities for local processing/manufacturing and commerce in Australia.

This question really becomes three interrelated ones. Firstly, given the increasing orientation towards British imports, what was happening to British prices in the relevant goods range? Secondly, what was happening to British freight rates? And thirdly, how did the rate of increase of arriving ships (or their tonnage) relate to the physical ability to deliver goods cargoes to Australia?

As to the first issue, British price indexes relevant to the range of Australian imports suggest a flat U-shape over time (Mitchell, 1988). Prices peaked in 1818 during the post-Napoleonic inflation and then fell heavily by about one-third to the mid-1820s. They fluctuated around this low-point to the end of the 1820s and then rose steadily about 20 to 25 per cent up to 1839–40. It is likely that, through competitive pressures, there may have been some external depressant on Australian industry and commerce in the second half of the 1820s. But from the late 1820s, the rise in British price levels significantly reversed any such tendency and helped to sustain Australian competitiveness.

Before commenting on ocean transport costs, it is convenient to look a little more closely at the implications of the rising overseas ship arrivals. Most long-distance ships could pick up freight from Australia so that increasing arrivals appeared to provide an encouragement to exports. But inward goods movements were not nearly so correlated with ship arrivals. The large trend rise between 1815 and 1840 might be disaggregated into convict ships, whalers and those carrying free immigrants apart from freighters. It was the first of these three groups that dominated the increased flow of shipping. To that extent, Australia remained, throughout the 1810–40 period, much more isolated in freight terms than it might appear — in other words, distance and isolation continued to encourage local import competition. Moreover, convict and later immigrant ships carried a rising local demand to be satisfied partly by local production.

That distance from the increasingly important British sources of imports implied, even with declining freight charges, relatively high transport costs. We know little of the specifics of freight (or insurance) charges by British shippers. One of the outstanding gaps in British economic history is the absence of a substantial study of the British marine industry. As data become available we know that freight charges on wool exports from Australia varied remarkably little in terms of charges per unit volume. To the extent that this is any indicator of freight costs on imports, it would suggest that transport costs on the value of imports may have risen between 1815–25 and then fallen but comparatively little during 1825–40.

But what was more significant was the fact that the total costs of shipping freight from Britain over such long distances were high. This implied a strong discouragement to the inflow into Australia of bulky, low value commodities. From the point of view of Australian importers, given the presence of skills in Australia, it was far more efficient to import either high-value finished goods (spirits were an outstanding example) or to introduce processed and semi-processed materials that could be compacted in transit and amplified into more cumbersome final products in Australia. This specification conforms to the basic and persistent pattern of imports during the three decades to 1840. The ability to compete with imports was reinforced by the fact that skilled immigrants from Britain were combining their labour with materials with which they were directly familiar.

Natural Resource Development, Consumption and Exports

Introduction

Regardless of the level of public support that was offered or claimed by the colonies, British intrusion into Australia posed the task or opportunity of exploiting available natural resources. British government pressures to make the colonies self-supporting emphasised the task aspect. Private individuals were also preoccupied with sheer survival in conditions of isolation. But early private enterprise also responded to the opportunities.

The innovative and directed responses of private individuals and of colonial governments found a potential in agriculture, in pastoral industry, in marine harvests, in timber-getting and in mining in particular, all reflecting the supply side of Australian natural resources. These were the accessible staples. How effectively did these staple products contribute to Australian economic development? Were they primarily support for local consumption? Were there significant linkages with other activities? Were these natural resources the foundation for exports that could allow Australians to enlarge their market through external trade?

One of the basic problems in answering these questions is: what, in these peculiar conditions, does one mean by external trade and local consumption? External trade is normally defined in relation to goods passing across national boundaries. Local or domestic consumpticn or production occurs within national boundaries. These distinctions became shadowy in early Australia for several reasons. Explicit external trade as an interchange of exports and imports developed early and grew rapidly after 1815. Visiting ships and their crews became progressively more important as a source of foreign exchange earnings (or as a means of barter). But most of all, the role of the Commissariat in acquiring or purchasing local production to be consumed locally opened the way for quasi-exports. These purchases were concentrated on farm and pastoral products, particularly grain, potatoes and meat. They could be and were made wholly within the colony. Or they could prompt a flow of what would otherwise be treated as intercolonial trade, as in the case of NSW official purchases of agricultural produce from Van Diemen's Land. But, as intercolonially traded goods produced officially, they ended in an entitlement either to overseas goods or to liquid foreign exchange.

Once we take official intra- and intercolonial trade into account, agriculture in Australia assumes a meaning different from the direct local production of goods to meet the immediate and basic consumption needs of the colonists. The same conclusion applies to foreign ship visits. Yet, in conditions of isolation and with precarious links with the outside world, agriculture was basic to individual and group survival. Given the meats derived from the pastoral industry, the same applies to the early growth of livestock. An important question then arises as to what tensions existed between public purchases and private interests and between exports and quasi-exports as a means of acquiring access to foreign imports.

Despite its immediate relevance as a basis for colonial survival, agriculture cannot be treated merely as an industry related to local consumption even when output was consumed locally. Indeed, particularly until the early 1820s, it appears as the single most important local output used in acquiring access to foreign supplies or exchange. Its limitations were, however, major ones. Apart from restrictive problems arising from harvest variability and the narrow range of achievable products, agricultural and meat sales to the Commissariat (and probably often to visiting ships) could be constrained by the degree to which proceeds could be flexibly used to purchase imports. Barter arrangements, the limitations on convertibility of Commissariat notes or the sheer shortage of colonial currency for domestic purposes could limit the import capability flowing from quasi-exports to the Commissariat even though those purchases were ultimately funded by the British Treasury.

In one way or another, then, we have to take the full range of natural resource exploitation into account, though in different ways, to display the full range of colonial 'exporting' potential.

The character of major export and quasi-export earnings and industries

Wool, oil, deliveries to the increasing flow of overseas ships and quasi-exports were the dominant items as Australian export capability developed after 1810. Let us put these in some general perspective relative to each other.

Maritime activity provided oil as the major product. This offshore enterprise had begun with sealing and continued with a miscellany of sea products including timber, shells, skins and seal oil during the 1810s. These products were sufficient to encourage colonists to persist with the sea even though the peak of seal cargoes appears to have been reached in 1812, after which sealing declined rapidly. Investment in local ships and their operation paid off by the early 1820s for NSW as they participated in (mostly close) offshore whaling. In Van Diemen's Land, whaling was delayed until later and depended greatly on estuarine catches of black whales during the 1820s. However, efforts were rewarded by rapid increases in whaling catches, including some sperm whales, so that from the late 1820s and by the mid-1830s Van Diemen's Land rivalled NSW in the output and export of whale products. This was one major turnaround over the 30 years in the early development of colonial exports.

One needs to avoid reading history backwards or focusing undue attention on wool. Whaling development, in particular, was led by foreign intervention in the southern fisheries. From these foreign ships came a rising demand for support services. As local colonial populations expanded, the ports of Sydney and Hobart became prime havens for revictualling and repairs (Cumpston, 1977) throughout the 1830s.

In the circumstances, colonial catches and revenues from these visitors may well have significantly exceeded the export proceeds from the Australian pastoral industry throughout the whole period to 1840. It was far from unreasonable for some colonists to look to the sea as their prime source of export income right up to 1840. Nevertheless, foreign visitors placed the colonists in a highly dependent condition and, indeed, almost immediately after 1840 there was a drastic decline in visitors, with especially depressive effects on Hobart. The alternative of exploiting land resources had, of necessity, been imposed on the colonists during the first 25 years after the first settlement. From those land resources, a miscellany of products, comparable to the maritime miscellany in the early years, came in the form of timber, coal, skins and curios (sic) for export. This continued to be the effective horizon until after the Napoleonic Wars even though ambitious hopes and promises for a prospective wool export were held and made. The wool trickle of the 1810s became a firm flow during the 1820s and moved by the mid-1830s to be the major single Australian export.

In the meantime, however, rural resource development was induced by other imperatives and other incentives. Until 1830, for the mass of landholders farming in Australia typically meant some combination of agriculture and animal husbandry. Though pastoral enterprises became increasingly specialised after 1830, all types of farming in Australia were strongly geared to consumption within the colonies, whether of crops or of meats. In contrast with maritime ventures, rural resource development presented fewer risks despite Aborigines, climatic variations and the need to come to terms with the new environment. It was possible for small farming by persons with little capital to coexist beside large landholders. This was particularly so of Van Diemen's Land where climate and soil conditions were more appropriate to small-scale farming and conditions were more akin to those understood in Britain (Hartwell, 1954). As pastoral activity expanded after the late 1820s, it became progressively less feasible for small pastoralists to be leaders in the industry and particularly so in NSW. For small landholders, non-specialised farming that included not merely crops but also some small number of animal populations and timber production was a common pattern. But it was predominantly a coastal pattern, not one that was widely feasibly in the hinterland.

For the larger pastoralists, however, a different set of incentives prevailed and particularly so during the 1820s and 1830s. They, too, tended in the 1820s to combine some agriculture with pastoralism. But the pastoral industry offered prospects quite apart from immediate sales of wool and carcass products. Substantial real estate holdings, supported by assigned convicts, were a major incentive to investment. And livestock generated natural increase that gave scope for further enterprise expansion or the sale of live animals. These prospects, and not merely wool sales, were major factors, in substantial, though not complete, contrast with the local whaling industry, in attracting British private capital and reducing the local dependence on own capital accumulation in both NSW and Van Diemen's Land.

Whereas up to 1810 and, indeed, into the 1810s, larger landholders tended to combine farming interests with commerce and maritime ventures, after 1815, an increasing separation of investment followed. With extensive spread of settlement out of the Cumberland Plain and the estuaries of Van Diemen's Land into the interior, the paths of the two growing export industries diverged particularly during the 1820s and 1830s. Though, as has been suggested, the colonies became less isolated during these two decades, the pastoral industry, in particular, was moving for a large part of this time away from ports, confronting mounting transport problems to deliver exports. As they moved into the Port Phillip area by the mid-1830s, the expanding fringe moved once more back into contact with the sea. But until then, it seems implausible to see much of pastoral expansion as driven by short-term wool prices and immediate sales. A long-term investment commitment was fundamental to building up an eventual pastoral export industry. It may have been fortunate then that local consumption of carcass products and foodstuffs provided a large and probably the major part of total pastoral sales throughout the whole 30 years.

Maritime producers did look to external sales and to this extent the conditions of external markets were more immediately relevant. In the few cases of offshore whaling, this is somewhat qualified by the long duration of whaling voyages but the major shipping asset was more readily deployable outside whaling so that reallocation due to price changes was more feasible. For bay whalers, adaptation could be more rapid. External conditions for wool and other minor pastoral exports had no immediate implication except where wool was sold locally to merchants and accumulated assets were not so readily transferable. Colonists were clearly alert for news of wool sale successes or failures in Britain by the mid-1820s (cf. the early sales listings in the *Sydney Gazette*), if only to determine long-term strategy. In considering demand conditions for these two major industries, we need to read the evidence rather differently for each. It is convenient, with this proviso, to turn to the evolving overseas demand conditions during 1810–40.

In doing so, let us recall the intellectual baggage of the colonists whether free or convict. Coming throughout 1800–40 from an increasingly urbanised Britain, many would have been aware, if only by handling the relevant objects as domestic servants, of the value placed on whale oil for lighting. More obviously, British whaling interests like the Enderbys provided direct initiative in colonial whaling (Hartwell, 1954). Other arrivals would have had some awareness of the growing mechanisation of British industry and the increasing importance of oil for machinery. More generally, in the early years of the century, oil and whaling products were well recognised as saleable articles not only in Britain but also in Asia.

In the case of wool, the woollen textile industry was widely accepted as the 'premier' industry of Britain. Sheepgrowing was a major rural activity and wool, as a textile fibre, penetrated the homes and lives of both rural and urban people in Britain. Marsden from Yorkshire and Macarthur, the son of a draper, are merely two obvious candidates who would have had this understanding. Textile workers were strongly represented in the flow of convicts from Britain (Nicholas, 1988). As the Australian pastoral industry developed towards an export capability, absentee investment and corporate investment by British residents increasingly tied the understanding of British demand to Australian conditions. Initially, the British market prospects can have been little more than an ambitious future prospect. By the mid-1810s, entry into that market was beginning to be a realisable objective.

Intellectual baggage was, however, only one part of the explanation. The evidence of the formation of the South Australia Company and the Van Diemen's Land Company, for example, shows the origins of such proposals existing back before 1820. Proposals for corporate interest in pastoral activity in Australia appear related to individuals in Britain who had an interest in the textile industry, in finance and in wider imperial growth. These persons and the capital that they assembled were an important contributor to the eventual development.

We can take up the question of growing export capability by dealing with the development of agriculture and quasi-exports or we can move directly to those commodities that became the major overt exports. There is a case for doing the latter despite the necessity to establish a food supply base within the colony(ies). One reason lies in the very early preoccupation of settlers with the development of an independent export capability. The other arises from the possibility that quasi-exports may not have been an unmixed blessing in the development of that capability. This is an important matter — that quasi-exports may have retarded independent exports needs to be discussed in the supply side response within Australia to perceptions of overseas demand. It is convenient to look at this matter after discussing demand conditions as they evolved over the three decades to 1840.

Formal Exports: British demand for imports of wool and oil

Britain was a major producer of wool and oil, both long-established industries by 1810. Oil competed with animal fats, and tallow in particular, as both lighting and lubrication. Oil from marine animals was, subject to price, income levels and the increase of mechanisation, strongly preferred over alternatives for both lighting and lubrication.

Wool faced substitutes in animal skins, linen and silk and increasingly in the rapidly growing cotton textile products, particularly after 1750. All of these substitutes were supplied in large volumes from British industry. Wool, however, was a strongly entrenched product in British preferences, from tradition, scale of supply and climate, and cotton provided substitutes essentially for lighter clothing, undergarments, sheeting etc.

Britain and America, in particular, had competed for oil supplies from the Atlantic fisheries during the second half of the 18th century. The scale of international competition in whaling at that stage was making considerable inroads into Atlantic supplies and the 'southern fisheries' prospects may have been part of the stimulus to the British settlement in Australia. The American Revolution had one fallout in displacing much of the American whaling interests to the European continent. Subsequently, the massive shipbuilding activity prompted by the Napoleonic Wars (peaking in 1812) provided Britain with the resources to extend its whaling activities (Mitchell, 1988). The terms of the settlement after the end of the Napoleonic Wars assured a high degree of freedom for British ships to roam the world, including whaling in their activities. Accordingly, they were prime actors in the development of the 'southern fisheries' and, in the second half of the 1810s, had displaced many earlier American venturers in the waters around Australia.

Britain remained the dominant producer of whaling products throughout 1810–40 and a powerful whaling lobby protected their interests in the British market through the imposition of customs duties, limiting imports. Increasing real incomes in Britain, increasing urbanisation and increasing mechanisation promoted an escalating demand for oil. In trend terms, these changes outstripped British supply, even though a substitute, gas, was beginning to emerge in the early 19th century. The effects of overall demand increase for domestic and industrial purposes were subject to two major destabilising conditions. One was the series of fluctuations in business activity in Britain, with significant booms and slumps during 1810–40. Aggravating these fluctuations, the nature of the supply, depending on variable numbers of whaling ships engaged in long voyages and uncertain catches, created considerable volatility in prices. Competing suppliers, such as the Australian colonists, faced

Table 13.7: Estimated Wool and Oil Price Indexes

	Index UK Wool 1830=100	Oil Index 1830=100
1810	177.8	140.3
1811	144.4	141.9
1812	150.0	137.1
1813	166.7	122.6
1814	211.1	108.1
1815	244.4	104.8
1816	177.8	71.0
1817	166.7	98.4
1818	244.4	108.1
1819	183.3	104.8
1820	183.3	106.5
1821	155.6	64.5
1822	133.3	66.1
1823	125.0	67.7
1824	133.3	60.5
1825	194.4	83.9
1826	144.4	106.5
1827	127.8	93.5
1828	122.2	78.2
1829	111.1	83.1
1830	100.0	100.0

Sources: Wool, Mitchell (1988).
        Oil, Tooke (1857).

import duties, distant business fluctuations and supply gluts with a price variance that was not easily predictable.

The British market conditions suggest a considerable price decline in both commodities from the latter part of the Napoleonic Wars and a sharp, but brief, price increase in the mid-1820s. Both export industries were, in general, expanding in the face of a trend price fall prior to 1830.

These were tough market conditions for any foreign exporters let alone small-scale colonial operators, at best seeking a marginal niche. The wool market had a greater stability both in trend and fluctuation. In this case, however, Britain was constrained in terms of the type of wool it could produce domestically and for a range of purposes the British market depended on foreign suppliers. The British domestic wool clip between 1800 and 1820 averaged annually some 100 million pounds in weight, with an annual average income of around £10 million sterling. Domestic output rose steadily throughout the first half of the 19th century to an annual average of 110 million pounds (in weight) in 1820–24, rising to 120 million pounds in 1830–34 and 125 million pounds in 1840–44 (Mitchell, 1988). This was substantially long-staple soft wools, despite British efforts to introduce fine short-fibre merino animals.

Increased volume of consumption occurred despite the rising supply of substitutes, particularly cotton. Technological change in the cotton industry is, of course, generally accepted as one of the prime conditions of the Industrial Revolution, altering the structure and mode of operation as well as the range of cotton products available on the British and world markets. Mechanised methods were also applied increasingly after 1780 to woollen production gradually throughout the first half of the 19th century, shifting the output of woollens towards factory production. Although it could not keep pace with the expansion of domestically produced cottons, the output of woollens nevertheless continued to expand to meet British home demand and the rising volume of British exports particularly to North America and Europe.

Woollen products used short-fibre wool, not necessarily very fine, as the weft in woollen fabrics. This then provided one source of demand for short woollen fibres that Australia came to show itself capable of producing. But there was another demand for short-fibre wool in which quality was really not important. This was the worsted industry. Here products of variable qualities were produced, reaching up into the high quality market for which short-fibre wools were essential.

For short-fibre fine wools, Britain depended on continental supplies, initially from Spain and Portugal, and subsequently from Germany (Saxon wool). In volume terms, these provided a tiny supplement of 6.3 million pounds (weight) at the end of the Napoleonic Wars or about 6 per cent of British wool production by volume. These wools were, however, much more highly priced at 2 to 3 times British wools so that the import supplement by value was higher than, though still only around 15 per cent of the value of, British raw wool output. By 1820–21 the average volume flow from Germany and the Iberian peninsula had almost quadrupled without much change in relative prices. By 1830–1, the flow doubled again though at a significant relative price loss to imported wools. Thereafter the imports of these European fine wools levelled off and Spain had become a minor source. At the beginning of the 1830s, these wools equalled about 20 per cent of British domestic wool production by volume and approximately 25 to 30 per cent by value (Mitchell, 1988).

The low import level and rapid rise were due to two special conditions. Firstly, at the end of the 18th century, Britain had been particularly backward in worsted production of short-fibre fine wools. Interest in factory production of worsteds appears to have developed slowly by about 1780. But the technical leaders were French producers and British access to French technology was facilitated by the Napoleonic Wars. During the wars and for the next two decades after them, the number of British worsted factories and investment in them rose extremely rapidly. But supplies depended basically on German and Spanish merino flocks.

This merino wool, as high-priced wool, served the quality end of the British market. It was produced under conditions that imposed high cost — winter feeding, enclosing of animals — and it was transported in German transport conditions that significantly enhanced the landed price in Britain. Moreover, it came from traditional 'old enemies', a strategic and political issue that appears to have eventually influenced British attitudes about Australia's potential as substitute source of wools. Certainly, these conditions appear to have provided an opportunity in the long run for Australian producers to cut into these European supplies of wool. Despite distance, the fact that Australian sheep did not require such attention radically altered relative cost conditions. Ultimate success depended, however, on producing the appropriate quality competition. In the meantime, it was possible for Australia to deliver weft wool to the woollen industry.

Australian supply of oil and wool: trend issues of quantity and quality

In neither marine oils nor in wool did Australian producers succeed in matching the quality of competitors by 1840. Figure 13.5 (p.178) shows UK wool imports by origin and gives an appearance of a success story in which, from minute beginnings in 1816, Australian had surpassed the stagnant Spanish and Portuguese supplies to Britain by the mid-1830s and was on the verge of toppling the much larger German supplies. In 1845, Australia seems to be Britain's prime external supplier (Mitchell, 1988). Unfortunately, this does not take into account price and quality, or the relative cleanliness of the wools. When one does so, Australian supplies shrink considerably in significance. However, notwithstanding quality differences, German supplies were set on a downward trend from a peak in 1835. There was a German supply constraint. But, in addition, even though Australian wool was not then in the same class as the Saxon merino, its quality had greatly improved. If not yet serving the very top end of the British worsted market, it was fine enough to deliver a substitute that would satisfy many purposes. But to attain that qualified approval required a slow and relatively haphazard path. The design was a long time coming and faced a variety of obstacles in Australia. Some of these obstacles, as we will see, derived from the British Government itself, even if unintentionally.

Similar qualified comments apply to Australian marine products though, in this case, Australian exports to Britain were never more than a small component, although the exports were important to the Australian colonies. Distance was a prime obstacle to a great deal of Australian marine oil in that black whale oil was relatively strongly represented. Black whale oil tended to go rancid much more readily than sperm oil. While British whalers concentrated on sperm whales, colonists particularly in Van Diemen's Land depended much more on black whales, the oil from which was typically priced between one-quarter and one-half that of sperm oil and

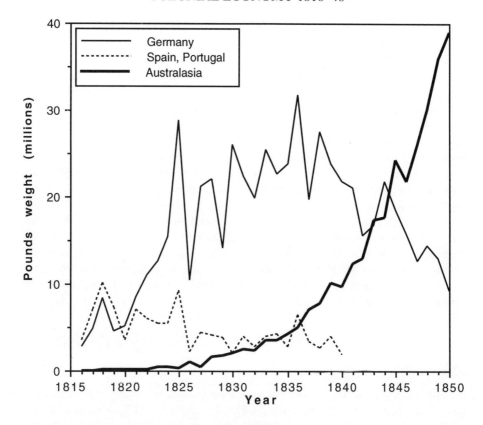

Figure 13.5: Origin of British Wool Imports, 1816–50

provided the major part of the colonial catch to 1840. In these respects, the colonial whaling industry regressed even though it provided a stimulus to colonial ship-building.

Fitful beginnings — A possible conflict of formal and quasi-exports

Supply conditions in both industries offered little immediate prospect for the first 20 years of the 19th century. We know little about Australian export activity before 1820. No economic history of whaling or of the pastoral industry before 1850 has been written. Detailed knowledge of farming in NSW is limited to the period up to 1820. There are major gaps that need to be filled by future research.

Until 1820, overt export efforts spanned a large variety of disparate activities. Sealing, kangaroo skins, Pacific timbers (particularly sandalwood), shells, amber-gris, occasionally other whale products, Australian cedar, coal and modest disposal of farm products to the small number of visiting ships completed the colonial horizon to 1810. After 1812, this horizon narrowed as sealing peaked with the first major depletion of Australian natural resources. Though wool began to emerge after 1812, the focus of Australian export endeavours, in practical terms, remained on

Asia and particularly on India even though Britain remained as a preferred alternative. Whaling was not yet ready to take the place of sealing until the early 1820s.

It is impossible to recover much statistically of these early disparate attempts in the colonies to earn foreign exchange. Severe constraints existed. Such newly formed settlements could not be expected to move rapidly into an export mode. A great deal of 'learning by doing' was necessary for survival. A large array of allocative demands were pressed on the colonists and it is, perhaps, surprising that so much was achieved by 1820. In addition, the East India Company's monopoly exercised limits on other than small ships trading in the Pacific until 1819. The rapid influx of convicts after 1812 added many more mouths to be fed rather than human capital to generate exports.

A partial recovery of export estimates — or 'guesstimates' — is useful if only as indicative of the limited horizons. Steven (1969b) has provided figures on exports to India though they are probably not complete. No means of estimating trade with China has been found. A somewhat heroic extrapolation of Australian wool export prices in the 1820s, tied to the most closely related British wool prices, gives an order-of-magnitude figure of possible wool export earnings in Britain to 1821. Omissions are, apart from China, other exports to Britain and sales to visiting ships. These omissions may add significantly to the absolute earnings, but do not alter the very small ratio of exports to gross domestic product (GDP) until 1821.

Whatever the omissions and errors, it is implausible that Australian exports before 1821 had attained more than 2 per cent or 3 per cent of GDP. By contrast with these figures, the annual purchases from the colony by the Commissariat in NSW were about twice the export earnings shown above for average 1810–11 and nearly three times that for the year 1821 for meat alone. Commissariat purchases of grain greatly

Table 13.8: NSW/Van Diemen's Land Export Records, 1807–21, (£)

	Australian Exports to India	Estimated Wool Exports to UK
1807		19
1808		42
1809	2 989	NA
1810	2 699	NA
1811	8 411	13
1812	2 542	NA
1813	10 132	NA
1814	2 396	NA
1815	3 214	3 500
1816	2 839	7 700
1817	7 026	1 300
1818	4 789	8 500
1819	14 250	7 300
1820	2 006	10 000
1821	6 422	14 000

Notes: (a) Exports to India from Steven in Abbott & Nairn (1969); volume of wool from Macarthur in Select Committee and wool values based on relativities of Australian realised prices and Lincoln Half-Hogg.
(b) Estimated at 1 rupee equals 2 shillings and 3 pence.

enhanced local sales to government, even though grain acquisitions rose more slowly than meat (Fletcher, 1976). During the 1810–21 period, the NSW Commissariat purchased 10 million pounds weight of meat, almost 350 000 bushels of wheat and some 125 000 bushels of maize for purposes of public distribution (Fletcher, 1976) in NSW. We do not know the corresponding purchases in Van Diemen's Land but the NSW levels are sufficient to indicate the massive scale of public demands relative to the total economy. Moreover, the rate of increase was extremely high. In NSW purchases of meat rose from an estimated £10 000 in 1810 to around £35 000 by 1820 (peaking at about £42 000 in 1817). Similarly wheat purchases escalated from £16 000 in 1811 (ignoring an exceptional low in 1810) to a peak of some £27 000 in 1819. Only maize, an inferior good, declined — from about £11 000 in 1810 to about £500 in 1820. These three items were the main but not the only quasi-exports, that the colonists effectively sent to the British government.

That these purchases helped to sustain local activity and provide an incentive to produce these goods can scarcely be doubted. This was accentuated for private settlers in that government had withdrawn almost completely from farming before 1810 and sustained only a slight pastoral activity between 1810 and 1820. There was another incentive to individuals — the threat of starvation. This was particularly so as the proportion of the population victualled by government in NSW declined from 40 to around 33 per cent between 1810 and 1819 (Vamplew, 1987). But the interesting question is whether these public purchases were an unqualified benefit in stimulating actual export endeavours.

NSW farming does not seem to have kept pace with these public pressures in NSW. The colony's wheat acreages, according to Fletcher (1976), rose from just under 10 000 acres in 1812 (data are missing for 1810–11) to just over 17 000 acres by 1821. The official tendency to keep the NSW settlement compact meant constraint on expansion. By contrast, however, wheat production was much more successful in Van Diemen's Land (*Statistics of Van Diemen's Land*, various issues). Wheat acreages increased from a mere 1500 acres in 1811 to almost exactly 13 000 acres in 1821, beginning to vie with the NSW total. With its small population, Van Diemen's Land was able to export grains, particularly wheat to NSW, by 1813. Here, the limited potential of the Cumberland Plain in NSW and the more amenable environmental conditions in Van Diemen's Land gave the latter a head start as a granary. Wheat was not the only crop for which the island colony was favoured. Root crops, particularly potatoes, became a major item of early intercolonial trade and quasi-export for Van Diemen's Land residents.

We know little of yields. Only a crude husbandry was practised. In NSW, farming relied on river flats exposed to frequent flooding, drought, diseases, pests and fire (sometimes set by Aborigines). In Van Diemen's Land, a shifting agriculture was adopted, cropping small areas of land as successively cleared, and moving away as soils were depleted. For both colonies, but especially in Van Diemen's Land, public purchases of grain and potatoes benefited particularly small landholders, able to convert some of their crops into bartered imports or into transferable notes.

So far as large landholders were concerned, the influence of public purchases seems very different. They were no longer able to dominate the dealings of small farmers with the Commissariat as they had done before 1810. But more importantly, after 1810, the officials (now in the main ex-officials) that had earlier led in farming endeavours largely abandoned grain production in favour of livestock (Fletcher,

1976). Though meat was purchased in small unit volumes from the tiny flocks of small farmers after 1810, the mass official purchases were made from the comparatively small number of large landholders (the *Sydney Gazette,* various issues). These dominated the pastoral industry of the Cumberland Plain, joined by a handful of successful ex-convicts (Fletcher, 1976). With their expanding livestock populations, they were still, during 1810–21, a driving force towards loosening the physical limits of the settlement and in expanding and consolidating pastoral holdings. In their hands lay the potential for developing wool exports.

In this context, Commissariat meat purchases were two-edged. They encouraged livestock activity and supplied large landholders with access to Commissariat resources either through barter or access to foreign exchange. They enhanced pastoralists' incomes substantially. But with these two positive implications, official purchases had opposing consequences. The scale of these purchases kept natural increase in check, limiting the expansion of livestock populations, particularly of sheep. And they provided a strong incentive to the growing of meat-producing animals, again particularly sheep. This may not have mattered immediately in Van Diemen's Land where the introduced sheep were dominantly long-woolled meat producing animals (Hartwell, 1954). However, in NSW, the consequence was to significantly retard the development of fine wool, particularly as the surge of convict arrivals between 1812 and 1820 led to escalating meat demands for convicts, officials and their dependents. Notwithstanding the demolition of the 'Macarthur myth' (Garran & White, 1985), there is no doubt that at least dim awareness of the potential for wool production existed at the turn of the century and grew in the closing stages of the Napoleonic Wars. Equally, by force of necessity or otherwise, the variety of sheep introduced early had the potential, provided a sufficient gene pool existed, to be culled into fine-woolled slighter-framed sheep. The Bengal sheep, the English coarse woolled sheep and an admixture of merino or merino-cross introduced before, and shortly after 1800, provided a genetic base that might have yielded fine or at least finer wool. Even when presented with the opportunity to give preference to merino, the colonial pastoralists tended to prefer 'larger and stronger' animals, restraining interest in developing the gene pool. An important reason lay in their access to a large and rising public demand for meat from whose sales access to imports could be achieved.

This was not the only retarding influence on the evolution of the pastoral industry. The colonists in NSW had chosen one of the worst locations in which to attempt to grow sheep and they continued to do so while they remained in a coastal environment on the mainland. Despite the fecundity of Bengal sheep, survival rates were poor in damp coastal conditions. Once again, public constraints operated as an impediment in endeavouring to limit settlement, initially to the Cumberland Plain and later even to the Nineteen Counties of the east coast and mountains up to the end of the 1820s.

As corporate British investment was made by the Australian Agricultural Company after 1824, the misreading of the Australian environment continued. The company's representatives were fully aware of problems of sheep growing in the wetter parts of Britain. Astonishingly, they chose, for their initial grant location an area that was little better than a swamp. The restricted transfer across the mountains to Bathurst placed the colonists for the first time into a location highly adapted to fine wool — once the genetic and climatic secrets were realised. Then the colonists were in a position to reap the benefit of both climate and the inheritance of thousands of years of 'fire-stick' farming practised by the Aborigines. But for more than a decade, expansion in that direction was constrained by government control. It remained for individuals to burst those bonds by illegal squatting in the interior.

Extensive Resource Use and Export Development
External Capital Support

The British government's decision, after 1821, to transfer the mass of convict arrivals into private assignment had two important implications. Firstly, it quickly reduced the significance of quasi-exports through declining purchases by the Commissariat. It still left the task of feeding and clothing convicts, but increasingly as a private responsibility. Secondly, it delivered an increased flow of unfree labour to be allocated, among other colonial competing ends, to interior settlement. That decision was accompanied by another of comparable or even greater substance. This was to declare Australia as an area for private investment. From that decision followed a flow of corporate and individual absentee investment and the migration of individuals with capital to fund the establishment of large-scale enterprises. This does not necessarily imply that these investors were the prime 'entrepreneurs' in Australian pastoral export activity. Some can claim that title (Statham, 1989). Several were interested in introducing more Saxon merino sheep into Australia, particularly in the 1820s. But it will be suggested that either many British investors lost much of their capital or they waited an extremely long time for substantial rewards. It is possible that the main gainers were colonials who acquired developed properties cheaply or exploited the British investors in other ways.

To measure these flows, we need to combine estimates of balances of payments with direct British outlays. There are two basic sources. One is the direct British subvention to the colonies in the early years. This began and continued into the early 1820s when some, but almost certainly very little, private capital inflow occurred. We can use this British subvention as a measure, albeit as some undercount, of capital inflow and as a proxy for the balance of payments from 1810–22.

It is unfortunate that we have a gap in the early to mid-1820s This was the period during which Britain began to reduce its fiscal commitment to the colonies, looking to both domestic fiscal arrangements and to private employment of convicts as a means of budgetary constraint and of altering the complexion of the colonial economies towards private enterprise. As local export capability built up rapidly during the 1820s, the real balance of payments and real capital dependence relative to gross domestic product shrank sharply, moving at around one-sixth to one-seventh of gross product up to 1840. The most striking reduction was, however, in the relative importance of the British government subvention which fell, generally, to around half these fractions. Its place was taken by private capital inflow which, with some aberrations, roughly approximated (at times fell below and at times exceeded) British official support to the colonies.

Despite these structural shifts, external capital appears as a primary driver of Australian expansion throughout the 1810–40 period. Total capital inflow rose faster than local domestic activity until the early 1820s but declined somewhat from the later 1820s. The fact that external capital support became less significant relative to

Table 13.9: NSW/Van Diemen's Land Public and Private Capital Inflow, 1810–50, (Current prices, £'000)

	Public British	Private
1810	139.3	NA
1811	213.9	
1812	155.7	
1813	147.7	
1814	168.5	
1815	149.0	
1816	181.9	
1817	201.7	
1818	145.3	
1819	160.5	
1820	313.0	
1821	248.8	
1822	NA	
1823	NA	
1824	324.1	
1825	354.2	
1826	430.2	NA
1827	234.1	196.1
1828	285.3	424.6
1829	281.1	391.4
1830	256.8	151.6
1831	247.7	22.2
1832	244.0	215.0
1833	282.8	167.1
1834	321.5	357.1
1835	361.2	327.4
1836	399.2	250.1
1837	351.3	196.4
1838	319.8	703.8
1839	295.7	1 052.9
1840	368.1	1 796.8
1841	354.2	1 808.2
1842	363.0	198.9
1843	364.2	440.2
1844	416.7	−425.1
1845	366.7	−491.6
1846	367.3	−111.2
1847	355.3	83.1
1848	292.8	−220.0
1849	294.9	−65.4
1850	259.2	−142.5

Note: NA — Not available.

the domestic economy, and the timing at which this change occurred, should be noted. Fundamentally, however, external capital, firstly public and then jointly public and private, appears as a major contribution of the ability of the colonies to sustain a high level of activity in the process of forming the early substitute for the original Aboriginal economy.

Extensive Settlement

A third change followed throughout the 1820s and 1830s, related to these two flows, in the formal decision to allow, subject to constraint, a large expansion of the area of colonial settlement. This began the move towards the truly extensive settlement of Australia and into a broad collision with Aborigines. Supposedly, it was controlled by the system of land grants until the late 1820s. Those land grants defined areas where settlement was approved. In practice, this meant all but the south-west corner of Van Diemen's Land. In NSW, the concentration was on the areas towards Bathurst–Monaro in the west, Illawarra in the south and the Hunter and Manning River valleys in the north (Roberts, 1935). These areas were formally delineated as the Nineteen Counties in 1829. Substantially, they were coastal riverine valleys and the mountain chain moving to the western foothills.

Within these geographical limits, notwithstanding some early efforts to sell public lands, grants now regularly altered their character. In place of the common pre-1820 small land grants to ex-convicts, the areas granted in NSW and to a lesser extent in Van Diemen's Land, frequently became substantial, typically of 1000 to 2000 acres and upwards (Roberts, 1935). The 1 million acre grant to the Australian Agricultural Company in 1824 was exceptional, but other very substantial grants were made, supposedly to accord with the capital possessed by immigrants or by absentees who delivered resources to the colony and took convicts out of public hands. Van Diemen's Land was particularly active in attempting to attract migrants and investors. Nevertheless, NSW also, in addition to the major project of the Australian Agricultural Company, attracted a significant inflow of free immigrants with capital and individual absentee investors during the 1820s. Grants of land proceeded apace in both colonies outside the early bridgehead areas. In Van Diemen's Land, they took colonial settlement inland along the main river systems and well into the interior of the island; in NSW, the dominant grant area spread along the reaches of the Hunter River and into the mountains (Hartwell, 1954).

By the beginning of the 1830s, substantially the whole of Van Diemen's Land except the south-west forest area was occupied. In NSW, the illicit use of land adjoining or near grant areas enlarged effective holdings. This 'squatting' extended rapidly as settlers broke the bounds of the settlement limits and passed into the NSW plains, moving illegally north, west and south. As they did, settlers from Van Diemen's Land joined in the squatting process to occupy the rich lands of southern and western Port Phillip and moved north to meet the southward flow of settlers from NSW. During the second half of the 1830s, the flows merged and pushed westward to reach the Darling River.

This rapid absorption of Van Diemen's Land and the south-eastern mainland presented the settlers with major environmental changes and new problems of 'learning by doing'. Limited largely to riverine coastal areas during the 1820s on the mainland and with Van Diemen's Land settlement still strongly concentrated in riverine conditions, the new style of capitalist landholder could revert to the pre-1800 mode of combining pastoral and agricultural activity. Even in the mountains, where agriculture was less attractive, distance largely compelled some combination of agriculture with other endeavours. On the mainland, the Hunter and Manning Valleys came to be a prime agricultural area in which the larger farmers were able to employ more capital intensive and innovative farming methods (the *Sydney Gazette*). But here, still, as on the Cumberland Plain, their agricultural and pastoral efforts were plagued by diseases and pests, drought and flood. Crop yields were highly variable and uncertain. Sheep were subject to coastal diseases, particularly footrot. In the mountains, with poor soils, only a low yield agriculture was achieved.

Van Diemen's Land still continued to sustain a higher rate of agricultural expansion thanks to a more secure, mild climate and better soils (Hartwell, 1954). In this case, however, the very large number of small grants made to ex-convicts limited the application of capital and technology, despite the influx of free immigrants. Farming methods remained poor and a mobile form of agriculture continued. Nevertheless, the island sustained its role as a vital source of crops for the mainland. This became the more important as settlement spread into the interior and conditions changed once more to favour, as it had done during the period 1800–20, the pastoral specialisation of large landholders. The joint endeavours of NSW coastal and Van Diemen's Land agriculturists were vital in sustaining the burst of relatively specialised expansion during the 1830s.

It is important, then, to appreciate the scale of this agricultural development and the dependence of NSW on imports of crops, particularly grain crops, as a condition of pastoral development. Unfortunately, the statistics are limited. The major farm activities were wheat and maize growing, orchard products and potatoes, with supplements provided by other grains and vegetables. Given its key significance, the following table indicates the joint development of the two colonies in the production

Table 13.10: Production and NSW Wheat Imports, 1821–40

	NSW Acres Under Crop	NSW Wheat Acres	NSW Wheat Bushels	VDL Acres Under Crop	VDL Wheat Acres	VDL Wheat Bushels	NSW Wheat Imports Bushels
1821	32 273	17 356	NA	14 940	12 967	168 571	
1822		NA	NA		13 200	171 600	
1823		NA	NA		13 314	173 082	
1824		NA	NA		14 500	188 500	
1825	45 515	NA	NA		15 500	201 500	
1826		NA	NA		17 000	221 000	
1827		NA	NA		19 000	247 000	
1828	71 523	NA	NA	34 038	20 357	264 641	85 716
1829		NA	NA	38 802	24 423	318 641	107 929
1830		NA	NA	55 977	31 155	511 000	70 904
1831		29 442	476 334	54 219	31 007	350 000	74 892
1832	60 520	36 580	406 690	56 626	26 346	390 000	44 908
1833	60 520	36 679	559 225	61 400	26 568	232 548	19 507
1834	74 811	48 667	780 700	69 041	26 974	218 348	15 568
1835	79 256	46 237	510 226	87 283	33 931	508 965	122 908
1836	87 432	51 616	884 153	89 528	40 389	485 969	263 956
1837	92 125	59 975	692 620	79 429	32 012	509 569	114 416
1838	92 912	47 977	469 140	108 000	41 796	550 189	79 166
1839	95 312	48 211	802 540	100 348	40 350	571 703	470 971
1840	126 116	72 193	1 066 394	124 103	60 813	839 985	289 436

Note: NA — Not available.
Sources: NSW from *Returns of the Colony*, Van Diemen's Land from *Statistics of Van Diemen's Land*.

of wheat and NSW dependence on imports of wheat, a great deal of it from Van Diemen's Land.

The linkages between agriculture and pastoral activity may then be seen as going through three phases. Broadly, these fall into successive decades. During the 1810s, with settlement still constrained in the vicinity of the original bridgeheads, the two 'industries' were divided to a large extent by size of landholding. During the 1820s, agricultural and pastoral activity was widely conjoined particularly in the expanding riverine valleys, each providing income flows to given producers and particularly large landholders. During the 1830s, coastal and to some extent mountain agriculture supported the specialisation of pastoral producers in the interior; and, to repeat, Van Diemen's Land assisted the greater pastoral specialisation of NSW, particularly in the 1830s.

Pastoral Expansion and Wool Quality

Until settlers burst their coastal bounds, pastoral development remained strongly geared to local meat consumption. At given ration rates and prevalent prices throughout the 1820s and 1830s, meat sales (including the imputed value of on-property consumption) considerably surpassed incomes from wool. Estimating on the basis of a viable slaughter rate of both sheep and horned cattle, NSW is unlikely to have been self-sufficient in meat until as late as 1835. In this case, Van Diemen's Land could not supply fresh meat though it did deliver some preserved meats to the larger colony.

In the movement towards an expanded mainland colony, there were then several tensions in the development of pastoral enterprise, particularly from the late 1810s to the mid-1830s. So long as expanded settlement concentrated on coastal environments, climatic conditions did not favour sheep, particularly fine wool sheep. The overt demand for meat continued to induce emphasis on large-framed meat-producing animals in contrast with the smaller-bodied fine wool sheep. For the same reason, there were market pressures to produce cattle that could thrive on coastal conditions. On the other hand, the inflow of new British entrants into the pastoral industry confirmed the link between Australian pastoralism and British wool import demands. Those demands were almost entirely for fine wool and some at least of the new entrants in both NSW and Van Diemen's Land were aware of that British demand orientation.

Van Diemen's Land appears as having a greater task of adaptation to confront these tensions than did NSW. The island began with a concentration on large long-woolled sheep, possibly mainly Leicesters and only gradually received a few merinos or merino crosses. Hartwell (1954) has recorded that for many producers, at least in the first half of the 1820s, wool was simply discarded and left to rot after shearing. Wool was an added cost in the process of meat production. Moreover, despite the improved conditions as the industry moved into the interior of the island, Van Diemen's Land was not as well adapted to fine wool sheep as was the interior of NSW. That qualification was not vital during the 1820s. Coastal NSW was similarly unsuitable. In the first half of the 1820s, the Van Diemen's Land pastoral industry was able to produce only poor quality, very low-price wool. This experience created an incentive to alter the genetic mix and it was with this aim that the Van Diemen's Land Company was formed in 1825. The company was pivotal in providing Saxon wool imports into the island.

Nevertheless, in NSW, the mixtures of sheep introduced between 1800–20 had already shown a potential for at least finer wool. It is more than doubtful whether very conscious or consistent efforts were made before 1820 to plan for fine wool sheep on a consistent basis. The biggest shift in emphasis came with the introduction of new British entrants, among them the large corporate undertaking, the Australian Agricultural Company. This company introduced Saxon merinos and merino crosses and also sold parts of its expanding flocks sequentially to other pastoralists. None-theless, the Company's initial plans to buy Saxon sheep were dramatically scaled down and its immediate impact was consequently well below its original intent. The sales meant more than merely the disposal of individual sheep but included what might be described as small 'start-up' flocks that included rams, ewes and wethers. The Australian Agricultural Company was not the only concern interested in improving the quality of flocks for the British market but it initially became a particularly important innovator (Garran & White, 1985).

Some of the company's experiences are indicative of the initial ignorance of con-ditions and the high costs of learning by doing. The company chose as its initial grant a specially poor area, much of it swamp or near-swamp land. With explicit connections of some of its London directors with the British wool industry, it sought to establish high-grade wool along with agriculture. But it relied largely upon buying colonial sheep for this purpose. Appropriate farm machinery was introduced, along with indentured British farm workers to supplement a large number of convict assignees. Apart from moderate agricultural success, its pastoral efforts were extremely poorly rewarded although it did engage in conscious efforts to introduce merino sheep. Poor lambing rates, high death rates, footrot and other sheep diseases meant substantial lost capital in the pastoral side of the undertaking.

In the early 1830s, the company was able to exchange much of its grant in and west of the mountains in the Liverpool Plains. Here was an ideal situation in which it could combine efficient wheat farming with high-grade wool. It was during the 1830s that the company's conscious efforts to upgrade Australian wool achieved a substantial success. That success was not achieved quickly. Establishment of such an enterprise was a slow business. Massive internal capital formation was required. The company had largely to rely, for volume production, on introducing a few high-grade animals to mate with large numbers of indifferent ones and gradually to cull. Culling and selective breeding required close oversight and control and separation of animals. It was not until the mid-1830s that the company was sufficiently organised on the Liverpool Plains for such planning to be effective. By 1840, the Australian Agricultural Company was launched towards fine wool sheep and was helping to spread their progeny. But this was sixteen years after its first establishment.

The company was not alone in conscious attempts to improve sheep quality. Like it, local and overseas investors in the pastoral industry faced similar genetic con-straints and similar climatic problems throughout the 1820s. Absentee investors from Britain relied on the integrity and efficiency of managers. In some cases at least (Statham, 1989), those managers appear to have been the prime beneficiary of these projects, selecting progeny for themselves and claiming personal supplementary land grants. Also, in some respects, absentee investment served to project those who acquired local understanding into pastoral ownership and development (Statham, 1989). Some absentees experienced financial failure. Their funds supplied the means to the establishment of pastoral assets that were acquired at low prices for local benefit. But again, flocks were improved, and were moved on and dispersed, to the gradual benefit of Australian export capability.

Once squatting began in earnest in the interior mainland, the squatters had access through initial sheep purchase to a gradually and somewhat haphazardly improving gene pool. Squatting in the interior relocated sheep in an environment in which fine wool was naturally favoured. Moreover, even with inefficient flock tending and Aboriginal depredations, lambing and survival rates rose markedly. The rate of expansion was accelerated by the climatic conditions. To that extent, serendipity may have contributed some further improvement in quality during the 1830s, though this was so only on the mainland, not in Van Diemen's Land. On the other hand, the speed of movement into the interior during the 1830s was such as to prevent much attention to selection and flock improvement. Inadequate labour supply, absentee ownership, the reliance on ex-convict overseers with little skill, poor flock control, and dependence on supplies of start-up flocks at marginal quality all militated against rapid improvement in wool quality. It was fortunate for the squatters that sufficient of merino or merino-cross genes had been established by 1830 to make some mark on the type of wool produced and to give Australian producers the qualified reception that they achieved in the British market.

To qualify disposal problems even further, extensive settlement implied rising transport costs to port locations. There was little possibility, with prevalent technology, capital and labour, to sustain the level of cleanliness of wool delivered to market. Movement away from the coast appears to have reduced, rather than improved, quality in this respect, increasing land transport costs and restraining eventual price realisation. Moreover, more limited shearing skills were available in the interior, implying wastage of wool or animals. Nevertheless, the surge of expansion into the interior clearly enormously enhanced the capacity of the Australian industry to deliver wool in large volumes of varied quality to the British market. The very nature of labour supply problems, combined with climate, limited wage costs. Added to the minimal capital deployed in fixtures in the interior, these conditions meant the ability to produce wool in volume at low costs. If they could not match German or Spanish quality by 1840, Australian producers were able to deliver wool cheaply at a degree of fineness that no British producer could match. However, the establishment of a high-grade merino industry did not occur until later in the century with the application of capital, through fencing and water supply, to permit flock separation and selection.

By the mid-1830s, the extensive spread appears to have approached its limits on both the mainland and in Van Diemen's Land, with given resources, capital and labour. Settlement on the mainland had experimented with squatting on the Darling River and retreated in the face of climatic constraint in the late 1830s. In principle, there was ample scope for further expansion. But the personal, if illegal, claims of individual squatters enclosed large areas, limiting access by new entrants. This is indicative of the 'real estate' incentive behind much of the squatting movement (Roberts, 1935). Expansion depended on the capital resources of first entrants into preferred areas. But this expansion was constrained by the limited resources of individual squatters. With slowing expansion came a slackening in the market for livestock. But this was accompanied also by a retardation in the expansion of the British demand for imported wool as 1840 approached. In its primitive foundation form, the pastoral industry was facing major instability that was part of the 'depression of the 1840s'. The problems that the industry then faced were that the inland squatters had no title to land, no legal rights of occupation and little to offer as credit to sustain their activities. This was a major problem to be resolved during the 1840s.

In the meantime, wool exports and livestock numbers had increased greatly from the position of 1810. It is unfortunate that so few statistics of animals in NSW exist and seem to be open to a good deal of question. Once substantial movement began out of the Cumberland Plain, it is scarcely plausible that accurate counts could be sustained even at Muster and Census times. In principle, the elasticity of supply of livestock numbers was significantly increased with settlement north along the NSW coast, but, as already suggested, there were still disease and climatic constraints on the rates of increase of sheep. From the late 1820s, as the movement into the interior developed on a large scale, that elasticity was greatly improved. Sheep were not only in good, if still pastorally primitive, conditions but flock numbers were in a position until the second half of the 1830s to expand more or less exponentially. In NSW, the official numbers, if they can be believed, for 1821 were a mere 73 000. By 1843, the official record was over 4 million. However one may attempt this re-estimation, there is no doubt but that expansion was extremely rapid even if subject to some climatic and disease retardation from time to time.

In Van Diemen's Land, success in expanding flock numbers came earlier and was well sustained through the 1820s. Here the official numbers are almost continuous. If the NSW reconstructions are not too implausible and the Van Diemen's Land numbers are reasonably accurate, they suggest that the wool yield per sheep *as exported* was, in modern terms, very low. Whereas in 1820, the fleece weights exported were of the order of two-thirds of a pound in weight per sheep they exceeded one pound weight per sheep by 1843. A great deal appears to have been discarded initially. Rapid expansion of flocks implied a high proportion of lambs and a high proportion of old, low-yield sheep. It is improbable that there was not a great deal wasted as rapid expansion occurred, if only for reasons of labour shortage, isolation and transport costs overland. However, it is impossible to determine what productivity per animal, age and type adjusted, was achieved.

Whaling

Before assessing the export outcome of rural resource development, it is useful to turn briefly to maritime performance, particularly of whaling. Statistically, there is little information on Australian whaling before the mid-1820s. The subsidence of sealing after 1812 left a major gap in fisheries activity as distinct from other maritime pursuits. It is doubtful whether the colonists of their own initiative and using available capital achieved much in the way of a substitute for seals before 1820. Though shipbuilding began early in the colony, capital was a major constraint on the production of seagoing vessels capable of engaging in whaling in deep sea terms. Moreover, until 1819, the East India Company monopoly restrained colonial deployment of ships of substance for whaling purposes. Despite these limitations, through British gifts, colonial public purchases of ships, local building and private purchase, a considerable if miscellaneous 'fleet', mostly of small ships, had been assembled during the decade after 1810. Only a small fraction appears to have engaged in whaling, the mass being committed publicly to essential overseas carriage or publicly and privately to strictly transferring troops, prisoners and stores between NSW and Van Diemen's Land and carrying produce locally.

In part, this allocation reflected sheer size and maritime capability of the available 'fleet'. But these more mundane activities offered small shipowners a more secure return than the risky and uncertain pursuit of maritime rewards. In contrast with pastoral development, where capital could literally be accumulated by 'waiting' (cf. the old concept of capital), in whaling, participation in deep sea whaling required the immediate injection of substantial capital and its exposure to considerable physical and market risk. Few colonists with such capital were prepared to engage in whaling. Some prefered other maritime ventures in such activities as the sandalwood trade with Pacific islands. Yet, a very considerable export in whale products was achieved early — certainly by the beginning of the 1820s.

One might suspect that perhaps the reputed exports were predominantly re-exports of catches made by foreigners, either purchased by colonists and resold abroad or processed onshore by foreigners. It is clear that a little of both such activities occurred. The trade statistics of NSW, as already indicated, may invite this interpretation in that large imports and exports, not very dissimilar in value, are recorded in the official statistics. The following table shows the available records of imports and exports and output of colonial produce for both NSW and Van Diemen's Land for the years from 1826. There may be some suspicion remaining about the precision in definition of 'colonial produce'. Clearly, there is no exact annual correspondence beween exports, imports and output but each series averaged over a few years gives quite similar totals.

Hartwell (1954) has described the dominantly bay whaling practised in Van Diemen's Land. His picture is one of localised 'whaling stations' — strictly lookouts — in bays at several locations around the Van Diemen's Land coast, deploying tiny boats and small numbers of employees summoned to pursue predominantly black whales when sighted entering the estuaries, as they often did in considerable

Table 13.11: NSW and Van Diemen's Land Oil Exports, Imports and Output, 1826–40, (£)

	NSW Oil Domestic Prod.	NSW Oil Imports	NSW Oil Exports	VDL Value Fisheries	VDL Fish Exports	NSW Oils % Gross Exports
1826	NA	NA	26 300	NA	NA	8.44
1827	NA	NA	24 825	NA	NA	26.94
1828	27 011	NA	18 558	11 268	NA	19.38
1829	NA	44 292	41 652	12 313	NA	25.42
1830	NA	41 200	52 613	22 065	NA	30.71
1831	120 752	115 780	89 401	33 549	20 883	24.23
1832	87 558	86 320	142 937	37 176	37 177	31.94
1833	169 278	165 625	144 564	30 620	29 914	34.69
1834	139 498	134 438	152 541	56 450	57 414	23.35
1835	147 373	163 168	171 984	64 858	64 858	22.34
1836	126 085	116 826	133 809	57 600	67 369	13.55a
1837	116 744	107 182	176 071	135 210	88 905	20.07a
1838	117 474	101 716	181 894	98 660	137 470	15.50a
1839	242 768	228 122	157 252	65 600	119 413	11.88a
1840	135 562	129 702	205 545	71 600	93 892	9.30a

Notes: (a) Port Phillip included in total exports.
(b) Statistics for NSW exclude whalebone and sealskins in all columns.
(c) NA — Not available.

numbers. There was comparatively little capital or equipment required though some physical risk. Occasionally, the intrusion of a sperm whale added handsomely to the value of the catch.

Officially, the number of ships of all types belonging to the two main Van Diemen's Land ports rose from one ship of 42 tons in 1824 to a preliminary peak of 27 ships of 1625 tons in 1828 (*Statistics of Van Diemen's Land*, selected issues). After a brief decline, the numbers reached 104 in 1838, with an aggregate tonnage of 8382. In all, 86 ships were reputedly built in Van Diemen's Land during 1828–38, in the latter year attaining an average for ten ships of around 130 tons each.

Of the registered ships, only seven were whaling in 1829 and 19 in 1838. Boats employed rose from 23 in 1828 (the first available record) to 155 in 1835 and then fell to 79 by 1838. Prior to 1836 some of these ships and boats may have been foreign-owned (but possibly resident in Van Diemen's Land). Over the 1828–38 period, for only part of which sperm catches were recorded separately from black whales, the preponderance of the latter is shown by the fact that the black whale catch was recorded at an aggregate 2980 whales while only 231 sperm whales were captured (*Statistics of Van Diemen's Land*, various issues).

NSW whaling appears slightly different. Certainly a few large ships did indeed engage in deep sea whaling (*Returns of the Colony,* various years), but NSW whaling appears to have been mainly very close into the coast. Black whales were less frequent and the catch was more likely to be sperm. Rather more capital or equipment was required for the limited colonial participation in the NSW whaling industry. Where a detailed count is available, the small number of ships engaged in the fisheries in NSW in the second half of the 1820s do not indicate a strong inclination to engage in deep sea whaling.

Thus, in 1827, with an available total colonial fleet of nine government vessels and 93 privately owned, only seven were reported occupied in 'the fisheries' and of a total employment of men and boys in that year of just on 500, only 96 persons were employed on these ships. Of the seven ships, only three or four could rate as ocean-going. The rest were capable, at best, of hugging the coast. (*Returns of the Colony*, 1827: 188). In this case, no 'boats' as such are recorded. Yet, by that year, whaling products of NSW are represented as exceeding pastoral exports. We know (Shineberg, 1967) that Australian ships at sea disposed of part of the sandalwood cargoes to foreign ships and it is possible that similar oil transfers were made or, alternatively, that catches were transferred from foreigners. This leaves the true Australian export open to some doubt. However, NSW whaling activity expanded throughout the 1830s at much the same rate as in Van Diemen's Land. Whaling establishments were dotted along the NSW coast from Sydney southwards and whaling 'factories' were established as boiling-down plants (see Hartwell, 1954). Sydney, indeed, acquired several such plants during the 1820s and 1830s, contributing a strong aroma to the harbour.

Major Export Earnings

With reservations about sea interchanges and the true ownership of ships engaged, we can then compare the official outcome, in export terms, of the two main natural resource industries (see table 13.12, p.192). The third natural resource industry for Van Diemen's Land, agriculture, is included though its implications are different from the other two. Agricultural products, in this case, were exported intercolonially and to the rising number of visiting ships. Only part of the exports of agricultural produce earned the 'Australian economy' overseas exchange. Intercolonial sales were an important — in the early 1820s, a vital — source of support to the domestic economy of the island. It is unfortunate that we cannot adequately separate overseas and intercolonial agricultural exports.

For data on major export items, we have to be content with Van Diemen's Land records from 1822 and from 1826 for NSW. The one trade item that has been recovered before 1822 is the volume of wool exports to Britain derived from British import returns. There were miscellaneous packages up to 1812 but thereafter volume flows rose rapidly from 36 971 pounds in 1814 to 172 880 pounds by 1821 (the *Sydney Gazette*, various issues). However, this increase occurred at a time of greatly falling prices so that the rate of increase of export earnings was not nearly so obvious. It is doubtful whether wool exports by 1820 accounted for as much as

Table 13.12: Value of Major Exports, NSW (including Port Phillip) and Van Diemen's Land, 1822–50

	NSW Pastoral (£)	NSW Fisheries (£)	NSW Pastoral % Share	NSW Fisheries % Share	VDL Pastoral (£)	VDL Fisheries (£)	VDL Pastoral % Share	VDL Fisheries % Share	VDL Agric. (£)	VDL Agric. % Share
1822					4 162	22 873	7.2	39.5	30 536	52.7
1823					4 887	2 002	19.8	8.1	17 595	71.1
1824					NA	NA	NA	NA	NA	NA
1825					12 984	2 758	54.5	11.6	4 245	17.8
1826	49 374	36 414	50.0	36.9	16 246	2 855	43.3	7.6	13 559	36.2
1827	25 473	32 605	34.7	44.4	14 444	10 669	24.1	17.8	8 665	14.5
1828	43 202	28 674	49.4	32.8	25 891	11 268	28.3	12.3	28 181	30.8
1829	74 239	56 200	48.1	36.4	41 072	18 321	32.3	14.4	35 587	28.0
1830	50 325	61 277	39.8	48.5	38 897	21 904	26.7	15.0	37 406	25.6
1831	100 044	97 990	45.7	44.8	62 131	20 883	43.8	14.7	36 266	25.6
1832	111 683	147 440	39.5	52.1	67 129	37 177	42.5	23.5	32 130	20.3
1833	136 249	147 245	43.5	47.0	68 976	29 914	45.1	19.6	30 596	20.0
1834	266 591	157 849	56.6	33.5	109 392	57 414	53.8	28.2	18 544	9.1
1835	350 248	180 463	62.3	32.1	154 741	67 301	48.3	21.0	67 738	21.1
1836	413 894	134 975	71.2	23.2	NA	NA	NA	NA	NA	NA
1837	352 353	184 128	60.6	31.7	331 936	90 773	61.4	16.8	48 710	9.0
1838	417 910	201 080	63.9	30.8	250 750	142 318	43.1	24.5	76 219	13.1
1839	485 627	175 692	70.2	25.4	358 369	127 140	41.0	14.5	257 508	29.4
1840	640 671	227 244	67.4	23.9	341 030	109 618	39.3	12.7	274 706	31.7
1841	625 789	174 522	75.0	20.9	290 169	102 257	46.0	16.2	140 410	22.3
1842	658 252	81 806	84.5	10.5	255 209	68 204	43.8	11.7	169 502	29.1
1843	762 782	74 484	87.0	8.5	208 177	51 859	47.3	11.8	113 594	25.8
1844	813 622	57 633	89.0	6.3	187 859	61 181	46.0	15.0	100 462	24.6
1845	1 225 774	97 297	90.0	7.2	204 995	49 077	48.6	11.6	80 491	19.1
1846	1 155 204	70 226	91.0	5.5	243 030	56 560	41.6	9.7	179 124	30.7
1847	1 511 532	80 553	91.9	4.9	269 996	72 459	44.9	12.1	157 462	26.2
1848	1 518 147	69 189	93.8	4.3	217 416	53 333	44.0	10.8	120 588	24.4
1849	1 597 617	45 698	94.3	2.7	230 477	47 128	41.3	8.4	144 222	25.8
1850	2 044 522	29 426	94.0	1.4	271 849	57 829	44.3	9.4	153 011	24.9

Note: NA — Not available.
Source: Derived from *Returns of the Colony*.

one per cent of the GDP of NSW. In terms of other exports, wool was still subject to competition from the (dying) sealing output and from the emergent whaling. Moreover, it is clear that opportunities were seized during 1810–20 to ship such objects as might be available — timber, coal, 'curios', 'natural history items', kangaroo and other skins, seal oil etc. — to Asia to earn some foreign exchange in order to enhance import capability. We have only the haziest idea, in quantitative terms, of the composition of this trading activity. Moreover, given the transshipment of many goods from Van Diemen's Land at Sydney until 1819, it is out of the question to disentangle the two colonies.

Only from the mid-1830s did pastoral exports begin to take a leading position in NSW exports and it was not until after 1840 that the pastoral industry was the dominant export earner. In Van Diemen's Land, the inclusion of agriculture and hence some intercolonial trade in the aggregate confuses the percentages. It is better to compare the absolute export values of the separate pastoral and whaling industries. On this basis, despite Van Diemen's Land's prominence as an agricultural producer and despite the romance attached to whaling, pastoral exports appear to have been far more important than whaling throughout. For a brief period, primarily in the second half of the 1830s, whaling picked up relatively only to be checked severely after 1840 (*Statistics of Van Diemen's Land,* 1841–4).

The increasing arrival of foreign ships in Van Diemen's Land during the 1830s, with a large whaling component, added an air but also an effect of a different sort, associating Van Diemen's Land with whaling. Of the deliveries, victuals and repair services briefly, but substantially, enhanced export earnings in that way (*Van Diemen's Land Census,* various issues). But, in the middle of the 1830s, another change was beginning to have an impact on Van Diemen's Land, altering its total export structure, the structure of its industry and, indeed, its whole economy. This was the establishment of Port Phillip. After 1835, very large and highly varied flows of physical assets, goods and people were made from Van Diemen's Land to Port Phillip, both participating directly in settlement there and supporting settlement by others. Migrants on the one hand, with their sheep and workforce, moved across the Strait. On the other, a large miscellany of exports followed in the form of agricultural produce, complete houses, timber, bricks, tiles, furniture, and other items to fuel the settlement of Port Phillip. For some, particularly those migrating, this was a beneficial change. For the Van Diemen's Land economy as a whole, it was part of a total change that quickly spelt basic economic retrogression.

Conclusion

From a domestic colonial point of view, one might perceive of the economy as initially British-driven. But it was also one in which colonial arrivals proceeded to transfer what they knew and understood of the most advanced economy on earth, 13 000 miles away in the isolation of the Antipodes. There was indeed a great deal of this transference and, in a real sense, a transplantion of the attitudes, mores, institutions, market practices and rights that existed and evolved in Britiain at the time. Of course, there was no simple transplantation. Convictism was one constraint though less strong than may immediately be thought. Factor endowments were radically different. Population size, urban–rural structures, the scale of the market were all manifestly different. And it was a new pioneering process, not just transplanting but carving an economy out of what was to the colonists a distant wilderness.

Nevertheless, this process of transplantation of the style of a British economy in terms of market principles is a fundamental part of the story of the formation of the early colonial economy.

The structuring of the economy(ies) revolved around three basic courses of adaptation. Without suggesting a three-sector economy, we have an initial view of a changing and, in trend terms, declining public sector with a corresponding rapid escalation of private activity. Beside this, there was the process of acquiring access to natural resources and utilising them for beneficial economic purposes. And thirdly, there is the partly linked, partly distinct, evolution of urban-oriented trades, commercial and services activities.

The interplay of these three component parts is by no means clear-cut. Under the influence of the classical theory of international trade and of the staple thesis, it is an easy leap from a small population nucleus of colonists to an explanation of growth and development through population. resource ratios, factor endowments and staple linkages. Part of this thesis is relevant. But it is far from clear-cut even in its own terms. And there are a series of distinct issues that draw attention to the urban-oriented activities that emerged, became important at an early stage and remained a major dynamic element in the economies throughout.

The early imposed constraints on settlement were partly for security and control reasons. These, combined with surrounding Aborigines, limited any easy relationship between population and natural resource ratios. Once the Aboriginal threat from the Cumberland Plain was cleared shortly after 1800, a freer but still limited population/resource combination was feasible. Even then, settlement containment held the ratio in quite severe check. Only gradually, as the settlements burst their early bounds, was a more expansive relationship between resources and population more meaningful. One qualification arose at an early stage. This was the use of the sea and its resources and certainly here the colonists found early access to substantial if rapidly depletable resources.

Rural resource development was initially driven by the pressures for sheer survival and subsequently the potential for agriculture and pastoralism opened the gates to rural resource development. In due course, this was prompted not by government but by rejection of government. The rapid growth of squatting on the mainland and large-scale granting in Van Diemen's Land threw open vast areas of extensive settlement. Private interest, the search for profit, capital inflow and local capital accumulation all contributed to this adaptation. So too did the rapidly increasing number of ship arrivals and the ability to move cargoes, and supply changes in Germany and Spain also encouraged the use of Australian wool to serve in the expanding export opportunities.

Private incentive granted, it is important, however, not to accept notions of the validation of private property rights in this process. Squatting did not yield these rights and it was one of the major outstanding issues up to 1840 as to what property rights, if any, squatters acquired. The more cautious accepted grants or purchased within official limits and extended squatting interests from these more secure bases. But it was not until the end of the 1840s that some degree of resolution through temporary land leasing validated the early squatters' ambitions.

Pastoralism was not the only or even the dominant basis of natural resource development. Quasi-exports of foodstuffs, including carcass products, were major items. But so too were the products of the seas and it was as much whaling in the

1820s and 1830s that contributed to the export earnings of the colonies. As a major adjunct of whaling locally, the arrival of increasing numbers of foreign whaling ships made large, if obscure, contributions to balance of payments credits and, indeed, by the end of the 1830s may have helped to briefly rescue Van Diemen's Land from a threatened retrogression.

We do not know the rate of return on capital invested in primary activities. There may be some guide in the form of the extremely low rates yielded — often losses occurred — by absentee investors. But it is not clear how far their efforts were turned to local advantage as assets built up in this way were absorbed into resident colonial hands for local benefit. In any event, the build-up of any of these pioneering investments necessarily looked to long-range rather than short-term yields.

There is no possibility of suggesting a divorce between primary resource development and urban-oriented activities. There were clearly intimate and considerable linkages between the two. But to suggest that one dominated, determined or directed the other is equally untenable. Port towns were basic as entry and exit points for rural developers. So, too, they were important as government centres and there were major general expenditure linkages involved. As trades activities developed in the towns, the products of primary activity found a locale there. However, there are many reasons for believing that the staples did not drive the urban sector even though their success was important to the process. Rather, a joint urban–rural development formed the early colonial economy,

Urban activities had their roots in a variety of factors. So long as Britain supplied considerable subventions to the colonies, a substantial contribution was made to sustaining the standards of living. Hence effective demand for a wide range of goods could be exercised on the expenditure side. Similarly, inflow of private capital further enhanced this capability. These stimuli could have leaked into imports. But there were several reasons why they did not do so.

First and foremost, Britain supplied (particularly after 1812) large numbers of relatively well-skilled convicts as skilled young males. They were dominantly urban, accustomed to living and working in towns and on skilled trades. They provided a mass of human capital offsetting the array of natural resource endowments and had many of the skills necessary to deliver, in situ, the goods and services demanded by persons with effective demand for those outputs. These included not only skilled trades but often relatively high-level services. Moreover, habit was important. As persons accustomed to towns, they preferred urban life. As convicts, many could be directed. As freed persons, they could exercise choice in increasing the elasticity of supply of labour to urban activities. They might often work on resources supplied from natural resource advantages and to that extent a staple linkage arose. But it is clear that a great many penetrated areas outside these simple linkages.

Even so, could they compete with imported goods? The answer lay partly in their skills. But it was underscored by the limitation of ship flows for a considerable period and the natural isolation of several thousand miles of ocean carriage combined with insecurities in supply conditions generally. Isolation was a fundamental advantage in these conditions in promoting urban-oriented activities. Customs taxation added a minor, limited range protection.

Even within rural producers and seafarers, the tendency to look to part of their life satisfactions in urban environments was a matter of habit and not simply staple success. There were more than merely general expenditure linkages implied by this.

Indeed, the more successful of the pastoralists, in particular, tended to recreate a village community surrounding large ornate dwellings. From this flowed a variety of linkages to urban areas, particularly through imports and the fabrication of more complex household commodities. And, of course, all looked to the main ports as exit and entry points for goods, persons and central government.

Fundamentally, a combination of artificially supported living standards, foreign private capital, the possession of urban skills, habits of urban living, the protection of isolation and the presence of tastes and incomes to permit effective demand for skilled products were basic ingredients in the strong incentive to the growth of urban activities side by side with the exploitation of the natural environment. There were undoubtedly linkages between both, but it would be false to propose that either strong expansive tendency drove the other. The form of the economy, stressing both, reflected a fundamental if implicit policy problem. The settlers chose both options. They continued to do so throughout and they persisted, even to today. Times changed and circumstances differed but many of the original ingredients hang over the rest of modern Australian history to the end of the 20th century.

14

GROWTH PERFORMANCE: 1810–40

Introduction

What can we say of the Australian colonists' economic performance between 1810 and 1840? One achievement was the establishment of a reasonably flexibly operating market economy, despite convict origins and the absence of much in the way of political representation of the private sector in government decision making. Another was the development of a relatively complex structure of economic activities, combining natural resource use and urban-oriented industry, trade and services. A third achievement was the establishment of a substantial capability to export and to attract private capital from Britain. A fourth indicator of performance was the maintenance, with some instability, of extremely high rates of economic expansion or, alternatively, extremely high rates of labour absorption as convicts and, eventually, free immigrants flooded in.

These might all be taken as indicators of colonial 'success'. Moreover, they might be more significant than the usual tests of performance in terms of productivity and standards of living, given that we are dealing with a foundation process. Nevertheless, these usual tests remain to be made. What levels of labour productivity, of gross domestic product per unit of factor input or of product per head of population were achieved? Did these levels grow over the thirty years and, if so, at what rate? Similarly, we might ask, in standard of living terms, what was the level and rate of growth of income, consumption or gross national expenditure per head of population? These are core 'growth' issues within a social accounting framework. (Obviously, there are other broader 'growth' issues of increasing freedom, vertical social mobility, life expectancy, health, education etc. The discussion here is explicitly confined to the narrower focus.)

These indicators of growth performance might be treated in parochial colonial terms, examining the fortunes of the colonists once arrived in Australia. It would, perhaps, be wise, to confine attention to this narrow horizon because it is a more manageable and statistically safer perspective. In what follows, the growth performance of the colonists is discussed, so far as we can. Nevertheless, there are two reasons for taking greater statistical and conceptual risks.

Firstly, as an immigrant society, whether coerced or free, it is important to try to evaluate whether the colonists gained or lost by the long-distance transfer to Australia. In other words, some effort is needed to compare colonial performance with that in Britain. This has a special nuance given the large numbers of coerced immigrants. To the extent to which they gained by transfer, the colonists became a social as well as an economic success. In this light, it is intriguing that the British government saw the condition of convicts in NSW as too advantageous to sustain transportation there but chose to continue shipping convicts in large numbers to Van Diemen's Land. Do our performance indicators cast any light on this British choice?

Secondly, as immigrants, the colonists were, to the resident Aborigines, an invading army. However we attempt to 'explain' colonial economic growth, a crucial 'factor input', land, was absorbed into colonial productive activity by transfer from Aborigines. Aggregate Aboriginal output declined, Aboriginal productivity fell along with Aboriginal living standards. Is it possible, then, to draw up even a rough balance sheet of 'net' growth? In other words, was British colonisation a positive, negative or zero sum game for the totality of human beings in Australia? As we will see, the question yields some curious 'answers'.

Readers may think that this reflects some peculiar 'compassion' for the losers. One might risk more suspicions by going even further and drawing out the directions of ecological change set in these foundation years, thereby introducing an even broader balance sheet of the colonial benefits and costs of growth. But there is a different issue, fundamental to the whole of Australian economic history to the end of the 20th century and into the future.

How far have Australians been able, in the long run, to move from dependence on exploitation of natural resources transferred from Aborigines? Put in another way, how far has long-term Australian 'success' been dependent on these natural resources and how has our long-term use of them affected the viability of our long-term performance? One might widen this perspective by asking, what implications were there for the structure of the British economy and its growth performance arising from the accession of Australian natural resource products? (The European acquisition of North American resources and the implications for European development as a whole pose this question on a grand scale.) For both Australian and British economies, the typical 'internal' production function is, one might suggest, seriously misleading in not taking into account a basic resource redistribution away from indigenous peoples. For the moment, however, we confine our attention to the foundation years to 1840 but these longer term and broader issues need to be borne in mind in considering the implication of this early colonial period.

Colonial and modern Australians, in the long run, have had two important bases for development — natural resources and immigrant human capital. How far has our exploitation of both been dependent on the transfer of resources from Aborigines and how has our long term Australian 'success' been directed by easy access to natural resources and external human capital?

Let us, firstly, try to place colonial performance during 1810–40 in a temporal and international context.

Comparative and Growth Measures

There are a good many constraints on measures that can be provided both comparatively and over time to indicate levels and change in productivity and standards of living. For Britain, we have Feinstein's estimates of gross domestic and national product from 1830 (in Mitchell, 1988). In the case of Australia, we have gross domestic product for separate colonies and gross national expenditure for NSW and Van Diemen's Land jointly. In neither the British nor Australian case do we have annual input series, not even of labour. We do have population estimates throughout and the simplest basic measure that allows some preliminary indication of productivity levels is gross domestic product per head of population for the United Kingdom, NSW and Van Diemen's Land.

Comparisons with Britain

Rebasing Feinstein's deflated series to conform to the 1830 Australian base, Australian 'productivity' levels appear extravagantly high. Averaged over the ten years 1830–9, British product per head of population is given at approximately £19 sterling compared to an Australian aggregate domestic product per head, in round figures, of £30 sterling! This, however, includes the imputed value of livestock increase. If we exclude this, the Australian level is about £26 sterling.

Of course, these simple comparisons cannot be taken seriously. In principle we need, if only we had the data, to achieve systematic exchange pricing for the two economies, allowing for differences in the composition and quality of products. This is impossible. But we can significantly improve the comparison by adjusting for differences in age and sex composition (we lack age data for Ireland), for transfer costs between the two economies and for exchange rate differences. This rough and ready procedure brings Australian and British product per head, averaged over 1830–9, to substantially the same level when one includes livestock increase in the Australian calculation. Omitting livestock significantly increases British product per head but not greatly above the Australian level. By far the major factors in this adjustment process are the age and sex differences, indicative of the masculinity of the Australian population, its limited number of dependents and the benefit in terms of per capita product accruing from demographic structure.

One should not place too much faith on this comparison but it is a useful point of reference. It is doubtful whether one should make much adjustment for quality (i.e. lower quality in Australia) though the product mix of the two economies leaves a major problem. What might be said is that, in this decade, Australian labour productivity may have achieved standards that were not far short of those in Britain. Population/resource ratios and relatively high skill standards applicable to urban activities were important advantages in the Australian case. And, of course, the (not quite costless) natural accumulation of livestock was a peculiar and important benefit, achieved over this period with minimal capital equipment. It is perhaps consistent with this broad brush comparison that rising numbers of British families were willing to make the unassisted transfer to Australia during the 1830s. This transfer was made despite substantial costs, the known background of convictism and the fact that, for most, it was a one-way trip.

Colonial Comparisons and Temporal Change

When we turn to the Australian colonies there appears to be a striking contrast in growth achievement in terms of domestic product per head. Averaged over the same ten years as before, NSW product per head including livestock increase stood, in round figures, at an average of £40 sterling per person in 1830 prices compared with only £25 sterling for Van Diemen's Land. To some extent, this contrast illustrates the benefits and the dangers of incorporating livestock increase. For the second half of the 1830s, Van Diemen's Land was transferring livestock to NSW in large numbers so that NSW standards appear to gain from Van Diemen's Land's loss. When we exclude livestock increase, NSW output per head falls, rounded, to about £35 sterling and there is minimal change to Van Diemen's Land. Even so, it appears possible that productivity in Van Diemen's Land may have been as much as one-third below that in NSW over these nominated years.

Before trying to evaluate this particular difference, let us turn to the longer run and the annual sequence of changes in the two colonies over the whole period 1810–40. Table 14.1 (p.201) shows product per head in the separate colonies including and excluding livestock increase and figure 14.1 gives a simple picture of the time series with livestock increase included.

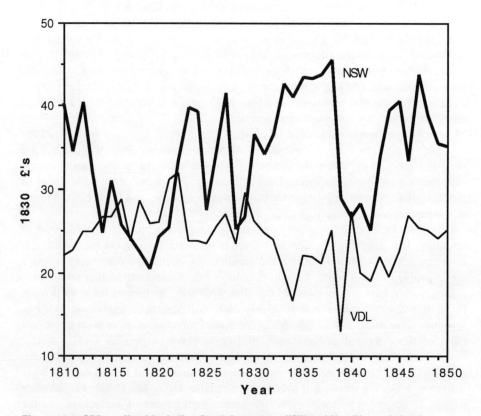

Figure 14.1: GDP per Head including Stock Increases, NSW and Van Diemen's Land (1830 prices, £)

Table 14.1: NSW and Van Diemen's Land GDP per Head, 1810–50 (1830 prices, £)

	New South Wales		Van Diemen's Land		VDL/NSW (%)	VDL/NSW (%)
	exc. Stock	inc. Stock	exc. Stock	inc. Stock	exc. Stock	inc. Stock
1810	37.6	40.2	21.2	22.0	56.4	54.8
1811	30.7	34.4	21.6	22.7	70.4	65.8
1812	37.5	40.4	24.2	24.9	64.5	61.6
1813	28.9	32.0	24.2	24.9	83.9	77.7
1814	25.4	24.8	26.1	26.7	102.6	107.5
1815	30.7	31.0	26.1	26.7	85.1	85.9
1816	22.9	25.6	28.2	28.7	123.4	112.0
1817	21.5	24.0	21.5	23.8	100.2	99.2
1818	20.1	22.5	26.5	28.6	131.8	127.2
1819	18.2	20.4	22.2	25.9	122.2	127.2
1820	19.6	24.3	25.0	26.0	127.9	107.2
1821	20.2	25.3	29.8	31.1	147.5	123.1
1822	27.3	33.3	28.4	31.9	104.2	95.9
1823	31.1	39.8	21.9	23.8	70.5	59.8
1824	28.5	39.3	21.5	23.7	75.4	60.2
1825	22.1	27.4	21.1	23.5	95.6	85.7
1826	27.5	34.8	22.6	25.5	82.4	73.1
1827	30.7	41.5	25.4	27.0	82.5	65.1
1828	21.9	25.2	20.9	23.4	95.6	92.8
1829	24.0	26.7	24.0	29.6	100.3	110.7
1830	32.4	36.6	27.3	26.1	84.2	71.2
1831	32.3	34.2	23.9	24.7	74.1	72.1
1832	33.3	36.6	23.6	23.9	71.0	65.4
1833	34.0	42.7	20.5	20.1	60.4	47.1
1834	33.4	41.1	16.2	16.5	48.6	40.1
1835	42.7	43.4	21.2	22.0	49.5	50.8
1836	39.5	43.3	21.3	21.9	54.0	50.6
1837	37.9	43.7	21.0	21.0	55.4	48.1
1838	35.0	45.5	22.5	25.0	64.2	55.1
1839	25.3	28.9	16.7	12.9	66.0	44.7
1840	25.0	26.7	24.8	27.2	99.0	102.0
1841	26.0	28.3	19.6	20.0	75.5	70.6
1842	22.7	25.0	18.5	19.0	81.8	76.0
1843	29.7	33.8	20.8	21.9	70.0	64.6
1844	33.9	39.5	21.3	19.5	62.9	49.2
1845	33.3	40.6	21.9	22.5	65.8	55.3
1846	29.4	33.3	26.5	26.8	90.0	80.5
1847	32.8	43.7	22.4	25.3	68.1	57.9
1848	36.8	38.8	25.4	25.1	69.1	64.6
1849	33.8	35.4	24.3	24.0	71.7	67.9
1850	35.1	35.1	24.5	25.1	69.9	71.5

The short-term variance in output per head might be recognisably the experience of economies in which primary activities, exposed to climatic changes, are prominent. Leaving this characteristic aside, the two most striking features of figure 14.1 and table 14.1 are:

(a) the appearance of inverse behaviour by the two colonies, with NSW 'productivity' falling to 1819 and Van Diemen's Land's rising to 1822. A trend reversal occurred thereafter to the closing years of the 1830s, with NSW moving strongly upwards (subject to major fluctuations) and Van Diemen's Land tending to sag downwards; and

(b) the failure of either colony to attain, in the closing years of the 1830s, a level of output per head very much above the levels of 1810.

Within these trend characteristics, there are several other subsidiary features — the instability, particularly in NSW, of the 1820s and the strong upward surge essentially in the 1830s; and the eventual more deeply seated instability from the late 1830s ending in the 'depression of the 1840s'. The fluctuations in the 1820s appear to be exaggerated because of likely errors in the underlying population estimates, most importantly in 1825. Even so, plausible adjustments to the population of NSW still leave a significant productivity decline in that year. Let us concentrate, here, on the first two points, leaving aside questions of instability.

Lines of Possible Explanation of 'Productivity' Performance

It is unfortunate that we have only quinquennial estimates of potential male workforce and hence only quinquennial series of labour productivity directly. It is important to try to track the annual productivity movements, using the crude measure of output per head of population. Some adjustment is needed to isolate the fact that the ratio of workforce to population changed significantly over the 30 years examined and to allow us to move closer to a labour productivity measure.

The population and workforce projections in part II suggested that the ratio of workforce to population of NSW and Van Diemen's Land, combined, stood at a little over 80 per cent throughout 1810–20. Thereafter, it declined gradually to about 60 per cent at the end of the 1830s. Both percentages were abnormally high even though the trend was downwards. This means that the trend rise in NSW should be adjusted further upwards so that labour productivity would be about one-fifth higher at the end of the 1840s. A similar adjustment upwards should be made to the trend decline in Van Diemen's Land. In both cases, then, the endpoint comparisons in point (b) above need to be qualified.

There was, on this basis, a rather more definite labour productivity improvement between 1810 and 1835 (but not 1840) in both colonies, as shown in figure 11.4 (see chapter 11). But the endpoint comparisons are dominated by the contrary change in trends in the two colonies.

The crucial shift is the first decade, approximately, of NSW decline and Van Diemen's Land rise followed by some 15 years of upward trend in NSW and a declining trend in Van Diemen's Land. This appears to be the major problem to try to explain in order to understand long-term experience.

What might be plausible *a priori* expectations? We have, apparently, a high natural resource to population ratio in both colonies. Do we expect, then, relatively high productivity? On the other hand, population and workforce increases were extremely rapid. Were there problems of labour absorption, with inefficiency and declining productivity? Were there major constraints and changes in population/ resource ratios? These questions presuppose the dominance of natural resource use. Once we accept the relatively high degree of urban orientation of both colonies, different questions arise. Were the colonies able to sustain the efficient use of urban skills? In terms of productivity as perceived by economists, were there marked changes in the relative prices of products of skilled labour as compared with the prices of natural resource products? It seems that any explanation must be relatively complex. The most important proposition to appreciate is that losses and gains of productivity are not accounted for by some sweeping simple explanation. Rather, variations were due to a large number of detailed influences that need to be comprehended.

Contrasting Experience: New South Wales 1810–19 and Van Diemen's Land 1810–23

Let us examine natural resource considerations first. These divide into land use and maritime issues. So far as land use was concerned, the differences between the two colonies in 1810 were striking. NSW, still with a small and slowly growing population, had been able to develop the resources of the Cumberland Plain during 1802–10 more efficiently once threats from Aborigines had been disposed of by 1802. As the population began to grow rapidly after 1810, the policy options and private choices for the ensuing decade tended strongly towards declining productivity. The efforts to limit settlement predominantly to the Cumberland Plain meant that, increasingly, marginal lands were brought into production.

Macquarie's attempts to utilise more skilled convict labour for social infrastructure actually accentuated this trend by providing greater ease of access to the land resources of the Cumberland Plain thereby accelerating the decline in the marginal product of land. This was underscored by the fact that land grants during the 1810s were concentrated on small ex-convict farmers, with limited skills or capital to exploit or adapt to local natural resource conditions. Moreover, the emphasis on social infrastructure in itself tended to favour, in the short term, a low productivity outcome. Added to these considerations, the tendency for large landholders to specialise towards animal husbandry and to leave agriculture to small ex-convict farmers added to restraints on productivity. This was partly because of the diversion of potential capital investment from agriculture, but also because in the 1810s, the peculiar problems of sheep farming showed up in the failure to expand the genetic pool of sheep with the consequential low and declining wool yields over that decade.

So far as NSW was concerned, the 1810s were not, then, a decade of advantageous population and land resource ratios. It awaited the gradual relaxation of efforts to contain the settlement to the small controllable area and to allow occupation of coastal valleys to the north and the plains across the mountains to provide for more advantageous population/resource ratios. From this point of view, then, the early bridgehead achievements were exposed to short-term risks and reversals until the policy of containment was changed formally following the Bigge recommendations. But even before then, in the late 1810s, Macquarie was slowly relaxing that containment.

A different narrowing of productive horizons occurred in maritime undertakings. Leaving aside the less substantial maritime activities, the fact that sealing reached its peak at or about 1810 meant that there was a consequential decline in the main maritime activity in which comparatively little capital was required. As sealing declined, considerable numbers of men continued to be deployed with inevitable reductions in average productivity. But the colonists were not yet in a position to make a signifi-cant entry into the alternative maritime activity of whaling. Again, productivity benefits from whaling largely awaited the end of the 1810s when both men and capital could be increasingly exploited to this end.

Before discussing the urban-oriented activities of NSW, let us look at natural resource considerations in Van Diemen's Land. This is a period of extremely rapid livestock and agricultural production on the island. Here one should note that we are not concerned only with a rapidly rising productivity in the island but also, accord-ing to these estimates, with the possibility that Van Diemen's Land's overall output per head seems to have exceeded that in NSW in the few years surrounding 1820.

In part, the low initial levels in Van Diemen's Land might be seen as due to the fact that the island had been settled only in 1803. Several years of near-starvation, preoccupation with penal infrastructure and lack of knowledge in farm selection, threats from Aborigines and considerable activity by escaped convicts disrupting settlement activities helped to keep productivity low before 1810. Nevertheless, Van Diemen's Land had several important advantages, particularly into the early 1820s. A substantial proportion of convicts transferred to the island had acquired some farming understanding in NSW and some of the directing military had similar NSW backgrounds. The island received a benefit from the transfer of some 500 farming settlers from Norfolk Island during 1807–8 and their experience, once resettled, helped to raise productivity standards.

Most importantly, accessible river flats in the north and south of the island, com-bined with more secure rainfall and a climate generally more appropriate to farming than on the Cumberland Plain, helped to make adaptation easier. Even the crude shifting agriculture practised on the coastal flats was more efficient than in the area around Botany Bay. To enhance incentive in Van Diemen's Land, the island settlers had a nearby market for many farm surpluses in the form of the NSW Commissariat.

Even though Van Diemen's Land population quadrupled during the decade after 1810, it had a much more advantageous population/resource ratio in terms of land resources than was the case of the NSW settlement, which was largely confined to the Cumberland Plain. Physical conditions and the more limited tasks of learning by doing in those conditions appear to have allowed an increasingly efficient absorption of the arriving population. Similarly, in terms of maritime activities, despite the decline of sealing grounds, the persistent arrival of black whales and the emergent opportunity for bay whaling on a scale not available in NSW meant that the full range of natural resource endowments permitted a readier settlement and produc-tivity response.

Van Diemen's Land appeared, for a time, peculiarly attractive for convict settle-ment where self-support for convicts held on a relatively small island could be expected. With prevalent pre-1820 policies of containment, this appeared as a more appropriate outlet than the extension of mainland settlement. Nevertheless, Van Diemen's Land output per head rose by the late 1810s and early 1820s only to surpass a deep trough level of the artificially restricted NSW settlement. However simplified by natural conditions, Van Diemen's Land farming was highly inefficient. Agriculture was dependent on clearing small areas and moving to new locations. Even though livestock increased rapidly, wool from sheep was almost entirely wasted. Black whales were a poor alternative to sperm whales or seals. With predominantly small land grants to ex-convicts possessing little capital, one might suggest that Van Diemen's Land was an attractive, and for a time an increasingly attractive, place in which convicts and ex-convicts might be self-supporting. But this was a limited merit.

So far as urban-oriented trades and services were concerned, divergent considerations applied in the two colonies, yielding additional tendencies to declining productivity in NSW and rising trends in Van Diemen's Land in the first decade or so. In 1810, NSW had reached a peak in the extent to which free and freed persons were allocated by personal choice, with the deployment of many skilled workers to special private urban trades and services. These had been encouraged, among other things, by the high level of British support that leaked into private demands.

During the 1810s, however, there were strong factors reversing this position. Macquarie's reservation of the more skilled of arriving convicts to his social infrastructure program, limited assignment of these skilled persons to private trades employment so that their relative importance tended to decline, while skills expanded only slowly in the private sector. Moreover, the production of infrastructure by convicts under public supervision emphasised long-term benefits through externalities rather than short-term productivity gains, tending to lower productivity in the short run. In addition, Macquarie's deployment of convicts in this manner meant that available British government subsidies tended to be retained more within the public sector, with less leakage into private demands than before 1810, even though some specific private industries were encouraged. One offset to this was that infrastructure demands with fewer skilled convicts assigned to private employment appears to have encouraged increased capital equipment in a limited range of activities. This applied primarily in a small range of manufacturing, but with little overall impact on total labour productivity.

There appear then to have been significant influences in NSW tending to lower productivity from quite exceptional levels in both natural resource use and in urban trades and services during the decade after 1810. The reverse appears to have applied in Van Diemen's Land. However, although there appear to have been tendencies to encourage increased productivity in urban trades and services on the island in 1820, the relative importance of these activities remained significantly below that in NSW. They provided an influence towards increasing productivity but were not substantial enough to contribute strongly to very high productivity levels.

A major factor supporting the rise of productivity in Van Diemen's Land between 1810 and 1823 was the profound relative shift away from the public sector, contrasting with the slight NSW restructuring towards the public sector up to 1817. This also meant a major relative decline in strictly military and penal construction. Proportionately, more available resources were deployed into natural resource use and trades and services. The potential for the latter group was, however, more restricted than in NSW. The size of the Van Diemen's Land population was too small to provide a wide and varied market for trades and crafts in the first decade. The British external subvention, which supported private choice in NSW before 1810, was never allowed to operate strongly in Van Diemen's Land which remained under relatively tight fiscal constraint by way of its tutelage under the NSW authorities. Nevertheless, as convicts were freed, increasing numbers were in a position to present their products and services on a slowly expanding private market. The combined effect of a large relative shift away from penal infrastructure and a limited

development of private crafts and services combined to contribute significantly to a
lift in Van Diemen's Land productivity in contrast with the NSW experience. The
movement towards private crafts and services appears to have accelerated sharply in
the early 1820s, helping to carry productivity in Van Diemen's Land above that
in NSW.

Divergent Productivity Performance to late 1830s

In the two decades after 1820, and particularly during 1820 to 1835, many of these
productivity tendencies in the two colonies were reversed, helping to restore levels
in NSW and to degrade those in Van Diemen's Land. Though the mainland population continued to expand rapidly, its rate of growth slackened significantly during the
1820s. At the same time, the brakes on the extension of settlement were greatly released during the 1820s and increasingly ignored from the late 1820s. Despite population increase, then, the effective population/resource ratio was greatly improved.

No longer largely constrained within the Cumberland Plain, the colony initially
spread firstly to the large river plains on the coast where, in particular, a far more
productive agriculture was presented (the marginal product in agriculture in the
Hunter Valley far exceeded that on the Cumberland Plain). Subsequent extension
into the interior was the crucial factor opening up large-scale pastoral expansion.
Inefficient as much of this pastoral development may have been, and largely independent of capital inputs as it was, the opening up of the territory allowed, if nothing
else, a vast proliferation of livestock numbers. Here, then, was a major individual
element in increased productivity: the opportunity for livestock accumulation on a
large scale.

At the same time, the movement away from immediate coastal environments
combined with genetic changes, even though not highly planned or carefully organised, implied a rise in productivity per sheep in terms both of quantity and quality.
This was accompanied by increased scale of operations and increased capital, not for
the purposes of physical capital inputs, but to support genetic improvements and to
provide waiting time for flocks to expand and improve. This is not an easily measur-
able change, partly because of the absence of continuous underlying numbers, and
partly because of the changing age structure of a growing livestock population and
the changing significance of exports as against domestic consumption.

It seems possible, too, that there may have been increased wastage as the industry
moved inland, given labour constraints and transport problems. One should be
careful about overstating the physical productivity in terms of fleece per sheep.
Fleece weights remained small relative to later 19th-century standards. Nevertheless,
on the basis of export statistics, it would appear that fleece weights per average
animal in the population may have doubled between 1820 and 1840. The two components of livestock increase and fleece weights, combined with quality improvement, meant a very substantial contribution to NSW productivity levels overall.

On the maritime side, the development of whaling in NSW was accompanied by
some increase in capital investment in physical assets in shipping and whaling gear
and in onshore stations. These allowed a modest participation in offshore whaling
and hence access to valuable sperm whales with substantial productivity improvements. This contribution appears to be similar to that arising from the expansion and
improvement of wool production particularly during 1825–35.

The changing flow and composition of human capital and its use within NSW operated similarly to provide for a resurgence of productivity, most particularly during 1825–38. The social overhead capital provided during 1810–20 subsequently had a long-term contribution by facilitating the urban grouping of populations in more ordered communities. The substantial cessation of the provision of social infrastructure after 1821 allowed an initial long-term benefit to flow on but also transferred a much higher proportion of skilled employment into privately assigned or freely employed and self-employed activities. But there was an even more important productivity outcome. It was really after 1815 that the full flow of British skills to Australia occurred, with an increasing representation of the human capital generated in Britain from the flowering of technical change and training. So the range and variety of skills in Australia widened and were updated as new convicts arrived. There was, it is true, a brief retardation: the numbers arriving declined during 1820–5. But thereafter, transportees arrived in large numbers and continued to do so to the late 1830s. Moreover, the sex composition favoured males much more than females as compared with pre-1815, implying a concentration on male skills.

Despite the tendencies to 'concealed unemployment' arising from the assignment system and the use of many convicts in natural resource activities, here was a greatly enlarged flow of human capital to contribute to a wide range of private manufacturing, crafts, trade and service activities. Initially, they provided an employed workforce. Once freed they also contributed to the ranks of employers and self-employed as well as free wage-earners in these 'urban-oriented' activities.

Scale of manufacturing and commercial activity rose as the total market increased rapidly and, with it, capital investment in plant and equipment. Physical assets allowed the transfer of embodied technology in fixed equipment, enhancing labour productivity. But scale and equipment were not overriding. It seems likely that the mass of manufacturing, crafts and trade activities were carried out by one or a very few persons with little capital, relying basically on their skills and available materials. In doing so, another related change appears to have been important in supporting a productivity rise. This was the shift in the direction of trade away from Asia and towards Britain. Asian imports were rapidly replaced by British imports, many of them requiring further processing. Hence an increasing flow of human skills were deployed with the materials with which the workers had been accustomed in Britain.

Here we should note the symbiosis between natural resource and urban-oriented activities. As the former expanded with increasing productivity and incomes, there was a general expenditure feedback to urban-oriented activities. Similarly the expansion of urban activities encouraged, even if only in a general way, the extension of land settlement. Improving productivity on either side tended indirectly to encourage productivity increases on the other. To the extent that this interactive process was important, one should note, then, that extensive land settlement came to depend increasingly on the inflow of private capital. So long as conditions persisted to sustain that inflow, a combined surge of productivity could be expected. In fact, private capital inflow escalated rapidly in the closing years of the 1830s in such a way as to create an unstable condition leading subsequently to a reversal of the prior productivity achievements. But that is a topic for the next chapter.

From the tiny colonial population base in 1810, Van Diemen's Land colonists had quadrupled in the 1810s. During the next decade, population quadrupled again so that by 1830 it was a little more than 50 per cent of the NSW population. In the next five years, the population continued to rise rapidly, increasing by some 65 per cent. Then expansion faltered and in two years of the second half of the 1830s, the Van Diemen's Land population is estimated as falling in absolute terms. This demographic experience contrasts with that in NSW. Here population was also expanding rapidly by about 140 per cent over the decade to 1820 (based on contemporary returns, see table 3.1, p.34), by about 80 per cent in the 1820s and, reversing the contrast with Van Diemen's Land, speeded up to rise in the ten years to 1840 by 180 per cent. If the expansion during the first decade from a tiny base still allowed Van Diemen's Land a beneficial population/resource ratio, the continued injection of population at a high rate may have begun to press on the island's resources as early as the mid-1820s.

At that stage, however, there was another major contrast between the two colonies. Van Diemen's Land population was pushing into the interior of the island, just as the NSW population was beginning to spread into the interior plains. In both cases, the colonists collided with Aborigines and one needs to perceive the significance of two societies seeking to occupy the same territory. The differences in this collision were marked. In NSW, expansion into the interior occurred when the Aborigines were widely stricken by smallpox (1828) with resulting large-scale depopulation and destruction of the social order. Though they resisted colonial expansion, they were not in a position to offer strong opposition. It is, in fact, possible that, until colonists absorbed their lands on a broad scale, food supply per Aborigine may have increased so that there could have been less sense of resource competition. There is considerable evidence that Aborigines, at an early stage, guided settlers to beneficial locations, reducing establishment costs and enhancing marginal productivity for colonists.

In Van Diemen's Land, no comparable disease epidemic smoothed the way for settlers. Aboriginal populations had clearly been reduced by the early 1820s when colonial population expansion led to the occupation of the interior of the island. For the Van Diemen's Land population as a whole, Aborigines at around the beginning of the 1820s probably numbered one for every two colonists. For those colonists attempting to occupy the interior, the Aborigines probably opposed them in superior numbers. Moreover, the Aborigines were supported by escaped convicts and stolen firearms. In addition, Aborigines appear to have used more systematically the interior of the island than was the case of the wide spread of the mainland interior. What all this meant, as conflict rose to its height in the second half of the 1820s, was, firstly, a considerable diversion of colonial effort into protection, fighting Aboriginal attacks and a more systematic effort to destroy the Aboriginal population through organised conflict. It meant, too, episodes of withdrawal by individual settlers, the loss of property and life and the destruction of output. It encouraged close grouping of settlers and hence restricted the ability to make optimal choice of productive locations. It was not until the beginning of the 1830s that these obstacles were lifted.

Very rapid population growth during the 1820s in Van Diemen's Land confronted special problems of labour absorption that the mainland did not face. Moreover, despite a still small population, the population/resource ratio was not as advantageous as it may seem, when contention for resources is taken into account. The one advantage that Van Diemen's Land had, as compared with the mainland, was that climatically there was less learning by doing for persons accustomed to British conditions.

On the other hand, in natural resource terms, the island settlers encountered a good many limitations. Firstly, the conditions that had favoured rapid expansion of pastoral activity in the 1810s, particularly through the introduction of long woolled meat-producing sheep, turned out to be a disadvantage by the middle of the 1820s as pastoralists sought to complement meat with wool. There was no prospect of Van Diemen's Land competing in the British market in long wools, and without a massive injection of merino or merino crosses the ability to translate the island's pastoral industry into exportable wool was a slow and difficult business.

This transition was one of the objects of the Van Diemen's Land Company in the late 1820s and 1830s but efforts by the company and others made only a slow adjustment in the quality and exportable volumes of wool overseas. It is often suggested that during the 1830s, the Van Diemen's Land pastoralists faced limited resource potential and this may have been a factor in its poor productivity performance (see, for example, Hartwell, 1954; Robson, 1965). In any event, as efforts to improve stock quality proceeded during the 1830s, a new prospect opened in the opportunity to transfer pastoral enterprises, livestock, labour and equipment to Port Phillip. So, during the second half of the 1830s, a major drain occurred on Van Diemen's Land's pastoral resources, with some of its leading pastoralists and a substantial proportion of its preferred sheep moving across the Strait to NSW. The loss in productivity, as measured, followed from reduced and sometimes negative increase in livestock and from the decline of overall wool quality during 1836–40.

The most marked quality problem for Van Diemen's Land arose in 'maritime' industries. Whaling around the island, once sealing was depleted, was exposed to severe competition from foreigners (and New South Welshmen). Lack of capital severely restricted the islanders' ability to engage in offshore whaling and they were largely forced to be content with 'bay whaling' which delivered essentially low-grade black whale oil. The dominance of this low-quality end of the market spelled low productivity in an industry which, for the whole of the Australian colonies, was as important as the pastoral industry until the end of the 1830s.

Extremely little is known of Van Diemen's Land manufacturing and service activities despite the recorded numbers of factories and shops. However, given the extremely high rate of population and labour inflow between 1820 and 1835 and the tendency of a high proportion (averaging one-third of the total inflow according to Rimmer, 1969) to seek employment in towns, it seems implausible that the island could sustain rapid expansion of these activities while also preserving a high marginal product, at least so long as the producers depended on internal incomes and demand.

Although one can only guess, it seems plausible that the marginal product of urban-oriented activities would, at best, have mirrored the productivity (earnings/expenditure) constraints in natural resource and maritime industries. This position seems likely to have changed, however, once the large-scale influx of visiting ships in the second half of the 1830s provided a booming market in provisioning and repairing. It is possible that there was a major turnaround in prosperity and productivity, particularly in Hobart, in the 1835–40 period. This boom was clearly accompanied by a related burst of demand as population left the island but, in the process, demanded the production of goods and chattels for transfer to Port Phillip. A similar market arose in Port Phillip as other settlers congregated there. However, the stimuli were short term and ended in reversal and depression by the end of the 1830s.

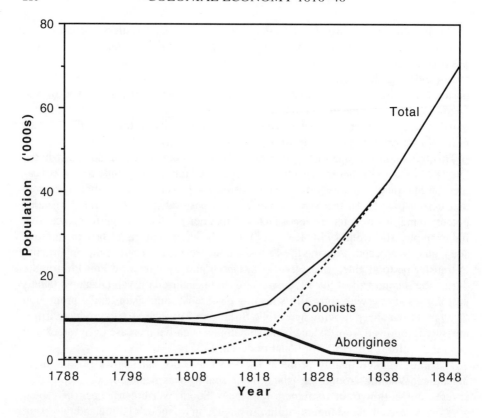

Figure 14.2: Van Diemen's Land Population, Two Societies

Net Colonial and Aboriginal Outcomes

In my book, *Our Original Aggression*, I attempted to exploit a system of population dynamics that subjected an assumed stable stationary population of Aborigines to a series of shocks due to disease, killing and resource loss. This procedure was applied to populations of the present NSW and Victoria. Taking such estimates of surviving Aborigines as existed at or about 1840, this method allowed an approximate projection backwards to possible levels of pre-contact Aboriginal numbers. To do so depends on subjecting Aborigines to disease shocks at the appropriate historical dates, to subjecting them to resource loss in accordance with the spread colonial settlement and to time the killing of Aborigines similarly with colonial settlement. This is far from being a perfect replication of the demographic shocks actually experienced by Aborigines but keeps the process of depopulation reasonably in accord with history.

Since the publication of *Our Original Aggression*, I have adopted the same techniques, in principle, for Van Diemen's Land (with a more limited disease regime and a higher killing rate) and for the rest of Australia. One of the implications of disease experience is that several diseases could spread far beyond points of colonial–Aboriginal contact and this is particularly relevant to the rest of Australia other than Van Diemen's Land, NSW and Victoria. In making these projections, I have assumed that the mass of the Aboriginal population was 'exposed', i.e. had no

This early decline, partial recovery and subsequent downturn was offset by an average 9 per cent per annum compound growth rate in colonial population. Despite this high rate of increase, it was not until the mid-1840s that the colonial population equalled the pre-contact indigenous numbers. It was only by about 1838 that the combined colonial and Aboriginal populations had grown to the pre-1788 level of Aborigines. The net effect was to produce a crude W-shaped curve of total population, the shape dominated by three factors:

- the massive early loss by Aborigines;
- aboriginal recovery and colonial expansion into the 1820s; and
- further Aboriginal loss and rapid colonial increase from the mid- to late 1820s.

The third picture is the all-Australian one (see figure 14.4, p.212).

Here the essential supplementary point is the long-distance impact of disease on Aboriginal populations with whom colonists had made no direct contact. Resource taking and killing had only a slight effect on Aboriginal populations outside NSW, Victoria and Van Diemen's Land (local problems occurred around Adelaide, the south-west corner of Western Australia, at Moreton Bay and Port Essington). So, Aboriginal populations are modelled as having recovered significantly better by the 1820s after the impact of smallpox (and spreading venereal disease) so that by the mid-1820s, they may have recovered to about 75 per cent of the pre-contact numbers and then been depleted again by the second smallpox epidemic. The whole weight of Aboriginal populations was then thrown on the northern half of Australia, free from close contact but under a disease shadow.

Even though the mass of colonial population as late as 1850 was still in Van Diemen's Land, NSW and Victoria, the net effect can be defined as:

(a) An attenuated version of the W-shaped curve in figure 14.3 (p.211);

(b) In contrast with the prime areas of colonial settlement, the aggregate population of Australia, both colonists and Aborigines, was significantly less in 1850 than it had been in 1788 with Aborigines alone comprising about 80 per cent of the 1788 numbers.

Should we go any further than this demographic picture of Aboriginal loss and colonial gain? Can we make any sensible comparison and coalescence of the two societies in terms of output? In adding up activity for one society to derive an aggregate gross domestic product we are already comparing and adding unlikes. This is done as a matter of convention and convenience. But to bring Aboriginal and colonial societies together requires, it would seem, a much bigger logical and conceptual jump. One is regarded as 'primitive' and the other 'advanced'. Tastes and preferences of the two societies appear radically different, with little means of equating them through any pricing or shadow pricing of the commodities produced in the two cases. Colonial society sought the basic land resource of Aborigines and was, so it seems, ready to discard Aboriginal technology and Aboriginal products.

When anthropologists attempt to demonstrate that Aboriginal society was not, in many respects, 'primitive', they tend to stress the differences between the two societies. There are basic differences in attitude to land, special systems of order in individual and cooperative effort in food gathering and hunting, sharing rules, complex kinship arrangements, devotion to traditional beliefs and rites, ritualistic punishment and so on. There is no doubt that Aborigines prized (placed a high price on) some activities that would leave little room for exchange relations with colonists. The overt or alleged reasons for behaviour can, on this approach, dominate to emphasise the peculiarities of Aboriginal society.

One can accept these reasons and still interpret behaviour *as if* it were divorced from the explicit system of beliefs and traditions. We are then interested in what is implied by behaviour, not what motivates it. Thus kinship rules, among other things, may be interpreted as resulting in arrangements for resource sharing or access to resources. Ritualistic punishment becomes a process of law and order to preserve groups as a unit. Ceremonial activity achieves an educative effect, and in the process, integrates groups as economic units. This does not mean that motivation is irrelevant. On the contrary, motivation (preferences) are important in explaining how highly-prized certain activities are. But we are not concerned with motives for their own sake.

It was suggested in *Economics and the Dreamtime* that one might approach the Aboriginal economy through a system of time budgeting. On this basis, it is possible to order Aboriginal time allocation in terms of a range of categories along the lines of:

• Food collection;
• Environmental management and adaptation;
• Food preparation and distribution;
• Clothing, bedding and household utensils;
• Production planning, including decisions to relocate;
• Travel and transport;
• Housing;
• Equipment production and maintenance;
• Education;
• Law and Order;
• Defence;
• Religious observance;
• Ritual ceremonies;
• Art; and
• Recreation and entertainment.

No doubt such a list could be amended and extended. But once we move beyond the ancient travesty of Aborigines as naked nomads, any plausible list looks as if it has a reasonable match with colonial society even if the priorities may be different. Aborigines may seem to be more prone to the pooling of resources and to sharing rules though even in this case, the definition of 'convict rations' and, even in the free labour market the typical provision, in kind, of 'board and lodging', brings the two societies closer together than one may at first think.

Most importantly, there were many items that were consumed in both societies. Game meats, wild fowl, eggs, wild fruits and nuts, fish, shellfish and crustaceans illustrate a cross-cultural food transfer that accounted for a large part of Aboriginal diets (even if colonists drew the line at snakes and lizards). Animal skins and seal skins were prized by both sides. Aborigines took sheep and cattle meat when they could. One prime difference between the two societies was the Aboriginal technical superiority in the capture of game and birds and the colonial superiority in production of domesticated livestock.

The greater degree of specialisation by colonists and the fact that they produced specific articles for trade and beyond personal consumption needs (note that Aborigines did engage in some trade) meant, in the case of the colonists, the specific allocation of persons to functions rather than group time to those functions. Thus law and order, education, religion, for example, were functions attaching to specific colonial professionals. The delivery of these services were often dispersed widely among Aborigines, absorbing group time rather than the attention of specialised individuals. In either case, resources were allocated and it is with the efficiency of this allocative process that we are fundamentally concerned in endeavouring to relate the relative productivity of the two societies.

Without domesticated animals or plants (at least in general terms) and with limited storage provisions, Aborigines depended substantially on daily food collection (indeed there is evidence (*shell midden*) that they prized fresh food highly). We have widespread observations of good health and physique in early years, particularly by explorers, the presence of ample food in their camps and the repeated propositions that, averaged for men and women, food collection took about five hours a day. This has to be qualified by winter being a period of stress and, of course, intermittent droughts altered the budgeting from time to time. Possibly, then, half their available time budget of a hypothetical ten-hour day was absorbed in food acquisition and some side-products such as skins.

Time budgets are not immediately appropriate to colonials. However, given that neither society deployed large amounts of capital equipment, colonial workforce shares are a useful first step. The 1828 Census suggests that approximately 50 per cent of the male and female workforce were deployed in farming in NSW. This allocation, however, did not satisfy the food demands of the colonists since substantial volumes of grains, potatoes and meats were imported. Were the colonists able to expand their farm production with no change in productivity to meet these additional demands, about one-sixth more of the total workforce would have been needed. However, not all time of on-farm labour was absorbed in farm production. Shepherds and others tending various forms of livestock were required throughout the whole year, seven days a week. Agricultural labour in ploughing, weeding, seeding, harvesting is unlikely to have exceeded more than the equivalent of six months. However, with shifting farming practised, continuous farm formation was required throughout the year, with sustained effort year-round in land-clearing. Since this was the condition on which their agriculture depended, it is appropriate to include this farm formation effort. There were two basic offsets — often only an eight-hour day and a six-day week in agriculture. Even though limited capital was deployed, colonists certainly used more than did Aborigines so that some additional time was required in maintenance activity.

For what this notional balance sheet is worth, it would suggest that colonists were a little more efficient in producing the basic foods they desired than were the Aborigines. Assuming an even split between animal husbandry and agriculture, the preceding argument would suggest that colonials satisfied their basic food tastes with about 10 per cent less labour than the Aborigines deployed to satisfy their food demands. Clearly, we need a much more careful time budget for Aborigines. In particular, the external descriptions of time taken in food acquisition do not include consideration of activities that went on in conjunction with the major activity. Thus child supervision, training and education, the observation of special rites might all be examples of outputs concealed within the food time budget. In this context, with little comparable among colonists where these activities were functionally separate, one might conclude tentatively that there may not have been much difference between the two societies in their relative efficiency in satisfying basic food demands.

Aboriginal food intake was an omnivorous one while colonists' diets were very limited in range. *Ex post*, one might say that Aboriginal diets were more healthful and this might be important in understanding comments on their physique. But would one side exchange the other's diet and at what exchange rate? We have some limited information on this. In colonial markets, wildfowl and their eggs appear to have traded interchangably with colonial poultry and their eggs. Certainly, at times, kangaroo meat was priced above mutton. Aborigines were induced to work in exchange for mutton and flour. Competition for fish, shellfish and crustaceans was at times intense. It is implausible that had Aborigines been allowed to put fish on markets they would not have received the going price. On the other hand, Aborigines are reported as simply giving fish to travellers. This should not be interpreted as implying zero value for fish — Aborigines were accustomed to mutuality of gifts and we do not know the expected return.

It is impossible to be conclusive. But it is equally unreasonable to regard the two societies at this level as simply alien to each other. For example, edible meats, eggs and fish made up a large part of the diets of both groups and the two societies were prepared to allocate roughly the same proportion of their resources to food acquisition. At this level, a rough equation does not seem unreasonable.

One cannot accept Sahlins' view (1972) that with easily available food, Aborigines spent the balance of their time in idleness. We know a little more than that. There is evidence that they were highly efficient in producing animal skin blankets and cloaks as needed. Though their seagoing capability was limited, they impressed colonists with their facility to fashion watertight river craft from bark with great speed. The stone axes which fashioned these craft and other objects may have lacked some of the versatility of metal axes but were produced very quickly (less than an hour per axe head). Similarly many food eating utensils were fashioned, on the spot, from shells and animals so easily that they were typically left discarded. Netting of vines or bark rope were similarly produced with facility for hunting and fishing purposes and for netting birds. Much larger challenges were met and faced in the production of stone fish traps and the specialised eel canals of Western Victoria. Possibly one major item, the grindstone, presented a major challenge of laborious effort, typically a marriage present to a new bride. All in all, one cannot think of Aboriginal effort in these and similar directions as being at a low level of productivity.

What the Aborigines appear to have done was to embellish their 'basic' activities with complex systems that included order, ritual, education, ceremonies and art. These activities cannot be disregarded as 'non-productive'. To ignore them in a production context is comparable to the traditional disregard, in advanced societies, of the 'services' component of economies. Equally, to stress their social and cultural implications is to trivialise their economic implications. They served to hold productive units together, to achieve production planning, to preserve the heritage of understanding of the surrounding environment and sustain continuity.

One might object that there was a high degree of inequality and a hierarchy of rewards in colonial society lacking in Aboriginal groups. Can we imagine an

Aboriginal hierarchy of rewards comparable to that which stretched downward from the governor through various officials to the meanest constable, teacher or curate? There were no overt Aboriginal trappings of power and wealth corresponding to those among the colonists. Indeed, the stress is on the absence of 'chiefs'.

There does seem to have been, nevertheless, a great deal of inequality in Aboriginal society, an inequality that is often concealed and even secretive. Differential rights to numbers of wives had crucial economic and social implications as did authority in the exercise of justice and punishment, the ordering of ritual and control of ceremonies, rights of bestowal of women and so on. The fact that the 'senior' individual or individuals chose to share food and other objects is irrelevant. The two societies simply had different mechanisms to induce some individuals to perform the functions (produce the services) that created an ordered society sustaining its traditions and preserving its human capital. There may have been some differences in priorities: Aborigines appear to have placed greater value on education and training, but fundamentally the same principles of social integration and continuity were at work.

Despite the conceptual problems, practical considerations suggest that we might reasonably equate, in 'rough and ready' terms, the output per worker in the two societies. This is intended to suggest equality of Aboriginal workers in pre-contact conditions with colonists once established with a functioning economy. But let us remember the special age and sex composition of the colonists. Equality per worker is not intended to suggest equality per person. In conditions of a stable stationary population, Aborigines had a relatively high proportion of dependents so that equality per worker meant a much lower level of output per person in the total Aboriginal population pre-contact; roughly half that of colonists per head during, say, the 1820s. This is not high. Interestingly enough, such an assumption would yield an output per Aboriginal person approximating the average of the colonists during the first decade of settlement. If anything, this is probably conservative. We can be reasonably confident that Aboriginal standards cannot have been much lower, except in times of stress and are likely to have been somewhat higher.

It is the occasions of stress that we have to be concerned with when an attempt is made to trace a plausible path of gross domestic product for Aborigines after 1788. Three basic problems arise. One is the impact of disease and exceptional mortality on productivity. A second is the withdrawal of resources from Aborigines by colonists, including the denial of traditional practices including fire-stick farming. The third was the killing of Aborigines. Not all of these meant productivity loss. Indeed, subject to questions of economy of scale, population reduction (subject to age and sex composition of mortality) might, in certain conditions, have yielded an increase in productivity per worker and even more so of output per person.

In attempting to identify a plausible path of Aboriginal output during 1788 to 1850, it is essential to bear in mind that there was a differential and changing impact of colonists on Aborigines in terms of Van Diemen's Land, NSW and the rest of Australia. This has already been indicated in dealing with likely demographic experience. It became more complicated in productivity terms.

Smallpox had a particularly heavy mortality incidence for pregnant females, children and the old. Venereal disease reduced the proportion of children in the population. The reduction in numbers may have made resource supplies more plentiful. On the other hand, it reduced the potential for economies of scale in group activity in, e.g., fire-stick farming. It also reduced the ability to sustain training and education, particularly with the demise of the elderly. It produced a population with a relatively high proportion aged five to 15, semi-trained but increasingly vigorous and productive and a source of potential increase in productivity per person.

Let us abstract, firstly, from resource contention with colonists and killing. One might model the smallpox outcome, then, as a short-term decline in productivity followed by a gradual increase over, say, two decades, to the point at which output per person actually increased as compared with the base level. The spread of venereal disease, subject to female morbidity, would tend to accentuate this longer-term trend outcome by reducing the proportion of children. This omits any consideration of Aboriginal morale. Within about 30 years after a smallpox outbreak, one might hypothesise that productivity per person might have subsided to approximate the base level. Since this approximates the experience outside NSW and Van Diemen's Land, it is the course that is applied to the 'rest of Australia', assuming the impact of two smallpox epidemics and the gradual spread of venereal disease.

In NSW including the present Victoria, the same short-term and trend response is assumed up to 1820. Then the introduction of additional disease, resource taking and killing is brought to bear on productivity experience. Early additional disease chiefly affected children so that the immediate effect may have been an acceleration in output per head of population. But this was, at best, a short-term outcome as resource competition and killing intensified during the 1820s.

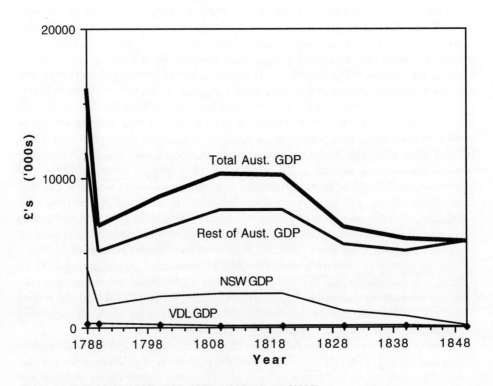

Figure 14.5: Aboriginal GDP, 1788–1850, (1830 prices, £'000)

By the 1830s, resource competition was overwhelming Aboriginal productive ability. Destruction of Aboriginal fishing grounds, refusal to allow the firing of the bush, rejection of the rights of women to gather yams on 'colonial property', and denial of rights of passage for men progressively narrowed productive potential. Killing or deaths of Aborigines had little consequence for productivity to the extent that mass killing often occurred. Deaths were also occurring increasingly from diet-related diseases affecting all ages and both sexes. By the beginning of the 1840s, Aborigines were described widely as in a miserable, starving or dying condition. The decline in output per head between 1825 and 1840 was then extremely rapid. A trend decline from 1825 to approximately one-quarter of the level then achieved by 1840 is assumed. It cannot have been a much better outcome.

In Van Diemen's Land, no comparable disease experience occurred. But there was a gradual loss of women and children to 1820 with probably a slow decline in output per head. Rapidly, during the 1820s, contention rose to extreme levels as Aborigines were diverted into battle or avoidance mode and rapid population loss. By the early 1830s, population and output fell substantially to zero.

Figure 14.5 shows, valued in 1830 prices (£), the rough approximations of Aboriginal gross domestic product for Van Diemen's Land, NSW, the rest of Australia and the total for the three areas on these supposed examples. It should be stressed that these are, at best, rough measures and can only be treated as indicative. They are intended not to stand in isolation but to give us some impression, as distinct from

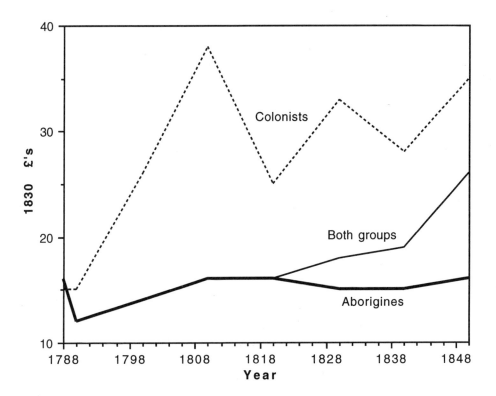

Figure 14.6: Output per Head, Two Societies, (1830 prices, £)

mere demographic change, of the possible impact over time of colonial settlement on the Aboriginal economy and, through that, on the joint economic activity of Aborigines and colonists.

Figure 14.6 (p.219) accordingly compares productivity per head of population for colonists, Aborigines and the two societies together for the whole of Australia. The three essential points are:

(a) Colonial output per head rose rapidly from a level below that of Aborigines in 1788 and initially moved to more than twice the Aboriginal level by 1810, thereafter dropping in the period to 1840 closer to, but still above, the original Aboriginal level;

(b) Aboriginal output per head fell drastically in the beginning but recovered to close to its initial level by 1810, thereafter sagging slowly in the period to 1840; and

(c) Until 1820, it was Aboriginal output per head that dominated the two-society performance but thereafter the joint level, averaged, rose above the Aboriginal level.

Figures 14.7, 14.8 and 14.9 show real aggregate gross domestic product, and may usefully be compared with the purely demographic representations in figures 14.2, 14.3 and 14.4. In effect, we are now asking the question: From available resources and with available human capital did the colonists achieve a higher aggregate output

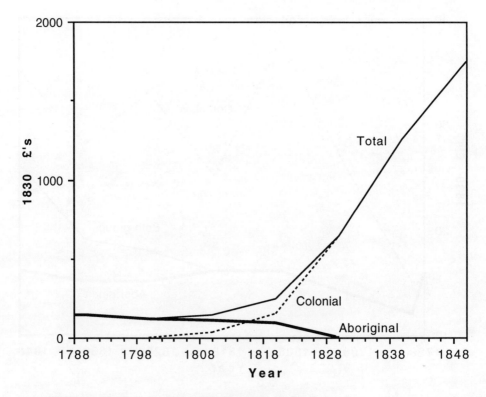

Figure 14.7: Van Diemen's Land GDP, Two Societies, (1830 prices, £)

than Aborigines; and was the aggregate output of the two societies greater or less than the Aboriginal output had been in 1788?

In Van Diemen's Land, the answer is very clear-cut (see figure 14.7, opposite). Firstly, colonial gross domestic product exceeded that of the 1788 Aboriginal level within a mere eight years of arrival. By 1840, the colonists' product had risen to approximately eight times the original Aboriginal achievement by which time the colonists had completely displaced the Aborigines. Ironically then, the less productive colonial economy showed itself clearly superior in this sense, essentially because of the speed of colonial population growth and the completeness with which the Aborigines were disposed of.

By contrast, figure 14.8 for NSW (including the present Victoria) suggests that the colonists just managed to equal the original Aboriginal product in 1844, despite the relatively high level of mainland colonial productivity; and, given the radically degraded Aboriginal economy particularly during the 1830s, the joint product of the two societies together surpassed the original Aboriginal one only by 1840.

For Australia as a whole, two conclusions are suggested. Firstly, colonial product had not attained the 1788 Aboriginal level by 1850. Secondly, the joint product of the two societies had restored the separate Aboriginal level of 1788 only by the mid-1840s.

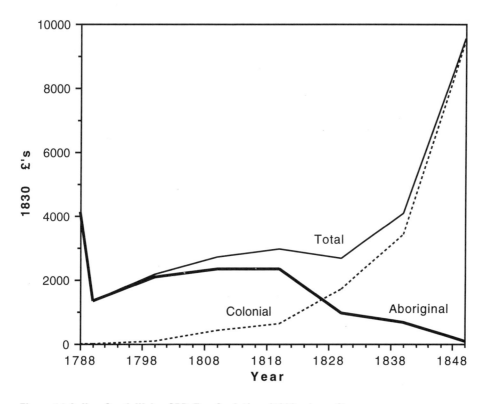

Figure 14.8: New South Wales GDP, Two Societies, (1830 prices, £)

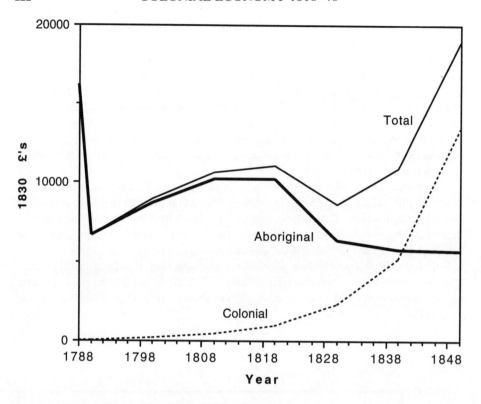

Figure 14.9: Australian GDP, Two Societies, (1830 prices, £)

15

INSTABILITY AND ECONOMIC FLUCTUATIONS WITH SPECIAL REFERENCE TO THE DEPRESSION OF THE 1840s AND RECOVERY

Introduction

The Australian economies of New South Wales and Van Diemen's Land were expanding geographically in terms of aggregate activity at an enormous pace after 1812. To these were added, in 1828, the tiny Swan River settlement and the beginnings of the South Australian corporate undertaking in 1836, combined with the surge of expansion at Port Phillip from 1835, initially as an adjunct of NSW. At an average population and workforce growth rate compounded in excess of 10 per cent per annum, it would be surprising if a high order of stability could have been sustained. Curiously, Van Diemen's Land, with by far the fastest rate of expansion, indeed seems to have achieved a relatively stable expansion path, particularly by comparison with NSW. The risk of instability in rapid expansion was accentuated by the novelty of the whole Australian development project, the underlying importance of adapting to a new rural environment, exposure to climatic variations and other farming problems, variations in British policy in relation to human and physical capital.

The speed of expansion and its continued geographical spread led to a severe check in the form of the so-called 'depression of the 1840s'. This was the approximate point at which Australia was experiencing its first major halt to long-run expansion. The depression of the 1840s stands in a line, historically, with that in 'the 1890s' and in 'the 1930s'. This periodicity has tempted several scholars to look to a Kondratieff-type thesis or alternatively to Kuznets' building cycle, with Australia a prominent representative, given the 40–50 year gap between the peaks of the booms or troughs of the slumps. There is then perhaps a question of whether this thesis is relevant, or whether Australia happens to have had a peculiar experience, spuriously supporting the Kondratieff picture.

From some points of view, the early Australian experience could be slotted into a Schumpeterian version of the Kondratieff cycle, based, in part, on the introduction of domesticated animals and farm products into a formerly Aboriginal environment. This was, at least, an extension of new technology and a new mode of business operation. But the underlying supply of convicts and public resource supplies, together with the basic importance of British policy, makes any simple application of such a thesis extremely difficult. Much more importantly was the essentially pioneering and long-term attitudes that had to be adopted in the development of the colony. This long gestation period is, to a large extent, the key to understanding the series of booms and slumps that occurred up to 1850, because they led to the need for long-term planning and exposed the decision makers to a great many short-term risks that could force the delays or closures of any long-term projects.

Thus, in this context, one might trace the development path of Van Diemen's Land following on behind, and partly catching up with NSW, and the injection of Western Australia, South Australia and Port Phillip, into an overall Australian development process. Certainly there appears to be a tendency to rise to a crescendo (and vice versa) in all these areas simultaneously that helped to account for the severity of the depression of the 1840s.

In the meantime, the writings on Australian economic history reveal numerous references to a series of recessions and depressions prior to 1840. Thus, we have the commercial crisis as of 1810–13 that curiously enough appears to ignore some significant livestock disturbances in the period 1814–15. We have, too, the so-called 'depression of 1826' which leads a curious life in some cases, a commercial crisis extending to the second half of that year, and, in other cases, deepening into 1827–8.

While these incidents need to be taken into account, they may only have been speed variations on an extremely fast expanding track. Alternatively, and this applies particularly to the 1826–8 period, they may reflect the gathering problems associated with rapid aggregate and geographic expansion that contributed so strongly to the depression of the 1840s. What is striking is the lumpiness of experience, relatively speaking, of NSW compared with Van Diemen's Land, and it is possible that there is some contracyclic experience operating between the two colonies.

The expansion paths of all the colonies are significantly influenced by the importance of livestock changes and in the case of NSW and Van Diemen's Land, the estimated contribution of the imputed value of livestock increase to GDP varies as wildly as plus 30 per cent to minus one per cent.

Postscript

Noel Butlin died before he could complete this chapter, and I have not sought to go beyond the material he actually wrote. His intention in this chapter — based on conversations shortly before his death — was to explore the volatility of Australian business cycle experience in the 40 years to 1850, with particular emphasis on the depression of the 1840s, which he saw as Australia's first large, sustained downturn. Other fluctuations to that point had been minor interruptions to an underlying, extremely vigorous pace of economic growth in the colonial economies.

In his view, past accounts of Australia's performance in the depression of the 1840s (including S.J. Butlin, 1953; Coghlan, 1918; Fitzpatrick, 1941; and Shann, 1930) had captured the domestic factors affecting the local economies well. By contrast, he felt that the impact of events external to the domestic colonial economies, especially the timing and severity of the business cycle in the United

Kingdom, had not been adequately factored into those earlier accounts. His intention was to fill what he considered to be a major gap in the understanding of the economic interdependencies between Australia and the external world — especially the United Kingdom — in that period.

The Australian economies expanded rapidly in the 1830s, with the frenetic pace of growth reflecting, in particular, an emphasis by British investors, the colonial born and new settlers on developing the pastoral industry. In the words of Fitzpatrick

> ... Australian economy, hitched to a wool waggon (sic), moved forward at a rate which would not be exceeded between 1840 and the early gold period a dozen years later ... And wool, on which the boom was based seemed quite capable of supporting it: the colonial wool cheques in 1834 were four times as great as in 1831. In 1840 more than seven times as great (Fitzpatrick, 1941: 33).

The settlement of Port Phillip and the occupation of its hinterland originally grew out of a rapidly expanding pastoral industry in Van Diemen's Land. It was rapidly followed by a pincer from the north flowing from the old confines of the New South Wales settlement, successively southward across the Murrumbidgee and the Murray Rivers.

The decade of very rapid growth had been stimulated by the British government's policy of the sale of Crown land to stimulate immigration, the growing importance of the wool industry as supplier to British manufacturers, and extensive imports of development capital (Fitzpatrick, 1941). A decade of depression then ensued, with rapid economic expansion returning after the discovery of gold. There are two conventional views of the collapse and its causes.

Fitzpatrick identifies five factors that triggered the depression of the 1840s: the fall of English wholesale prices (by 23 per cent over four years to 1843); the gradual fall of NSW export wool prices; the economic crisis in Britain in mid-1839; severe drought in NSW from 1838; and the withdrawal of funds by the colonial government to meet the costs of immigration. The chief factor was 'a sudden failure of capital, after 1839, to bring from England further support of the land boom which had accompanied the pastoral extension' (Fitzpatrick, 1941: 71), triggered by the Bank of England's lifting of the discount rate in May 1839, which 'heightened panic in the English money market' (Fitzpatrick, 1941: 72).

This primacy of external factors was challenged by S.J. Butlin (1953) who argued that the evidence of wool exports (volumes and values) showed a relatively modest drop in prices between the peak of 1840 and 1842 and, otherwise, every sign of a strong industry in the early years of the 1840s. Butlin proposed that the key issue was the emerging evidence of bad returns in the colonies, as the great expansion of the past decade had taken up all the best opportunities and that increasingly what land remained 'appeared to offer poorer yields and higher costs, especially for transport' (S.J. Butlin, 1953: 317). Indeed, he saw the 'great drop in capital transfer as occurring in 1842 with 1840 as the great peak' (S.J. Butlin, 1953: 318), and the success of several capital raisings in Britain after the crisis of 1839, meant the fall in British investment was triggered by news of poor returns in the colonies and that it exacerbated a slump that had already begun.

It was intended that this chapter analyse the Australian business cycle experience of the 1830s and 1840s and compare it with the evidence from the United Kingdom.

That task was to draw on the themes of export development and increasing integration of the Australian colonies to the international economy (through the domestic economy of Great Britain); and the financial and migration links with which this second volume began were also to be brought into the explanation of business cycle performance in Australia over the period 1810–50. Events in the United Kingdom cast a longer shadow than their impact on the supply of private capital to finance pastoral expansion and the terms under which that finance was made available. Those events were also reshaping the conditions of immigration from Britain, the economic linkages between the colonial colonies and Britain, and the public finance of the colonies. Unfortunately, Noel Butlin could not complete the task. Having stated the intention of this remaining chapter, it now remains a matter for other scholars of Australian economic history.

M.W. Butlin

BIBLIOGRAPHY

Abbott, G.J. (1969), 'The Pastoral Industry', in G.J. Abbott & N.B. Nairn (eds) *Economic Growth of Australia 1788–1821*, Melbourne: Melbourne University Press

Abbott, G.J. (1971), *The Pastoral Age: A Re-examination*, South Melbourne: Macmillan, with the assistance of Dalgety Australia

Abbott, G.J. & Nairn, N.B. (eds) (1969), *Economic Growth of Australia 1788–1821*, Melbourne: Melbourne University Press

Ashton, T.S. (1959), *Economic Fluctuations in England, 1700–1800*, Oxford: Clarendon Press

Australian Agricultural Company, MS records, Noel Butlin Archives Centre, Australian National University, Canberra

Bathurst, H., 3rd Earl Bathurst (1822), 'Copy of the Instructions given ... to Mr. Bigge on his proceeding to New South Wales ... 6th January, 1819', in J.T. Bigge, *Report of the Commissioner of Inquiry into the State of the Colony of New South Wales*, London: Colonial Office

Baxter, C.J. (ed.) (1987a), *General Muster of New South Wales, 1814*, Sydney: Australian Biographical and Genealogical Record (ABGR) in association with the Society of Australian Genealogists

Baxter, C.J. (ed.) (1987b), *General Musters of New South Wales, Norfolk Island and Van Diemen's Land, 1811*, Sydney: ABGR in association with the Society of Australian Genealogists

Baxter, C.J. (ed.) (1988a), *General Muster and Land and Stock Muster of New South Wales, 1822*, Sydney: ABGR in association with the Society of Australian Genealogists

Baxter, C.J. (ed.) (1988b), *Musters and Lists, New South Wales and Norfolk Island, 1800–1802*, Sydney: ABGR in association with the Society of Australian Genealogists

Baxter, C.J. (ed.) (1989), *Musters of New South Wales and Norfolk Island,*

1805–1806, Sydney: ABGR in association with the Society of Australian Genealogists

Beattie, J.M. (1986), *Crime and the Courts in England, 1660–1800,* Princeton: Princeton University Press

Bigge, J.T. (1822), *Report of the Commissioner of Inquiry into the State of the Colony of New South Wales; With which is bound Bathurst, Henry, 3rd Earl Bathurst: Copy of the Instructions given by Earl Bathurst to Mr. Bigge on his Proceeding to New South Wales … 6th January, 1819,* London: Colonial Office

Bigge, J.T. (1823), *Report of the Commissioner of Inquiry on the Judicial Establishments of New South Wales and Van Diemen's Land; With which is bound Bathurst, Henry, 3rd Earl Bathurst: Copy of the Instructions given by Earl Bathurst to Mr. Bigge on his Proceeding to New South Wales … 6th January, 1819,* London: Colonial Office

Bigge, J.T. (1983), *Report of the Commissioner of Inquiry on the state of Agriculture and Trade in the Colony of New South Wales; With which is bound Bathurst, Henry, 3rd Earl Bathurst: Copy of the Instructions given by Earl Bathurst to Mr. Bigge on his Proceeding to New South Wales … 6th January, 1819,* London: Colonial Office

Binney, J.E.D. (1958), *British Public Finance and Administration, 1774–92,* Oxford: Clarendon Press

British Almanac 1847, The (n.d.), London: The Society for the Diffusion of Useful Knowledge

Broxam, G. and Nicholson, I.H., *Shipping Arrivals and Departures, Sydney,* vol. 3: *1841 to 1844, and Gazetteer,* Canberra: Roebuck Society

Butlin, N.G. (1962), *Australian Domestic Product, Investment and Foreign Borrowing 1861–1938/39,* Cambridge: Cambridge University Press

Butlin, N.G. (1983), *Our Original Aggression: Aboriginal Populations of Southeastern Australia, 1788–1850,* Sydney: George Allen & Unwin

Butlin, N.G. (1985a), 'What a way to run an empire, fiscally!', *Working Papers in Economic History,* no. 55, August, Canberra: Australian National University

Butlin, N.G. (1985b), 'Free lunches antipodean style: N.S.W. economy 1788–1810', *Working Papers in Economic History,* no. 57, October, Canberra: Australian National University

Butlin, N.G. (1993), *Economics and the Dreamtime: A Hypothetical History,* Melbourne: Cambridge University Press

Butlin, N.G., Cromwell, C.W. & Suthern, K.L. (eds) (1987), *General Return of Convicts in New South Wales, 1837,* Sydney: ABGR in association with the Society of Australian Genealogists

Butlin, N.G., Ginswick, J. & Statham, P. (1987), 'The Economy Before 1850', in W. Vamplew (ed.), *Australians: Historical Statistics,* Broadway: Fairfax, Syme & Weldon

Butlin, S.J. (1953), *Foundations of the Australian Monetary System, 1788–1951,* Melbourne: Melbourne University Press

Coale, A.J. & Demeny, P., with Vaughan, B. (1983), *Regional Model Life Tables and Stable Populations,* New York: Academic Press, 2nd edn

Cobley, J. (1970), *The Crimes of the First Fleet Convicts,* Sydney: Angus & Robertson

Coghlan, T.A. (1918), *Labour and Industry in Australia: From the First Settlement in 1788 to the Establishment of the Commonwealth in 1901*, vols 1–4, Oxford: Oxford University Press

Colquhoun, P. (1800), *A Treatise on the Police of the Metropolis, Containing a Detail of the Various Crimes and Misdemeanours by which Public and Private Property and Security are, at Present, Injured and Endangered and Suggesting Remedies for their Prevention*, London: H. Baldwin and Son for Joseph Mawman, 6th edn

Commonwealth Bureau of Census and Statistics (1947), *Demography 1945: Bulletin no. 63*, Canberra: Commonwealth Bureau of Census and Statistics

Convict indents, 1788–1842, Archives Office of New South Wales, Sydney

Corcoran, K. & Nicholas, S. (1988), 'Statistical Appendix: Convicts Transported to New South Wales 1817–40', in S. Nicholas (ed.), *Convict Workers: Reinterpreting Australia's Past*, Cambridge: Cambridge University Press, 1988

Cumpston, J.S. (1977), *Shipping Arrivals and Departures, Sydney, 1788–1825*, Canberra: Roebuck Society

Deane, P. (1965), *The First Industrial Revolution*, Cambridge: Cambridge University Press

DeLacy, M. (1986), *Prison Reform in Lancashire, 1700–1850*, Stanford: Stanford University Press

Dowd, B.T., (1966), 'A.T.H. Alt', in D. Pike (ed.), *Australian Dictionary of Biography*, vol. 1: *1788–1850*, Melbourne: Melbourne University Press

Durham, Earl (John George Lambton) (1912), *Report on the Affairs of British North America*, vol. 1, Oxford: Clarendon Press, 2nd edn

Ekirch, A.R. (1987), *Bound for America: The Transportation of British Convicts to the Colonies, 1718–1775*, Oxford: Clarendon Press

Fitzpatrick, B.C. (1939), *British Imperialism and Australia 1783–1833: An Economic History of Australasia*, London: George Allen & Unwin

Fitzpatrick, B.C. (1941), *The British Empire in Australia: An Economic History, 1834–1939*, Melbourne: Melbourne University Press in association with Oxford University Press

Fletcher, B.H. (1976), *Landed Enterprise and Penal Society: A History of Farming and Grazing in New South Wales before 1821*, Sydney: Sydney University Press

Garran, J.C. & White, L. (1985), *Merinos, Myths and Macarthurs: Australian Graziers and their Sheep, 1788–1900*, Rushcutters Bay: Australian National University Press

Gatrell, V.A.C. & Hadden, T.B. (1972), 'Criminal Statistics and their Interpretation', in E.A. Wrigley (ed.), *Nineteenth-Century Society: Essays in the Use of Quantitative Methods for the Study of Social Data*, Cambridge: Cambridge University Press

Gayer, A.D., Rostow, W.W. & Schwartz, A.J. (1953), *The Growth and Fluctuation of the British Economy, 1790–1850: An Historical, Statistical, and Theoretical Study of Britain's Economic Development*, vols 1 & 2, Oxford: Clarendon Press

Ginswick, J. [unpublished manuscript containing statistics of New South Wales compiled by Jules Ginswick]

Guy, A.J. (1985), *Oeconomy and Discipline: Officership and Administration in the British Army, 1714–63*, Manchester: Manchester University Press

Hainsworth, D.R. (1981), *The Sydney Traders: Simeon Lord and his Contemporaries 1788–1821*, Melbourne: Melbourne University Press

Hartwell, R.M. (1954), *The Economic Development of Van Diemen's Land, 1820–1850,* Melbourne: Melbourne University Press

Historical Records of Australia (HRA), series 1: Governors' Despatches to and from England (1914–1925), 26 vols, Sydney: Library Committee of the Commonwealth Parliament

Historical Records of New South Wales (1892–1901), 7 vols in 9, Sydney: Government Printer

Hoffmann, W.G. (1955), *British Industry, 1700–1950,* Oxford: Blackwell

Ignatieff, M. (1978), *A Just Measure of Pain: The Penitentiary in the Industrial Revolution, 1750–1850,* Columbia: Columbia University Press

Jones, R. (1969), 'Fire Stick Farming', *Australian Natural History,* XVI, September

Jones, R. (1975), 'The Neolithic, Paleolithic and the Hunting Gardeners: Man and Land in the Antipodes', *Quaternary Studies,* IX, INQUA Congress, 1973, in the Royal Society of New Zealand Bulletin, no. 13

Jones, R. (1977), 'Man as an Element of a Continental Fauna: The Case of the Sundering of the Bassian Bridge', in J. Allen, J. Golson & R. Jones (eds), *Sunda and Sahul: Prehistoric Studies in Southeast Asia, Melanesia and Australia,* London: Academic Press

Jones, R. (ed.) (1980a), *Northern Australia: Options and Implications,* Canberra: Research School of Pacific Studies, Australian National University

Jones, R. (1980b), 'Hunters in the Australian Coastal Savanna', in D.R. Harris (ed.), *Human Ecology in Savanna Environments,* London: Academic Press

La Nauze, J.A. (1948), 'Australian Tariffs and Imperial Control', *Economic Record,* vol. 24, no. 47, December

Madgwick, R.B. (1937), *Immigration into Eastern Australia, 1788–1851,* London: Longmans & Green

Mansfield, R. (1841), *Analytical View of the Census of New South Wales for the year 1841, with Tables Showing the Progress of the Population during the Previous Twenty Years,* Sydney: Kemp & Fairfax

McDonald, P., Ruzicka, L. & Pyne, P. (1987), 'Marriage, Fertility and Mortality', in W. Vamplew (ed.), *Australians: Historical Statistics,* Broadway: Fairfax, Syme & Weldon

McMartin, A. (1983), *Public Servants and Patronage: The Foundation and Rise of the New South Wales Public Service, 1786–1859,* Sydney: Sydney University Press

Mills, R.C. (1915), *The Colonisation of Australia (1829–42): The Wakefield Experiment in Empire Building,* London: Sidgwick & Jackson

Mitchell, B.R. (1988), *British Historical Statistics,* Cambridge: Cambridge University Press

Musters of New South Wales, 1805/6 to 1825

Musters of Van Diemen's Land, 1811 to 1822

Musters (see Baxter, C.J.)

New South Wales (—), *Blue Book* [variously titled], Sydney: various years

New South Wales, Colonial Secretary, *New South Wales Census* (1833, 1836, 1841, 1846 & 1851), Sydney

New South Wales, Colonial Secretary (—), *Returns of the Colony,* Sydney: various years

Nicholas, S. (ed.) (1988), *Convict Workers: Reinterpreting Australia's Past,* Cambridge: Cambridge University Press

Nicholas, S. & Shergold, P.R. (1988), 'Convicts as Migrants', in S. Nicholas (ed.), *Convict Workers: Reinterpreting Australia's Past,* Cambridge: Cambridge University Press

Nicholson, I.H. (1977), *Shipping Arrivals and Departures, Sydney, 1826 to 1840,* vol. 2, Canberra: Roebuck Society

Nicholson, I.H. (1983–85), *Shipping Arrivals and Departures, Tasmania,* vols 1 & 2, Canberra: Roebuck Society

O'Brien, E.M. (1950), *The Foundations of Australia, 1786–1800: A Study of English Criminal Practice and Penal Colonisation in the Eighteenth Century,* Sydney: Angus & Robertson, 2nd edn

Palmer, S.H. (1988), *Police and Protest in England and Ireland, 1780–1850,* Cambridge: Cambridge University Press

Philips, D. (1977), *Crime and Authority in Victorian England: The Black Country 1835–1860,* London: Croom Helm

Rimmer, W.G. (1969), 'The Economic Growth of Van Diemen's Land 1803–1821', in G.J. Abbott & N.B. Nairn (eds), *Economic Growth of Australia 1788–1821,* Melbourne: Melbourne University Press

Roberts, S.H. (1924), *History of Australian Land Settlement, 1788–1920,* Melbourne: Macmillan, in association with Melbourne University Press

Roberts, S.H. (1935), *The Squatting Age in Australia, 1835–1847,* Melbourne: Melbourne University Press

Robinson, P. (1985), *The Hatch and Brood of Time: A Study of the First Generation of Native-Born White Australians, 1788–1828,* Melbourne: Oxford University Press

Robson, L.L. (1965), *The Convict Settlers of Australia: An Enquiry into the Origin and Character of the Convicts Transported to New South Wales and Van Diemen's Land, 1787–1852,* Melbourne: Melbourne University Press

Robson, L.L. (1983), *A History of Tasmania,* vol. 1: *Van Diemen's Land from the Earliest Times to 1855.* Melbourne: Oxford University Press

Sahlins, M. (1974), *Stone Age Economics,* London: Tavistock Publications

Sainty, M.R. & Johnson, K.A. (eds) (1980), *The Census of New South Wales, November 1828,* Sydney: Library of Australian History

Shann, E.O.G. (1938), *An Economic History of Australia,* Cambridge: Cambridge University Press

Shaw, A.G.L. (1966), *Convicts and the Colonies: A Study of Penal Transportation from Great Britain and Ireland to Australia and Other Parts of the British Empire,* London: Faber & Faber

Shaw, A.G.L. (1970), *Great Britain and the Colonies, 1815–1865,* London: Methuen

Shaw, A.G.L. (ed.) (1989), *Gipps–La Trobe Correspondence, 1839–1846,* Melbourne: Melbourne University Press at the Miegunyah Press

Shineberg, D. (1967), *They Came for Sandalwood: A Study of the Sandalwood Trade in the South-West Pacific, 1830–1865,* Melbourne: Melbourne University Press

Shipping arrivals at Hobart, 1829–52, Archives Office of Tasmania

Smith, A. (1776), *An Inquiry into the Nature and Causes of the Wealth of Nations,* London: W. Strahan & T. Cadell

Statham, P.C. (1986), 'Peter Augustus Lautour: absentee investor extraordinaire', *Journal of the Royal Australian Historical Society,* vol. 72, part 3, December

Statham, P.C. (ed.) (1989), *The Origins of Australia's Capital Cities,* Melbourne: Cambridge University Press

Steven, M.J.E. (1965), *Merchant Campbell, 1769–1846: A Study of Colonial Trade,* Melbourne: Oxford University Press

Steven, M.J.E. (1969a), 'Enterprise', in G.J. Abbott & N.B. Nairn (eds), *Economic Growth of Australia 1788–1821,* Melbourne: Melbourne University Press

Steven, M.J.E. (1969b), 'Exports other than Wool', in G.J. Abbott & N.B. Nairn (eds), *Economic Growth of Australia 1788–1821,* Melbourne: Melbourne University Press

Steven, M.J.E. (1969c), 'The Changing Pattern of Commerce', in G.J. Abbott & N.B. Nairn (eds), *Economic Growth of Australia 1788–1821,* Melbourne: Melbourne University Press

Sydney Gazette, The (various issues)

Tobias, J.J. (1967), *Crime and Industrial Society in the 19th Century,* London: Batsford

Tooke, T. (1857), *A History of Prices, and of the State of the Circulation, from 1793 to 1837*, vols 1–6 London: Longman, Orme, Brown, Green, & Longmans

United Kingdom (1970, 1971), '1841 Census Great Britain' (*P.P.*, Sessions 1842–1844), in *Irish University Press Series of British Parliamentary Papers— Population, 3–5*, Shannon: Irish University Press

United Kingdom (1970), '1851 Census Great Britain' (*P.P.*, Sessions 1852–1854), in *Irish University Press Series of British Parliamentary Papers—Population, 8–11*, Shannon: Irish University Press

United Kingdom, Colonial Land and Emigration Commission (1969), 'General Report of the Colonial Land and Emigration Commissioners', (*P.P.*, Sessions 1842–1852), in *Irish University Press Series of British Parliamentary Papers— Emigration, 10–11*, Shannon: Irish University Press

United Kingdom, Colonial Office (n.d.), 'Return from the Period since the Establishment of the Colony of New South Wales up to the Year 1817 …', in 'Appendix to Commissioner Bigge's Report, 1822 …', Australian Joint Copying Project (AJCP) Public Record Office (PRO), London: CO201/130

United Kingdom, Exchequer and Audit Department (n.d.), Declared Accounts (in Rolls), Colonies, New South Wales, National Library of Australia and the Library of New South Wales, AJCP: PRO, London: AO1/1295 [1786–91], AO1/1296–99 [1791–1827]

United Kingdom, Exchequer and Audit Department (n.d.), Declared Accounts (in Rolls), Commissariat (Abroad), New South Wales, National Library of Australia and the Library of New South Wales, AJCP: PRO, London: AO1/556–9 [March 1791–December 1822]

United Kingdom, Exchequer and Audit Department (n.d.), Declared Accounts (in Rolls), Commissariat (Abroad), Van Diemen's Land, National Library of Australia and the Library of New South Wales, AJCP: PRO, London: AO1/578–9 [July 1803–February 1810]

United Kingdom, Exchequer and Audit Department (n.d.), Declared Accounts (in Rolls, Commissariat (Abroad), Norfolk Island, National Library of Australia and the Library of New South Wales, AJCP: PRO, London: AO1/559–60 [January 1801–March 1810]

United Kingdom, Exchequer and Audit Department (n.d.), Declared and Passed Accounts (in Books), Commissariat (Abroad), Van Diemen's Land, National Library of Australia and the Library of New South Wales, AJCP: PRO, London

United Kingdom, Home Office (n.d.), General Muster, 1825, National Library of

Australia and the Library of New South Wales, AJCP: PRO, London: HO10/19–20

United Kingdom, House of Commons (1970), 'A Return of the Annual Expenditure in the Colony of New South Wales ... 1st January 1818', in *Irish University Press Series of British Parliamentary Papers—Colonies: Australia, no. 3,* Shannon: Irish University Press

United Kingdom, House of Commons (1970), 'A Return of the Annual Expenditure of the Colony of New South Wales ... 1st January 1821', in *Irish University Press Series of British Parliamentary Papers—Colonies: Australia, no. 3,* Shannon: Irish University Press

United Kingdom, House of Commons (1970–71), 'Report from His Majesty's Commissioners for Inquiry into the Administration and Practical Operation of the Poor Laws ... 21 February 1834', *P.P.*, Session 1834, no. 44, vols 27–39, in *Irish University Press Series of British Parliamentary Papers—Crime and Punishment: Transportation, nos. 8–18,* Shannon: Irish University Press

United Kingdom, House of Commons (1969), 'Report from the Select Committee appointed to consider the Poor Laws', *Parliamentary Papers*, Session 1818, no. 107, vol. 5; 'Second Report', *Parliamentary Papers*, Session 1818, no. 237, vol. 5; 'Third Report', *Parliamentary Papers*, Session 1819, no. 358, vol. 5, in *Irish University Press Series of British Parliamentary Papers—Crime and Punishment: Transportation, no. 1,* Shannon: Irish University Press

United Kingdom, House of Commons (1969), 'Report from the Select Committee appointed to consider the expediency of erecting a Penitentiary House ... and who were instructed to inquire into the effects which have been produced by the punishment of Transportation to New South Wales, and of Imprisonment on board the Hulks, *P.P.*, Session 1810–11, no. 199, vol. 3; 'Second Report', *P.P.*, Session 1810–11, no. 217, vol. 3; 'Third Report', *P.P.*, Session 1812, no. 306, vol. 2, in *Irish University Press Series of British Parliamentary Papers—Crime and Punishment: Transportation, no. 1,* Shannon: Irish University Press

United Kingdom, House of Commons (1968), 'Report from the Select Committee on Transportation ... 3 August 1838', *P.P.*, Session 1837–38, no. 669, vol. 22, in *Irish University Press Series of British Parliamentary Papers—Crime and Punishment: Transportation, no. 3,* Shannon: Irish University Press

United Kingdom, House of Commons (1969), 'Report from the Select Committee on Transportation ... 10 July 1812', *P.P.*, Session 1812, no. 341, vol. 2, in *Irish University Press Series of British Parliamentary Papers—Crime and Punishment: Transportation, no. 1,* Shannon: Irish University Press

United Kingdom, House of Commons (1968), 'Report from the Select Committee on Transportation ... 14 July 1837', *P.P.*, Session 1837, no. 518, vol. 19, in *Irish University Press Series of British Parliamentary Papers—Crime and Punishment: Transportation, no. 2,* Shannon: Irish University Press

Vamplew, W. (ed.) (1987), *Australians: Historical Statistics,* Broadway, NSW: Fairfax, Syme & Weldon

Van Diemen's Land, Colonial Secretary (1843), 'Van Diemen's Land Census of the Year 1842', *Hobart Town Gazette*, 11 April

Van Diemen's Land, Colonial Secretary (n.d.), 'Van Diemen's Land Census of the Year 1843', *Statistics of Van Diemen's Land, 1841–1844,* Hobart Town: Government Printer

Van Diemen's Land, Colonial Secretary (1848), 'Van Diemen's Land Census of the
    Year 1848', *Hobart Town Gazette*, 28 March
Van Diemen's Land, Colonial Secretary (—), *Statistics of Van Diemen's Land*
    [various titles], Hobart Town: various years
Van Diemen's Land, Colonial Secretary (n.d.), *Van Diemen's Land Census, March 1,
    1851,* Hobart Town
Wakefield, E.G. (ed.) (1914), *A View of the Art of Colonization in Present Reference
    to the British Empire, in Letters Between a Statesman and a Colonist, with an
    introduction by James Collier,* Oxford: Clarendon Press, 2nd edn
Wakefield, E.G. (1929), *A Letter from Sydney and Other Writings,* London: Dent
Wakefield, E.G. (1833), *England and America: A Comparison of the Social and
    Political State of Both Nations,* vols 1–2, London: Richard Bentley
Wentworth, W.C. (1824), *A Statistical Account of the British Settlements in
    Australasia, including the Colonies of New South Wales and Van Diemen's
    Land,* vols 1–2, London: Whittaker, 3rd edn
Wrigley, E.A. (ed.) (1972), *Nineteenth-Century Society: Essays in the Use of
    Quantitative Methods for the Study of Social Data,* Cambridge: Cambridge
    University Press
Wrigley, E.A. (1988), *Continuity, Chance and Change: The Character of the
    Industrial Revolution in England,* Cambridge: Cambridge University Press
Young, D.M. (1961), *The Colonial Office in the Early Nineteenth Century,* London:
    Longmans

APPENDIX 1

COLONIAL AGENT'S TRANSFERS

The Colonial Agent was an important figure in respect of New South Wales and Van Diemen's Land partly because of his role in receiving British Parliamentary Appropriations for civil salaries and transmitting the appropriate sums, and also partly because he became, in due course, an important source of information in Britain about colonial affairs. The Agent's role changed in 1827 with the withdrawal of the relevant appropriations; it became increasingly related to migration and his transactions became a mix of public and private affairs. The present estimates are therefore confined to the period 1787 to 1827.

Bigge's estimates (see table 7.1, p.62) of civil costs take merely (but not quite perfectly) the series of appropriations; and they do not deal with the balances accumulating in the Agent's hands. The appropriations are far from representing either the civil costs or the transfers to the colonies on civil account. The Agent was a British tax gatherer; he paid pensions of retired civil officials; he transferred sums to dependents or personal agents in Britain; he adjusted the appropriations to accord with due earnings; he corrected for past over- or underclaims; he charged fees for his work; and he paid out fees for various approvals of transactions.

The estimates below include all earnings, fees and pensions to approximate the 'cost' of the colonies to Britain. A different series would be required to estimate transfers to the colonies.

Table 1: Colonial Agent's Transfers, 1787–1827, (£)

	Received from Exchequer	Expenditure inc fees	Colonial Agent Balance
1787	2 877		
1788	2 877	2 502	374
1789	2 877		
1790	4 559		
1791	4 758		3 453
1792	4 726	3 369	5 307
1793	4 658	2 960	6 894
1794	4 795	4 417	8 210
1795	5 241	4 320	9 282
1796	5 241	3 819	11 099
1797	5 524		
1798	6 157	17 939 }	13 166 }
1799	6 017		
1800	6 310	6 992	12 813
1801	7 146	3 967	16 321
1802	5 908	4 063	18 242
1803	9 125	10 575	16 926
1804	10 049	7 287	19 811
1805	7 226	4 721	22 612
1806	12 934	15 088	23 235
1807	12 705	16 125	22 745
1808	11 165	10 198	24 147
1809	15 135	13 870	25 625
1810	13 269	15 008	24 885
1811	NA	NA	NA
1812	13 329	11 628	1 782
1813	12 701	11 763	2 341
1814	20 593	16 732	6 944
1815	6 000	11 996	2 547
1816	12 788	12 070	3 911
1817	12 924		
1818	12 315	32 678 }	0 }
1819	2 000		
1820	30 430	22 119	8 376
1821	16 581	21 063	3 894
1822	15 581	14 907	4 667
1823	21 569	17 775	8 470
1824	8 000	16 008	461
1825	19 294	17 525	2 231
1826	23 876 }	25 718 }	389 }
1827			

Note: NA — Not available.
Source: United Kingdom, Exchequer and Audit Department, AJCP: PRO, AO1/1295, AO1/1296–1299.

APPENDIX 2

THE NSW COMMISSARIAT ACCOUNTS TO 1827

The New South Wales Commissariat Accounts, as presented to audit, have been included in the text in terms of the years shown in the various Commissaries' statements. As they stand, they do not allow full annual estimates. It is useful to attempt annual estimates. In doing so, some of the Governors' Accounts have been incorporated (eliminating double-counting) in order to make the statements more complete.

In appendix table 2 following, a complete annual series has not been possible; and to achieve the break-up shown, it is necessary to be content with a single aggregate. Even so, the procedure adopted will seem strange, at least at first sight. What has been done is to confuse revenues and expenditures. Moreover, some of the series have had to be compiled on a pro rata basis.

The confusion of revenues and expenditures would be impossible were there significant outstanding balances. In practice, there is little in the way of balances to create problems. This does not altogether suffice in the case of the long periods covered, but there are inherent reasons why only small annual balances would arise. The reasons lie in the difficulties which compel confusion of the two sides of the accounts. Frequently, but not always, expenditures are shown only in very aggregated terms. But the issue of bills as a means of raising charges on Britain (equals revenues) typically was done to pay for purchases. Revenue raising and expenditure were necessarily simultaneous. Where the transactions in one side of the accounts were summarised and in the other itemised and dated, it is possible to shift from one to the other to derive a reasonably continuous calendar year series of aggregate 'operations'.

Fortunately, so far as these accounts go, bills dominated. Other revenues, such as sales, were small and typically undated. In the main, these small components can be linked to non-goods purchases, particularly salaries, where an approximate dating can be made provided, one assumes, that earnings were paid in the year due and not as occasional lump sums. Even so, this is not a major issue. Governors' bills must be brought into account and, indeed, greatly facilitate an annual estimation because, almost entirely, they were passed to the Commissaries and help to date the Commissariat's activities. Where they were not so passed, they have been added to the annual series.

Not all the years are true calendar years. Often they were December–December accounts and have been left as such. Deviations from strict calendar year accounts are noted in the footnotes to the table. On two occasions, no break-up is possible. Two additional points should be noted. Firstly, as indicated in the text, the accounts are net, not gross, statements. Secondly, they are handwritten and there is at times some difficulty in deciphering the script.

Throughout, the operations in Norfolk Island and Van Diemen's Land are included. Sometimes these could be unscrambled, but usually they are represented as net NSW obligations, not as the true transactions (even as net transactions) within these two areas. The Norfolk Island Commissariat records, as audited, are shown below at the date at which the settlement was abandoned. In Van Diemen's Land, the Commissariat accounts have been found up to 1810 and shown below.

Table 2: NSW Commissariat Operations, 1787–1827, (£)

Year	Operations
1787	211
1788	4 346
1789	831
1790	1 309
1791	1 075
1792	5 127
1793	15 807
1794	3 572
1795	32 103
1796	41 736
1797	19 465
1798	27 035
1799	41 588
1800	50 910
1801	10 786
1802	16 468
1803	16 975
1804	10 192
1805	17 442
1806	9 083
1807	10 483
1808	13 800
1809	25 199
1810	
1811	259 972 }
1812	
1813	
1814	NA
1815	NA
1816	120 673
1817	112 691
1818	188 700
1819	
1820	428 986 }
1821	

Note: NA — Not available.
Sources: Re-estimated from Commissariat Accounts and Governor's bills.
        AJCP: PRO, AO1/556–9.

APPENDIX 3

EXTRA-NSW COMMISSARIAT OPERATIONS, 1791–1810

The New South Wales and Norfolk Island Commissariats were separated in 1827 and only the 1827–30 accounts for Van Diemen's Land have so far been located in legible form. The series below stop at 1810. For those inclined to use the record, it cannot be too strongly stressed that the Van Diemen's Land Commissariat had a life of its own and one cannot subtract the Van Diemen's Land (or Norfolk Island) series from that for the NSW Commissariat to derive a mainland series. The accounts do not work in that manner. The early Norfolk Island and Van Diemen's Land accounts are given in appendix table 3.

Table 3: Extra-NSW Commissariat Operations, 1791–1810, (£)

	Norfolk Island	Van Diemen's Land	Port Dalrymple
1791			
1792	4 516 }		
1793			
1794	NA		
1795	NA		
1796			
1797	1 486 }		
1798			
1799			
1800	2 846		
1801	4 602		
1802	4 334		
1803	4 468	7 770	
1804	7 033	6 887	
1805	5 046	14 664	
1806	3 590	16 221	7 012
1807	2 047	19 756	4 908
1808	2 569	NA	
1809	1 537	NA	4 341 }
1810	—	NA	

Note: NA — Not available.
Sources: AJCP: PRO.
Norfolk Island — AO1/559–60.
Van Diemen's Land — AO1/578–9.

APPENDIX 4

NSW COMMISSARIAT REVENUE, 1822–50

Table 4(a): NSW Commissariat Revenue, 1822–50[a], (£'000)

Year	Treasury Bills	Sale Goods	Specie Colonial	Loans Colonial Treasury	Supplies Port Phillip Depts.	Provisions etc.	Balances	Other	Total Including Balances
1822	230.1	4.4	NA	NA	NA	NA	NA	21.0	255.5
1823	119.0	4.7	NA	NA	NA	NA	NA	10.4	134.1
1824	NA	NA	NA	NA	NA	NA	NA	NA	NA
1825	193.9	4.4	NA	NA	NA	NA	NA	NA	198.3
1826	59.3	3.9	NA	NA	NA	NA	NA	NA	63.2
1827	164.6	1.6	NA	NA	NA	NA	NA	NA	166.2
1828	98.5	NA	NA	NA	NA	NA	NA	NA	98.5
1829	154.4	NA	NA	NA	NA	NA	NA	4.5	158.9
1830	138.7	NA	NA	NA	NA	NA	NA	0.9	139.6
1831	117.8	5.8	20.5	NA	NA	NA	34.1	4.4	182.6
1832	114.8	9.3	5.0	NA	NA	NA	24.3	12.3	165.7
1833	81.0	8.1	15.0	2.8	NA	NA	33.0	6.6	146.5
1834	114.9	3.9	20.8	3.8	NA	NA	22.7	8.1	174.2
1835	176.9	2.5	40.0	4.8	1.3	NA	15.5	9.2	250.2
1836	223.4	9.8	60.0	2.6	NA	NA	51.2	7.2	354.4
1837	173.9	3.3	NA	28.9	NA	NA	26.7	22.0	254.8
1838	292.5	4.1	NA	62.8	1.3	NA	14.1	8.9	383.7
1839	248.0	7.6	NA	90.6	2.9	10.1	103.6	11.9	474.7
1840	205.6	5.0	NA	39.1	0.9	4.0	117.0	17.9	389.5
1841	92.1	2.7	NA	7.4	0.3	0.8	159.8	15.5	278.6
1842	171.5	1.8	15.0	8.4	0.1	0.2	36.7	13.4	247.1
1843	146.9	0.9	NA	8.7	0.1	0.2	32.4	16.8	206.0
1844	142.8	1.3	10.0	1.5	0.1	NA	6.1	14.7	176.5
1845	91.2	4.7	100.0	3.0	0.1	NA	11.0	62.5	272.5
1846	213.7	3.5	85.0	87.1	0.2	NA	54.3	11.0	448.8
1847	120.4	3.5	4.0	56.9	NA	NA	121.2	12.0	318.0
1848	85.4	4.1	NA	118.8	NA	0.6	30.1	25.5	264.5
1849	101.9	1.8	10.0	123.5	2.3	0.3	15.1	8.3	262.5
1850	37.7	1.5	NA	161.8	0.8	NA	49.5	5.4	256.7

Notes: (a) Includes VDL 1822–7.
     (b) NA = zero except 1824.
Source: Summarised from J. Ginswick (unpub.) MS.

Table 4(b): NSW Commissariat Expenditure 1822–50[a] (£'000)

Year	Not NSW	Supplies	Police	Clergy	Paid to Colonial Treasury	Charity	Other Convict Service	Total Convict Service	Military	Retire. T.Bills	Other	Total NSW	Repay Public Loans	Balance	Total Inc. Balance
1822	4.4	175.9	NA	NA	NA	NA	4.1	180.0	27.8	NA	NA	207.8	NA	NA	212.2
1823	2.1	110.7	NA	NA	NA	NA	6.2	116.9	27.7	NA	NA	144.6	NA	NA	149.7
1824	NA	NA	NA	NA	NA	NA	NA	NA	NA	NA	NA	NA	NA	NA	NA
1825	2.9	13.8	NA	NA	NA	NA	68.0	86.8	35.9	NA	NA	122.7	NA	29.4	155.0
1826	4.7	68.8	NA	NA	NA	NA	NA	68.8	29.8	NA	NA	98.6	NA	NA	103.3
1827	5.0	81.6	NA	NA	NA	NA	10.0	91.6	37.0	NA	0.1	128.7	NA	NA	133.7
1828	7.6	69.0	20.6	NA	NA	1.7	27.1	118.4	60.3	NA	NA	178.7	5.0	40.6	238.0
1829	8.0	71.4	21.6	NA	NA	1.0	21.4	115.4	68.2	NA	6.3	189.9	NA	45.3	243.2
1830	7.3	46.0	22.6	NA	NA	1.0	20.1	87.7	59.5	NA	NA	149.2	NA	34.1	196.8
1831	13.8	46.9	22.2	NA	NA	0.6	19.8	89.5	61.3	NA	14.7	165.5	NA	24.3	203.6
1832	8.8	NA	NA	NA	NA	NA	77.0	77.7	67.4	NA	7.3	182.4	NA	33.0	194.3
1833	8.7	42.2	19.9	NA	NA	1.3	14.7	78.1	53.2	NA	2.8	134.1	NA	22.7	165.5
1834	7.0	64.6	15.8	NA	NA	1.6	16.2	98.2	65.0	NA	3.1	166.3	NA	15.5	187.0
1835	8.8	79.1	5.5	NA	NA	2.7	18.0	105.3	82.7	NA	13.4	201.4	NA	51.2	250.2
1836	23.9	103.8	5.7	NA	NA	1.7	22.6	133.8	98.1	NA	12.2	243.8	50.0	26.7	344.4
1837	14.6	92.6	7.5	NA	NA	2.9	22.8	125.8	83.2	NA	17.2	226.2	NA	14.1	254.8
1838	24.8	97.9	4.8	0.3	0.5	2.7	21.2	127.4	81.0	10.0	16.9	253.3	NA	103.6	363.7
1839	24.2	132.6	0.4	0.5	NA	2.4	23.3	159.2	86.1	65.0	23.2	333.5	NA	117.0	474.7
1840	25.6	126.5	0.4	0.8	NA	2.5	19.3	149.5	88.4	NA	21.0	258.9	NA	105.0	389.5
1841	13.5	93.4	0.2	0.9	NA	3.3	21.0	118.8	86.4	NA	23.2	228.4	NA	36.7	278.6
1842	28.9	61.5	0.1	0.7	2.6	3.2	20.3	88.0	81.4	NA	21.4	190.8	NA	27.3	247.1
1843	53.1	4.7	0.1	0.7	2.5	2.5	18.0	66.5	61.7	NA	18.6	146.8	NA	6.1	206.0
1844	20.9	26.6	0.1	0.7	2.9	2.5	21.6	54.4	80.5	NA	9.7	144.6	NA	11.0	176.6
1845	77.0	13.4	0.1	0.7	2.0	1.9	13.5	31.6	56.5	NA	9.1	97.2	NA	54.3	272.5
1846	229.0	11.4	0.1	0.7	2.2	2.6	10.7	27.7	81.3	NA	9.9	88.9	9.7	121.2	448.8
1847	151.4	9.4	0.1	0.8	0.7	2.0	12.5	25.5	53.3	NA	10.4	89.2	45.3	30.1	318.0
1848	138.7	4.3	NA	0.7	0.6	1.5	7.6	14.7	45.3	NA	11.3	71.3	39.4	15.1	264.5
1849	152.4	2.7	NA	0.5	0.3	1.3	6.6	11.4	41.4	NA	7.9	60.7	NA	49.5	262.5
1850	200.2	2.1	NA	0.4	0.3	1.0	6.9	10.7	35.0	NA	6.4	52.1	NA	4.4	256.7

Notes: (a) Including Van Diemen's Land 1822–7
(b) NA = zero except for 1824.
Source: Summarised from J. Ginswick (unpub.) MS.

Table 4(c): NSW Colonial Fund Revenue 1822–50, (£'000)

Year	Arrears	Customs	Other Indirect	Fees and Fines	Postal	Income Public Assets	Misc.	Transf. from UK	Public Loans Repaid	Transf. & Sales Commt.	Loans Military Chest	Special Appropns	Balance	Other	Total inc. Balances
1822	10.0	37.9	5.9	NA	NA	2.8	NA	9.5	NA	NA	NA	NA	NA	0.6	66.7
1823	7.6	23.7	6.8	0.2	NA	6.8	NA	8.0	NA	NA	NA	NA	NA	0.3	53.4
1824	6.6	28.8	5.3	1.3	NA	7.0	7.8	NA	NA	NA	NA	NA	NA	NA	NA
1825	11.8	48.4	6.5	1.3	NA	12.1	NA	16.6	0.7	NA	NA	NA	NA	NA	97.3
1826	3.0	47.7	7.2	1.9	NA	5.2	NA	91.7	NA	NA	NA	NA	NA	0.2	156.9
1827	2.6	49.5	10.2	2.7	NA	14.8	NA	15.2	1.0	NA	NA	NA	NA	NA	95.6
1828	7.3	64.8	10.7	3.7	0.6	16.5	NA	NA	1.4	11.4	5.0	NA	4.0	NA	119.5
1829	6.6	73.2	9.2	6.7	1.2	9.0	1.7	20.0	0.4	0.1	NA	NA	83.9	0.7	182.7
1830	4.0	78.7	9.5	6.3	1.6	6.6	1.1	NA	0.1	0.3	NA	NA	48.8	NA	159.6
1831	NA	87.8	11.1	8.0	2.2	10.8	1.4	NA	1.0	NA	NA	NA	12.4	0.4	135.3
1832	NA	93.9	12.7	6.0	2.6	20.0	0.5	NA	NA	NA	NA	NA	NA	0.2	135.9
1833	NA	108.5	14.8	6.3	3.0	4.7	1.3	NA	NA	NA	NA	NA	9.0	0.1	147.7
1834	NA	124.5	17.1	9.9	3.7	5.0	1.7	25.0	NA	NA	NA	NA	16.5	0.1	203.5
1835	NA	140.4	17.7	8.8	4.3	7.5	5.3	55.0	NA	NA	NA	NA	30.8	0.2	270.0
1836	NA	153.7	18.6	9.7	5.0	7.7	3.4	50.0	NA	NA	120.9	NA	18.8	NA	387.8
1837	NA	163.3	20.8	11.6	5.6	9.5	12.5	20.0	NA	NA	48.2	NA	16.8	NA	356.3
1838	NA	145.3	23.5	13.6	8.4	4.5	4.2	25.0	NA	NA	NA	265.3	NA	3.1	492.9
1839	NA	153.4	42.5	17.4	11.0	15.4	8.9	NA	NA	NA	NA	NA	285.4	5.5	540.5
1840	NA	192.8	56.1	33.1	14.2	19.8	32.5	NA	NA	NA	NA	NA	144.8	NA	486.6
1841	NA	216.2	54.4	43.1	19.1	19.8	7.5	NA	NA	0.9	NA	NA	266.2	16.0	643.2
1842	NA	215.3	49.3	41.4	20.0	28.8	7.5	46.0	NA	1.2	NA	NA	6.9	3.3	419.7
1843	NA	164.9	54.8	27.5	18.9	25.0	1.0	NA	NA	NA	NA	NA	26.2	2.2	320.5
1844	NA	151.9	45.8	20.2	17.2	30.7	0.2	NA	NA	NA	NA	NA	7.6	0.7	274.3
1845	NA	157.5	56.8	10.3	18.0	39.7	0.6	NA	NA	0.1	NA	NA	28.3	0.8	309.1
1846	NA	151.1	86.2	11.2	17.9	27.5	0.5	NA	NA	0.1	NA	NA	58.0	NA	322.5
1847	NA	170.6	87.2	14.9	19.3	9.4	0.4	NA	NA	NA	NA	NA	52.9	1.2	328.9
1848	NA	168.7	52.7	16.7	20.7	31.7	0.3	NA	NA	NA	NA	NA	36.2	4.0	331.0
1849	NA	186.0	53.0	16.7	21.8	44.5	0.3	NA	NA	NA	NA	NA	23.6	1.4	347.3
1850	NA	219.3	56.7	22.6	20.2	48.5	0.2	NA	NA	NA	NA	NA	71.3	2.9	441.7

Note: NA = zero except 1824.
Source: Summarised from J. Ginswick (unpub.) MS.

Table 4(d): NSW Colonial Fund Expenditure 1822–50, (£'000)

Year	Arrears	Civil Estab-lishment	Judic-iary	Clergy & Schools	Trustees Clergy & Schools	Police & Gaols	Constr-uction	Works & Survey	Supp-lies	Military	Colonial Agent	Loans to Commt	Other Loans	Appropns not Charged	Balances	Other	Total inc. Balances
1822	NA	20.1	5.0	2.5	NA	8.1	3.9	1.9	1.1	0.2	NA	19.0	NA	NA	NA	5.1	58.0
1823	NA	16.8	4.0	3.0	NA	8.5	2.5	3.2	2.2	0.2	0.6	8.3	1.1	NA	NA	4.5	46.8
1824	NA	NA	NA	NA	NA	NA	NA	NA	NA	NA	NA	NA	NA	NA	NA	NA	NA
1825	NA	47.9	17.0	10.6	NA	14.4	NA	22.1	NA	1.6	0.9	NA	0.4	NA	35.3	16.8	142.2
1826	7.5	37.2	13.5	14.6	NA	18.3	NA	12.7	20.0	NA	NA	NA	NA	NA	NA	4.5	113.2
1827	2.6	47.4	15.2	0.6	NA	19.3	NA	19.8	7.6	5.1	NA	NA	NA	NA	11.7	0.9	118.4
1828	9.1	46.4	15.9	0.6	19.8	NA	NA	20.7	NA	7.6	4.9	NA	NA	NA	23.5	NA	107.6
1829	4.4	54.1	18.9	0.7	19.3	NA	NA	24.4	NA	0.6	5.2	NA	NA	NA	21.8	NA	98.3
1830	1.0	52.9	19.6	0.5	20.5	NA	NA	24.9	NA	0.6	NA	NA	NA	NA	36.6	NA	103.0
1831	NA	26.4	22.3	NA	17.2	0.1	17.0	NA	NA	3.5	NA	NA	NA	NA	9.0	14.7	135.3
1832	1.8	27.5	19.2	NA	17.1	NA	28.7	NA	NA	1.4	NA	NA	NA	14.3	16.5	16.9	135.9
1833	0.9	28.3	20.9	NA	16.8	NA	28.3	NA	NA	0.6	NA	NA	NA	16.9	30.8	18.5	147.7
1834	1.6	32.7	21.9	NA	18.8	8.0	33.8	NA	NA	0.5	NA	25.0	NA	20.8	18.8	9.6	203.5
1835	1.0	34.7	23.6	NA	23.7	26.4	36.4	NA	NA	0.6	NA	55.0	NA	37.0	66.8	12.8	270.0
1836	1.8	38.9	25.5	NA	25.6	39.5	48.0	NA	NA	0.4	NA	NA	NA	72.4	NA	68.9	387.8
1837	1.5	50.3	25.5	NA	23.1	43.0	66.8	NA	1.1	NA	NA	2.0	NA	104.0	285.4	25.6	360.9
1838	7.1	55.1	28.8	NA	31.0	63.2	128.6	NA	1.3	1.0	NA	NA	NA	NA	144.8	15.9	617.4
1839	6.0	65.1	29.2	NA	37.3	86.7	112.3	NA	0.8	1.0	NA	NA	NA	NA	266.2	45.1	528.3
1840	3.4	72.1	28.2	NA	38.0	97.6	106.6	NA	1.2	NA	NA	NA	NA	NA	6.9	57.2	670.5
1841	4.3	80.8	32.5	NA	49.4	103.8	108.2	NA	1.1	1.5	NA	NA	NA	NA	26.2	33.6	421.3
1842	NA	73.6	35.6	NA	46.0	93.7	106.4	NA	0.5	2.0	NA	NA	NA	NA	7.6	14.2	398.2
1843	NA	71.4	35.7	NA	41.8	80.9	63.9	NA	NA	14.5	NA	NA	NA	NA	6.2	15.6	331.4
1844	NA	64.3	34.1	NA	36.6	67.8	27.6	NA	NA	10.8	NA	NA	NA	NA	64.1	10.0	257.9
1845	NA	6.4	26.3	NA	38.8	67.3	27.6	NA	NA	11.0	NA	NA	NA	NA	57.4	9.3	309.1
1846	NA	68.4	26.1	NA	43.2	6.9	32.0	NA	NA	12.0	NA	NA	NA	NA	26.2	13.3	322.5
1847	NA	71.4	36.1	NA	47.7	69.1	58.0	NA	0.2	8.3	NA	NA	NA	NA	21.4	8.9	328.9
1848	NA	83.4	33.4	NA	42.0	79.7	56.9	NA	0.2	NA	NA	NA	NA	NA	72.6	14.1	331.1
1849	NA	77.0	30.8	NA	43.6	69.8	41.2	NA	0.1	NA	NA	NA	NA	NA	105.7	12.2	347.3
1850	NA	75.4	33.5	NA	49.9	72.1	54.0	NA	1.1	NA	NA	NA	NA	NA	NA	50.0	441.7

Note: NA = zero except for 1824.
Source: Summarised from J. Ginswick (unpub.) MS.

Table 4(e): NSW Crown and Land Fund Revenue 1833–50, (£'000)

Year	Land Sales	Other Land Rev.	Total Land	Licenses and Assess.	Loan Repay Commt	Balances	Debentures	Church and Schools	Other	Total inc. Balances
1833	25.0	1.1	26.1	0.2	NA	NA	NA	NA	NA	26.3
1834	41.8	1.4	43.2	0.3	NA	NA	NA	NA	0.1	43.6
1835	80.8	8.2	89.0	0.4	NA	42.5	NA	NA	0.1	132.0
1836	126.5	4.9	131.4	1.0	10.0	120.9	NA	NA	NA	263.3
1837	120.2	3.4	123.6	4.2	NA	126.0	NA	NA	1.1	254.9
1838	116.3	3.9	120.2	4.5	NA	197.3	NA	NA	6.8	328.8
1839	153.0	7.8	160.8	8.4	NA	NA	NA	NA	3.1	172.3
1840	314.6	10.7	325.3	14.9	NA	NA	NA	NA	0.5	340.7
1841	90.4	15.4	105.8	14.5	NA	NA	NA	NA	NA	120.3
1842	14.6	29.5	44.1	17.4	NA	NA	48.7	NA	0.1	110.3
1843	10.8	18.5	29.3	17.6	NA	NA	NA	2.4	7.3	56.6
1844	7.4	13.5	20.9	20.4	NA	NA	75.7	2.7	0.2	119.9
1845	16.7	11.5	28.2	32.9	NA	23.5	NA	3.5	18.2	106.3
1846	27.1	11.7	38.8	35.4	NA	64.6	NA	4.2	3.5	146.5
1847	60.3	17.1	77.4	40.9	NA	110.4	NA	4.7	0.3	233.6
1848	46.0	5.7	51.7	45.9	NA	110.3	NA	4.1	0.3	212.3
1849	75.3	15.2	90.5	43.4	NA	59.4	77.2	5.6	19.9	296.0
1850	51.6	13.7	65.3	41.1	NA	109.8	57.9	4.8	94.2	373.1

Note: NA = zero.
Source: Summarised from J. Ginswick (unpub.) MS.

Table 4(f): NSW Land and Crown Expenditure 1833–50, (£'000)

Year	Immigration	Land Administration	Aborigines	Port Phillip Estate	Debent. and Interest	Clergy and Schools	Loans Adjust. to Com.	Transfer to Colonial	Balances	Other	Total inc. Balances
1833	9.0	NA	NA	NA	NA	NA	NA	NA	NA	NA	9.0
1834	7.9	NA	NA	NA	NA	NA	10.0	NA	42.5	0.4	60.8
1835	10.6	NA	NA	NA	NA	NA	NA	NA	120.9	0.5	132.0
1836	11.8	NA	NA	2.2	NA	NA	NA	120.9	126.0	2.4	263.3
1837	36.5	2.0	NA	5.9	NA	NA	NA	NA	197.3	13.2	254.9
1838	101.7	4.5	4.6	13.7	NA	NA	25.0	48.2	285.4	6.6	489.7
1839	156.9	0.2	5.9	20.1	NA	NA	NA	NA	NA	1.4	184.5
1840	146.0	0.1	7.5	NA	NA	NA	NA	NA	NA	4.2	156.8
1841	329.3	0.2	10.2	NA	NA	NA	NA	NA	NA	2.5	342.2
1842	110.1	6.0	10.4	NA	3.0	NA	NA	NA	NA	2.3	131.8
1843	11.5	0.9	4.8	NA	27.8	0.5	NA	NA	NA	0.2	45.7
1844	70.3	10.0	3.0	NA	4.2	0.4	NA	NA	NA	NA	87.7
1845	15.6	9.8	2.2	NA	8.7	0.4	NA	NA	64.6	5.0	106.3
1846	1.1	14.9	2.1	NA	15.8	0.4	NA	NA	110.4	1.8	146.5
1847	0.6	23.0	2.5	NA	92.0	0.6	NA	NA	110.3	4.6	233.6
1848	113.1	32.7	2.6	NA	NA	0.4	NA	NA	59.4	4.1	212.3
1849	137.4	35.8	3.6	NA	1.9	2.4	NA	NA	109.8	5.1	296.0
1850	165.7	48.6	2.1	NA	5.2	5.9	NA	NA	140.4	5.4	373.1

Note: NA = zero.
Source: Summarised from J. Ginswick (unpub.) MS.

APPENDIX 5

VAN DIEMEN'S LAND ACCOUNTS

In Van Diemen's Land, three accounts are relevant — the Colonial Fund, the Land Fund and the Commissariat, the first beginning in 1824, the second in the second half of the 1840s and the third covering September 1826 to 31 March 1840.

These are all defective sources of information, much more so than the corresponding New South Wales accounts. Contrary to Hartwell's view (1954) that the Commissariat and Colonial Fund Accounts were separate, the two were intimately intertwined. Any discussion of Van Diemen's Land accounts and their implications for the economy is seriously flawed unless the two are considered together.

Unfortunately, any such consideration is very difficult. So far as the present representation goes, the records of the Colonial and Land Funds are based not on detailed data but on the summaries presented in Hartwell (1954). These summaries are explicitly defective, in particular, acknowledging that there was inadequate entry of loans from the Commissariat. This admission is a considerable understatement of the problem. The Colonial Fund, as summarised, does not acknowledge the quite massive transfers between that and the Commissariat Account. For its part, the Commissariat records fail to admit loans to the Colonial Fund but show a great many other and very large transfers to and from the Colonial Fund. Moreover, they include very large retrospective adjustments as between the two accounts, imposed by British auditors, when the Commissariat support to certain activities, particularly relating to convict children and education, were disallowed (see Commissariat accounts).

There is another very practical problem. The extant Commissariat records are by no means always legible and there must be some doubts about the expenditure amounts and more particularly the objects of expenditure and the sources of revenue. There is also a word of warning. The Van Diemen's Land Commissariat Accounts are operations within that colony. One cannot compare the Van Diemen's Land and NSW Commissariat accounts in 1826/27 and 1825/26 to attempt to gauge the scale of Commissariat spending in NSW alone in the latter year. While the two were combined to 1825/26, the so-called NSW accounts contain net NSW obligations for Van Diemen's Land, not the true operations of the latter.

Until more work is done on Van Diemen's Land in particular, there is not much point in extended comment. One can, however, already observe considerable interaction between the two funds, the broad similarity with NSW expenditure objects and revenue sources, and a definite tightening of British fiscal commitment to the Van Diemen's Land colony. Land revenues were more significant in Van Diemen's Land relative to NSW but appear to have been accepted by Britain as applicable to colonial purposes. There is considerable evidence of declining British subsidies through Commissariat bills in the last two years of the 1830s, a decline that occurred as problems of instability developed in the Van Diemen's Land economy. This may be a significant factor in the downturn, however, the fiscal influences on them are clouded by referring only to the Colonial Fund.

The summary accounts are given in appendix tables 6(a) (Land Fund) and 6(b) (Commissariat). Because of the problem of legibility of the Commissariat records, only very general summaries are presented.

APPENDIX 6

VAN DIEMEN'S LAND FUND: REVENUE AND EXPENDITURE 1847–50

Table 6(a): Van Diemen's Land Fund, (£'000)

		Revenue			
Year	Balance	Rent of Crown Land	Sale of Crown Lands	Other	Total
1847	NA	NA	NA	NA	NA
1848	10.8	17.5	4.5	1.7	34.5
1849	24.3	12.4	1.8	1.9	40.4
1850	NA	NA	NA	NA	NA

			Expenditure			
	Survey Dept	Surveying Loans	Aborigines	Other	Balance	Transfer to General Revenue	Total
1847	NA	NA	NA	NA	NA	NA	NA
1848	4.3	3.2	2.2	0.6	24.3	-	34.5
1849	6.2	3.5	1.5	2.7	13.1	13.1	40.4
1850	NA	NA	NA	NA	NA	NA	NA

Note: NA — Not available.
Source: Statistics of Van Diemen's Land.

Table 6(b): Van Diemen's Land Commissariat 1826/27–1840, (£)

Year	Balance	Receipts Bills	Other	Total	Expenditure Current	Balance	Total
1826/27(a)	–	103 914	23 948	127 862	105 530	22 332	127 862
1827/28(b)	22 332	98 208	1 235	121 775	106 672	15 102	121 774
1828/29(b)	15 102	83 799	10 476	109 377	97 464	11 913	109 377
1829/30(b)	11 913	105 656	6 598	124 167	107 577	16 590	124 167
1830/31(b)	16 590	87 757	18 235	122 582	96 967	25 616	122 583
1832(c)	25 616	88 351	5 163	119 130	98 887	20 243	119 130
1833/34(d)	20 243	NA	NA	158 733	151 473	7 260	158 733
1834/35(e)	7 260	149 618	34 713	191 591	158 256	33 334	191 590
1835/36(e)	33 334	133 385	30 319	197 038	173 248	23 789	197 037
1836/37(e)	23 789	136 817	36 457	197 063	167 607	29 456	197 063
1837/38(e)	29 456	181 890	10 404	221 750	142 652	79 099	221 751
1838(f)	79 099	99 362	5 553	184 014	111 018	72 996	184 014
1838/39(g)	72 994	25 061	6 519	104 574	50 359	54 216	104 575
1839(h)	54 216	92 674	25 508	172 405	130 202	42 202	172 404
1840(i)	42 202	30 361	7 604	80 167	38 556	41 611	80 167

Notes: (a) Sept. 1826–27 Dec. 1827.
       (b) Dec.–Dec. years.
       (c) Calendar year.
       (d) Jan. 1833 to Mar. 1834 (A/cs are incomplete).
       (e) 1 April to 31 March.
       (f) 1 April 1838 to 27 Nov. 1838.
       (g) 1/12/1838–31/3/1839
       (h) 1/4/1839–31/12/1839
       (i) First quarter only.
       NA — Not available.
Sources: AJCP: PRO, A02/19, A02/21, A02/27 (wrongly titled NSW), A02/49, A02/52, A02/32–4, A02/36, A02/38, A02/40.

INDEX